UNFIXABLE FORMS

UNFIXABLE FORMS

DISABILITY, PERFORMANCE, AND THE EARLY MODERN ENGLISH THEATER

KATHERINE SCHAAP WILLIAMS

CORNELL UNIVERSITY PRESS
Ithaca and London

Copyright © 2021 by Cornell University

All rights reserved. Except for brief quotations in a review, this book, or parts thereof, must not be reproduced in any form without permission in writing from the publisher. For information, address Cornell University Press, Sage House, 512 East State Street, Ithaca, New York 14850. Visit our website at cornellpress.cornell.edu.

First published 2021 by Cornell University Press

Library of Congress Cataloging-in-Publication Data

Names: Schaap Williams, Katherine, 1983– author.
Title: Unfixable forms : disability, performance, and the early modern English theater / Katherine Schaap Williams.
Description: Ithaca [New York] : Cornell University Press, 2021. | Includes bibliographical references and index.
Identifiers: LCCN 2020056455 (print) | LCCN 2020056456 (ebook) | ISBN 9781501753503 (hardcover) | ISBN 9781501753510 (epub) | ISBN 9781501753527 (pdf)
Subjects: LCSH: Disabilities in the theater—England—History—16th century. | Disabilities in the theater—England—History—17th century. | Disabilities in literature. | English drama—Early modern and Elizabethan, 1500–1600—History and criticism. | English drama—17th century—History and criticism.
Classification: LCC PN2179.D57 S33 2021 (print) | LCC PN2179.D57 (ebook) | DDC 808.8/03561—dc23
LC record available at https://lccn.loc.gov/2020056455
LC ebook record available at https://lccn.loc.gov/2020056456
ISBN 978-1-5017-8684-6 (pbk.)

For Emily, Jackie, and Ann:
three thinkers who—at the very beginning—
flung open the door and welcomed me inside

Contents

Acknowledgments ix
Textual Note xiii

Introduction: Unfixing Early
Modern Disability   1

1. Deformed: Wanting to See Richard III   25
2. Citizen Transformed: Being the
   Lame Soldier   55
3. Performing Cripple in Theatrical
   Exchange   86
4. Changing the Ugly Body   120
5. Playing Time, or Sick of Feigning   154
6. Making the Monster   186

   Coda: Inviting Performance   219

Notes 229
Bibliography 275
Index 303

Acknowledgments

Thank you. Those words feel impossibly inadequate to account for the individuals and communities who have helped to make this book a real thing in the world.

I dedicate this book to a trinity of scholarly mentors, with profound gratitude (I am not sure I would have stayed in grad school without them): to Emily Bartels (the sine qua non), for discerning the heart of the argument with magnificent wit, every time; to Jackie Miller, for shaping my scrutiny with keen questions; and to Ann Coiro, for responding to my ideas with invigorating, enthusiastic skepticism. I am especially grateful to Henry Turner, a model of scholarly inquiry, for guidance that enriched every bit of my writing, and to Elin Diamond, whose generative thinking about performance reoriented what I thought I knew about the theater. I am also grateful to other faculty at Rutgers whose complicated questions (and reassurance) still rang in my ears as I wrote this book: Alastair Bellany, James Delbourgo, Lynn Festa, Thomas Fulton, Colin Jager, Ann Jurecic, Meredith McGill, Sarah Novacich, and Carolyn Williams. During a formative year, François-Xavier Gleyzon and Sandy Hartwig welcomed me into their community at the American University of Beirut, and I thank them for their hospitality. I could not have been more fortunate in smart and supportive colleagues in my grad cohort, and I thank Sarah Balkin, Joshua Gang, Octavio Gonzales, Erin Kelly, Nimanthi Rajasingham Perera, Brian Pietras, and Scott Trudell.

At New York University Abu Dhabi, I gladly acknowledge vital support from two deans, Judith Miller and Robert J. C. Young, and two program heads, Bryan Waterman and Deborah Williams, who offered tireless guidance and enthusiastic encouragement. Jesusita Santillan, Nisrin Abdulkhadir, and Suze Heinrich networked the globe with ease. Aysan Celik remains my favorite Hamlet. Debra Levine taught me to think politics and performance differently. Cyrus Patell and Shamoon Zamir, perpetual Shakespeare interlocutors, supported my work at every turn. Marion Wrenn (emergency contact in two weeks and forever) ballasted me. I am indebted to colleagues in the departments of literature and theater and beyond for an enlivening community: Marzia Balzani, Bill

Bragin, Andrew Bush, Diana Chester, Kevin Coffey, Toral Gajarawala, Lindsey Goss, Wail Hassan, Stephanie Hilger, Maya Kesrouani, Masha Kirasirova, Ilana Kogen, Jill Magi, Sheetal Majithia, Ken Nielsen, Erin Pettigrew, Nathalie Peutz, Rubén Polendo, Maurice Pomerantz, Joanna Settle, Matty Silverstein, Heidi Stalla, Andrew Starner, Justin Stearns, and Simon Webster.

At New York University, I thank English department chairs Christopher Cannon and Thomas Augst, and I am especially grateful to Una Chaudhuri, Valerie Forman, Sonia Posmentier, Kate Stimpson, Jini Kim Watson, and Suzanne Wofford for their collegiality, savvy, and welcoming cheer. Mara Mills and Faye Ginsburg drew me into the circle of the NYU Center for Disability Studies for timely conversations. The Department of English supported a manuscript conference award, and I am grateful, above all, to John Archer, John Guillory, and Ato Quayson, and especially to Melissa Sanchez and Ellen MacKay: I hope they will detect how much their collective wisdom and—characteristically—brilliant insights helped me to perceive the form of arguments I could not have foreseen.

In the final stages of this project, I joined the intellectual community at the University of Toronto, and this book was made better by support and provocations from colleagues here, especially Jeremy Lopez, who always recommended the right play to read, and Chris Warley, who reminded me to keep close-reading it. For their welcome and insight, I thank Alan Bewell, Brian Corman, Marlene Goldman, Elizabeth Harvey, Linda Hutcheon, Katie Larson, Lynne Magnusson, Mary Nyquist, Cannon Schmitt, Paul Stevens, Holger Syme, and Karen Weisman. I thank the lively community of junior faculty, especially Tania Aguila-Way, Thom Dancer, Rijuta Mehta, Jacob Gallagher-Ross, Kara Gaston, Melissa Gniadek, Anjuli Rasa Kolb, Terry Robinson, Avery Slater (electron extraordinaire), Misha Teramura, Anna Thomas, Audrey Walton, and Danny Wright, for their kindness and good company. I am especially grateful to Liza Blake and Urvashi Chakravarty, who saw me through the final stages with moral support and unfailing wisdom.

This book bears the imprint of so many people who lighted my way with ideas, questions, long discussions, offhand comments, bibliographical references, dazzling insights, and pep talks: in particular, I thank Susan Anderson, J. K. Barrett, Elizabeth Bearden, Susan Bennett, Claire Bourne, Andrew Bozio, Kerry Cooke, Jane Hwang Degenhardt, Cora Fox, Jonathan Gil Harris, David Hershinow, Allison Hobgood, Adam Hooks, Daniel Keegan, Andy Kesson, Emily King, Matt Kosuzko, John Kuhn, Sonia Massai, Emily McLeod, Gordan McMullan, Madhavi Menon, Lucy Munro, Vin Nardizzi, Noémie Ndiaye, Deborah Payne, Joanna Picciotto, Richard Preiss, Kevin Riordan, Marjorie Rubright, Andrea Stevens, Ayanna Thompson, Maggie Vinter, Brian Walsh, Sarah

Werner, Will West, Katie Will, Nora Williams, Mike Witmore, Marshelle Woodward, and Sam Yates.

Stephanie Hershinow gets her own line (LUNGS).

Curtis Perry taught me about dramatic form in the first place. Dan Shore's intellectual generosity helped me through the process of writing. Conversations about performance with Musa Gurnis, Erika Lin, Paul Menzer, and Kathryn Vomero Santos got me unstuck without fail. Michael Littig and Gregg Mozgala opened up their luminous craft to me. Finally, my deepest thanks go to Genevieve Love, Colleen Rosenfeld, and Debapriya Sarkar. Each of them read this book, in part or whole, at nearly every stage of development, a task that feels unimaginable even to its author. Their insights inflect every idea on these pages, and every page is better for them.

It is a pleasure to acknowledge my great debt to institutions that have nurtured and sustained my intellectual life. This project was shaped in early stages by interlocutors whose insights astound me years later: the Center for Cultural Analysis at Rutgers University (especially Henry Turner and Meredith McGill and members of the "Public Knowledge" seminar), the Mellon School of Theater and Performance at Harvard University (especially Martin Puchner and members of the "Theatre and Philosophy" seminar); and the School of Criticism and Theory at Cornell University (especially Michael Bérubé and members of the "Narrative, Intellectual Disability, and the Boundaries of the Human" seminar). The Folger Shakespeare Library has been a constant scholarly refuge during many peripatetic years; this project was supported by a short-term fellowship grant and, in the final stage of preparation, benefitted immensely from participation in the seminar "What Acting *Is*," convened by the inimitable Joseph Roach. Material from this project has been presented at the Medieval-Renaissance Colloquium, Rutgers University; New York University; New York University Abu Dhabi; Queen's College, Oxford University; George Washington University; University of Toronto; the London Shakespeare Seminar; and meetings of the Shakespeare Association of America, the Renaissance Society of America, the American Society for Theatre Research, and the Blackfriars Conference at the American Shakespeare Center. I thank these audiences for their generative responses. A portion of chapter 1 appeared in *English Studies*; an early version of chapter 3 appeared in *English Literary History*. I am grateful to these journals for permission to reproduce this material and to the David L. Kalstone Memorial Fund for support. I am delighted that Theater Mitu allowed me to use an image from their production of *Hamlet/UR-Hamlet* at the NYUAD Arts Center, Abu Dhabi (UAE), in 2015.

I thank two anonymous readers for the press who generously offered incisive comments that helped me to reimagine and reframe the argument. At

ACKNOWLEDGMENTS

Cornell University Press, Mahinder Kingra believed in this project from the beginning, and his support, thoughtful questions, and endless patience have been invaluable. I am especially grateful to Bethany Wasik for expert guidance, and I thank the team associated with the press who helped to bring this book across the finish line, including Jennifer Dana Savran Kelly, Mary Ribesky, Anne Davidson, and Brock Schnoke. In the final stages of manuscript preparation, my writing and thinking benefitted from Puck Fletcher's editing acumen, Aidan Selmer's illuminating attention, Nate Crocker's exuberant insight, and Alexandra Atiya's succinct precision, along with Sarah Osment's considerable indexing skill.

I thank friends who have offered joy and shelter in every conceivable form, especially Amy Bastian, Ed Connor, Wendy Jager, Eleanor Keppelman, Jonathan Koefoed, Ruth Ann Logue, Shelly Ogren, Carol Springer, Ian Trevethan, and Ken White. For keeping me on track: endless gratitude to Havi Brooks, and to the MFF Bowery and Formation Strength crews. All my love to the original crowd of siblings—Ben, Hannah, Meg, and John—and many beloved additions to the family: Ashley, Madilyn, Zachariah, Jackson, John Henry, Mary James, Nathan, Charlotte, Oliver, Wes, and Kristina, along with Mary Elizabeth, Wayne and Laurel, and Michelle, Henry, and Ingrid. My parents, Jeff and Debbie, encouraged me to check out the maximum number of library books every week: thank you. Tim has lived through every bit of this project with me (and then some) and remained cheerfully and endlessly supportive. Thank you for championing this book without ever reading a word of it, and for enriching my life in precincts far beyond academia.

I began by thanking my teachers, and I want to conclude with gratitude to my students and companions in inquiry. My collaborators in the NYUAD Global Shakespeare Student Festival—students and faculty from institutions in Abu Dhabi, Beirut, Cairo, Delhi, New York, Sharjah, Singapore, and Staunton—reminded me of the improbable communities that performance can generate, and demonstrated what theater can be, at its most urgent and most joyful. I thank these interlocutors with all my heart.

Textual Note

Where possible, I quote primary texts from modern scholarly editions. Otherwise, I cite page signatures from early modern printed texts by edition (with information about specific copytext in the note, as relevant), with ESTC numbers listed in the bibliography. I have primarily consulted early printed texts at the Folger Shakespeare Library and the British Library; references have been checked by consulting EEBO.

When quoting from early modern printed texts, I have usually retained spellings and typography. I have silently emended the long *s* and *vv* (to *w*), changed *v* to *u* and *i* to *j* (and vice versa), and modernized superscript letters and tildes; I have occasionally shortened long titles.

With rare exception, all dramatic texts are cited parenthetically in the text by act, scene, and line number or by page signature.

UNFIXABLE FORMS

Introduction
Unfixing Early Modern Disability

> I don't say the *Stage* Fells all before them, and disables the whole *Audience*: 'Tis a hard Battle where none escapes. However, Their *Triumphs* and their *Tropheys* are unspeakable.
>
> —Jeremy Collier, *A Short View of the Immorality, and Profaneness of the English Stage*

> What we've learned from exposure of the mechanisms is that the problem of any form is the form itself. The medium by which we think is the problem of which we think. The problem with the theater, as I see it, is that there is always somebody there thinking, or a piece of him.
>
> —Herbert Blau, *Take Up the Bodies*

William Shakespeare's *Julius Caesar* has barely gotten off the ground. In the second scene of the play, Casca enters with news that Caesar "fell down in the marketplace, and foamed at mouth, and was speechless" (1.2.252–53).[1] Recounted as a compact series of actions, this event is up for debate, refracted through ideas about the body grounded in political, medical, and moral interpretations. Casca blames the crowd pressing upon Caesar ("rabblement" [244] and their "deal of stinking breath" [246]) with a Galenic commonplace about the danger of infected air. Brutus diagnoses the convulsion as a symptom of a disease: Caesar "hath the falling sickness" (254). Just as quickly, Cassius reframes this medical insight as a metaphor for subjection ("No, Caesar hath it not; but you and I / And honest Casca, we have the falling sickness" [255–56]), wresting its significance into an appeal. The event reorganizes clues of vulnerability earlier in the scene—Cassius's memory of Caesar's "fever" (121) and "fit" (122) during a military campaign ("'Tis true, this god did shake" [123]); Caesar's own navigation of hearing loss (telling Mark Antony, "Come on my right hand, for this ear is deaf" [214])—into

1

a trajectory of disqualification. The episode evokes and multiplies the cultural meanings of epilepsy.[2] For the men, these instances of physical disability certify Caesar unfit for rule, an incapacity that the fickle crowds cannot perceive, and their exchange suggests that to have seen Caesar's fit would be to know something true about Caesar's person. The fit appears to confirm the past and predict the future, as if disability secures knowledge about who a person *is* from how a body functions.

Yet the problem of the marketplace fit is not only what Caesar's falling sickness means, but what it *does*: prompt spectatorship that may fail to detect whether Caesar is feigning. Casca relates the crowd's avid response, for "if the tagrag people did not clap him and hiss him, according as he pleased and displeased them, as they use to do the players in the theater, I am no true man" (1.2.258–61). Their judgment heightens interpretive scrutiny: Caesar's fit might just be a theatrical technique he learned from actors. Casca continues, "And so he fell. When he came to himself again, he said, if he had done or said anything amiss, he desired their worships to think it was his infirmity. Three or four wenches where I stood cried, 'Alas, good soul!' and forgave him with all their hearts" (268–73). Casca's *nuntio* function lets *Julius Caesar* off the hook for staging the episode, though his deictic "and so" may imitate Caesar's incapacitation. If the fit were performed, the action would require physical work suggested by the cues "falling" and then coming "to himself again," constellating the actor's presentational feat of a fall, the character's fiction of a swoon, and the spectator's scrutiny of the epileptic fit. Enacted within the play, such a theatrical event far outpaces the stage direction; the action is an air bubble in the linear time of the plot. Even without such performance, however, Caesar's fall makes it difficult to discern an action from the imitation of an action. Does the fit reveal Caesar to be vulnerable, helpless against the multitude's press? Does the event, instead, emphasize Caesar's swift recovery of stateliness as he employs his "infirmity" to establish sympathy with the people? Does Caesar simply fake the fit to distract his audience when he realizes they are bored? In the gap between Caesar's fall and recovery, what event do spectators think they are witnessing?

In this book, I explicate the formal and conceptual problems compressed in examples such as this one—the disabling event that exceeds the individual body in social significance, the temporal act of deciding whether and when bodily difference *is* disabling, the hinge between the embodied presentation of the actor and the representational work of the character, and the recruitment of collective witnessing to scrutinize and diagnose features of the body. Taking up these problems, I pursue two major claims: first, that representations of disability point us, counterintuitively, to social formations and cultural problems that do not seem to be *about* disability. My second claim is that disability operates as a formal aesthetic for the early modern theater, by which I mean that the work of performing bodily difference enables the theater to theorize theatricality itself as a medium. Each of the chapters in this book begins with a discursive marker, such as "deformed," "lame," "crippled," "ugly," "sick," or "monstrous," that flags visible anomaly and, simultaneously, requires an actor's performance. Disability is an idea for theatrical representation: dramatic fictions engage ideas about bodies from early modern physic treatises and surgical manuals and they also, unexpectedly, expose demands for able bodies at the heart of concepts of political power, urban citizenship, and financial exchange. Yet disability is also a problem *of* representation, requiring the human actor's vulnerable body, which transforms that which it performs. The early modern theater insists—as performance theory and disability studies will later articulate—that the capacity to represent is also always a making, and disability is not a static attribute of a body but a dynamic interaction that happens in space and time. Put another way, my readings in this book attend both to what the theater demonstrates about disability in early modern culture and to what the performance of disability in the early modern theater makes possible on and beyond the stage.

I use the concept of disability, therefore, to bring together several different operations. First, I identify disability in moments when bodily impairment, incapacity, or variance is fixed as disabling through interaction with an unaccommodating world. In this sense, I draw on the social model of disability in disability studies, which distinguishes between impairment and disability. The core insight is that the source of disability is not within the body itself but in the world that transforms impairment into disability.[3] Targeting an inaccessible physical environment—the sidewalk without a curb cut, the door with no push button, the kitchen countertop that is too high—the social model shows how the world is built for some bodies and not others. Disability is an external roadblock rather than an innate defect; disability happens when a wheelchair user encounters a building without a ramp. Further critical work nuances the social model and consolidates this key idea: constructed through interaction, disability is a *temporal* phenomenon and therefore radically contingent.[4] Turning to early modern drama with this perspective, I track the contingent fixing of bodily difference into disability in an array of contexts as varied as, for example, political libels about a "crookbacked" shape, legal provisions for aid that scrutinize a "crippled" beggar to determine capacity for work, and surgical manuals that highlight prosthetic devices to correct the bodies of "lame" soldiers. The theater makes visible the interactive nature of this encounter by showing disability as conspicuously situational rather than innate. Of disability in early modern culture, I ask not *who* counts as a disabled person, but *how* disabled bodies cast social formations into sharp relief.

Furthermore, I consider moments of discursive pointing at bodily difference within a dramatic fiction. Disability operates in this sense as a stage semiotic for theatrical conventions, inflecting performed dialogue, material properties, and stage prosthetics, as well as paratextual indicators such as stage directions, titles, and speech prefixes. My method of reading, I confess, is stubbornly literal minded in explicating these discursive traces of performed disability. I ask: What exactly can the description "monstrous" or "deformed" look like on the stage? How does a character enter, *"being lame"*? I understand such a denotation as a kind of micro-compression of cultural assumptions about how bodies should look and function. Unfolding the significance of these disability representations, I find that their prevalence is not confined to a single character type or playwright's preoccupation or dramatic genre. From revenge tragedies that amass severed limbs and bleeding bodies as spectacles of corporate horrors of the body politic, to city comedies that display corpulent, sweating, and pockmarked bodies, the theater's disability discourse offers a capacious register of semiotic possibility. As early modern plays script bodily difference, their discursive making pulls social conceptions into the orbit of theatrical practice.

Finally, and most abstractly, by disability, I mean moments when an actor's body troubles the line between feigning and being, when the temporal relay of fixing and unfixing thwarts the process of codifying disability. In this sense, disability is an organizing logic of the theatrical world, the engine of social drives, as if disability signifiers have started speaking their own language. Disability constitutes a live-wire reordering of the signifying circuit between actor and character. The examples I explore in this study source theatrical pleasure in the encounter with the glitchy *mimos* who makes mimesis happen, the actor who renders dramatic representation endlessly liable to missed cues and missteps. A lightning rod for social scrutiny, disability vexes spectatorship through contingency, both radically overdetermined and underspecified at the same time. The early modern theater's work with disability reveals how incoherent and variable are standards for bodies—and illuminates the most exciting experiments with the actor's form. By foregrounding the ontology of theatrical doing, the performance of disability complicates theatrical seeing.

In this book, therefore, I find that the early modern theater's notion of disability is not the settled abstraction of a noun but something like a gerund, a verb that acts like a noun.[5] No instance of "disabling"—a temporary fixing of a body—can be fully stable because the temporal instability of performance unfixes the perception of disability as legible difference. Moments of disabling, like the one I have traced in *Julius Caesar*, offer a kind of embedded formal crux through which to explicate the theatrical, historical, and cultural meanings with which disability is freighted. My title's pun on "unfixable" gestures to how dramatic representations of disability resist normative imperatives to cure, correct, or otherwise fix a body. The early modern theater contests the impulse to return a disabled body to an imagined past of wholeness or prepare it for an imagined future of perfection. Yet "unfixable" also captures the dynamism of early modern phenomena that cannot be consigned to the past as mere precursor to our modern concept of disability. In the theater, disability is an instrumental disordering that opens up the shaky order of things that will harden into norms, and a way to experiment with performance's unsettling demands and electrifying eventfulness. In performance, disability opens a channel between the theater and the epistemologies that govern and explicate bodily difference in early modern England.

Not Only Richard III: Theorizing Early Modern Disability

Unfixable Forms expands our account of what disability can mean in early modern culture by demonstrating how theatrical form remakes—and is remade by—the performance of disability. Disability studies has typically understood disability as an identity category that emerges in the late eighteenth century coterminously with what Michel Foucault calls "a discourse about a natural rule, or in other words, a norm."[6] The norm is staked on a medical model of disability, which views disability as a problem to be cured or corrected, an individual catastrophe of the mind or body. Critics have argued that, prior to this notion of an abstract norm from which bodily deviation could be quantified, physical disability was primarily understood as a moral judgment: bodily difference signified inner depravity. Reading Shakespeare's *Richard III*—with hump, limp, and withered arm—as a powerful didactic metaphor, scholars of early modern literature tended to agree that Richard Gloucester's physical features spelled out his moral evil.[7] Early modern disability thus appears an atavistic concept against which we can map the more complex category of disability that emerges in modernity.

Over the past decade, scholars of early modern and medieval literature have complicated this reliance on Richard III and the "allegory of interpretation" his character inaugurates.[8] The burgeoning field of early modern disability studies, from Allison P. Hobgood and David Houston Wood's foundational call to recover "insights into the material, lived experiences of disabled individuals in the distant past" to Sujata Iyengar's perceptive invitation to explore "the ontological interface between human bodies and emotions within their material environments," has moved our account of disability well beyond protocols of moral interpretation.[9] The engagement goes both ways: as Elizabeth B. Bearden observes, "grand narratives of disability's past" in disability studies may be usefully particularized by attention to the historical specificity of texts that represent, classify, and reimagine bodily difference.[10] My attention to dramatic texts elaborates disability through the early modern theater's rich archive of experiment with disability as a formal aesthetic.[11] I contribute to our account of the aesthetic *"work*—in and for the theatre" that disability does, building on Genevieve Love's trenchant reading of "disability and/as theatricality" in early modern drama.[12] In the plays I consider here, the early modern theater produces a concept of disability that is interactive, temporally in flux, and constituted through the volatile form of the actor's body.

Early modern dramatic texts productively complicate modern theories of disability identity, which have prioritized first-person narrative forms to recover disabled subjectivity. The urgency of reclaiming disability as a lived experience is well founded: disability theory emerges from the disability rights movement and its political critique of a long history of efforts to control, cure, and eliminate people with disabilities. David T. Mitchell and Sharon L. Snyder's groundbreaking account of narrative prosthesis founds its critique of literary texts on the charge that representations of disability—as metaphor, as shortcut to characterization, as difference that demands a story—always stand for something other than actual disability.[13] Against a world structured to exclude, and against literary representations that reduce disability to metaphor or reinforce stereotypes of pity and fear, critics call for positive reclamations of disabled identity and literary forms with "more realistic representations" rooted in the ethics of disability justice.[14] Early modern texts, however, are not easily identified through the literary conventions of realism or the first-person memoir. Figuring monstrosity as extravagant bodily difference, marking lines with "limping" meter, and inventing lyric poems about deformed mistresses, sixteenth- and seventeenth-century English literature brims with unfamiliar registers of disability representation.

Especially in the early modern theater. Herbert Blau's insight, in my epigraph here, that "the problem of any form is the form itself" reminds us that the formal thinking of the theater is inextricable from the body of the actor.[15] For Blau, "the medium by which we think is the problem of which we think." In a form that thinks through the medium of an actor's body, disability is not an abstraction. As I noted earlier, on the stage, the denotation of terms such as "deformed" or "lame" or "crippled" demands an actor do—and show—

something, and this enactment calls attention to the cultural conventions by which disabled bodies are understood. Beyond simply disturbing a spectator's certainty about the stereotype of the crippled beggar she encounters when she leaves the theater, theatrical performance unsettles the very act of pointing to a fixed shape from which a body deviates. The actor's body disrupts a static concept of bodily norms because an "able" body is just as much a performance as a "disabled" body—and must likewise be flagged by theatrical conventions. There is no singularly ideal body or binary between abled and disabled bodies; there is simply bodily variance.

Early modern concepts of performance, as I discuss in detail later in the introduction, therefore reconfigure foundational claims about theatrical representation in contemporary disability theory. The strongest critique of the theater is the contention that mimetic practice exploits disability as "disability drag" or "cripping up": a nondisabled actor plays a disabled character.[16] Cripping up reduces the lived identity of disability to a temporary impersonation by an able-bodied actor. This representational artifice often inspires pity or applause for overcoming a disability—and the bitter jest is that any actor who wants to win an Oscar should play a disabled character. From Daniel Day-Lewis to Hilary Swank to Dustin Hoffman to Colin Firth (to list only a few of the actors with celebrated portrayals), accolades bear out the idea that the performance of disability is a notable test for a gifted actor. When actors crip up, the theater reproduces the logic of the medical model of disability, locating disability as a problem within a particular body, rather than an encounter with a disabling world, much less a variation of human flourishing. This logic, furthermore, undergirds prescriptions about the body imagined as capable of performing in the first place. Modern Western notions of acting begin from a "neutral" stance, Carrie Sandahl observes, which disqualifies a disabled actor on the grounds that her distinctive embodiment disrupts characterization.[17] In the theater's space of witnessing, disability oversignifies.[18] A scar, a limp, or a stutter operates as a metaphor or tells a story about the character's history—a fiction that depends on spectators distinguishing such a feature as the property of the character rather than the actor. Casting protocols, Sandahl argues, demand the actor with "not only the able body, but also the extraordinarily able body," a figure with the capacity to assume—and then discard—extravagant markers of somatic difference at will.[19] This expectation of neutrality means that disabled actors are rarely cast for the parts of disabled characters, and almost never cast to play a character who is not explicitly scripted as disabled.[20] The corollary of cripping up is the presumption, as Petra Kuppers puts it, that "the disabled body is *naturally* about disability."[21] The disabled actor risks having her performance taken for reality, as if she were simply onstage "being disabled" rather than—in a demonstration of skill, like any other actor—acting.

These important critiques indict performance traditions that have long excluded disabled actors—traditions that are thrillingly upended by new work composed by and for actors with disabilities.[22] Yet the critique of cripping up depends on an actor who extracts herself from one character and moves to another with skillful volition—in short, the modern aspirations of actor training. Let me underscore this point: the early modern theater has no such faith that the body of the actor can be a stable template. Early modern antitheatrical discourse harps on the idea that acting alters the body, insisting that theatrical metamorphosis might lead to unpredictable effects, even irreversibly transforming the actor. In anecdotes about actors who cannot stop playing a part, such texts fear, as Joseph R. Roach puts it, that "he who can assume any shape is in danger of losing his own."[23] In these worst-case scenarios, theatrical verisimilitude produces the thing itself—the actor who, feigning madness, actually goes mad.[24] More broadly, treatises against the theater, sumptuary laws, and gossipy harangues about women in men's clothing converge in fears about the body's unaccountable plasticity. Discussions of the theater (to which I will return shortly) are distinctly skeptical of the view that an actor can easily extricate himself, unchanged, from a part that has deformed him into another shape.

My reappraisal of the early modern theater does not proceed, therefore, on an ethical impulse to identify positive representations of disability, nor will I attempt to recuperate the theater as a site of empathy through identification with disabled characters. The theater's real-world links with actual disabled people, when we have been able to trace them—like Robert Armin's *The History of the Two Maids of More-clacke*, which stages Armin's famous comic persona of "John of the Hospital," modeled on a person with a form of intellectual disability—frequently appropriate incapacity for jokes.[25] Plots often use feigned disability as a narrative trigger, as Lindsey Row-Heyveld has deftly explored, fulfilling cultural prejudice about appeals for charitable aid.[26] Entire subplots revolve around mocking characters for their blindness, lameness, or foolishness, and, as Love discusses, disability metaphors are routinely invoked to characterize dramatic texts in the bibliographical history of early modern plays.[27] Despite the best efforts to discipline a disabled character into a recognizable stereotype (as in the case of Cripple in chapter 3), a play may still spark an audience member's sympathy, but my premise here is not that we should turn to the early modern theater to affirm the representations of disability we find there.

Instead, I argue that the early modern theater understands the social model's insight that disability is the product of encounter, and offers a different analytic for bodily norms. The early modern plays I read in this book offer valuable insights because, by putting such ideas on view as *fictions* of disabling rather than innate truths about bodies, they let slip the contingency of fictions of disqualification. In this sense, the early modern theater offers something like what Robert McRuer identifies as a "crip" perspective on disability: a perspective that foregrounds the "processes that unsettle, unravel, and unmake" rather than affirming concepts of "substance or authenticity."[28] The theater *formally* refuses authenticity, for every identity on the stage has to be made up. The labor of the actor's theatrical marking required to flag disability contests the self-evidence of disability as an apparent fact. The early modern theater, therefore, dissents from the "binary division of the world into able-bodied and disabled" because it works from the radical particularity of the actor's body rather than from a stable norm.[29] The formal process of representing disability discloses social judgments about bodies, even those pronouncements of disqualification that appear uncontestable. And, by foregrounding the contingent vulnerability of the actor in time, the theater implicates every body in that vulnerability too, admitting that (to put it in the parlance of disability theory) even an able body is only ever temporarily able.

The early modern theater, in other words, not only reflects cultural ideas about bodily capacity but generates new ways of looking at and through the human form of the actor. This innovation is aligned with the notion of disability aesthetics, the idea that, as Tobin Siebers puts it, disability "acquires aesthetic value because it represents for makers of art a critical resource for thinking about what a human being is."[30] I find a critical resource in the early modern theater's disablings, vital and elusive, constrained by the temporality of performance but unpredictably flashing up to unsettle the plotted sequence of the dramatic fiction. Acting is a process in time, a four-dimensional art that challenges how perceptions of disability work. The actor's ability—to present, to disfigure, to deform, in a few early modern verbs for acting—blurs the distinction between original and copy because the body will not stay fixed. On the stage, disability does not neatly metaphorize because the medium of the actor's body is never fixed enough to limit the transfer of meaning to the signified "disabled," and because "disabled" itself is a category that encompasses the broadest range of human difference. In early modern performance, theatrical mimesis thrives on unfixing signification: the actor's body is not a stable signifier and disability is not a stable signified. The early modern theater redefines disability because the form's dependence on the unfixable bodies of actors—virtuosic, fallible—changes disability representation.

"Strange Recompences": Fictions of Bodily Form

Early modern usage of the word "disable" reflects both impaired bodily function and the slipperiness of social scrutiny. Specifically, "disabled" denotes the inability to work. Elizabeth I's 1592 act prescribing care of returning soldiers addresses those who have "aventured their Lyves and loste their Lymmes or disabled their bodies," and statutes direct state relief for those who are "poore olde blynde lame & ympotent person or other poore person not able to worke."[31] These legal definitions of those eligible for aid are linked to a complex network of state-structured care and governance, including hospitals and workhouses, as statutes define a population that shifts into and out of institutional control. If this legal context for disability suggests that the concept is limited to impairment, however, "disable" also encodes a genealogy of rhetorical complexity. Surveying uses of "disable" and its cognates, Iyengar notes that the term connotes the experience of "a physical, moral, or economic slowdown, but the word is rarely used as a participial adjective or to connote a pre-existing or unchangeable or tragic condition."[32] As Vin Nardizzi perceptively discusses, George Puttenham's treatise on rhetoric, *The Art of English Poesy* (1589), identifies the "Disabler," or the "figure of Extenuation," as meiosis, a figure of speech that minimizes an object or its importance. Puttenham's example is a captain who expresses "contempt" for an enemy, "disabling him scornfully" to give courage to his soldiers and "make light of every thing that might be a discouragement to the attempt."[33] "Disabling" is a rhetorical diminishment bound up in perception.

Although early modern texts employ the word "disable," early work in disability studies identified deformity and monstrosity as the key analogues to a modern concept of disability. As Lennard J. Davis puts it, deformity is "a major category, a dramatic physical event or bodily configuration"; therefore, prior to the concept of the norm, "unless the deformity is wondrous, it is ignored or erased."[34] My book opens with a chapter on deformity and closes with one on monstrosity, and I have argued elsewhere that the concept of deformity offers productive friction to our contemporary accounts of disability.[35] Yet I use "disability" in order to foreground my investment in disability studies, especially disability aesthetics. The discursive process of constituting bodily difference goes beyond the self-evidence of disqualification, and the aesthetic power of human variation is not reducible to stigmatized impairment.[36] Excavating unfamiliar terms and habits of thinking in sixteenth- and seventeenth-century English texts, I track disablings by turning to concepts from disability theory, which illuminate how fictions of bodily anomaly are constituted by unpredictable encounter, no matter how fixed they appear.

For early modern writers given to sweeping pronouncements on the human condition, disability tests the limits of discerning interpretation by making it difficult to draw the line between settled differences and those that may be corrected. We associate this predictive scrutiny with beliefs about physiognomy, or what Martin Porter calls the "hermeneutic process" of interpreting the body's signs in order to determine natural tendencies, understood as a *"way of looking"* at a person in order to read the evidence of who they are.[37] Such a gaze assumes that disorder is undesirable, that "defect or excesse" in a body "must needs breed griefe, because it createth trouble." That assertion is Thomas Bedford's conclusion when, reflecting on a "strange-birth" in a sermon in 1635, he urges his hearers to "consider the discomfort of Deformitie," the visible anomaly of a "prodigious" child that evokes deformity, a broader category of unelective physical difference.[38] When Robert Burton, likewise, lumps many kinds of bodily difference together, he does so not by distinguishing between the ontology of the disability—whether congenital or acquired or periodic—but by the shared affective response they are understood to prompt. Noting that "deformities and imperfections of our bodies, as lameness, crookedness, deafness, blindness, be they innate or accidental, torture many men," Burton includes a range of negative forms of bodily variation that we think of as disability today.[39]

Despite the assumption that impairments are a kind of "torture," however, Burton resists the idea that the body's fixedness governs the person. He notes that "this may comfort them, that those imperfections of the body do not a whit blemish the soul, or hinder the operations of it, but rather help and much increase it."[40] Burton distinguishes between soul and body to reassure the reader that even though he is "lame of body, deformed to the eye, yet this hinders not but that thou mayest be a good, a wise, upright, honest man."[41] Making this point, he offers a compendium of examples of historical figures whose bodies offer no clue to their famed wisdom. Dispatching their descriptions in haste ("Aesop was crooked, Socrates purblind, long-legged, hairy, Democritus withered, Seneca lean and harsh, ugly to behold; yet show me so many flourishing wits, such divine spirits"), Burton collates many forms of bodily difference under the sign of "discontents" that nonetheless may be overcome.[42] His depreciation of visible appearance returns repeatedly to Socrates, a commonplace example of a great philosopher "deformed, crooked, ugly to behold" that nonetheless could have "those good parts of the mind denominate them fair" (which Burton glosses via Gregory of Nazianzen: "deformed most part in that which is to be seen with the eyes, but most elegant in that which is not to be seen").[43] Appealing to a distinction between what is unseen and what is visible, Burton's concept of disability exceeds a fixed moral frame of interpretation. The stress on appearances that are "deformed to the eye" and "ugly to behold" admits that perceptions of bodily difference are inextricable from the perceiver. Addressing his reader, he slides from "our bodies," to "comfort them," to "thou mayest," shifting between a notion of vulnerability that is common to all bodies and a disabling feature that disqualifies a person on the basis of apprehension.

The variability of deformity reflects the alterity of early modern concepts of the body itself. As a wealth of scholarship over the past three decades has shown, bodies were understood as radically permeable, subject to passions, composed of humors, and responsive to occult forces of sympathies and antipathies.[44] Against this template of the body's fluid and volatile substance, writers, from physicians and natural philosophers to schoolmasters and courtiers, frequently uphold an ideal of embodied mastery. John Bulwer's assertion that the "rich jewell of the soule" was "placed in a body reciprocally answerable to its merit, where the exact symetry of every part enjoyed so ample an aptitude to what it was designed, that the result became an ocular harmony of that rare composure," evokes an entirely commonplace image of the body's decorum.[45] This neoclassical fantasy—the body as symmetrical and proportional—prizes visible order as that which is perceptible, an "ocular harmony" apparent to all.

These fantasies of order, of course, demarcate exclusions too. Fictions of natural rule are wielded against bodies presumed to be incapable of self-regulation, often imagined in early modern discourse through figures of leakiness, weakness, intransigence, impotence, and failure. These tropes of disability or incapacity are often allied and intersect with identifications of race, gender, sexuality, and status, whether or not they refer to bodies that are actually impaired.[46] Disability may take the form of a "stigmatized somatic mark," to follow Patricia Akhimie, participating in a hierarchy by which some bodily differences appear impossible to amend.[47] As an expression of human vulnerability, disability is both subject to social orderings that discriminate between bodies and invoked to ground assertions of incapacity in bodily difference *as if* bodies are—or could be—fixed as disabled.[48] Yet in nearly the same breath in which they acknowledge the natural imperfections of the body, early modern thinkers express an equally conventional ambition to refine and fix an appearance perceived as deficient. As Castiglione's *The Book of the Courtier*, the most influential manual for courtiers of the sixteenth century, puts it: "Those who are not perfectly endowed by Nature can, through care and effort, polish and to a great extent correct their natural defects."[49] Bearden has shown how the courtly technique of sprezzatura, the prized skill of effortlessly graceful conduct, "produces disability by carving out the proper balance of courtliness from the extremes of disabled types."[50] I am interested in both aspects of these "natural defects": the power of "natural" to render judgments about bodies inevitable, and the unspecified "defects" that offer corrective opportunities. Modernity's concept of the "normal" body may still be inchoate, but early modern "norming effects"—concepts of the "ideal" and the "natural"—express ambitions to regulate and discipline the body.[51]

Beyond and alongside redress, however, early modern writers insist that disability may also be unexpectedly compensated. Bulwer's proposal for Deaf education, the application of his work on gesture for which he is perhaps best known to modern critics, addresses Edward and William Gostwicke and "all other intelligent and ingenious Gentlemen, who as yet can neither heare nor speake."[52] And yet, Bulwer refuses to interpret their disability as only deprivation, insisting that "although some who understand not the mystery of your condition, looke upon you as *misprisions* in nature; yet to me who have studied your perfections, and well observed the strange recompences Nature affords you, I behold nothing in you but what may be a just object of admiration!"[53] "Strange recompences" rather than "misprisions": Bulwer commends the embodied knowledge and somatic possibilities of skilled communication that bodily difference has produced. Deafness may offer useful advantages, and Deaf rhetorical capacity compels "admiration"; as he notes, the capacity to lip-read offers an estimable financial advantage on the noisy floor of the Royal Exchange. Bulwer's admiration for the "perfections" of the Gostwickes' communication takes stock of unexpected affordances that challenge a simple equation of disability with limitation or incapacity.

This quick tour of attitudes toward bodily variance signals why the staging of disability is a catalyst for the theater's practice: because disability is constructed through encounter, even the apparent fact of bodily difference keeps shifting. Self-evident anomaly slips into social effects that depend on perception. For every Richard III, with an apparent correlation between hunchbacked shape and evil, there is a Socrates, icon of philosophical wisdom and extremely ugly, whose appearance is not traceable to a clear cause or prediction. The disjunction between interior and exterior is disconcerting: as Burton notes, Socrates's deformity might be either a sign of his natural inclination toward wickedness he has resisted through virtuous discipline (as Socrates himself is said to have told his physiognomy-practicing disciple) or the refusal of correlation, proving that appearance is no reliable indicator of a person's virtue. Visible physical difference prompts questions such as: What can be deduced from the appearance of the body? Are deformities fixed and innate, or may they be altered, corrected, or improved? Is disability an accident or a revelation? Divine judgment or human consequence? Cause or effect? Does the body indicate a person's natural aptitude or ambitious discipline? Disability is both limit of and occasion for the exercise of refinement, at times an apparent deficiency that a person amends, and at other times, an unelective difference he cannot overcome. The rhetorics of disability throughout the early modern period provide a vocabulary for the paradoxes that follow from the belief in a self simultaneously ordained and contingent on shaping.

Deforming the Actor

The contingency of the actor's body and the spectator's perception is crucial, in fact, in George Puttenham's early modern genealogy of the theater. Puttenham explains how the classical actor Roscius Gallus, "the most excellent player among the Romans," reinvented theatrical practice. Roscius "brought up these vizards which we see at this day used, partly to supply the want of players when there were more parts than there were persons, or that it was not thought meet to trouble and pester princes' chambers with too many folks."[54] Playing barefaced, the actors constrain the dramatis personae through scarcity of number or lack of playing space. The number of bodies constitutes the limit of theatrical form. By contrast, when Roscius introduces the practice of wearing a mask, "by the change of a vizard one man might play the king and the carter, the old nurse and the young damsel, the merchant and the soldier, or any other part he listed very conveniently." Puttenham's origin story for the theater celebrates the mask's potential to multiply a single actor's form into diverse characters. The theatrical prosthetic enables one performer to play many different roles, traversing status, gender, and age, from "king" and "carter" to "old nurse" and "young damsel." The actor adopts the fixed form of each mask in turn, animating one after another to generate the theater's power to unfix persons from roles.

But Puttenham cannot stop there. He offers a second ontology of theater, one that derives from the actor's form, or rather, the actor's bodily deformity: "There be that say Roscius did it for another purpose, for being himself the best *histrion* or buffoon that was in his days to be found, insomuch as Cicero said Roscius contended with him by variety of lively gestures to surmount the copy of his speech, yet because he was squint-eyed and had a very unpleasant countenance, and looks which made him rather ridiculous or rather odious to the presence, he devised these vizards to hide his own ill-favored face." Roscius is the model actor, as great as Cicero in gesture ("lively") and speech ("copy," or copiousness), but his "squint-eyed" and "ill-favored" appearance fixes him into a type. Spectators apprehend Roscius's physical difference, perhaps a facial deformity, as "odious," a specificity that disables acting.[55] Roscius risks turning every play into a comedy because he prompts laughter no matter what part he plays. He is too much himself in a form that demands the actor's transformation into a new part. Roscius resorts to the mask's unfixing powers, a prosthetic that turns his body into many different forms.

Quietly tucked into Puttenham's offhand history of the greatest actor is a theory of theatrical form. Theatrical form is a circuit between the body of the actor (unfixing each mask and also fixed in his own specific form) and the theatrical mask (fixed as a single character and also unfixing the body of any actor). Generating resistance in this circuit because of his specificity, Roscius's "squint-eyed" deformity turns theatricality into disability aesthetics.[56] This account of the theater, I am suggesting, foregrounds the twin pistons that motor theatrical performance: singularity (the mask, the body) and iterability (the body, the mask), pulsing between the operations of fixing and unfixing. Roscius's appearance is perceived as a negative departure from an expected form—yet his physical distinctiveness generates theatrical innovation. Turning to theatrical prosthetics that multiply the roles beyond the material limits of the personating bodies, he invents a mode of playing that does not reduce him in advance to a single feature; in the process, he demonstrates virtuosic skill. Roscius's limitation creates limitless variation precisely because of his particularity. If disability is the product of witnessing that converts human variation into disqualification, it is also the engine of theatrical forms that pulse new life through familiar constraints.

As this reading of Puttenham suggests, attending to disability in the theater reminds us that performance is a material making that is never simply reducible to text.[57] In the chapters that follow, I find that the staging of disability activates a major affordance of the early modern theater's "entwining of the fictive in the actual, the drama in its *doing* that animates (our appetite for) dramatic performance."[58] As Erika T. Lin observes, "Performance is unique in that it itself is also the *act* of production; the medium *is* the process of transformation."[59] This tenet of theater theory is expounded by early modern plays themselves, specifically in the relation of the actor to his part, or role. The induction to John Marston's *Antonio and Mellida* begins by bringing the actors onstage *"with parts in their hands,"* thinking about performance's demands beyond the script.[60] They have memorized their lines but have yet to master their personations: "We can say our parts: but wee are ignorant in what mould we must cast our Actors" (sig. A3r). For the rest of the scene, they offer each other advice about how to act their roles, suggesting "thus frame your exterior shape, / To hautie forme of elate majestie," and lamenting that "I was never worse fitted since the nativitie of my Actorshippe" (sig. A4r), with deictics that indicate they are testing postures that will suit their parts. The "forme" of a character requires the actor's body to personate a dramatic character, to reframe his own "exterior shape." Beyond simply reproducing the part, a prescripted role, Roach reminds us, the actor acts on himself, on the theatrical environment, and on spectators, so that early modern acting theory chiefly aims to "control and restrain" the actor's self-transformation.[61] The actor's body is the pressure point for the theater because the actor's labor grounds mimetic reproduction in his person.

The most strident voices of alarm about the labor of the actor's person, as I noted earlier, were those of antitheatrical writers. Stephen Gosson's *Playes Confuted in Five Actions* (1582) identifies the actor's feigning as a dangerous falsehood, for "to declare our selves by wordes or by gestures to be otherwise then we are, is an act executed where it should not, therefore a lye."[62] Gesturing like a woman, declaring himself a king, the actor's "act executed" indulges the dramatic fiction's untruths and accomplishes something "otherwise." William Perkins posits that the body should be a stable "outward forme and favour" and condemns those who "devise artificiall forms and favours, to set upon their bodies and faces."[63] Likewise, when William Prynne, decades later, inveighs against *"the acting of anothers part or person on the Stage,"* he channels theological and classical authorities to insist that humans should likewise *"seeme that outwardly which they are inwardly."*[64] Theatrical making demands that an actor put on the "part"—the term for a role—of another and requires players to assume "prodigious deformed habits and disguises, as are unsuitable to their humanity."[65] Yet the falsehoods that theatrical transformations require in the "act executed" may turn out to alter the very forms that enact them. John Rainolds laments that actors engaged in "earnest and much meditation of sundry dayes and weekes, by often repetition and representation of the partes, shall as it were engrave the things in their minde with a penne of iron, or with the point of a diamond."[66] The script etches the actor's mind, a pun on character as writing that figures the role's reiterative power to wear a groove into the person. To play a part requires focus ("much meditation"), time ("sundry dayes and weekes"), and action, again and again ("often repetition"): personating warps the personator. We might be tempted to read these indictments of performance's alterations as armchair quarterbacking by preachers far from the theater's doors, but Gosson worked as a playwright for two years, and Rainolds acted in university drama at Oxford. Protesting the transforming power of performance, these writers understand that the theater's appeal—visible, audible, sensible—is rooted in the actor's making, even if that making is unpredictable.

Some trace of performance's electrifying charge remains in what printer Richard Jones, in his preface to Christopher Marlowe's play *Tamburlaine* in

1590, calls "graced deformities," noting that he has excised certain "fond and frivolous jestures" that were "shewed upon the stage" but "wuld proove a great disgrace" in print.[67] "Deformity" is his term for what actors do; a deformity is the actor's making that escapes the fixed form of the printed text. Deformity thus captures—or evokes while it fails to capture—the doing of the actor in time. This unfamiliar usage of deformity reminds us that, although the primary meaning indicates a departure from form, to "deform" may also mean "to form or fashion."[68] The contronym indexes the precarious distinction between forming and disforming—and shows how difficult it may be to discern a deformity's putative departure from form. Indeed, following the Latin prefix, Colleen R. Rosenfeld observes that "deformity means not only 'misshapen' (Lt. *de-forma*) but also 'difformity,' from the medieval Latin *dis-forma*, meaning 'of diverse forms.'"[69] The negative prefix conceals a radical asymmetry: deformity is not form's opposite but its multiplicity. A deformity, an action or form tenuously stabilized into a noun, is *any* of the many possible fixings that permit contingency. In the theater, this genealogy of deformity gestures to the very basis of acting itself, which William N. West describes as "the reforming, or deforming, or performing, of the player's substance into a series of new forms."[70] I understand deformity in both senses, as a negative departure from form and as a form's instantiation in time, which may also become another form. Like Roscius's body, a deformity evinces fixed particularity and unfixing multiplicity; it is a site of limitation and scope for limitless variation. In the account of disability I offer in this book, the early modern theater depends on generative deformities produced by and through the mutable body of the actor.

Considering theatrical form, I draw on recent work in literary studies that understands form as an epistemological instrument; that is, in Rosenfeld's incisive articulation, as "'a doing' that is always also capable of doing otherwise."[71] Excavating form as a process of poetic making, Rosenfeld turns to Ben Jonson's distinction in *Timber: or, Discoveries*.[72] Jonson writes: "A poem, as I have told you, is the work of the poet, the end and fruit of his labour and study. Poesy is his skill or craft of making; the very fiction itself, the reason, or form of the work. And these three voices differ, as the thing done, the doing, and the doer; the thing feigned, the feigning, and the feigner; so the poem, the poesy, and the poet."[73] Alongside the predictable categories of maker and object made, Jonson adds a third, the "craft of making" or the "form of the work." The emphasis on "making," Rosenfeld notes, introduces a crucial temporality, a "doing" that is not the same as the "thing done." Taking this insight into the theater, we notice that the ontological force of the "craft of making" returns us to the body of the actor, where the doing and the thing done appear indistinguishable. Beyond playwright ("poet") and play ("the work"), the "very fiction itself" depends on a player who engages in the temporal process that Jonson's theory of art highlights, the "feigning" that stabilizes into "thing feigned." This emphasis on the craft of making and object made likewise appears in Elin Diamond's foundational formulation of performance: "In the blink of an eye," Diamond writes, "performance is always a doing and a thing done."[74] Diamond's reading highlights "a reiteration of norms" ("a doing") and the "discursive conventions that frames our interpretations" ("a thing done") that enables analysis.[75] That "blink of an eye," I would suggest, returns us to a witness, to the perception that implicates theatrical making in the construction of disability as an encounter. Oriented to form as process, we understand the construction of bodies and ideas—and, therefore, concepts of disability—in performance as the result of the actor's making just as much as the poet's craft. A disabling may appear stable, a deformity that is *this* and not otherwise, but the act is always liable to the doing as much as the thing done.

My rereading of Jonson's early modern theory of form alongside a modern theory of performance might not please Jonson himself, who was notably unhappy with actors who failed to live up to his scripts. Yet this is the point I want to stress: if our readings attend only to the written product of the poet's making, we risk smuggling a platonic ideal of abstraction into our concept of form. Rather than disappearing the stage into a metaphor, early modern plays ask us to attend to how theatrical form may snag on the actor's materiality. From the perspective of theater semiotics, the actor's body is a unique set of signs, which are resignified through the language of the scripted role.[76] In turn, the language of the role is transformed by the unique morphology of the actor who embodies—or bodies forth—theatrical language.[77] Early modern plays, however, experiment with theatrical representation, testing when and how and whether the actor's body shows through the character. The early modern theater was still in the process of developing distinctions between presentational (or nonrepresentational) action, which foregrounds the body of the actor, and representational action, which foregrounds the dramatic character in the fictional world of the play.[78] The staging of disability is a seam between actor and character; thus, as Love argues, disabled characters teach us about theatrical personation because they evoke the theatrical body, actor and character apprehended together, in prosthetic surplus and extravagant dynamism.[79]

Building on this insight, I suggest that the theater's work with disability offers a limit case of the negotiation between the actor's bodily particularity and the mechanisms of reproducibility—from script to dramatic character to stage properties—that drive theatrical practice. Critical accounts of the early modern theater often turn to the example of the character of "An Excellent Actor," almost certainly composed by John Webster and collected in Sir Thomas Overbury's collection *New and Choice Characters* (1615). The sketch praises the "full and significant action of body" with which the actor "charmes our attention," and gestures to the encircling audience of a "full theater" that surrounds this captivating form ("what we see him personate, we thinke truely done before us").[80] In this familiar elaboration of the actor's craft, however, the description turns to another body waiting in the wings. The actor "doth not strive to make nature monstrous, she is often seen in the same Scene with him, but neither on Stilts nor Crutches" (sig. M5v). This sidelong glance perceives a figure who threatens to steal the scene through the extravagant display of "monstrous" bodily difference. Alongside the actor, the account conjures a figure associated with stilts and crutches, properties that heighten and supplement the body. Peripheral to, and possibly supplanting, the ideal actor, another form suggests that deformities are the source of theatrical form's unfixing possibility.

To put this another way, the negative fantasy that appears alongside the ideal actor testifies to the attraction of the deforming capacities of the actor's body and stage properties, the materials on which the theater capitalizes in the doing of disability. When the property list of the Lord Admiral's Men in Philip Henslowe's diary records "Kentes woden leage," a wooden leg brings together an actor, a character, and a play, perhaps *The Wise Man of West Chester*.[81] Such an instance of archival residue reminds us that the very process by which disability is legible emerges in the context of the early modern theater's uneven settling into institutional conventions. Like the stage properties that produce other identity distinctions—the wig and costume through which a boy signifies a "Lady," or the paint or cloth that produces skin color as racialized distinction—disability signification appears to be fixed, plainly signaled by the objects that literally make it up.[82] Theatrical prosthetics lend force to disability caricature, from crutches and wooden stumps to ointment encrusting the eyes, to scales and claws, to a special effects suit donned to thicken a body. Although I focus in this book on physical disability, intellectual disability demands signification in the theater too: a character's madness or foolishness must be exteriorized on the stage, whether through disordered language that introduces temporal delay in the plot, appearance (*"with her hair about her ears"*), or clothing (*"attired like a madman"*).[83] And even a cursory glance at the production history of *Richard III* indicates how abiding is the hope that a prosthetic hump could convey a fixed meaning: Samuel Johnson's well-known caricature of an actor, likely referring to David Garrick, identifies him as a "fellow who claps a hump on his back, and a lump on his leg, and cries 'I am Richard the Third.'"[84]

In the readings that follow, however, I trace a curious paradox in the material objects that construct visible anomaly. Theatrical prosthetics are often ostensive; they point at the body of the actor. Yet plays traffic in the impossibility of perceiving where the body ends and the prosthetic begins. Disability signifiers may blur into the actor's body so far as to be indistinguishable. When Cripple's "crooked habit" hesitates between body and garment (as I will consider in chapter 3), or when Ralph's *"being lame"* in *The Shoemaker's Holiday* does not specify between locomotion and wooden leg (as I will consider in chapter 2), the theater exploits the indeterminacy of disability as a bodily property. In some examples, as in the case of a limp or an epileptic fit, no property may be required beyond the virtuosic body of the actor. Love's trenchant reading of characters with theatrical prosthetics has demonstrated how figures of disability enact doubleness, oscillating between actor and character.[85] Rather than oscillation, the movement I isolate in the study is closer to the gerund's in-between, when phenomenological apprehension is resolving or has not quite resolved—indeed, might not fully resolve—into semiotic signification.

Ultimately, I find that the theater's disability fictions exceed the frame of disabled character.[86] In Mitchell and Snyder's important account of narrative prosthesis, disability functions both as "a stock feature of characterization" that furnishes a "distinctive idiosyncrasy" to a character and as an "opportunistic metaphorical device" that employs disability to spark a story about how and why that idiosyncrasy matters.[87] Disability offers a literary strategy of marking a character as anomalous, employing her to make meaning within a story, and curing or erasing her disability for narrative closure.[88] Visible idiosyncrasy, to be sure, is irresistible to the theater, and disability fictions in the early modern theater often look like type characters, or "recognizable figures of literary imagination and social fantasy."[89] Encountered only through a narrative logic that prioritizes the end of the plot, disability appears to determine the character's predictable disqualification or rehabilitation through cure. A play, however, unfolds in time, and a dramatic character is never only one thing. Some figures I consider here are deemed congenitally "deformed" or "ill-favoured" from birth, but others are transformed over the course of the play, like the shoemaker who returns from war lame, or move in and out of visibility with a periodic disability like palsy or epilepsy. Constituted through interaction, disability poses the question of *when* a character may be described as "disabled" and whether that designation—"this is a disabled character"—arises from the character's embodiment or the spectator's perception.[90] My readings begin from what Michael Bérubé calls "radical individuation," in which "disability does not work toward one determined end," as a starting point for theatrical fictions.[91] In the chapters that follow, I place particular stress on the textual apparatus that singles out bodily anomaly. But it is precisely the theatrical openness of the relay between script and body that challenges the work of abstraction required to designate a character "disabled." Disability is the product of deformities that begin from the actor's form but never reside within a single body.

Enabling Theatrical Making

The sense that disability operates as a relay of fixing and unfixing in the early modern theater accounts for my analytic priorities in this book. With each chapter organized around a keyword of disabling—*deformed, lame, crippled, ugly, sick,* and *monstrous*—I examine moments when the script points at physical difference and cues theatrical making from an actor's practice. Putting plays into conversation with other early modern texts and with contemporary disability theory, my inquiry attends to how disability fuses social formation, semiotic pointing, and theatrical form. The readings therefore focus on temporal slices of a play, on scenes, on moments, on encounters; I slow down to privilege spectacle over narrative closure. I have selected sketches of theatrical doing and seeing that render vividly the conjunction of performance and disability. I treat with equal fervor familiar heavy hitters—*Volpone, The Changeling,* and *The Tempest,* to name a few, in addition to *Richard III*—and unattributed plays such as *The Fair Maid of the Exchange* and *A Larum for London* that have garnered few performance histories, few scholarly editions, and still fewer readers. This method is motivated by the conviction that if we approach drama only as evidence for what was thought about disability in early modern England, we risk reducing performance into text, and fictions of disability into records of what Philip Sidney calls the "bare *Was*" of history, in teleological lockstep on the road to modernity.[92] I am interested instead in how the early modern theater thinks about disability through the form of the actor, and what, in turn, the staging of disability allowed the theater to think about its own practices.

My first chapter, "Deformed: Wanting to See Richard III," considers the most recognizably disabled body in the early modern period, that of the "deformed" Richard Gloucester. I set Shakespeare's *Richard III* alongside historical sources and Elizabethan antecedents such as the unattributed *The True Tragedie of Richard III* to show how Shakespeare's Richard is anything but fixed. Turning to popular verse libels written on the death of Robert Cecil and Francis Bacon's essay "Of Deformity," I consider how the these literary forms crystallize deformity into an explicitly "crookbacked" shape. Richard's proclamation that he is "deformed," by contrast, lights up the intersection of discursive script and the actor's unfixing embodiment. To put it in terms of the unitalicized title of my chapter, the play leaves us wanting to watch what emerges from deformity—between Richard Gloucester and *Richard III*—and offers a concept of theatrical disability that begins from the deformations of the actor.

The second chapter turns to the type character of the "lame" soldier, whose disabling foregrounds the conflict between martial labor and artisanal labor in the urban civic structure of early modern London. In "Citizen Transformed: Being the Lame Soldier," I find disability embedded within the early modern structure of citizenship, which makes the laboring bodies of artisans available for conscription to war and subjects them to uncompensated loss. Yet from the unattributed plays *A Larum for London* and *The Trial of Chivalry* to Thomas Dekker's *The Shoemaker's Holiday*, the lame soldier troubles a key ambition of medical rehabilitation. Surgeons such as Ambroise Paré and John Woodall celebrate the possibility of remaking injured veterans, in medical texts that champion innovative prosthetic devices to repair the wounded soldier. On the stage, however, theatrical representations refuse to embrace the fixing potential of a wooden leg. Through the material of the actor's body, the theater points insistently at the lame soldier, against official discourse that looks away from the maiming the state authorizes.

By contrast, the stereotype of the "crippled" beggar, the subject of my third chapter, is a character incessantly scrutinized for faked disability in jest books and begging prohibitions. In "Performing Cripple in Theatrical Exchange," I consider how the character of Cripple, in the unattributed play *The Fair Maid of the Exchange*, offers a concept of disability that challenges the cultural equation of begging with pretended impairment. Unlike humorous figures of feigning in plays such as George Chapman's *The Blind Beggar of Alexandria* and John Fletcher and Philip Massinger's *Beggars' Bush*, Cripple is actually impaired and can work, the legal standard for distinguishing disability. Cripple's disabling, therefore, exposes social negotiations that depend on duplicitous impersonation performed by able bodies rather than productive labor. Cripple inaugurates and grounds the circuit of imitation, but the dynamic transfer of bodies and prosthetics only goes one way. The play demarcates Cripple's body as incapable of performing other roles, while Frank can borrow Cripple's prostheses as props for one of his many deceptions. Cripple's reproducibility, I argue, gestures to unequal punishment for feigning and demonstrates how mimetic representation blurs the distinction between seeming and being.

My fourth chapter, "Changing the Ugly Body," takes the problem of scrutiny into the realm of aesthetics to consider a disabling that moves from what a body does to how a body looks. In the Renaissance discourse of the "gifts of the body," which includes beauty and health alongside ability as bodily properties that must be maintained and refined, the social meaning of ugliness is inscrutable. Looking first at Francis Beaumont and John Fletcher's *The Captain*, which aligns spectators with the pleasure of witnessing a distinctive body, I then turn to Thomas Middleton and William Rowley's *The Changeling*, which conscripts spectators into the gaze of the ugly character, whose dissent from a normative standard of beauty corrodes the very basis for reading bodies. If the theater renders an "ill-favoured" appearance transparently interpretable and illegible at the same time, John Bulwer's "Artificiall Changling," in his sprawling proto-anthropological treatise, *Anthropometamorphosis*, pushes this logic of surface reading to its polemical conclusion: whether in "cosmeticall physic" or theatrical practice, the distinction between natural and artificial collapses entirely. Drawing a spectator into the vertiginous undoing of apparently stable truths about the body, disability undermines what can be determined about a person on the basis of appearance.

Whereas the ugly body compels a mode of surface reading, the fifth chapter takes scrutiny of the symptom to the problem of cause. In "Playing Time, or Sick of Feigning," I consider the "sick" body, examining bodily phenomena such as palsy, epileptic fits, and convulsions that disrupt a dramatic fiction. Disability troubles the distinction between what can be seen and what can be feigned. While discussions of such diseases in Philip Barrough's *The Method of Physic* and Reginald Scot's *The Discoverie of Witchcraft* attempt to demystify the symptoms that grip the body, the theater uses them for virtuosic effect. Turning to plays like Shakespeare's *The Second Part of Henry the Sixth* and *Othello* and Middleton's *Hengist, King of Kent*, I consider how a display of palsy or fit of epilepsy affords the theater the opportunity to experiment with the gap between the body of the actor and the body of the character. Ben Jonson's *Volpone* is the centerpiece example of this chapter, for Volpone constructs stage properties and faked symptoms into an imposture that then imperils him, stricken with a "dead palsy" when his feigning becomes public. Bearing out the dire claims of antitheatricalists that performance alters the actor's body, the play fixes Volpone in the act, a disabling that turns witnessing spectators back to their own bodily vulnerability.

The sixth and final chapter, "Making the Monster," turns to the "monstrous" body, the other term (along with "deformity") through which critics have most often wanted to historicize early modern disability. Monstrosity is the cultural discourse that has seemed most remote, easily relegated to a premodern past that took the fact of a physical anomaly for a wondrous sign. Representing the monster as a static image, monstrous birth pamphlets and medical texts emphasize the nonhuman alterity of the monstrous body. Yet I find that the theater counters such ontological claims in performance, because the monstrous characters must be made—and made up—through the palpably human form of the actor. Plays such as Jasper Mayne's *The Citye Match*, William Rowley's *The Birth of Merlin*, and Shakespeare's *The Tempest* assemble monstrosity out of stage properties. The theater's practice confounds interpretive assumptions about what a "monster" can mean by generating performed monstrosity from the unfixable body of the actor. Ultimately, I argue, theatrical form tacks across the official discourse to scramble the discursive fervor that monstrosity is supposed to incite.

In his account of the stage at the end of the seventeenth century, Jeremy Collier laments that the theater's affective power "disables the whole *Audience*." In the quotation that is my other epigraph here, Collier qualifies the stage's "*Triumphs*," but worries that its power to sway a spectator's discernment is still "unspeakable."[93] My coda, "Inviting Performance," reads this disabling as the electrifying endpoint of the theater's aesthetic experimentation with formal unfixing. The early modern theater, in a moment before the typical settles into the normative, enjoins us to a speculative theater history that defamiliarizes theatrical form. Taken together, the case studies I offer in this book demonstrate how inextricable are the thinking of disability and theatricality in early modern culture.

Most of all, I want to say that if this study prompts you to wonder about another play or example that, for want of world enough and time, I do not here discuss—what about blinding in *King Lear*? what about ugliness in *The Witch of Edmonton*? what about sickness in *A Wife for a Month*? what about deafness in *Fair Em*? what about wounds in *Coriolanus*? what about madness in *The Nice Valour*?—my answer is: yes. Disability is everywhere in early modern plays, contributing to dramatic convention, character, and plot and exceeding these frames too, opening up dramatic fictions and theatrical form to the jolts of temporal uncertainty. The performance of disability implicates the actor: Was the stutter or slip a missed cue or an intentional flourish? Does the limp reveal an actor's gait or accrue to a character's history? Is the scar a meaningful clue to character or a trace of the actor's particularity? In moments of disabling, the theater lets slip the social formations that fix bodily diversity into disability, the habits of witnessing that may be pried from predictable grooves, and the animating excess of signification that shocks theatrical form into new life. Bringing together discursive pointing and morphological showing, disability is a joint in theatrical making that allows us to perceive the incoherence of criteria that selects for disqualification—and the generative aesthetics of bodies that refuse to stay fixed. When we are looking at disability in early modern culture through the theater, we are reckoning with unfixability, with the doing and the done of performance, and the doing of disability that will never be completely done.

Chapter 1

Deformed
Wanting to See Richard III

> It may be asked, then, why all great actors choose characters from Shakespeare to come out in; and again, why these become their favourite parts? First, it is not that they are able to exhibit their author, but that he enables them to show themselves off.
>
> —William Hazlitt, *Hazlitt on Theatre*

Early modern disability studies began with William Shakespeare's *Richard III* and has not yet been able to leave the play behind. This staying power is partly due to *Richard III*'s prominence in foundational formulations of disability theory, which found "Richard" to be shorthand for "Shakespeare," who in turn is shorthand for Renaissance ideas about disability—namely, the idea that physical deformity is a powerful metaphor for moral evil. Reading through the lens of Shakespeare's villain, early work in critical disability studies understood deformity as visible evidence of depravity rather than as disabled identity. Shakespeare's Richard Gloucester "is a hunchback, but his disability represents deceitfulness and lust for power," Tobin Siebers observes, and, noting that because disability "acts as a metaphor to mark anomalous social states," Ato Quayson suggests that the play foregrounds "the question of whether Richard's deformity is an insignia of or indeed the cause of his villainy."[1] Disability operates as a powerful, if negative, sign that invites spectators to interpret the distinctive body and extrapolate to the person. Richard offers an "almost, but not yet" example of disability, emblematizing a prior historical moment, a "Renaissance version of late medieval attitudes toward deformity," in which Shakespeare's play is exemplary because he "initiates a host of many other mutable and *social* meanings for disability."[2] Richard's distinctive hunchback formation anticipates our modern understanding of disability because, in Shakespeare's play, he seems aware of the social implications of his form. The social model of disability distinguishes between the impaired body and the environment that disables the body: disability is not a fixed property of a body but the product of encounter with a world not shaped to accommodate that body. Critics emphasize the "modern" in readings of Richard that stress the mutable significance of his form, and the "early" in readings that identify Richard's deformity as precursor to the development of disability as an identity category. Richard is prior to the moment when techniques of biopower and industrialized labor in modernity produce a quantifiably "normal" body against which other bodies may be deemed "abnormal" and selected for correction.[3] He is crucial to the stories we tell about the history of disability, but infamously so, an archaic example of the past that generates the stereotype of disabled revenger that still reverberates today.

Richard III has proven to be a sticking point for early modern scholars too. A long critical history has tracked the political, theological, moral, and dramaturgical lessons that the play's title figure provides.[4] These readings often stake their claims on assumptions about the significance of visible disability. Scholars assert, for example, that the play's early modern audiences "would immediately have recognized Richard's physical deformity and moral depravity as a synecdoche for the state" and, seeing his physical appearance, would have understood Richard as the "vehicle for the doctrine that villainy in the soul was predicated by a correspondent deformity in the body."[5] Critics have also been quick to describe what exactly the Richard of Shakespeare's play looks like: "A twisted mind in a twisted shape, Richard, the crippled figure, has an unbalanced and unfinished body, a hump, a limp, and perhaps . . . even acquires a withered or shortened arm by the middle of the play."[6] The body is incontrovertible proof of his character's motivations: "In acting the body—hunched, limping, and creeping in the margins—the actor will automatically enact mind, manner, and motive."[7] The "deformed Richard Crookback" thus becomes an example of a whole class of dramatic characters whose "sheer physique is so extraordinary that their very bodies make a continuous implicit contribution on their own account, as powerful cultural signs, to the dramatic narrative."[8] These familiar interpretations demonstrate how easily we assume we know what "deformity" looks like, and therefore what Richard emblematizes, as we move from his deformed body to claims about the early modern period and back again: Richard's body seems to speak for itself, revealing evil, and his actions prove the stereotype his body evokes.

The field of early modern disability studies that has grown up around *Richard III* has challenged the moral interpretation of disability that moves so easily from appearance to evil. Richard has been read as a "dismodern" figure who wields his deformity as a performative technology of power.[9] He offers an important "nascent medical model of disability," heightening the diagnostic scrutiny his form invites.[10] Given the multiple significations of monsters in cultural discourse, his figure creates "interpretive indeterminacy" about the portent he offers.[11] His theatrical prosthetics figure the props of the state and threaten reproductive futurity by performing a kind of "genealogical disablement."[12] As a disabled character, he nonetheless dissembles his own disability by employing the stereotype of a rogue as part of a "counterfeit-disability tradition."[13] His bustling movement is the engine of the play's theatrical work with history, as his shifting form figures the relation between texts as a "degree of difference" between source and play, between quarto and folio, and between actor and character.[14] These critical arguments model generative possibilities: disability theory opens up Shakespeare's play to new perceptions of early modern ideas about embodiment, and Shakespeare's play complicates reductive assumptions about disability in the past.

And we are still talking about Richard. Although this book makes the case for moving beyond Richard III, beyond *Richard III*, and beyond Shakespeare, I begin with the conviction that there is still more to say.[15] Work in disability studies has productively questioned why an early modern play would "find it necessary for Richard to be impaired in order to make the point the text is trying to make."[16] In this chapter, I ask instead: How have we already codified the "point" of the text when we associate a stable discourse of deformity with Richard III? And, what exactly *does* Richard Gloucester's body look like on the stage? Asking these questions, I do not mean to recenter Richard III, which, as Siebers rightly points out, risks continuing to orient disability studies around the "embrace [of] standard-bearers who represent power."[17] Yet I argue here that we have not read Richard's body closely enough, moving swiftly into an "allegory of interpretation" rather than attending to the creaky joints and dazzling dexterity that define the actor's body in the act of deforming the role.[18] Over the course of this argument, I revisit Shakespeare's Richard, among other dramatic representations, and then consider libels on the death of Robert Cecil, and Francis Bacon's essay on deformity, which cement the association of deformity with evil into fixity. The knotted discourses of theatrical performance and political history, which thrive on the stereotype of his distinctive shape, point us to a richer concept of "deformity," the term that Shakespeare's Richard uses to describe his figure. By constructing physical difference through presentational action in time, theatrical performance of disability torques the relationship between the body of the actor and the body of the character.

Early modern writers use "deformity," as I noted in the introduction, to describe departures from expected form, and the concept extends far beyond bodily deficiency to encompass aesthetic, medical, and social judgments.

George Puttenham's treatise on poetry, *The Art of English Poesy* (1589), seeks to catalogue and correct "vices or deformities in speech and writing"; Philip Sidney's *A Defence of Poetry* (1595) claims that "we laugh at deformed creatures, wherein certainly we cannot delight"; and the pamphlet *Hic Mulier* (1620) cites deformity as the product of cross-dressing women who "mould their bodies to every deformed fashion."[19] Deformity is a departure from form, resulting from ignorance, or unelective incapacity, or ungovernable exercise of will. And as a verb, "deforming" also describes what an actor does. Robert Weimann has shown how the early modern theater specialized in practices of "deformity, rather than form, *dis*figurement rather than pure figuration," and William N. West observes that plays imagine the actor's performance "through a rich vocabulary of words like *disfigure, translate,* and *deform.*"[20] Richard's explicit reference to himself as Vice, one of the most popular characters from medieval morality plays, draws on an older form of presentational (or nonrepresentational) mimesis "that either preceded or at least partially precluded representation."[21] This presentational stress on the doing of the actor's body, in relation to the representational fiction of the dramatic character, foregrounds what Richard Preiss has identified as a key insight of early modern mimesis: "Theatrical authority never stops being a function of *bodies,* or being mediated by them."[22] Understanding performance as a species of deforming action, we notice the labor of the player, the actor who is both "recipient" of the form of the character and "agent that gives form to, or performs, his own frame."[23] To put this another way: we cannot examine Richard Gloucester's "rhetoric of deformation" without attending to the performance of deformation, the productive friction between the form of the actor and the form of the character.[24] Deformity is the text's litany and—crucially—deformity is the actor's license, the cue to acts of disabling that put theatrical form on view as a circuit of fixing and unfixing.

Richard's proclamation that he is "deformed" captures the unfixable indeterminacy of disability's particularity and, at the same time, the stubborn material presence of an actor's body that can never be fully abstracted. Shakespeare's play differs from his historical source in refusing to specify the exact details of Richard's body, and Richard confounds the desire for interpretive certainty that other characters express when they call attention to his bodily features. As a role played by many different actors, and as a character who acts in his own play, Richard Gloucester is never deformed in the same way twice. The long history of stage productions of *Richard III* reveals how easily the incoherent, conflicting discursive register of "deformity" codifies, under pressure, into legibility. At the end of this chapter, turning to poetic and narrative forms that publicize deformity as a referendum on the historical figure of Robert Cecil, I suggest that we must account for the complexity of theatrical form in our analysis of early modern disability. To do so requires rethinking disability around the unfixing power of deforming theatrical action. In *Richard III*, the putatively disabled body is also the most extreme expression of the performative body.

Enter Gloucester: Rereading Richard

The Tragedy of King Richard III was a blockbluster. Likely performed around 1593, printed in 1597, and then reprinted five further times before the 1623 Folio, Shakespeare's play helped to make Richard III arguably "the most dramatized English king" in the period.[25] I begin in this section by considering Shakespeare's precedents, which describe Richard as "crookback" and associate this shape with a distinct set of physical features: a hump, uneven shoulders, a limp, a shortened arm. The chief historical source for this depiction is Thomas More's *The History of King Richard the Third* (ca. 1513), also transmitted through sixteenth-century chronicle histories by Edward Hall and Raphael Holinshed. More sums up the appearance of Richard's body in a brief digression: "Richard, the third son, of whom we now entreat, was in wit and courage equal with either of [his brothers], in body and prowess far under them both: little of stature, ill-featured of limbs, crook-backed, his left shoulder much higher than his right, hard-favored of visage, and such as in states called warly, in other men otherwise. He was malicious, wrathful, envious, and, from afore his birth, ever froward."[26] Describing Richard as "crook-backed" and "ill-featured," the account suggests that Richard is short, he has some kind of limb difference, his back is bent into a hunchback formation, his shoulders are different heights, and his face is, in the unfamiliar term "hard-favored," unpleasant or ugly. The account emphasizes Richard's talent for dissimulation and his cruelty, and it also registers the variance of social perception, for this appearance is "warly," or "valiant," in princes but "otherwise" in less powerful men. Aside from this brief excursus on Richard's body and disposition, however, the narrative concentrates on Richard's political machinations and public performances. More is interested in what his audience can learn, not so much from Richard's body, but from his strategic statecraft in the consolidation of tyrannical power.

Nonetheless, the dramatic representations that precede *Richard III* seize on and amplify this physical description. The unattributed play *The True Tragedie of Richard III* (c. 1589) opens with a dialogue between the allegorical characters of Poetrie and Truth, who introduce Richard in the catechistic rhythms of question and response. Poetrie asks, "What maner of man was this Richard Duke of *Gloster?*" and Truth replies, "A man ill shaped, crooked backed, lame armed, withall, / Valiantly minded, but tyrannous in authoritie."[27] Truth's summation sounds like an excerpt from More's history, setting out the essential features of Richard's body and specifying the "lame armed" description of his limb. Truth delivers the didactic takeaway—"Valiantly minded, but tyrannous"—before Richard himself appears on the stage. Narrated in advance, Richard enters already described by a catalogue of physical features and a moral judgment that the audience is encouraged to inhabit. After all, this is Truth speaking, who has backed Poetrie into a corner with the question "What makes thou upon a stage?" Hearing Poetrie reply, "Shadowes," Truth asserts: "Then will I adde bodies to the shadowes" (sig. A3r). Truth lays claim to means of representation beyond the outlines Poetrie limns, suggesting that the bodies of actors materialize history into reality, making the past visible in the theatrical representation. This tussle between allegorical flight lines demonstrates what Brian Walsh has identified as "the philosophical and practical implications of performing the past," a conflict between chronicled past and embodied present of performance.[28] I locate the charge of this history play in the dialogue that rehearses, and heightens, expectations about Richard's appearance before the actor who plays him ever enters. By the end of the induction, the play has constructed specific expectations for the appearance of the emblematic figure of tyranny. Truth tells us what Richard looks like, simultaneously legislating and interpreting the "crooked backed" shape.

Shakespeare's *The Third Part of Henry the Sixth* (ca. 1591), the play whose subject matter precedes *Richard III* in the first tetralogy, similarly indulges in the epithet of "crookback" for Richard. Expanding on the introductory appellation as *"crookback Richard"* (s.d. at 1.1.0), Richard is called "valiant crookback prodigy" (1.4.76) and addressed as "crookback" (2.2.96), "scolding crookback" (5.5.30), "misshapen Dick" (5.5.35), "Hard-favored Richard" (5.5.77), and "an indigested and deformèd lump" (5.6.51).[29] Rehearsing "crookback," the play expands the lexicon of physical difference. In Richard's long soliloquy in 3.2, he announces his desire for the crown only to dismiss this political future ("I do but dream on sovereignty" [134]) with the lament that disability disqualifies him. Blaming "love," he claims,

> She did corrupt frail nature with some bribe
> To shrink mine arm up like a withered shrub,
> To make an envious mountain on my back—
> Where sits deformity to mock my body—
> To shape my legs of an unequal size,

> To disproportion me in every part,
> Like to a chaos, or an unlicked bear whelp
> That carries no impression like the dam.
>
> (3.2.155–62)

Richard's "deformity" is metaphorical, and it is also specifically located in a distinct feature: the hunchbacked shape is an "envious mountain" that resides on his back. The infinitives—to shrink, to make, to shape, to disproportion—are actions of maternal disforming that render the body both too little, "withered" and insufficient, and too much, the "chaos" or an "unlicked bear whelp" of matter without form. These lines simultaneously defamiliarize his human shape and discursively construct the body he presents, enumerating the features to which spectators should attend.

If his disproportionate materiality appears to determine his shape, however, Richard also announces his ability to transform his appearance:

> Why, I can smile, and murder whiles I smile,
> And cry, "Content!" to that which grieves my heart,
> And wet my cheeks with artificial tears,
> And frame my face to all occasions.
>
> (182–86)

Apparent fixity gives way to the theatrical power of unfixing deformations. Richard can appear to be anything he wishes. Now he is capable of affective responses that sever cause from effect; Richard's expressions of feeling (a "smile," "artificial tears") are technologies of imitation. His boast to "add colors to the chameleon, / Change shapes with Proteus for advantage" (191–92) relies on two familiar myths of acting in the Renaissance: Proteus, the god of the sea, whose ability to assume forms at will makes him an emblem of versatility, and the chameleon, a creature believed capable of changing to every color except white, and therefore a figure for deceit.[30] Within the same speech, Richard has nominated his body as fixed deficiency and unfixed potential; alternately, his body is an unfixed deficiency and a fixed potential. Even though his deformity is wholly negative, Richard asserts a capacity for performance that unsettles the linear plot of a future determined by a particular form.

The play, nonetheless, returns to the idea that his physical deformity is explicable as moral deformity. When Richard arrives to kill King Henry, Henry interprets Richard's features as signs of evil, from prenatal teeth that "signify thou cam'st to bite the world" (5.6.54), breaking off only when Richard, calling him a "prophet" (57), kills him to end the speech. Richard himself adopts a predictive framework that names his body as the cause of his disposition and future actions. After killing Henry, Richard returns to the question of his portentous birth with a belated answer:

> And so I was, which plainly signified
> That I should snarl and bite and play the dog.
> Then, since the heavens have shaped my body so,
> Let hell make crooked my mind to answer it.
>
> (76–79)

Like Henry, the Richard of *3 Henry VI* claims that his body should "signify," and wrests his form thus "shaped" into "plainly" visible providential history. In the scene that follows, he again cites his hunchback conformation:

> For yet I am not looked on in the world.
> This shoulder was ordained so thick to heave;
> And heave it shall some weight or break my back.
> Work thou the way, and thou shalt execute.
>
> (5.7.22–25)

In the aside, Richard identifies his distinctive embodiment as both "ordained" and the prompt for his actions. "Work thou the way" cues the actor to display his body to the audience and expresses physical force, a gesture that aspires to "execute" the template he bears. This depiction of Richard, like the others I have examined, stresses his form's determining power to produce a didactic judgment, as if the interpretation of his "crookback'd" shape is one on which both Truth and Poetrie may agree. Locating Richard's deformity as a fixed feature, these representations map a hunchback formation, a legible shape that signifies moral evil.

Richard Playing Himself: Deformations in *Richard III*

In startling contrast to this specificity, Shakespeare refuses to spell out the features of Richard Gloucester's body when he enters the stage for the opening lines of *Richard III*. Richard's soliloquy calls the play into being with a decisive and repeated "Now" (1.1.1, 5, 10), an adverb that pits the time of theatrical performance against the strictures of historical counting.[31] In the middle section of the soliloquy, Richard asserts a decisive rejection of communal relations in anaphoric refusals: rather than describing his appearance, he names his departure from expectations. He is "not shaped for sportive tricks / Nor made to court an amorous looking glass" (14–15), but "rudely stamped" (16), "curtailed of this fair proportion" (18), and "cheated of feature" (19). In abstractions that are negations, Richard announces that he is

> Deformed, unfinished, sent before my time
> Into this breathing world, scarce half made up,
> And that so lamely and unfashionable
> That dogs bark at me as I halt by them—
> Why, I, in this weak piping time of peace,
> Have no delight to pass away the time,
> Unless to see my shadow in the sun
> And descant on mine own deformity.
> *(20–27)*

Under the rubric of "Deformed" and "deformity," Richard's vocabulary of scorn—"unfinished," "cheated of feature," "unfashionable"—emphasizes his body's social defects. Yet these terms refuse the descriptive specificity of the source texts, and even Shakespeare's earlier play, in their abstraction. Where, for this Richard, is the "crookback" or "lame arm"? Recent readings of the play in early modern disability studies have perceptively noted the "performative lacuna" and "perplexing" absence of language that define the features of Richard's body.[32] This ambiguity, however, strategically deputizes the actor's deformations. Richard begins his play by directing attention to the body that he displays, but he does not tell the audience exactly what they see. The Richard Gloucester of *Richard III* is not the Richard of the unattributed *True Tragedie*, nor is he the Richard of Shakespeare's *3 Henry VI*. Instead of narrating his features, this Richard asserts what his body can—and cannot—do. He will "halt" and "descant," emphasizing movement, but his repetition of "deform," never limited to a specific hunchback formation, insistently negates the form the actor presents while putting his body spectacularly on view.

Never explicit about his appearance, Richard goes on to emphasize his body's features as he pleases. At first, Richard wants his audience to believe that his "deformity" is his identity, and that his body is disabling within his social world. However, although he claims he cannot "court," Richard's success in wooing Anne in the very next scene confirms that his distinctive body is up to the task of playing a lover.[33] Anne begins by lamenting her husband's death at the hands of Richard, whom she addresses as "thou lump of foul deformity" (1.2.57), an image that casts Richard's "deformity" as a negation of form. Yet this designation introduces a tension between fixity and unfixing that continues throughout their lengthy exchange. Richard shifts in Anne's rhetoric from object to be apprehended ("diffused infection of a man" [78]) to subject with unexpected agency ("Thou dost infect mine eyes" [148]). When Anne attempts to name the evil that Richard committed as legible proof of his moral deformity—"Thou wast the cause and most accursed effect" (120)—Richard distinguishes cause from effect in order to claim that her "beauty was the cause of that effect" (121), redefining himself as acted on, a "lump" of matter that may be formed into another shape. If Anne introduces the language of judgment with "foul," Richard not only appeals to her pity but also implicates her in the causation she introduced from the very moment she read his form.[34] In reinscribing his deformity as that which may be reformed, Richard—horrifically—redefines the terms by which his interlocutor scrutinizes his body as visible evidence for who he is as a person.

Successful in courtship, Richard celebrates the malleability of his form, even to the point of occupying the very spaces he rejected in his opening soliloquy. Once Anne concedes and Richard is alone again on the stage, he exults in his triumph, marveling that Anne will "abase her eyes" (246) on him "that halts and am misshapen thus" (250). The deictic ("thus") invites spectators to witness his form as he "halts" across the stage again, but the expectations that emerge from this shape are no more settled than before. He exclaims:

> I do mistake my person all this while!
> Upon my life, she finds (although I cannot)
> Myself to be a marvelous proper man.
> I'll be at charges for a looking glass
> And entertain a score or two of tailors
> To study fashions to adorn my body.
>
> (252–57)

Richard uses Anne's acquiescence to shape his future interpretations, revaluing his own ability to present himself as "marvelous proper." Suggesting that he can perform this persona, Richard's plan to engage tailors and "study fashions" articulates the body that, only the scene before, he imagined as "lamely and unfashionable" (1.1.22). "Fashion" registers the capacity of clothing to refine appearance, but we should not miss the emphasis on remaking his body too, which appears simultaneously fixed in particularity and infinitely malleable. Richard's new "favour" for himself in his closing couplet—"Shine out, fair sun, till I have bought a glass, / That I may see my shadow as I pass" (1.2.262–63)—not only descants on his shape but revels in his newfound fashioning as he acts in the world.[35] Richard's deformity refracts the shape-shifting possibilities of theatrical making.

By contrast, Richard also produces his deformity as exaggerated recognition, assuring others that there is nothing more to know about his body beyond its limitations. When he enters the conference with Queen Elizabeth and the other nobles, Richard decries his inability to act out the rituals of courtly sociability. He claims:

> Because I cannot flatter and look fair,
> Smile in men's faces, smooth, deceive, and cog,
> Duck with French nods and apish courtesy,
> I must be held a rancorous enemy.
> Cannot a plain man live and think no harm,
> But this his simple truth must be abused
> With silken, sly, insinuating jacks?
>
> (1.3.47–53)

This double move equates his anomalous body with evident "simple truth," unlike the "silken, sly, insinuating jacks" that surround him, whose bodies never reveal their true selves. Richard bases this appeal to honesty on the expectation he ascribes to his spectators, who believe he "cannot flatter and look fair." Visible disability, he suggests, is an invitation to surface reading. Describing the regard of others as "rancor" turns bodily insufficiency into a defensive maneuver, suggesting that it is impossible for him to counterfeit or conceal himself from their stares. Richard, to follow Rosemarie Garland-Thomson's insight, stages his own "scenes of staring" throughout the play; here he directs attention to his appearance while recoding it for his onstage spectators.[36] Aligning courtesy with artifice ("apish courtesy") and foreignness ("French nods"), his body virtuously resists untruth, precisely because deformity is incapable of pretense. His inability to "smooth, deceive, and cog" recasts impairment as self-evident sincerity. The contradiction is not lost on his offstage audience, who are well aware of Richard's capacity for deception, but in this scene Richard indulges the expectation that deformity is all there is to see.

As should be clear from this range of recastings—by only the third scene of the play!—Richard himself multiplies the possible interpretations of his body. He is unfit for social courtesies; he cannot be a skillful lover; he proves a convincing lover; he is plainly honest. Richard decodes his body in different environments, an incessant revelation that shifts his appearance with each description. Richard's onstage audience, to be sure, resists his interpretations. Anne rejects him as a "Foul devil" (1.2.50), "diffused infection of a man" (78), and "hedgehog" (102); and Margaret curses him as "elvish-marked, abortive, rooting hog" (1.3.228) and the "slave of nature and the son of hell" (230), calling him a "bottled spider" (242), "poisonous bunch-backed toad" (246), and "yonder dog" (289). The women's epithets—like the association with animality that Richard rejects ("I know none, and therefore am no beast" [1.2.72])—move down the scale of being in the search for fitting invective. Yet Richard evades these epithets, interrupting Margaret's curse to "make the period" (1.3.238) with her name rather than his own, so that her curse is "done" by Richard and "ends in 'Margaret'" (239). As the play progresses, this language appears ineffective at accounting for who Richard's body might reveal him to be or thwarting his political actions. The interpretations of providential curse and singular evil are too limited to explain the mobility with which Richard himself changes the interpretive structures that frame his body.

In fact, the play stages misinterpretations that highlight the illegibility of the body rather than the clarity of Richard's deformity as a sign of evil. Early modern beliefs about physiognomy premise their predictions on a person's appearance, a knowledge-making practice that speculates about a person from their body.[37] Persons with a "bunche on the shoulders," according to Thomas Hill's popular text, for example, are likely to be "rather trayterous, and verie wicked in their actions."[38] As Michael Torrey argues, Shakespeare's play activates this epistemological scrutiny even as it undercuts assurance of such interpretations.[39] Rather than confirming Richard's appearance as an obvious sign of evil, *Richard III* undermines physiognomic readings since other characters misinterpret Richard's own visage, to their political downfall. Just before the council that will end in his death, Lord Hastings proclaims:

> His grace looks cheerfully and smooth this morning;
> There's some conceit or other likes him well
> When that he bids good morrow with such spirit.
> I think there's never a man in Christendom
> Can lesser hide his love or hate than he,
> For by his face straight shall you know his heart.
>
> (3.4.48–53)

Hastings correctly interprets Richard's happy "conceit," but wrongly assumes a correlation between "face" and "heart." The offstage audience knows, as Hastings does not, that Richard will doom him, but this sentiment ratifies Richard's ability to sever the link between exterior appearance and inner self. Hastings reads Richard's "cheerfully and smooth" demeanor as assurance (and indeed, when Lord Stanley queries him about what he perceives of Richard's heart "in his face" [54], he replies that, if offended, Richard would have "shown it in his looks" [57]), only to recognize belatedly how wrongly he interpreted that face. The play invokes visual scrutiny as a predictive measure but reveals how easily appearances may be mistaken.

In this scene, Richard himself links deformity with monstrosity, but not in the way we might expect. Critics repeatedly term Richard "monstrous," or, noting that Richard is never actually called a monster in the play, identify him as "a composite of 'monstrous' markers and behaviors," and argue that "physical monstrosity manifests itself as social monstrosity."[40] Bodies identified as monstrous—the focus of chapter 6 in this book—were key sites of early modern political and religious judgments and of inquiry for natural philosophers. The critical assertion that Richard is monstrous derives in part from the common juxtaposition of deformity and monstrosity in early modern texts—as when the surgeon Ambroise Paré repeatedly describes the anomalous bodies he discusses as "monstrous and deformed."[41] But "deformity" and "monstrosity" are not necessarily interchangeable. The play, in fact, *resists* their proximity in Richard's own language: his opening soliloquy contains no trace of monstrous animality, and his lament about his unfinished form is as close as he comes to the boundaries of the human. If we conflate Richard's deformity with monstrosity, we miss the specificity with which he deploys the term. Hastings introduces the adjective when remarking on the deaths of Rivers, Vaughan, and Grey, "O monstrous, monstrous!" (3.2.64), but Richard never calls himself a monster, and Richard's body, with its multiplication of deforming indistinction, never becomes a clearly interpretable portent (to follow one etymology of the monstrous) because his body never stays the same.

Instead, Richard himself uses "monstrous" to register political opposition, demonstrating not the interpretability of his appearance but the effective display of power. Richard runs the timing of act 3, scene 4, creating delays as he enters belatedly for the conference of nobles, requests strawberries from the bishop of Ely, withdraws with Buckingham, and then bursts back into the gathering to ask "what they deserve" (3.4.59) who "conspire my death with devilish plots / Of damnèd witchcraft" (60–61). When Hastings volunteers "deservèd death" (66) as sufficient punishment, Richard brandishes apparent evidence of supernatural power to mar his body:

> Then be your eyes the witness of their evil.
> Look how I am bewitched. Behold, mine arm
> Is like a blasted sapling, withered up;
> And this is Edward's wife, that monstrous witch,
> Consorted with that harlot, strumpet Shore,
> That by their witchcraft thus have markèd me.
> (67–72)

Richard's "Behold" directs attention to his body once more, claiming his "withered up" arm as evidence of "evil"—but not of his own evil. Instead, he mobilizes "monstrous" against the women. The staging possibilities here could include the actor adopting a theatrical prosthesis offstage before he reenters, so that Richard displays an arm that does, in fact, look different. Yet such an accommodation to one textual cue misses the real power dynamic of the scene: Richard's arm looks exactly the same as it has throughout the play. This is a test to see whether his onstage audience is willing to participate in his fantasy of political power. The display does not confirm his body in a "monstrous" sign but reveals those who resist his interpretation. Indeed, when Hastings begins to respond, "If they have done this deed, my noble lord—" (73), Richard cuts him off, dismissing the conditional: "If?" (74), and "Talk'st thou to me of ifs? Thou art a traitor. / Off with his head!" (75–76). Richard's arm, West suggests, "snaps into deformity," a formulation that succinctly captures the temporal possibility of performance.[42] Richard's production of a deformed body highlights not the limitation of his shape but the frightening consolidation of his power.

Although the theatrical effectiveness of Richard's disability inheres in curated spectacle, his body falls out of focus, and at times he appears, contradictorily, not to be deformed at all. The Duchess of York, Richard's mother, laments that "deceit should steal such gentle shape, / And with a virtuous visor hide deep vice" (2.2.27–28), and Buckingham appeals to a visual resemblance in which Richard (whom he addresses, recounting the claim) is "the right idea of your father / Both in your form and nobleness of mind" (3.7.13–14), citing the corporeal evidence of Richard's bodily "form" for an ideal of patriarchal reproduction. Richard's body shifts into visibility, not to display deformity but to emphasize his fitness for kingship. Indeed, as Richard transforms himself into "King Richard" instead of "Richard Gloucester"—a shift in character borne out by the speech prefixes in the play's printed text—and seeks to preserve his kingship, the body that he had pronounced "deformed" drops out of his language completely.[43] The only hint of physical incapacity is his appeal to Buckingham, in the context of the coronation scene. Ordering his audience to "Stand all apart" (4.2.1), Richard calls Buckingham and commands, "Give me thy hand" (3), and then completes his line by announcing, "Thus high, by thy advice / And thy assistance is King Richard seated" (3–4). Richard produces the coronation scene as director and actor. This moment is especially open to scenic dilation because of the midline switch, for no other character speaks in the space between Richard's address to Buckingham and his pronouncement.[44] Richard scripts his own visibility as he controls the timing of the scene. Productions regularly amplify the gap between Richard's lines; he stumbles or sprawls attempting to ascend to the throne. If such a choice exposes the gap between idealized kingly form and materially deformed body, Richard also immediately adopts the rhetoric of divine right in support of his kingship. His first postcoronation words inquire, "But shall we wear these glories for a day? / Or shall they last, and we rejoice in them? (4.2.5–6); when he learns that Richmond is on the move, Richard asks, "Is the chair empty? Is the sword unswayed? / Is the king dead? The empire unpossessed?" (4.4.469–70); and later he invokes the title of king as a "tower of strength" (5.3.12). As the most properly public scene of the play, this moment of transformation from "Gloucester" to "King Richard" produces monarchy within the frame of a ritual that puts a kingly body on display.

Richard's improvisatory and contingent work with deformity becomes a liability in the representation of kingship. Richard's "theatricality" is his downfall, in Richard P. Wheeler's formulation, "because he believes the momentary illusion of reality that he creates by acting can be extended through time over the real sources of power."[45] Richard's surrender to the demands of representation recapitulates the problem of visibility: he does not look like a king. Even if Richard appropriates the concept of the king's "two bodies," the ideal body politic of the king fails to assimilate Richard's deformities.[46] Following Siebers's observation that "when a disabled body moves into a social space, the lack of fit exposes the shape of the normative body for which the space was originally designed," I find that the play's conclusion revisits the bodily essentialism that Richard's "deformity" refuses.[47] The keyword for the "normative body" of a king is "fair": clearly racializing in early modern usage, the term also maps onto ability, for Richard himself introduces "fair" as an adjective ("look fair" [1.3.47]) that his deformed body cannot inhabit.[48] *Richard III* repeatedly describes Richmond, the figure who ushers in the Tudor monarchy, as "fair," and Richmond's summary speech to conclude the play is peppered with the term. Proclaiming an end to civil wars, he avers that his "fair conjunction" (5.4.20) with Elizabeth will be a sign of "God's fair ordinance" (31), bringing "fair prosperous days" (34) to England, although his speech detours again to imagine "bloody days" (36) that "wound this fair land's peace" (39), as if "fair" cannot be conjured except by marring. If Richmond is the ideal king, he recasts England's rule in terms that borrow from Richard's own vocabulary, even though "fair" is no more descriptive than "deformed."

The play ultimately disavows Richard's attempt to redefine a future in which his deformed shape may be fixed but poses no impediment to his power. Yet *Richard III* indulges the desire to remain in Richard's murderous, impossible, transfixing present until the tragic conclusion. Even in the penultimate scene, Catesby marvels that "the king enacts more wonders than a man" (5.4.2) and Richard tallies up the Richmond look-alikes he has vanquished with relish: "I think there be six Richmonds in the field; / Five have I slain today instead of him" (11–12). Having bowed to the demands of historical record by introducing Richmond, Elizabeth I's ancestor, *Richard III* cannot hurry the victor off the stage swiftly enough. Richmond is necessarily present for fifth act's structural contrast between present and future kings; he rallies his troops in act 5, scene 2, and benefits from the ghosts who curse Richard but bless Richmond in act 5, scene 3. And Richmond utters the final words of the play, a coercive call for the audience to "say amen" (5.5.41).[49] This gesture of appeal effectively recasts as dupes the offstage spectators who applaud and asks them to witness the attempt to return to a bodily standard for kingship. Yet in the swiftness of Richmond's entry and the haste of his exit, the play structurally thwarts Richmond's assumption of the preeminence of his "fair" person, as if—in the time of theatrical performance—to contest its own inheritance from English history.

That *Richard III* keeps its titular character in action as long as it possibly can is clearest in comparison to the unattributed *True Tragedie*. There, although Poetrie and Truth do not return to instantiate the play's conclusion, the ending keeps going (and going) after Richard's death. Although Richard proclaims that he will "keep my Crowne and die a King" (sig. H3r), the play continues with Richmond's reentry, followed by Queen Elizabeth and her daughter; the crowning of Richmond as King Henry VII; Henry VII's proposal to Elizabeth (she accepts); and the desecration of Richard's corpse before it finally concludes by predicting a future that ends with thirty lines praising Elizabeth I. Ensuring that the audience condemns the tyranny portended by the "crooked backed" Richard, *True Tragedie* brings English history full circle to a present that underscores Richard's evil. In order to produce the lesson that equates physical deformity with moral depravity, the play tells its spectators what to expect, shows it to them, and then tells them what they saw. *True Tragedie* closes the loop on history, dismissing Richard III by removing him from the diegesis as well as mimesis in the final scene. Shakespeare's *Richard III*, by contrast, can barely wrench its conclusion away from the character: *Richard III* ends at nearly the moment that Richard III does. Richard began the play with "Now," deforming history in the theatrical present, and the ending confirms the deforming power of the actor who has stolen the show from the beginning.

Richard Playing Richard: Burbage and Cibber in Character

I have been suggesting that Shakespeare's Richard turns "deformed" into a cue that trades a familiar litany of features for generative unfixing. *Richard III* understands the appeal of deforming action. In performance, the play foregrounds the intersection of embodied actor and scripted character. This intersection—or competition—is echoed in the unattributed *The Second Part of the Returne from Parnassus* (c. 1602), performed by students at St. John's College at Cambridge University, which spoofs not only the title character of *Richard III* but also Richard Burbage, the actor who made him so popular. In the play, Richard Burbage and Will Kemp, another luminary of the Lord Chamberlain's Men known for his comic roles, appear briefly as characters who comment on theatrical practice. The two actors are dubious about how well scholars can act: Burbage concedes that "they have oftentimes a good conceite in a part" (sig. G3r), but Kemp suggests that "good sport" (sig. G3r) comes only from laughing at uncapable scholars who cannot speak their parts and walk at the same time.[50] When Philomusus and Studioso arrive to audition, they joke with Kemp about his morris-dancing feats and Burbage instructs Studioso to "take some part in this booke and act it, that I may see what will fit you best, I thinke your voice would serve for *Hieronimo*, observe how I act it and then imitate mee" (sig. G3v). The text records no further demonstration from Burbage, but Studioso responds, or imitates him, with a familiar line from Thomas Kyd's *The Spanish Tragedy*: "Who call [*sic*] *Hieronimo* from his naked bed? / And &c." (sig. G3v). The textual aporia of "et cetera" simultaneously invites improvisation and marks performance's ephemerality. Perhaps Studioso only repeats as much as Burbage has said; perhaps Studioso keeps going in Hieronimo's anguished speech with another few lines; perhaps Burbage's comment, "You will do well after a while" (sig. G3v), ends his imitation nearly where he begins. *Returne* conflates actor, character, and line, raising the question of whether authority resides in text or performance. Will Studioso "do well" because he is good at the part or because he is good at imitating Burbage?

This equivocation between actor and character culminates with *Richard III*. Kemp turns to Philomusus and suggests that he is apt for a clown: "Now for you, me thinkes you should belong to my tuition, and your face me thinkes would be good for a foolish Mayre or a foolish justice of the peace: marke me.—" (sig. G3v). The long dash in the printed playbook signals some presentational action, clear from Kemp's instruction, "marke me." Kemp's reference to the justice of the peace is yet another inside joke of theater history, but unlike Burbage, Kemp will not cede the floor, launching into a discourse on the commonwealth and civic virtue. When Philomusus finally begins to speak, he manages to utter one line before Kemp offers a verdict on his performance ("thou wilt do well in time" [sig. G4r]), and then Burbage cuts in, prolonging the audition with another request:

BUR.: I like your face, and the proportion of your body for *Richard*
the 3. I pray, M. PHIL.: Let me see you act a little of it.
PHIL.: Now is the winter of our discontent,
Made glorious summer by the sonne of Yorke,
BUR.: Very well I assure you, well *M. Phil.*

(sig. G4r)

Invited to "act," Philomusus promptly strikes a pose and begins the opening lines of Richard's famous soliloquy. With "Very well," Burbage interrupts him after two lines. There is no "&c" here, no prompt for more lines—suggesting, perhaps, that perhaps Philomusus would *not* be a good actor. The satire in this snippet is on his appearance as much as acting ability, for a "face" and bodily "proportion" that instantly suggest Richard III might not be a compliment, even as the figure Philomusus cuts appears to offer an advantage for this part. Yet when Burbage sizes up a possible actor to reprise his own great role, the joke is on him, too. Even if the command to extend Philomusus's audition is cruelty, the invitation to act Burbage's signature role collapses actor and character. Burbage is entangled in this web of performance history, for it is unclear whether Philomusus resembles—in appearance, gait, or gesture—Shakespeare's Richard III (whatever he looks like) or Burbage himself.

This exchange, fewer than fifteen years after the first performances of *Richard III*, in which Burbage had starred, suggests the popularity, conventionality, and iterability of Richard's role. Vamping on Burbage's memorable stage presence, the anecdote forecasts a theme in the subsequent stage history of *Richard III*. Actors—from Colley Cibber, David Garrick, and Edmund Kean to Laurence Olivier, Antony Sher, and Ian McKellen—have taken Richard's distinctive body as an invitation, if daunting, to show off their skill.[51] The part's emphasis on embodiment uniquely taxes the actor. The sheer length of the play is challenging, second only to *Hamlet* for number of lines in the 1623 Folio, and Richard appears in nearly every scene. Indeed, a familiar anecdote repeated by Sher, among others, emphasizes this intensity: Shakespeare is said to have written the play as a challenge for Burbage, and Burbage is said to have responded, "If you ever do that to me again, mate, I'll kill you."[52] Burbage's "unrecorded comeback," writes Paul Menzer, is an illustration of the theater's "barely suppressed rivalry between writer and player" tussling for firsts in theater history, an "endlessly recursive process that turns the event into the eventual."[53] We can hear that eventuality in the Burbage cameo, yet the specificity of the event—one actor's body, with its particular features—is just as forceful. The physical demand on the actor's body is part of the delight. The actor's form animates the fixed script and is also always animated by the fixing power of theatrical tradition. "Deformed" pushes the formal tension between the playwright's making and the actor's making to the limit.

While the actor's performance calls attention to the deformity of the character, the character's distinctive body calls attention to the physical ability of the actor. The performance tradition of Shakespeare's play takes Richard's scripted "deformity" as an invitation to stage arduous physical difference that may deform the actor's body.[54] The production history of *Richard III* is rife with mythologies of harm (or, as Ron Daniels, the director of the Royal Shakespeare Company, tells Sher: "Richard is notorious for crippling actors").[55] Indeed, this report is only one of a long history of reflections on the dangers of playing Richard—and the magnetic temptation of bodily contortions. Edmund Kean, who received glowing reviews when he opened as Richard III in 1814, succumbed to "a violent cold and exhaustion."[56] For Laurence Olivier in 1944, the toll of playing Richard in the stage production produced torn cartilage in his knee because, as he notes, "my limp in *Richard III*, in constantly fatigued conditions, had set up a weakness in the 'straight' leg."[57] Acting Richard poses physical risk because of the intensity of projecting the character's body.

These tales of harm reproduce, as if to prove, a key feature of antitheatrical invective in the early modern period. I noted, in the introduction, how the danger of warping the actor's body is central to the threat of the role. The act of performance contorts the actor's vulnerable body and sustains those contortions. For Gosson, the sustained effort required to "give life" to a good counterfeit poses the danger of a sticky effect: the actor may not successfully exit the character once engaged in the work of becoming. Richard Gloucester is one such character. An early modern anecdote recounts a "scholar who played Richard III in college in such a lively manner that 'ever after he was transported with a royall humour in his large expences, which brought him to beggery.'"[58] The account recasts the "transport" of performance as dangerous—possibly permanent—transformation. The danger of the role's potential effects delineates the vulnerability of the able-bodied actor. Theatrical disability poses a risk of real disabling; the disjuncture between the actor's body and the character's deformity must be effaced for a successful performance of disability and (contradictorily) maintained for a safe performance. If the play's production history is built around the challenge of a role that alters the actor, Richard's double-facing presence in the disability studies narrative reproduces the challenge of uniqueness inscribed within the role itself. This is the paradox of taking Richard as the key example of early modern disability: Richard's role depends on an actor's body that is especially, extraordinarily, able.

Without diminishing the important call to cast disabled actors, I want to observe that the theatrical history of *Richard III* troubles a clear line between disabled character and nondisabled actor in the first place. In journal entries about his preparation for the role, Antony Sher explicitly meditates on the danger of the physical technique required by the role, musing that "the problem in playing him extremely deformed is to devise a position that would be 100 percent safe to sustain over three hours, and for a run that could last for two years. Play him on crutches perhaps?"[59] Sher's performance did employ crutches as a tactic for characterization, incorporating his facility with prosthetic devices after his own physical injury from a prior role. Sher's preparation reflects offensive assumptions about disabled people: he puzzles over how best to show that "Richard's personality has been deeply and dangerously affected by his deformity" and covertly observes people with disabilities to imitate them, and demands a pronounced hump to motivate Richard's vengeance.[60] Yet he connects the role to his own experience of temporary disability, noting that "I was on crutches for months after the operation so they have a personal association for me of being disabled. They could be permanently part of Richard, tied to his arms."[61] Sher is not a disabled actor, but he is not exactly cripping up, either. The role encompasses the actor's changing and vulnerable embodiment, and we could say that Sher's embodied knowledge has been expanded through disability experience. The inventiveness of his performance would not have been possible without his temporary disability. Enacting Richard's "deformity," in a stunning performance characterized by facility with crutches and agile motion across the stage, Sher elaborated his own corporeal repertoire as a disability aesthetic.

Richard III's refusal to specify Richard's body is clearest in contrast to Colley Cibber's eighteenth-century rewrite, which shuttles deforming action into negative deformity with brutal efficiency. Cibber cut Shakespeare's play, pasted in material from *3 Henry VI*, and then starred in his version, attuning the language of deformity to his own body.[62] Writing his autobiography in 1740, Cibber reflects that the "Insufficiency" of his voice and his status as "an uniform'd meager Person" meant that he "had but a melancholy Prospect of ever playing a Lover."[63] Cibber modeled his performance of Richard on Samuel Sandford, another actor associated with the Theatre Royal company who played the "Stage-Villain . . . from Necessity; for having a low and crooked Person, such bodily Defects were too strong to be admitted into great, or amiable Characters."[64] For Cibber, resemblance between actor and character is crucial: he is certain that if Sandford had lived a century earlier, Shakespeare "must have chose him, above all other Actors, to have play'd his *Richard the Third*."[65] Sandford's skill in acting extends beyond his "bodily Defects" (his

"Person... would have been the least part of his Recommendation"), but Cibber correlates the body with the role, asserting that "the less comely the Actor's Person, the fitter he may be to perform them."⁶⁶ Richard demands a "low and crooked Person" because the "necessity"—or deficiency—of the actor's body determines the character just as much as, or more than, the discursive construction of the script.

This theory of acting informs the cuts, splices, and additions to the play. Cibber's Richard explicates exactly what his deformity means and how it looks. Cibber composed a new opening for the play (beginning with the scene of King Henry VI's murder), trimmed Richard's soliloquy, and changed key words to make clear that Richard's body is far from the norm: "But I that am not shaped for sportive tricks / I that am curtailed of Man's fair proportion" (sig. B4r).⁶⁷ Cibber's adaptation employs italics and scare quotes to register Shakespeare's lines, against which his changes appear. For Shakespeare's Richard, the line runs "this fair proportion" (1.1.18) a choice that leaves the demonstrative ambiguous—and, since Richard is alone onstage, there is no other proportion by which to judge. Cibber's version measures Richard against the sweeping category of all humanity, especially the king he has just killed. The end of the monologue interlaces lines from *3 Henry VI* into Richard's already-truncated self-presentation: "'Why then to me this restless World's but Hell, / 'Till this misshapen trunks aspiring head / 'Be circled in a glorious Diadem" (sigs. B4r–v). Cibber's play splits Richard's soliloquy between act 1, scene 2 and act 2, scene 1, adding two lines of his own to conclude:

> *Why Love forswore me in my Mothers Womb,*
> *And for I should not deal in his soft Laws,*
> *He did corrupt frail Nature with some Bribe*
> *To shrink my Arm up like a wither'd Shrub,*
> *To make an envious Mountain on my Back,*
> *Where sits Deformity to mock my Body,*
> *To shape my legs of an unequal size,*
> *To disproportion me in every part:*
> And am I then a man to be belov'd?
> O monstrous Thought!
>
> (sig. C2r)

This is a Richard reworked to fit the discursive tradition of Thomas More's *History*. Here is the arm as "withered shrub," the hump as "Mountain," tropes that are candidates for localized theater prosthetics. Julia Fawcett perceptively reads Cibber's reliance on the term "deformity" as a "process of deformation, the deliberate dissolution of the recognizable forms of identity."⁶⁸

Yet this Richard, explicitly linked to monstrosity, returns to the deformity that squats on the body. Disability operates as explanatory device for the character and—read through Cibber's theory of the role—impetus of the actor's own body. If Cibber's version "supplied linkages, transitions, and motivations that Shakespeare seemed at times almost perversely unwilling to supply," I do not read the refusal of Shakespeare's play to enforce this causal link as an oversight.[69] Cibber scripts Richard's unquestioned "crookback" and highlights his keen sense of the negative perceptions such a form inspires. This reading of deformity as motive collapses the presentational work of the actor's body and the representational attributes of the character. Shakespeare's play invites audience assumptions that we all know what deformity looks like without prescribing the features of the deformed character. Cibber employs deformity to emphasize the affective experience of disability disqualification, a characterization that dwells in the sentimentalizing register of pity.

Cibber's imposition of the crookbacked form onto *Richard III* demands our attention because of its influence in theater history. Cibber's text was the version of Shakespeare's play in use for almost two hundred years from its introduction in 1700. David Garrick and Edmund Kean, among others, made their debuts and reputations with Cibber's *Tragical History*. Indeed, John Philip Kemble, one of the most famous actors from the most famous theatrical family in England in the late eighteenth century, praises the play as "Mr. Cibber's admirable alteration of Shakespeare's *King Richard the Third*."[70] These actors, and subsequent stars who took up the play's challenge, do not conform to Cibber's assertion of the aptitude for villainy implied by a "meager Person," but they carry forward the sentimental adaptation that makes Richard's disability explicit and explicitly motivating. Even when Samuel Phelps—prompted by Charles Macready, Kean's rival, who employed a "restored" but heavily edited text of Shakespeare's play in 1821—returned to Shakespeare's *Richard III* in 1845, he maintained the tradition of incorporating lines from other plays (fifteen lines from *2 Henry VI* and seventeen lines from *3 Henry VI*), rendering concretely Richard's hunchbacked shape. *Richard III* remains a test of performative mettle, and the theatrical tradition silently imports Cibber's fixity, closing down the unfixing operations of deformity in Shakespeare's play.

Revising Richard: The Cecil Libels and the Politics of Deformity

John Scott Colley introduces his stage history of *Richard III* with a claim for the vanishing matter of the theatrical archive: "Once the final curtain falls, the body disappears."[71] The story I have been telling so far suggests that the abstraction "deformed" lights up—and is in turn illuminated by—the body of the actor. The tradition of a prosthetic that literalizes a hunch, reasserted against and through the actor's deforming shape, prompts a theater history that never disappears. Yet Richard's deformity is also invoked in the seventeenth century to decry the political power of Sir Robert Cecil, Earl of Salisbury, the son of Lord Burghley. A powerful advisor first to Elizabeth and then James, Cecil was known for his distinctive body, with a hunchback formation resulting from childhood injury, and his extremely short stature. Cecil's advancement to secretary of state, master of the Court of Wards, and lord treasurer meant that he held "the three greatest offices of state in an unparalleled monopoly of power."[72] This final section of the chapter considers the codification of deformity in short verse libels that read Cecil's disability as indication of political crimes, texts that adduce the "crookback" shape to motor social critique. In literary rather than theatrical form, these representations turn on the moral evil his shape suggests, the genealogy of disability as metaphor that persists today. The libels, moreover, ask us to reread Francis Bacon's essay "Of Deformity," often cited as evidence of early modern concepts of deformity. Early work in disability studies grounded claims about the equation of disability and moral evil in Bacon's meditation, which appears to be a philosophical exploration of an abstract topic. Reading the form of the libels together with the form of the essay, however, I consider how these literary representations of disability braid together political opportunism and reductive commonplaces, sharpening the contrast between dramatic form's unfixing power and literary form's fixing abstractions.

In the final decade of Elizabeth I's rule and the first decade of James I's reign, Shakespeare's *Richard III* went through multiple editions in quarto, alongside staple texts that took Richard III as an example, such as *A Mirror for Magistrates*, and drama, including *True Tragedie*, the Latin university drama *Richardus Tertius*, and—intriguingly, for my purposes here—a play, no longer extant, titled *Richard Crookback*, for which there is a record of payment to Ben Jonson.[73] Cecil's burgeoning political power correlates strongly with cultural interest in English histories and *Richard III*.[74] The generic trend for English history plays in the 1590s marked a shift in the theater's engagement with topical political commentary.[75] In a time when public theaters reflected on current events by looking to England's past, Cecil—known for his ambition—was widely perceived to have bested other political actors of his day such as Walter Raleigh, Francis Bacon, and Robert Devereux, the Earl of Essex.[76] For an audience "exceptionally alert to contemporary political applications," Pauline Croft observes, "it seems very likely that the drama of a ruthless hunchback, a younger son with vaulting ambition, gained extra appeal from its topicality."[77] The surge of interest in Richard III, even if entirely coincidental, gave way to explicit critique of Cecil through their shared shape. Caricatured in life, in plays such as John Day's *Isle of Gulls*, which reputedly allegorized him as "the monstrous and deformed shape of vice," Cecil was attacked on his death in 1612 in defamatory verse libels.[78] This popular form is identified by Andrew McRae as "perhaps the single most important textual site for interaction between political and literary cultures" in early Stuart England, and Alastair Bellany has demonstrated how the "crude, coruscating, scabrous verses turn out to be fascinatingly complex political performances."[79] The libels composed on Cecil's death return to Richard III to cite his "hunchback" as the overriding signifier of his evil. In this politics of the personal, the "themes which emerged most insistently and savagely were those of Salisbury's crooked back and his sexual appetites," figured in "remorseless images of deformity and moral corruption."[80] Invoking Richard III as historical precedent for contemporary political critique, the libels fix a moral interpretation of disability.

Of the many libels penned in response to Cecil's death, I focus on two that reach for a stable shape with which to indict Cecil, and find a basic correspondence between corrupt political rule and a "crookback't" body. The first verse begins with a comparison between Richard and Cecil and appears to reject it almost immediately:

> Heere lieth Robbin Crookt back, unjustly reckond
> A Richard the third, he was Judas
> In their lives they agree, in their deaths somewhat alter,
> The more pitty the poxe soe cousend the halter.
> Richard, or Robert, which is the worse?
> A Crookt back great in state is Englands curse.[81]

Referring to Cecil with the diminutive "Robbin Crookt back," the verse claims first that he is "unjustly reckond / A Richard the third," an enjambment that winks at revising the critique of Cecil only to push it further. Cecil is "Judas," with the implied rhyme "the second," a biblical allusion to betrayal that highlights Cecil's role in Essex's political downfall. While the final couplet returns to Robert and Richard to ask which figure is "the worse," the comparison undoes both of them. If Richard is a tyrant who usurps the throne, Cecil's deeds against the realm are heinous indeed. England's past becomes present, perpetuating a curse that relies on the metaphorical and material shorthand of the crooked shape.

The second libel that summons Richard for comparison begins by noting the similarities of their initials to their bodily shape, and then assigns this form to England's injury. The couplet reads: "Two R:R:rs twoe Crookebacks of late ruled Englands helme / The one spilte the Royall bloode, the other Spoylde the Realme."[82] The *R* bends into a "Crookeback" that ruins England's national power. The first line pares the two names down to the letter that serves as a shortcut for monarchical rule (*R* as in "rex"), and then finds, in the curve of the letter, a designation of bodily type, a "Crookeback." The second line individuates Gloucester and Cecil according to act, but the two clauses succinctly elide their historical difference, making them commensurate in destruction. Although Cecil never actually "ruled" the nation, the two are aligned in their perceived malignant power even before the second line divulges the analogy. Richard "spilte" and Robert "Spoylde," actions of plunder that share a common destruction of linear processes designed to perpetuate royal power and English wealth. The libel's rollicking rhythm attaches corrupt action to a specific body, a scale of compression that begins from an initial. "Crookeback" maps indirection, a refusal of the straight line, onto the bodies accused of political corruption, fixing the shape of a body into a type of character (and a character in type) to extrapolate to the imagined body of the nation.

These examples—and there are more—suggest a paradox of perception: a crooked shape is apparently evil but deceptive at the same time. Deformity is proleptic, pronouncing Cecil's crimes, but can be conclusive only in retrospect, when evidence of the "crooked" public body of a statesman hardens into truth. Cecil's reputation did not depend only on the libels; defenses, mostly in prose, were circulated to counteract the public condemnation. Unlike the anonymous libels, Cecil's defenses were composed and circulated by authors such as Samuel Daniel and William Herbert, Earl of Pembroke (who would be one of the dedicatees of the Shakespeare Folio in 1623), Sir Walter Cope, Richard Johnson, and Cyril Tourneur. These defenses avoid scrutinizing Cecil's body, alluding to his disability obliquely, if at all. Though it is immediately apparent that the libels enjoyed a broader circulation, Cecil's posthumous reputation, vigorously contested, depends on his form being overlooked by his defenders and incessantly scrutinized by his detractors.[83] Deformity's apparent description is exposed as interpretation, a work of fixing performed by the looking libeler rather than the deforming actor, an ontological claim masked as an epistemological insight. The matter of the poetic form's extremely compact short verse—even the rounded orthography of the letter *R*—abstracts meaning from a body to reduce deformity to evil. The libels indulge the fantasy that a deformed shape can reveal who a person is and metaphorize the political condition of a state.

Such tropes were circulated and recirculated to the point that the outpouring of libels on Cecil's death astonished even seventeenth-century writers accustomed to the prevalence of such defamations; as Bellany notes, a contemporary of Cecil's remarks that he "never knew so great a man so soon and so generally censured."[84] This vernacular disability discourse suggests a circular relationship between theater and culture that is vexingly, productively, mutually energizing. Was Richard Gloucester so popular because of Cecil's particular embodiment, so that the theater's endless reproductions operate as a comment on the contemporary political figure? Or does the cause and effect work the other way, so that the literary tropes popularized by cultural representations of Richard III fuel depictions of Cecil? Drawing an explicit analogy between present and past, the libels demand that we attend closely to historical context in our accounts of early modern disability representations, and of actual people described as "deformed," to perceive the fixing power of tropes of deformity. In the theater, an actor's physicality is always at least partly producing the meaning of Richard's "deformity," but the verse libels mobilize deformity far beyond the singular body.

What is more, Robert Cecil lingers in the background of the other text that early critical work in disability studies found most influential for interpreting *Richard III*: Francis Bacon's essay "Of Deformity," which has sourced important—and sweeping—claims about early modern disability. As Stephen Pender puts it, Bacon's innovation in reading deformity "as a *cause* (with its requisite effects) rather than as a *sign* (requiring interpretation) secures an explanatory paradigm in which deformity figures as impetus and end."[85] Bacon's reading of deformity challenges physiognomy's link between body and mind as a closed signifying circle, and critics such as Pender and Davis suggest that his influential essay remained the dominant interpretation of deformity until William Hay's *Deformity: An Essay* in 1754.[86] Foundational work on Bacon's essay shapes the critical discourse about early modern disability, and I suggest that we can be even more specific. Bacon's generalizing about "deformity" as an abstraction registers differently when we remember that Robert Cecil was Bacon's cousin. Bacon was vexed by Cecil's political success in contrast to his own failures at statesmanship (indeed, it was not until Cecil's death that Bacon became a prominent counselor to James, and then lord chancellor). From the very publication of Bacon's *Essays*, contemporary commentators suggested that his observations on deformity were influenced by personal animus. In December 1612, John Chamberlain wrote that "Sir Fraunces Bacon hath set out new essayes, where in a chapter of deformitie the world takes notice that he paints out his late little cousin to the life."[87]

Bacon's essay "Of Deformity" appears in the 1612 edition of *Essays*, an addition to the collection he had published in 1597. We might expect the essay to begin by defining "deformity," so the first sentence is a surprise: "Deformed persons are commonly even with nature."[88] The opening claim slips from the abstraction of the title into an adjective that allows Bacon to generalize about the characteristics of such persons as if they are already a preexisting group. They are known by their actions, Bacon posits, "for as nature hath done ill by them, so do they by nature; being for the most part (as the Scripture saith) 'void of natural affection'; and so they have their revenge of nature" (426). This cause and effect becomes a mobius strip of mutual animus: nature does "ill" to such persons, who then "have their revenge" by doing ill in turn. Once Bacon's link to Cecil and the barrage of invective that accompanied his form becomes clear, it is hard not to read Bacon's immediate move to ill-doing and revenge in the register of specific critique.

I am most interested, however, in how difficult it is for Bacon to define what constitutes the "deformity" of his title. Even the distinction that arrives in the second paragraph of the essay cannot distinguish between the person and the scrutiny that constructs him: "Whoseover hath any thing fixed in his person that doth induce contempt" (426). Bodily deformity is simultaneously characterized by fixity of feature and unfixing variance of social response. This "any thing fixed"—whatever it may be—compels "contempt" and serves as a "perpetual spur" to the deformed person "to rescue and deliver himself from scorn" (426). The stylistic indeterminacy of these observations escapes grammatical specificity, for if the passage settles on deformity as cause, the effects shift from others who respond to the person who is prompted to act. When Bacon writes, "Also it stirreth in them industry" (426), the logical antecedent of "it" is the "any thing fixed" within the person himself, but then "it" suddenly includes the perceptions of others and generates a collective of deformed persons: "Again, in their superiors, it quencheth jealousy towards them, as persons that they think they may at pleasure despise: and it layeth their competitors and emulators asleep; as never believing they should be in possibility of advancement, till they see them in possession" (426–27). Deformity becomes itself an effectual force as the pronouns multiply, and the sentence requires multiple readings to track the referent—for "it," for "they"—as each clause deforms the cause and effect Bacon tries to trace. "Of Deformity" suggests that "superiors," "competitors," and "emulators" of "deformed persons" can best chart the effects of deformity, a formulation that stresses the normative expectations of others to the point of scaling back from the deformed body altogether: the bodily given of deformity cannot be specified, only reduced to social effects.

Ultimately, the account is ambivalent about the extent to which deformity is, in fact, generalizable: "And much like is the reason of deformed persons. Still the ground is, they will, if they be of spirit, seek to free themselves from scorn; which must be either by virtue or malice; and therefore let it not be marvelled if sometimes they prove excellent persons; as was Agesilaus, Zanger the son of Solyman, Aesop, Gasca President of Peru; and Socrates may go likewise amongst them; with others" (427). The final sentence strings along clauses of condition that hover between possibility and destiny. "If" is the determining conjunction for the "deformed persons," but this collective group splinters into individual examples across temporal and national registers. While the injunction to the readers not to marvel peremptorily elides one affective response, Bacon also concedes a partial rehabilitation for the "sometimes . . . excellent persons" he has characterized as deformed. His list of examples, which ranges from biblical to ancient to contemporary figures, ends with a clause that trails off in elusive incompleteness. Although the genre is given to testing ideas, the essay's final "with others" gestures not to a formal limitation but to the impossibility of pinning down the topic. Bacon summons his audience to take note of deformity, but the causal production of "deformed persons" from "deformity" continually slips back to the individual. The essay evinces a fundamental irresolution about the relationship between deformity, the actions of deformed persons, and the social restrictions on a body. "Of Deformity" shapes Richard's characterization in critical discourse about disability, but a closer reading reveals instead that deformity is socially unfixing even when it appears most evident in particular bodies.

* * *

One of the anecdotes to which literary critics frequently turn when we think about the contemporary reception of *Richard III* emphasizes the extent to which the Richards—Burbage and Gloucester—become indistinguishable as a result of impersonation. John Manningham's diary entry dated March 13, 1602, records an anecdote from William Towse about a theater-driven tryst that depends on confusing the actor and the character: "Upon a tyme when Burbidge played Rich[ard] 3. there was a Citizen grewe soe farre in liking with him, that before shee went from the play shee appointed him to come that night unto hir by the name of Ri[chard] the 3."[89] Jean E. Howard asks, "In the anecdote, who is attractive: Richard III or the Burbage who impersonated him?"[90] The very undecidability of the referent—which Richard?—recalls the example from *Returne* that both roots Richard's body in Burbage's own form and also identifies that form in another actor. To read the Richard/Richard overlap in the citizen's reported request is also to extend Richard's irresistible identification to the spectator. The anecdote's structural misogyny will turn the woman's desire into a punch line. (Manningham continues, explaining that Shakespeare overhears this tryst and gets to her before Burbage, a joke that puts the playwright before the actor in preeminence, as if prioritizing script over performance.) Yet this triangulation of male competition through the desiring spectator misses the woman's own investment in the play. After watching Burbage play Richard, the citizen wants to participate in the play herself, taking on the role of Anne and asking to be seduced by Richard's compelling presence and the arresting spectacle of his deformed body.[91] Just Burbage is not enough; she wants him as the character he personates. Making the appointment, the citizen demands to have Richard III played offstage, the actor inextricable from the character in desirable deformations.

I have argued that *Richard III* expands our notion of early modern disability if we understand "deformity" as a register of Richard's astonishing mobility in and through theatrical form. While it is clear that historical precedents for Richard III and the legacy of theatrical performance reduce his character to a stereotype, Shakespeare's *Richard III* harnesses theatrical performance through deforming action and reveals the process of social construction. Richard mobilizes deformity as the object of interpretive fervor and leverages this attention to his shape for seductive power, challenging the critical and cultural impulses to codify his deformity into a specific, legible, bodily formation. Richard confounds moral exemplarity because his deformity is never fixed, never stabilized into a fully disabling conformation. This interpretation ossifies in theatrical practice when Cibber's forceful rewriting of Richard stabilizes a back-formation of this stereotype, bringing bodily difference, social perception, and characterial motivation into lockstep to produce the legacy of the most emblematic disabled character on the early modern stage. Historically, this calcification has as much to do with the coincidence of Robert Cecil's bodily conformation and Francis Bacon's jealousy of his cousin's political success—a generalizing taken for truth, even when it is at its most particular. The scripted "deforming" action is an unfixing that the libels deny, framing Cecil's deformity into exactly the moral interpretation that we have accorded to Richard.

If we read early modern drama to understand disability in the period, then *Richard III* is one of the right plays to read but the wrong play to take as exemplary of a limited moral interpretation of deformity. If, in the broadest definition, we understand theatricality as how a play's "text enables a performance that exceeds its written form," deformity is a vector for that indefinable excess.[92] "Deformed" initiates the circuit of the script's fixing and unfixing of the actor's body and the actor's fixing and unfixing of the script, inviting spectators to witness what the theater is making in front of them. Moments of disabling ask us to notice how the theater depends on the virtuosic, vulnerable human actor, and "deformed" reveals more about cultural expectations than bodily properties. Richard's dramatic character demands virtuosic acting because the play accretes a long history of speculation about his overdetermined body, inciting the desire to see this body. But in refusing to make this body explicit except through the actor's gestures and movement, the play reveals disability—here, as the bodily indistinction that Richard performs—as an unpredictable theatrical resource for the early modern stage.

The next chapter considers the "lame" soldier—unlike Richard, not a powerful noble who becomes a king, but one of the many soldiers who fights for England and then returns home wounded, newly disabled. Like "deformed," "lame" is discursively denoted but theatrically open, a bodily particularity that accrues social significance. Unlike Richard's deformity, however, the maiming of the lame soldier marks subjection to the mechanisms of state conscription for England's history of war. Where Richard III enters *solus* and never stops running his show, characters such as Ralph and Stump flag the refusal to countenance the injuries war produces. The lame soldier, so ubiquitous as to be a type, offers an example of characterization as transformation. His prostheticized presence, often marginal, discloses disability as a matter of social capacity as much as function.

Chapter 2

Citizen Transformed
Being the Lame Soldier

> A Captaine dispatching a lame souldiour out of his bande, the souldiour mal-content said unto him:
> The warres need no men that can run away, but such as can bide by it.
>
> —Anthony Copley, "Of Crookednes and Lamenesse"

The epigraph to this chapter, a jest from Anthony Copley's 1595 collection *Wits fittes and fancies*, plays on the possibilities of an apparent bodily deficiency. "Mal-content" about the captain's presumptive dismissal, the soldier reconfigures bodily lack into martial virtue, insisting he will stay put in battle. For the captain, the soldier's lameness is visible evidence that his body is unable; for the soldier, lameness is evidence he is able to meet the peculiar demand of "the warres," which "need no men that can run away."[1] One of John Bodenham's brief poetic "Examples" records the lines, "*Androclidas* derided being lame, / Said; Then in fight I hope I shall not flie," and a similar recasting of lameness is attributed to "a Souldier beying lame," in an epigram collected by Timothy Kendall, who is asked "wherefore, / lympeing to warre he went" and replies that "though lims be lame, / my mynde to fight is bent."[2] These verses read lameness as productive physical constraint, a bodily lack recompensed—even spurred on—by the mind "bent" to fighting and the "sound" spirit. The soldier's negative formulation revalues the demands of warfare. What matters are the evasions this body cannot perform: a lame leg makes a good soldier by immobilizing him against cowardice. Impairment produces embodied steadfastness. If his physical limitation is perceived as disqualifying, the lame soldier forecasts a different future of bravery. These verses invite us to ask: what, exactly, disables a lame body? How does a lame body signify?

CHAPTER 2

I take up the figure of the "lame" soldier, whose body bears the signs of his service, in order to understand how the social construction of disability exposes a contradiction at the heart of early modern discourses of citizenship. Focusing on a cluster of plays from around 1600, the unattributed works *A Larum for London* and *The Trial of Chivalry* and Thomas Dekker's *The Shoemaker's Holiday* (with a nod to *The Famous Victories of Henry the Fifth*), I chart the lame soldier's presence in dramatic fictions, against a civic history of war and a medical history of surgical restoration. In 1599, plays about war would have felt especially topical to English audiences, given the ongoing conflicts through the 1590s; in the summer of 1599, news of Spanish forces preparing to attack London gripped the court and city to the point that Queen Elizabeth ordered soldiers mustered for the city's defense until the threat dissipated at the end of the summer. My reading of the citizen conscripted to war begins from a curious detail in a stage direction: in *The Shoemaker's Holiday*, Ralph Damport departs for battle in the play's opening scene and later returns, *"being lame"* (s.d. at 10.52). The lame soldier evinces the potential contradiction between citizenship as a civic identity associated with the early modern guild system and citizenship as a national claim that conscripts soldiers to fight "in defence of Her Majesty and the State." While both senses of citizenship depend on the citizen's labor—the artisanal labor of the craftsman and the martial labor of the soldier—the injury that results from the soldier's service renders the citizen unrecognizable. In moments of disabling that call attention to the lame soldier's loss, the theater exposes the conflict between national and urban identity inherent within the category of the citizen.

The lame soldier complicates the idea, received from early formulations in disability studies, that impairment was understood as unremarkable deformity in early modern England. In a preindustrial moment, prior to the concept of a quantifiable bodily norm, this idea goes, physical difference would have seemed unremarkable: mere impairment that did not rise to the social scrutiny of disability. Thus impairments and illnesses, "perhaps because they were so much more common, expected and accepted than they are today," were not socially disqualifying, for they "used not to render individuals socially unfit or invisible, that is, excluded on the basis of their biological anomalies."[3] Perceptively identifying deformity as an analogue for disability, Lennard J. Davis nonetheless elaborates deformity as the expression of "variously marked unexceptional bodies" prior to the concept of the norm, suggesting that "unless the deformity is wondrous, it is ignored or erased."[4] Impairment—a missing finger, a limp, a pockmarked face, a crippled body—is simply quotidian bodily difference rather than what Rosemarie Garland-Thomson calls the "attribution of corporeal deviance" that defines disability.[5] This chapter contests the idea that lameness equates to unremarkable difference. Instead, I find that the lame solder's quotidian deformity illuminates disability as a problem of social significance rather than function. The lame soldier's marginal presence embodies an injury from which spectators recoil and look away.

The lame soldier exposes the state's refusal to consider the bodily cost of the citizen's lost work—indeed, he indicts a gaze turned away from that cost and toward fantasies of medical rehabilitation. In what follows, I affiliate such disablings with recent work in critical disability studies. "Debility," according to Jasbir K. Puar, is the result of biopolitical power exercised to produce "injury and bodily exclusion that are endemic rather than epidemic or exceptional."[6] Debility escapes a formulation of disability as a rights-bearing identity; Puar traces how the state engages in acts of maiming bodies while "capacitating" others—rehabilitating disabled bodies that are "available and valuable enough for rehabilitation."[7] This insight concurs with Robert McRuer's concept of "disability exceptionalism," the idea that nationalist rhetoric *"using disability as a vehicle"* simultaneously "positions threats . . . as external or simply elsewhere" while overlooking "the redoubled, and *internal*, neoliberal threat to disabled or impaired bodies and minds."[8] These contemporary analyses work from a frame of late global capitalism, a concept barely adumbrated in early modern England, but the notions of debilitating power and disability exception usefully illuminate the contradictions that inhere in the early modern figure of the lame soldier. The jests and quips with which I began this chapter positively revalue lameness as capacity rather than lack; more significantly, however, the disabled figure's claim to courage justifies the state's practice of injuring citizens. The jest's lame soldier exposes disability as a vehicle for nation-building—a body that returns from war diminished, but marked with singular valor—while it directs attention away from the civic structure that requires his service.

As I will demonstrate, the theater's staging of the lame soldier departs from early modern medical discourse. Surgical texts champion prosthetic devices, such as stilts or wooden legs, both to restore the limping body's movement and, just as significantly, to enable social recognition. While surgeons celebrate the possibility of fixing bodies wounded by war, the theater highlights lameness through theatrical prosthetics. Fixing the actor's body into the "lame" character, performance points at the body's disabling. The theater's formal practice defies the ambition of invisibility that characterizes the rhetoric of surgical rehabilitation. The citizen-veteran becomes remarkable not for his impairment—although the prospect of losing the ability to labor shadows every theatrical image of a citizen dispatched to fight—but for his unrehabilitated loss. He evinces the glaring lack of compensation for martial labor even as that labor irrevocably alters his body.[9] The dramatic examples I consider here ask us to perceive disability in the early modern period as embedded within, even a consequence of, foundational structures of citizenship, an intersection of dramatic form and the political form of the embodied subject. And if the plays dramatize a gaze turned away from the lame soldier's body, theatrical enactment insists on his visibility through the stubborn materiality of the actor'.

Compensating Lameness in *The Trial of Chivalry* and *A Larum for London*

In English literature of the sixteenth and early seventeenth centuries, wounded soldiers are figures of recent history and promising innovation, appearing in treatises on military theory and war, edicts for the care of returning soldiers, medical texts that recorded new techniques mined from battlefield experience, and dramatic representations of noble and common soldiers.[10] By the turn of the seventeenth century, the state's responsibility to soldiers had emerged as a pressing concern, given the relentless campaigns in which England had been engaged, and the state exertions that demanded troops.[11] The constellation of edicts for relief, revived and newly articulated, note the necessity of rewarding soldiers who fought and encouraging new recruits. Elizabeth I's 1592 "Acte for Relief of Souldiors" designated that "suche as have synce the twentie fyveth Daye of Marche Anno 1588, aventured their Lyves and loste their Lymmes or disabled their bodies . . . in the defence and service of Her Majesty and the State, shoulde at their retorne be relieved and rewarded, to thend that they maye reape the Fruyte of their good deservinge, and others maye be encouraged to performe the like Endevors."[12] Venturing lives, losing limbs, and disabling bodies—backdating relief and reward to 1588, the act recognizes that England's wars have produced a population of permanently disabled soldiers who may be unable to work on their return. In this provision, upheld in subsequent acts through the reign of Charles I, "disabled" registers the veteran's inability to work and warrants relief for work of "defence" and "service" to the monarch and state.

Yet the soldier returning to England after such endeavors was a vexed figure: unable to work because of his injury and thus eligible for relief; or able-bodied, but threateningly vagrant if he had no job to which to return.[13] A. L. Beier points out that "most of the thirteen poor laws passed between 1495 and 1610 had as a first premise the discrimination between those able and unable to work."[14] This distinction links care for the deserving poor with the punishment of those who feigned need for relief to which they were not entitled, and it admits the fear that imposters might claim the "reward" owed to disabled soldiers. The 1598 and 1601 statutes prescribed strict penalties for "all wandering persons and common Labourers being persons able in bodye using loitering and refusing to worcke," punishing "Rogues Vagabonds and Sturdy Beggars" with a public whipping and forced labor.[15] While soldiers were allowed to beg on the way home, a practice that, Beier suggests, increased the number of vagabonds and failed to reintegrate them into society, this informal practice of soliciting money was highly suspect.[16] Despite the aim to celebrate their service and encourage others to fight, provisions for returning soldiers flag battle wounds as an uncertain impediment to labor.

In a moment when war preoccupies the audiences of London theaters, plays continually return to the lame soldier as the crucial locus of concern. As scholars such as Patricia A. Cahill, Nicholas de Somogyi, Roslyn L. Knutson, and Genevieve Love have perceptively discussed, these dramatic representations bring England's wars into the playhouse, in tones that vary from victorious to traumatic.[17] I begin with that triumphal tone in the unattributed play *The Historie of the Tryall of Chevalry, With the life and death of Cavaliero Dicke Bowyer* (likely 1599, printed 1605), for the lame soldier identified in the subtitle complicates identification with the common English soldier. The title's emphasis on chivalry inspires nostalgia for wars of the past, and Dick Bowyer's surname—"maker of bows"—reminds the audience of a weapon that had given way to artillery by the seventeenth century. Part miles gloriosus, Bowyer is unapologetically English in a play concerned with conflict between the kings of France and Flanders, a conflict resolved by Pembroke, the sole English noble in the retinue. Bowyer refers to himself in the third person throughout the play in a distinctive refrain: "he that is a true soldier, and a Gent. as Dick Bowyer is" (sig. C2r); "Dick Bowyer knowes what belongs to service" (sig. C2v); "Dicke Bowyer is a Soldier, and a Cavaliero" (sig. D4v); and "tis well known, since Dick Bowyer came to Fraunce, he hath shewed himselfe a gentleman & a Cavaliero" (sig. C1v).[18] A cavaliero may be a gentleman trained in arms or a soldier on a horse, like a knight. The repetitions of "gentleman" and "cavaliero" send the play into the mode of romance, making the soldier's work a version of aristocratic service that avoids the problems of conscription and compensation.

Bowyer's somatic distinctions—his speech impediment and his limp—introduce a dynamic relation between lack and capacity, pointing at his injury but never preventing his speech or courage.[19] Peter, his rival in courtship, introduces Bowyer's anomaly before Bowyer ever enters the stage, lamenting "I am crost with a Sutor, that wants a piece of his toung" (sig. A4r) and explaining that Bowyer "limps, and he limps, & he devoures more French ground at two paces" (sig. A4v). The repetition makes Bowyer's body both excessive and notable ("he limps, and he limps"), reproducing the halting rhythm of his gait but recasting his movement as effortless consumption of French land. This description previews the incessant motion that characterizes Bowyer in the rest of the play (and Peter again laments Bowyer's "lame legs" and "his lisping toung" [sig. A4v]). Yet when Bowyer himself describes his disability, he mythologizes the material cause of his injury: "Once as I was fighting in S. Georges fields, and blind Cupid seeing me, and taking me for some valiant Achilles, he tooke his shaft, and shot me right into the left heele, and ever since, Dick Bowyer hath beene lame: but my heart is as sound as a bell, heart of Oake, spirit, spirit" (sig. C1v). This tale of mistaken identity is a tribute to his martial prowess. His lameness is due to inadvertent injury by the god of love ("blind Cupid"), who mistakes Bowyer for the nearly invincible epic fighter ("some valiant Achilles") in an arena that invokes the most heroic knight of English myth ("S[t]. Georges fields"). This is no sordid battle wound. Proof of skill rather than evidence of vulnerability, the cause of his lame leg emphasizes not his variance of gait but his internal solidity. His "halt" is not the work of nature but of valor. Like his rival, who reiterates "limp" in characterizing him, Bowyer repeats himself ("spirit, spirit"), but the repetition emphasizes ability undeterred by injury, for his "heart is as sound as a bell"; he has a "heart of Oake," an English tree. Bowyer's resolve remakes his body as a history of martial ability.

Claiming his lameness is exceptional proof of English bravery and dedication, the play only occasionally marks the injury as a sign of limitation. Bested in single combat for his shield, Bowyer admits, "Thou mayst thank my lame legge: theres my shield" (sig. G3r). Yet this failure only makes him like every other knight in the play, since everyone else loses in this contest to the disguised Pembroke too. In the play's (extended) final battle, pitting the kings of France and Navarre against each other, Bowyer mobilizes his exceptionalism in order to ward off deserters and establish martial community among the English soldiers specifically. Believing that Pembroke is dead, Bowyer orders them: "Heere's some of us knowes how to runne away, and they be put to it: Though wee have lost our brave Generall, the Earle of Pembrooke, yet here's Cavaliero Bowyer, Core and Nod, by Jesu, sound Cards; and Mahound and Termagant come against us, weele fight with them. Couragio, my hearts, S. George for the honour of England" (sigs. H4v–I1r). They fight for England without their "brave Generall," a military hierarchy expanded to status ("Earle"), because Bowyer urges them on, unlike those who "knowe how to runne away." Although he musters his men in support of another nation's army, the collective labor is resolutely English and decidedly Christian, with undivided national and religious allegiance.[20] The chivalric model of nobility-centered "gentleman's warfare" offers a snow-globe fantasy of a past in which even common soldiers fight for glory, not money, and require no compensation for their lameness when they return from war. Bowyer's limp is only ever a matter for the present of the campaign's foray. His disabling associates injury with courage, a social value that accrues to the military ideal because he never has to return home to England. Like the indignant soldier of the jest, Bowyer invites nationalist sentiment that obscures—and even renders sordid—the drafted citizen's unchosen obligation to military service.

Bowyer's lameness signals an English soldier who needs no compensation other than honor. The lame soldier in the unattributed play *A Larum for London: With the ventrous actes and valorous deeds of the lame Soldier* (likely 1599, printed 1602) models a very different relationship between the service of the lame soldier and the payment his work entails.[21] In *Larum*, war explodes into civic space. Based on George Gascoigne's *The Spoyle of Antwerpe*, an account of the Spanish attack on Antwerp in 1576 that is as much propaganda as documentary, the play redirects Gascoigne's sensationalist prose to warn London specifically. *Larum*'s fantasy extends in the direction of brutality. The play reports and even stages graphic scenes of violence during the attack: citizens are stabbed, stripped, tortured, hanged, stoned, shot, and threatened with rape. Critics have focused on the topicality of the play, tracing how *Larum* trades on the didactic power of the history play, how it engages with late Elizabethan fears about increasing militarization and the threat of Spanish attack, and, in Cahill's perceptive analysis, how the stage replicates the traumatic events it tries to explain.[22] Love argues that the "lame Soldier" of the play's title yokes a set of central analogies in the play, the "interplay of sameness and difference between body and prosthesis, actor and character, present and past, English and Dutch."[23] Stump is the figure of disability through which theatrical problems are articulated in constative oppositions; here, I consider how Stump focuses the critique of citizens who avert their gaze from the consequences of war.

Larum refracts its lessons to London through the "lame" character of the play's subtitle, whose "ventrous actes and valorous deeds" model the work of fiction encrusted onto the history. This soldier does not appear in the source, nor is he given a name until late in the play. Although the historical protagonists are identified by name from the beginning, the "lame Soldier" is identified as "Stump" in most speech prefixes and only addressed by name (*"Vaughan"* [sig. F2r]) and rank (lieutenant) near the end.[24] Indeed, Stump does not even speak in his first entrance, when he is introduced textually in a stage direction for another character, Van End: *"As he is going out Stumpe encounters him"* (sig. C1r). Stump's singularity in the play's title and speech prefixes, along with his prosthetic leg, Naomi Baker suggests, "signals a dislocation, ethical as much as physical, from social norms."[25] Yet in the interim between appearing onstage and being named, as Love and Vin Nardizzi have both discussed, Stump's presence is characterized by visual bodily synecdoche. Pointing out that "stump" could refer to the "veteran's wooden leg" or to "the portion of the limb that has healed after amputation, the rounded thigh or nub strapped into a wooden stump," Nardizzi observes that "Stump" names at once bodily loss, the prosthesis that the character employs, and the dramatic character himself.[26] Love extends this set of relations further to include the "sonic dimensions" of Stump's "onomatopoetic . . . locomotion"—the thud of his wooden stump tapping out the speech prefix he is accorded—in which "his body's nouns become his movement's verb."[27] The play consolidates Stump's character around a visual and sonic distinctiveness; Stump is body and part, making audible the negotiation with the environment of the theater.

Chief among the play's preoccupations is the idea that citizens ought to have been soldiers. The Spanish invaders themselves point this out, as their commander notes that the "remisse and negligent" citizens of Antwerp hired mercenaries to defend them, failing to have "fore-seene the daunger [that] might ensue" (sig. A2v). Unpracticed and unprepared, Antwerp's citizens themselves are slower to learn; for having heard of the Spanish attack, they still refuse to fight. Stump enters the stage to hear the citizens urged, "To armes to armes," and "Stand not amazed, but with couragious hearts, / And forward hands, fight for your libertie" (sig. C2r), a final injunction that prompts Stump's first words in the play. In a lengthy diatribe about the horrors of Spanish invasion, he asks, "Are yet your eye-lids open, are you yet / Awakt out of the slumber you were in? / Or will you still lye snorting in your sloath?" (sig. C2r). Constructing the citizens as sleeping spectators, Stump mobilizes the form of the question but never pauses to let the citizens respond before imagining the violence to come. In the speech that follows, he foretells their suffering when "naked swoords glide through your weasond-pipes," and eventually answers his own questions about whether the citizens are aware of their danger: "I tell ye burghers no" (sig. C2r). The lame soldier, an obvious veteran of war, indicts the negligent citizens for their failures, mirroring a propagandistic call to national arms.

The critique of citizens who will not be soldiers gives way to its corollary: outsourcing their duty to fight, citizens fail to compensate their surrogates for martial labor and fail to care for their veterans. Stump claims that he "prophesied" with "zealous words" about the dangers of the Spanish, only to be "revil'd and bafled for my loyaltie" (sig. C2v). The verb "bafled" hearkens to chivalric punishment, the knight's baffling being a rebuke of martial cowardice, but this ire is sparked by the citizens' refusal to recognize the bodily costs these soldiers have borne. When a citizen pleads with him to "helpe to fight for Antwerpes libertie," Stump asks whether he has "another groate to give me then" (sig. C2v), a pointed commentary on the lack of remuneration:

> I know your liberall mindes will scorne t'impose,
> The sweat of bloudie daunger on the brow
> Of any man, but you'l reward him for it:
> He shall at least (when he hath lost his limmes)
> Be sent for harbour to a spittle-house.
> How say yee, shall he not? Good reason then,
> But we should venture; yes, to laugh at you,
> Whilst we beholde the Spaniard cut your throates.
>
> (sig. C2v)

Even as Stump urges the citizens to war, he anticipates the consequences of the soldier's labor. Facing the possible harm of "lost . . . limmes" in exchange for a "groate" from the citizens, Stump retorts that the soldiers should "venture" not their bodies but their laughter. Citizens are not "liberall"; the soldiers do not receive a "reward"; finally, there is no "harbour" for those who lose their limbs. Although Stump is singular in this scene, his imaginative forecast moves from a hypothetical soldier ("he" that "hath lost his limmes") to invoke a speculative plural of all wounded soldiers ("we" who "should venture"). Stump projects future loss, looking ahead to the day when the soldier's labor is used up and there is no structure of care.

Larum makes clear that the soldier's body grounds martial labor and presents the problem of recompense. To Stump's objection, the Burgher, representative of the city, responds that "it is thy Countrie that doth binde thee to it, / Not any imposition we exacte" (sig. C2v). Although the Spanish invasion threatens the city, the Burgher suggests that Stump's military obligation is owed as his contractual obligation to his country, if not to Antwerp itself.[28] Stump responds with a scale of compensation that counts this cost literally:

> Bindes me my country with no greater bondes,
> Than for a groate to fight? then for a groate,
> To be infeebled, or to loose a limme?
> Poore groates-worth of effection; Well, Ile learne

> To pay my debt and to measure my desert
> According to the rate: a groate I had,
> And so much as a groate amounts unto you,
> My swoord shall pay ye in exchange of blowes.
>
> (sig. C3r)

How many blows and how many limbs of a soldier's body can a groat purchase? The "debt" and "exchange" of a leg grounds economic transactions in the body, a problem of loss that the early modern period's legal discourse recognized as a matter of financial recompense.[29] Yet Stump's questions reverse the logic of repayment for injuries received in war, formulating an impossible rate: if paid a groat, then Stump will carry out his obligation—whatever that is worth—with exactly that much fervor. I take Stump's "effection" as both "effect" and "affect," an account of the "bondes" of felt national obligation, the homonym a complex reckoning of compensation. What stands out most of all is the inevitability of harm. Bodily injury is only a matter of *when*, not *if*. The future imagined for a soldier is one of anticipatory injury, when he is "infeebled" or "loose[s] a limme," a loss for which the soldier will only ever be underpaid.

Despite his sharp critique, Stump takes the lead in the city's defense, wreaking revenge on the Spanish, and his wooden stump becomes the sign of his honor as a soldier. Just before he intervenes to save a woman harried by soldiers, he exclaims, "And still my olde rotten stump and I, / Trot up and downe as long as we can wag" (sig. C4v). Appealing to a soldierly code, Stump prompts other soldiers with his injury: "No roague Sir, but a Soldier as you are, / And have had one leg more then I have now" (sig. D1r). The stage direction's indexical disabling, *"Pointing to his leg"* (sig. D1r), overrides any detraction, though it signifies doomed bravery rather than comic possibility. When Stump comes upon two soldiers who hope to escape by disguising themselves as if they were "maimed" in fighting, Stump calls them back to the claustrophobia of the city ("Harke you hark you, whether wil you flye?") and to their incapacity: "what have you to carry with you, but your scurvie notch'd limmes?" (sig. F1v). Their limbs have become "notch'd" in his rejoinder, an anticipatory gesture of their wounding when the soldier's duty cannot be relinquished. Stump asks: "What will you doe then? here is my poore stumpe and I have stumbled through a thousand shot, & yet we halt together; there was never one poore peece of Timber has been so sindg'd as it has been: zbloud it has been foure times a fire under me, and yet we scramble together trotting, trotting" (sig. F2r). Stump's distinctive body, recomposed around his leg, is an artifact of military experience rather than loss. His "poore peece of Timber" converts would-be deserters to soldiers again.[30] The repetition "trotting, trotting," as we have seen in Bowyer's example, renders his gait and the wooden leg ostentatious. This resignification of his lame body takes effect, for the soldiers address him by his title when Stump urges them to "Dye like men," responding, "*Lieuetenant Vaughan, leade us and wee'll follow you to the death.*" Given a name at the moment he is unfixed from reduction to the stump ("my poore stump and I"), he urges them on: "Yes, Ile halt before you, follow mee as straight as you can" (sig. F2r). Stump dies on the battlefield, but the play concludes with even the Spanish general extending him honor.[31] Stump's bodily loss enables the defense of unthankful citizens and wins even the appreciation of the besieging invaders. The play's valorization of the lame soldier offers a disability exceptionalism even within the dramatic fiction, as Stump's stump secures—and reproduces—an ideal of military courage.

Yet the play embeds an analysis of the state's refusal to countenance the injuries of war, in the form of an explicit contrast between martial labor and artisanal labor. Addressing the citizens who plead for his aid, Stump responds:

> A swettie Cobler, whose best industrie,
> Is but to cloute a Shoe, shall have his fee;
> But let a Soldier, that hath spent his bloud,
> Is lame'd, diseas'd, or any way distrest,
> Appeale for succour, then you looke a sconce
> As if you knew him not; respecting more
> An Ostler, or some drudge that rakes your kennels,
> Than one that fighteth for the common wealth.
>
> (sig. C2v)

Stump opposes the "industrie" of the "swettie Cobler" with that of the "Soldier, that hath spent his bloud," to mark the stakes of each kind of labor. The cobbler and the hostler are clearly remunerated: the citizens recompense artisanal "industrie" in the work of the "swettie Cobler" and even acknowledge the manual labor of the "Ostler" or kennel "drudge," but they will not render the "fee" for the soldier's work. Just as significant as their refusal to pay the newly impaired soldier is their deliberate aversion to social regard: the citizens purposely fail to see the body "distrest" from martial service.[32] Looking askance, they disavow the wounded soldier "as if," in Stump's indictment, they "knew him not." They refuse even to witness the bodily harm he has endured.

Stump exemplifies this deliberate disregard of the "lame'd" body, but his plea is not only his own. A soldier, any soldier, is a spectacle from which citizens avert their gaze. Unwilling to countenance the sacrifice of the body on which their city's defense is premised, the "common wealth" not only shirks compensation but actively refuses to see the person. Bowyer's lameness indexes English valor on the battlefield to disaffiliate martial labor from payment, but *Larum* reveals the nonidentity between the soldier and the citizen, who will neither pay nor recognize the body that has labored in his stead. Bowyer's nostalgic fantasy and Stump's trauma rehearsal are ideological mystifications that valorize war, a carrot and a stick for drumming up citizen soldiers. Yet the plays disclose disability as a matter of social recognition rather than simply impairment, posing the problem of bodily loss and recompense.

The Citizen-Soldier in *The Shoemaker's Holiday*

The full title of Thomas Dekker's play—*The Shoemakers Holiday / Or The Gentle Craft / With the humorous life of Simon Eyre, shoomaker, and Lord Maior of London*—scripts an emblematic mix of citizen history and romantic comedy. Until the late twentieth century, the critical tradition routinely endorsed the play as "a dramatized folk-tale, a fantasy of success" and "a comedy which ends in a cheerful assertion of English unity, a unity embracing monarch, nobility, merchants, and apprentices."[33] Performed in 1599, likely contemporaneous with *Larum for London* and *Trial of Chivalry*, and printed in 1600, the play participates in the fashion for citizen comedies. In classic accounts of the genre, such plays offer the urban audience "the pleasures of familiarity," representing sights, spaces, and sounds to which they are accustomed, depicting urban life in a moment of London's burgeoning population and economic growth.[34] More recent work has noted how the emphasis on festivity papers over the ambivalence of social tensions and contradictions, obscuring actual labor in the celebration of artisanal craft and profitable reward.[35] Simon Eyre's rise to become Lord Mayor of London depends on a miraculous (if specious) deal in foreign goods, success that derives not from industrious work but from a ship that comes in and generates a fabulous profit for him. Focused on Eyre's trajectory, we might miss the subplot of Ralph, the journeyman shoemaker who leaves his trade for a war that is never staged, and then returns from it lamed. Ralph is a citizen stranded between a civic identity as an artisan and a martial identity as a soldier, his loss not obscured by the play, but rendered glaringly present.

The Shoemaker's Holiday's taxonomy of citizenship reflects the multivalent understandings operative in the period, beginning with the distinction between the soon-to-be Lord Mayor and the soon-to-be soldier.[36] Citizenship is a form of national belonging that requires service through public acts of virtue, one of which may be going to war. The Dutch humanist Cornelius Valerius defines the citizen this way in *A Casket of Jewels* (1571): "He is to be named a good Citizen of his countrie, who, being trimmed with civill virtues . . . may be able to perfourme very well not only Domesticall and familier offices, but also Publike both at home and in warre."[37] This "good Citizen" performs the "Publike" duties of masculinized, humanist aims, and the "offices" of "warre" are one part. In addition to the more general sense of being a member of a nation, citizenship also encodes a specifically urban meaning on display in early modern fictions of London life. Foundational to this "municipal" category, as Julia Reinhard Lupton observes, was the citizen's ability to work.[38] Called the exercise of "freedom," working in the guild required indentured labor in stages, from apprentice, to journeyman, and then to citizen, as the guild conferred obligations and rights to civic governance.[39] Within the guild, further distinctions pertained between "skilled workers" and "company elites," a division on the basis of physical labor as well as wealth.[40] In the broadest sense, "citizen" entails two competing claims in early modern thought: one to the nation, and one to the city.

The Shoemaker's Holiday activates the demands of citizenship in all of these senses from the outset. The play begins with an exchange between the wealthy Lord Mayor of London and the noble Earl of Lincoln, who collude to end the romance of Oatley's daughter, Rose, and Lincoln's nephew, Lacy, by determining that Lacy is bound for "honourable fortunes" (1.81) in the war with France, which will remove him from Rose.[41] Their discussion gives way to Lacy's entrance and disclosure to the audience that he will stay in London secretly in order to further his courtship, posing as Hans, an immigrant Dutch shoemaker. The offstage war is the mechanism for solving a fraught boundary-crossing marriage, but the only character who actually goes to war is a citizen, the journeyman Ralph Damport. A group enters from the workshop, and Simon Eyre (the shoemaker), his wife Margery, other journeymen, and Ralph's wife, Jane, all beg for Ralph to be excused from "service." Although they plead his new marriage and offer a bribe, Lacy declares, "Truly, my friends, it lies not in my power" (1.145) and "I cannot change a man" (1.147). While Lacy himself has confided his plan to dodge the command of drafted soldiers, no such option is available to Ralph. This scene of conscription is familiar from Shakespeare's *The Second Part of King Henry the Fourth* where Falstaff musters, in a comic key, "half a dozen sufficient men" (3.2.93) from the "roll" (96), beginning with Ralph Mouldy and proceeding to Simon Shadow, Thomas Wart, Francis Feeble, and Peter Bullcalf, who protests that he is "a diseased man" (178) and cannot fight.[42] The joke is that these men are truly unfit, with names that pronounce incapacity; they are "spare men," eked from a roster that offers a dim prospect of England's soldierly resources. But where Shakespeare's play uproots the authority of the muster in dubious self-interest (Justice Shallow, Justice Silence, and easily bought Falstaff), Dekker's play scripts Lacy's apology for the conscription but offers little critique of his judgment. The play's immediate division between citizen and gentry sharpens to contrast Lacy with Ralph, a journeyman without sufficient power or wealth to elude service in the war.

Indeed, the play verifies Ralph's citizen identity as he departs to fight for England at royal command. One of many Londoners who are "pressed, paid and set forth / By the Lord Mayor" (1.146–47), his first words certify his place in the "press" (150) of citizens bound by the City of London's corporate obligation to the Crown. When Lacy asks, "Is thy name Ralph?" (1.176), Ralph's reply ("Yes, sir" [176]) assents to the address that hails him as part of the city's contribution to the king's war. But the accent is on the "citizen" aspect of his service. Eyre's farewell address to Ralph codes his fighting as guild participation: "Fight for the honor of the Gentle Craft, for the Gentlemen Shoemakers, the courageous cordwainers, the flower of Saint Martin's, the mad knaves of Bedlam, Fleet Street, Tower Street and Whitechapel" (1.210–14). Moving from artisanal craft to specific locations in London, this litany of dedications affiliates Ralph with the city. As Robert Smallwood notes, Dekker's play mentions thirty-five places in London—some of which are anachronistic, and all of which existed in the play's contemporary moment.[43] Although the figure of the soldier is national (he goes to France, after all), *The Shoemaker's Holiday* insists on Ralph's urban and craft allegiances by recoding his martial labor as service to London. Fighting as a soldier becomes one mode of serving other shoemakers and working for the guild. Henry Turner has insightfully argued that corporate membership is crucial to distinctions in emerging early modern notions of class; building on Max Weber's distinction between "class" and "status," Turner contrasts class, or the "social position relative to economic circumstances" (as in the example of Eyre), with status, or the "social position relative to symbolic power" (as in the example of Lacy).[44] These competing group identities—the citizen's economic wealth and the aristocrat's symbolic honor—are equally out of reach for Ralph, whose social position leaves him powerless to contest the reassignment of his labor from workshop to battlefield.[45]

Ralph's occupation as a shoemaker-turned-soldier emphasizes the fraught position of the citizen in the relationship between civic mechanisms and royal authority. In the source for Dekker's play, Ralph's precedent is the story of a shoemaker, nonetheless of noble birth, who emerges victorious from a war. Thomas Deloney's popular prose narrative *The Pleasant and Princely History of the Gentle Craft* (1597) tells "how Crispianus was prest to the warres," fighting for the French against the Persians "like a second Hector."⁴⁶ When the French general demands to know his history, the English Crispianus (who, with his brother, had taken refuge with a shoemaker and learned the trade, although he is a prince in disguise) replies that his "birth is not mean" but he is by trade "a Shoomaker in England," to which the general responds that "well were it for us, if all the people in the Kingdome were Shoomakers."⁴⁷ Transmuted from artisan to soldier, Crispianus wins and wins again on the battlefield, brokering peace when the Persian commander, Iphicratis—himself the son of a shoemaker—learns of Crispianus's trade. The moral of Deloney's text is that a "Shoomakers son was by a Shoomaker foiled."⁴⁸ The bond of skill forges an elemental recognition that appears to cut across status differences and national enmity: Crispianus and Iphicratis understand each other as a shoemaker and a shoemaker's son rather than as opponents. Crispianus, knighted, makes "shoemaker" a communal identification that overcomes even the discord of war.⁴⁹ Unlike *The Shoemaker's Holiday*, *The Gentle Craft* emphasizes the seamless shifting between artisanal and martial labor as the identity of shoemaker reconfigures national allegiance.

The Shoemaker's Holiday never identifies the king who appears in the final scene, but it follows other plays preoccupied with the knotty relationship between England's king and the artisans of London he sends to the battlefield. The unattributed play *The Famous Victories of Henry the Fifth* (printed in 1598 but probably performed around 1588), generally considered the first English history play, introduces a group of citizens.⁵⁰ Their entrance identifies these neighbors by their occupations: *"Enter John Cobbler, Robin Pewterer, Lawrence Costermonger"* (s.d. at 2.0).

JOHN: All is well here, all is well masters.
LAWRENCE: How say you, neighbor John Cobbler? I think it best that my neighbor Robin Pewterer went to Pudding Lane End, and we will watch here at Billingsgate Ward. How say you neighbor Robin, how like you this?

(2.1–4)

As they parcel out city watch duties, the men's neighborly closeness confers collective responsibility for a nightly patrol that distinguishes them from the type of "slumbering" citizens in Antwerp that Stump castigates. They are bound by civic duty; their surnames designate their guild membership and their low status within the guild system, for none of the three is a member of one of the great livery companies (unlike the cordwainers of *The Shoemaker's Holiday*, "John Cobbler" works with old leather, repairing rather than making shoes).⁵¹ The play heightens the contrast between local obligations and national demands when the newly crowned King Henry V, provoked by the French dauphin's scorn, decides to go to war with France. John Cobbler, conscripted for war, begs the captain to release him, pleading: "I am not able to go so far" (10.2), and then "Oh sir, I have a great many shoes at home to cobble" (10.7). But even this claim to work fails to stay John Cobbler's summons, for the captain declares: "Thou must needs serve the king" (10.1). Even when John's wife begs, "I pray you let him go home again" (10.8), the captain refuses the excuse of labor: "I care not, thou shalt go" (10.9). Elongating the scene of impressment, the play makes the point that the king's war removes citizens from their work even as it requires their bodies.

Underscoring divided allegiances to craft and monarch, the play directs attention to the problem of recompense. The penultimate scene of *Famous Victories*, just after King Henry's wooing of Katherine, returns abruptly to the battlefield. Derick, the clown, enters *"with his girdle full of shoes"* (s.d. at 19.0), only to be met by *"John Cobbler roving, with a pack full of apparel"* (s.d. at 19.1). In desperate spoil, Derick and John canvass the battlefield to collect shoes from the bodies of dead soldiers. When Derick observes, "But what hast thou there? I think thou hast been robbing the Frenchmen" (19.20–21), John replies that he has "gotten some reparrel to carry home to my wife" (22), reclaiming from the battlefield the very shoes he could not "cobble" back in England. While "reparrel" might also suggest clothing, John later exclaims, "Derick, help me to carry my shoes and boots" (19.46) as they scramble to leave the battlefield before they are caught. The unauthorized appropriation of shoes is self-compensation, since these are all the wages John Cobbler will get in the play, while the king will conclude a lucrative alliance with France in the next and final scene. As Linda Bradley Salamon has discussed, conscripted soldiers, unlike mercenaries, "could not expect regular paydays," and even at the war's end, "while 75 percent payment was probably typical, as little as 30 percent might be granted."[52] In the play, John Cobbler's illegal compensation comprises the very objects he left behind in England. He substitutes soldierly labor for artisanal labor to the same end: he has a "great many shoes to cobble." The plight of the citizen forced to war is reduced to a joke; the cobbler's remonstrations pit service to the state against the citizen's work.

Unlike *Famous Victories*, *The Shoemaker's Holiday* does not accompany Ralph into battle. When Ralph returns to the shop ten scenes later, *"being lame"* (s.d. at 10.52), Hodge, another journeyman, marks his injury: "What, fellow Ralph! Mistress, look here—Jane's husband! Why, how now—lame? Hans, make much of him: he's a brother of our trade, a good workman, and a tall soldier" (10.53–55). Hodge introduces Ralph as the journeyman he was before, still a "brother" who is as much "good workman" as "tall soldier." Ralph initially discounts this artisanal identity:

> How does my Jane? When didst thou see my wife?
> Where lives my poor heart? She'll be poor indeed
> Now I want limbs to get whereon to feed.
>
> (10.71–73)

If Ralph worries that injury deters him from working, Hodge rejects this premise of disqualification: "Limbs? Hast thou not hands, man? Thou shalt never see a shoemaker want bread, though he have but three fingers on a hand" (10.74–76). He may no longer wear the shoes he makes, but the shoemaker's capacity for craft requires only hands. Ralph's reply confirms his ability to resume his labor: "Since I want limbs and lands, / I'll trust to God, my good friends, and to my hands" (10.102–3). Asserting that Ralph can work, although his war wounds are real, the play produces the most sympathetic ideal of a veteran injured by military service. All should be well, since nothing removes Ralph from the reciprocal bonds of his fellow journeymen and the guild's corporate obligation to charity means that he will never "want bread." Ralph's return to the workshop has been mobilized in service of the comedy's reparative social vision, for even the limit case of bodily wholeness may be accommodated by the interdependence of the guild structure and its care.[53] Although the play hints at the workshop's failure to care for Jane—Ralph returns only to find that they "know not what's become of her" (10.78) and that she "is a stranger here" (10.94)—the encounter between journeymen puts Ralph back in the workshop.

What, then, disables the lame soldier? Ralph's disabling is the social misrecognition that attends his impairment, unfixing him from his citizen identity even within the space of the workshop.[54] When Hodge introduces Ralph, Margery exclaims, "I knew him not" (10.57) and then explains: "Trust me, I am sorry, Ralph, to see thee impotent. Lord, how the wars have made him sunburnt! The left leg is not well; 'twas a fair gift of God the infirmity took not hold a little higher, considering thou camest from France—but let that pass" (10.61–64). His "sunburnt" appearance is a joke about impotence, implying both physical and sexual powerlessness, that highlights the erotic implications of this "infirmity." The pointed reference to France (and, by extension, the French pox, or syphilis) may also be a topical reference to the sixteenth-century French account of Martin Guerre, which reveals the precarity of identity staked on social proof. In Guerre's case, a soldier returns to his wife and farm after fighting for France in Flanders, only to be legally judged an impostor when in 1560, four years later, another soldier, with a wooden leg, returns and claims that he is Martin Guerre. The instance, discussed by Michel de Montaigne, among others, is a litmus test for the social confirmation of the self—and for the conflation of the veteran with the counterfeiting rogue.[55] If one man may so thoroughly feign the identity of another, Margery's failure to recognize Ralph works in the opposite direction: Ralph cannot even lay claim to himself. Although Ralph's concern for Jane ("oh, my wife!") asserts his fidelity, Margery recognizes Ralph through the type of the maimed soldier who returns from war in France. She does not refuse to look at his service—as in Stump's critique—but she can only see the "impotent," "sunburnt," "infir[m]" body of any soldier rather than the journeyman she knows.

Ralph's visible identification as a wounded soldier eclipses his identity as a citizen, an ontological confusion about Ralph's person that extends even to his most intimate relationship. Margery's mistake might be understandable—she enters the shop preoccupied with Eyre's advancement—but even Jane fails to recognize him when she brings shoes to the shop. A few scenes later, Ralph tells the other shoemakers that "this morning, when I stroked on her shoes, I looked upon her, and she upon me, and sighed, asked me if ever I knew one Ralph. Yes, said I. For his sake, said she—tears standing in her eyes—and for thou art somewhat like him, spend this piece of gold. I took it; my lame leg and my travel beyond sea made me unknown" (18.7–12). Ralph's description of his vertiginous and dreamlike encounter with Jane sources her failure to recognize him to his "lame leg," which, with his travel, renders him "unknown." In the opening scene of the play, Ralph gives Jane a pair of shoes, a product of artisanal labor that required the whole workshop in the making. He codes the shoes as citizen affiliation (the work of "our trade" [1.227]) and emphasizes the specificity and intimacy of the gift, sized to her feet and marked with her name. Ornamented and "pinked with" (230) Jane's initials, the shoes are a talisman of memory with which he enjoins her to "remember" (233) him just as he can recognize these shoes "from a thousand moe" (235). When Jane returns with the shoes to the workshop, Ralph identifies the product of his labor but Jane cannot recognize him as anything but a former soldier, irrevocably altered by the war. She believes that Ralph is dead, but this half-recognition goes far beyond loss, consolidating their exchange as charity rather than wages. Jane offers a piece of gold to the returned soldier, not the journeyman shoemaker. With "somewhat like," Ralph becomes his own simile, as if the lame leg has slotted him into the structural forgetfulness required by the pitying donation. This disabling strands Ralph between type and individual, even in the workshop, among the products of his craft, unrecognizable even to his wife.

Ralph's social misrecognition extends to the point that he is even cast as his deceptive double: the soldier who feigns a war injury. When Oatley and Lincoln enter and accost Ralph and Jane (who is masked), believing them to be Lacy and Rose in disguise, Lincoln exclaims, "my nephew, / To hide his guilt, counterfeits him lame" (18.114–15). This trope of mistaken identity is adjacent to broader cultural concerns about feigned disability, but the "looking askance," to borrow Stump's phrase, doubly negates the disabled body in this instance. To see Lacy faking a limp, Lincoln must overlook—stare at but refuse to perceive—Ralph's actual lameness.[56] Firk's joke, "Yea, truly, God help the poor couple, they are lame and blind" (18.116), spurs Lincoln to vengeance, who intimates that he will "cure" this "lameness" (117) by revealing the falsehood:

> O base wretch!
> Nay, hide thy face; the horror of thy guilt
> Can hardly be washed off. Where are thy powers?
> What battles have you made? O yes, I see
> Thou fought'st with shame, and shame hath conquered thee.
> This lameness will not serve.
>
> (18.121–26)

Ralph's wounded body is visible evidence of soldierly shame rather than valor, evidence of cowardice rather than honor. The speech of excoriation intended for Lacy fictionalizes Ralph's actual lameness and undoes the value of Ralph's war service to city and country. Presuming faked impairment, Lincoln reverses the poles of visibility, locating the misrecognition that has dogged Ralph in the "horror" of the discerning spectator. When his war wound is assumed to be fraudulent, Ralph's "lame" body nearly bears the punishment of Lacy's deceit despite the veracity of Ralph's injury.

This loss of identity recapitulates the essential interchangeability of every common soldier. Any report of casualties after a battle would not name Ralph among the notable dead to be lamented.[57] The play underscores both Ralph's absence from official reports and his unrecognition in the intimacies of personal loss, repeating Jane's initial assessment of Ralph as a "stranger." When Jane and Ralph are reunited, Hodge identifies Ralph explicitly: "Jane, dost thou know this man? 'Tis Ralph, I can tell thee. Nay, 'tis he, in faith. Though he be lamed by the wars, yet look not strange, but run to him, fold him about the neck and kiss him" (18.36–39). With the slipperiness of "look," a command that equivocates between spectator and spectacle, Hodge attributes Jane's "strange" response to Ralph's injury, "lamed by the wars," and cues action by reconfirming ("Nay, 'tis he"), suggesting Jane's reticence to see Ralph for the shoemaker he was. Yet the history of conscription, wounding, and unrepaired loss that persists in the designation "lame" remains pressingly present in the dramatic fiction through Ralph's limp. The injury distinguishes Ralph from his other shoemakers even though their bond is forged on the ability to work and his limp proves no impediment to labor. The shoemaker who may require only one shoe displays the consequence of martial labor that alienates the citizen from himself. Ralph's misrecognition as a lame soldier unsettles his identity through the very structure that demanded his service. Ralph's disabling is a matter of perception, the unmooring of social recognition that leaves him more identifiable as former soldier than as shoemaker.

Surgical Arts and Social Restoration

The play marks Ralph as a citizen when he goes to war and, once he returns, notes the cost of this service by showing his lameness. Strikingly, however, the prosthetic potential of a wooden leg is a signal achievement of surgical advances in early modern medicine. Early modern surgeons envisioned new techniques of amputation to accommodate a prosthetic leg, or stilt or stump, that would reconstruct a wounded soldier's appearance. Much critical work has attended to early modern fascination with prosthetic supplements, or what Nardizzi calls "the inhuman valence of prosthesis" that blurs the boundaries of the human body.[58] My interest here is in how the ambition to counterfeit missing body parts exceeded purely medical correction. Envisioning restoration of the wounded veteran's body, surgeons aimed to integrate the veteran back into society with an undetectable fix, demonstrating an awareness of social disabling premised on appearance rather than function. The most prominent French surgeon of the period, Ambroise Paré, devoted an entire book to prosthetic devices, which was published separately in 1561 and 1564 before a compendium appeared in *Oeuvres (Collected Works)*, published in 1575 and 1578. Paré's work entered the English medical canon when the physician Helkiah Crooke appended *An Explanation of the Fashion and Use of Three and Fifty Instruments of Chirurgery* to the second edition of his own well-known anatomical treatise *Mikrokosmographia* (1631) and Thomas Johnson translated *Oeuvres* into English as *The Workes of that famous Chirurgion Ambrose Parey* in 1634. Surgeons operated on the body with manual interventions—excising fistulas, shaving hair, lancing boils—that put theoretical knowledge of anatomy to practical use, especially innovations that addressed typical war wounds.[59] In John Woodall's prefatory note to his own volume, *The Surgeons Mate* (1639), he writes that the surgeon is the only one of the three recognized branches of medicine—physicians, surgeons, and apothecaries—that "practiseth in military occasions, as in ships and camps," and therefore he aims to express "the easiest and safest waies and meanes of healing the wounds and other great infirmities and diseases that warre usually produceth."[60]

The work of amputation was chief among surgical innovations, and Paré champions new procedures when experience has taught him better techniques than classical directives. In the chapter "Where Amputation must be made," he distinguishes instances when the surgeon should amputate against the "common rules of Art."[61] Trained to preserve as much good flesh as possible, the surgeon should instead remove more of the leg to ensure a prosthesis that fits, so that "the patient may more fitly use the rest of his Legge and with lesse trouble, that is, he may the better goe on a woodden Legge." If a surgeon follows the received practice, Paré explains, "the patient will be forced with trouble to use three Legges instead of two," relying on a cane. Paré cites the example of a captain who, when his foot is lost, has more of the leg amputated (to "five fingers below the knee") to employ a wooden leg, and "verily hee useth it with much more ease and facility than before in performance of any motion" (sig. 2R1v). This defense of surgical innovation prioritizes the patient's restoration of movement over bodily integrity, a rationale that Woodall repeats in "Of Dismembring or Amputation" when he offers detailed instructions that depart from classical advice. Like Paré, he encourages a counterintuitive approach, suggesting that "though the foot onely be corrupted, it is best to take off the leg some foure inches below the lower end of the rotule, or round bone of the knee," because "the paine is all one, and it is most profitable to the Patient, for a long stump were but troublesome."[62] The language of "profit" recurs throughout as a way of estimating the surgeon's approach; if the patient is missing part of the foot, the rest may become "unprofitable" and must be removed, "and no lesse of the legge also, for it will be but a hinderance to the Patient, considering that hee cannot stand thereon, and is full of grievous paine" (sig. 3M4r). Woodall advocates for a more drastic technique, he explains, because new prosthetic devices are now available for amputees. If the surgeon amputates "a little below the Gartering place," he will "leav[e] a fit roome for the stilt, to rest the body upon" (sig. 3M2v). Conceptually, the surgeons' investment in the parts of the body over the whole demonstrates what David Hillman and Carla Mazzio characterize as the "emergence in early modern culture of the new aesthetic of the part."[63]

As surgeons expound these techniques of amputation, furthermore, they suggest that the reconstruction of the part may alter the whole body, offering new possibilities to compensate for bodily loss. The artful surgeon demonstrates the most competence when his interventions appear "natural"; this is medical intervention measured by the patient's restoration. Paré's discussion of how "armes, legs, and hands may be made by art, and placed instead of the naturall armes, legs, or hands that are cut off and lost," emphasizes the surgeon's work to "help and imitate nature, and supply the defect of members that are perished and lost." These "means" are prosthetic devices, "made by art," that allow the patient to "perform the functions of going, standing, and handling" (sig. 4E2v). *Workes* emphasizes the availability of prosthetic devices to aid patients across a spectrum of modifications. With diagrams and instructions for prosthetic devices, such as *"The forme of a woodden Leg made for poore men"* (figure 2.1), the surgeon's manual envisions a prosthetic device that facilitates movement. Nardizzi observes that this wooden leg consists "mainly of a 'stump or stock' that the wearer straps tightly onto the thigh and which enables him to balance and to move around as if he were on two feet."[64] As Patricia Cahill notes, "In Elizabethan England, such a semi-mechanical apparatus could be purchased from a joiner for eighteen pence, a sum then roughly equivalent to a bit more than two days' pay for a soldier."[65] The surgical possibilities of recompense are geared to affordability, and the emphasis on function stresses the replacement of the limb as artifice available to the "poore" soldier. The "forme" of the prosthetic depicts the object twice: first, the empty form, and then in use, with a demonstration of the leg worn on "the thigh it selfe, that you may know after what fashion it must stand" (sig. 4E3r). The directions emphasize ease as well as function, demonstrating the "pillow or bolster whereon the knee must rest" in use, and showing the thigh secured within the frame to make visible how the "forme" of the wooden leg rehabilitates the motion of a missing leg. The stilt registers the patient's body only in the synecdoche of the thigh in the second image, showing how it enables the wearer to stand. The form of the wooden leg, as a stilt, does not reproduce the appearance of the leg but the function of one.

In addition to describing their function, Paré stresses the hope that prosthetic devices render disability unapparent. The chapter on *"amending or helping lamenesse or halting"* concludes with the image of a stilt prosthesis that effects a proleptic restoration for the body shown using the crutch (figure 2.2). The stilt or crutch, labeled with letters to describe each part, is depicted in the center of the image. On either side, an extremely muscular nude male figure models its use, viewed from front and back. The accompanying description explains the practical value of the crutch's "forme" to repair the "great deformity" of "halting" (sig. 4E4v), a difference that would otherwise become apparent in the gait. The fixed form supplements the body, not standing in for the leg

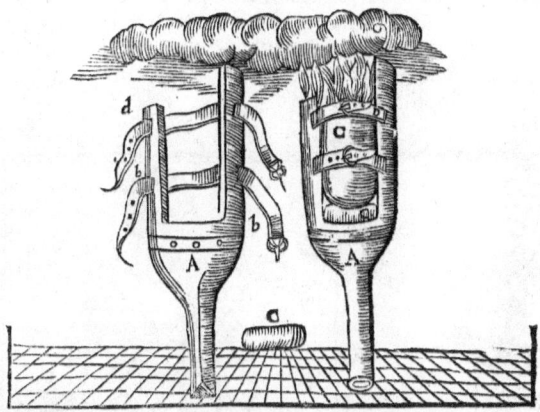

FIGURE 2.1. Ambroise Paré, *The Workes of that famous Chirurgion Ambrose Parey* (London, 1634), 883. Call#: STC 19189. Used by permission of the Folger Shakespeare Library under a Creative Commons Attribution-ShareAlike 4.0 International License.

but enabling movement. The description begins by asserting that halting is "not onely a great deformity"; it is "also very troublesome and grievous." (sig. 4E2v). Elaborating on the problem that halting poses, the surgeon's account moves deformity beyond injury. Assisted by the crutch, the image's idealized male body is a visual expression of the aesthetic value that Paré asserts a few pages earlier, describing prosthetic devices as "not onely profitable for the necessity of the body, but also for the decency and comelinesse thereof" (sig. 4E2v). Beyond simple "necessity," prostheses "profit" the wearer in appearance, enabling the body to appear decent and comely, or beautiful. These virtues reorient the surgeon's work from mobility to aesthetic appearance, social rehabilitation that produces bodily wholeness as a kind of moral value. As David Wills observes in his classic account of prosthesis, Paré's treatise "is extensive in its explanations of the use of prosthetic devices, all of them accompanied by diagrams, taking into account aesthetic as well as orthopedic concerns."[66] What is at stake in the concept of prosthesis for Wills is "the discovery of an artificiality there where

78 CHAPTER 2

Of amending or helping lamenesse or halting.

Alting is not onely a great deformity, but also very troublesome and grievous. Therefore if that any man be grieved therewith by reason that one of his legs is shorter than the other, it may be holpen by putting under his short foot this sitting crutch, which we are now about to describe. For by the helpe of this, he shall not onely goe upright, but also more easily and with little labour or no pain at all. It was taught mee by *Nicholas Picard* Chirurgian to the Duke of Loraine. The forme thereof is this.

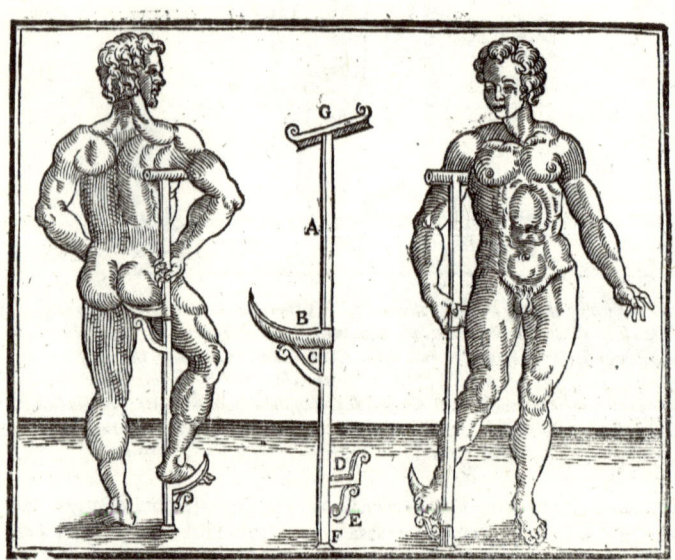

A. Sheweth the staffe or stilt of this crutch, which must bee made of wood. B. Sheweth the seat of iron whereon the thigh resteth, just under the buttocke. C. Sheweth a prop which stayeth up the seat whereon all the weight of the patients body resteth. D. Sheweth the stirrop, being made of iron, and bowing crooked upwards, that the foot may stand firm, and not slip off it when the patient goeth. E. Sheweth the prop that stayeth or holdeth up the stirrop to strengthen it. F. Sheweth the foote of the stilt or crutch made of iron with many pikes, and compassed with a ring or ferule, so to keepe it from slipping. G. The crosse or head of the crutch which the patient must put under his arme-hole to leane upon, as it is to be seene in the figure.

FIGURE 2.2. Ambroise Paré, *The Workes of that famous Chirurgion Ambrose Parey* (London, 1634), 884. Call#: STC 19189. Used by permission of the Folger Shakespeare Library under a Creative Commons Attribution-ShareAlike 4.0 International License.

the natural founds its priority"; here, the artifice of the leg makes identity legible.[67] The surgeon eases the patient's injury and reconstructs the body for the perception of others, understanding that the disabling effects of the war wounds go beyond "necessity" of movement. This ambition to "supply" a defect extends beyond simply correcting physical loss, revealing a concept of disability that anticipates the social model's emphasis on contingent encounter with the world.

Woodall's praise of the prosthetic device celebrates the restoration of bodily wholeness as a mode of social integration. After successful surgeries, the prosthetic conceals injury, for the surgical patient "went most neatly on an artificiall legge not easily discovered" (sig. 3N1v). Expounding on this accommodation, Woodall writes: "For the noblenesse of each member of mans body, and namely of the legge, is highly even in humanitie to be tendred and regarded, being a great honour and comfort to the man, when, if without a foot, by the helpe of Art, namely, of a hollow Case, or the like, with an artificiall foot adjoyned, a man may decently and comely walke, and ride, goe over a style, yea, and runne, and sit streight, and behave himselfe man-like in Bed, and at Boord, and doe good service for the defence of his Countrey, or of himself" (sig. 3M4v). The surgeon begins with the body and ends by praising the prosthetic devices, from "hollow Case" to "artificiall foot," that enable the patient to resume his activities. Echoing Paré's stress on "decency" and "comelinesse," Woodall's patient "may decently and comely walke," a benefit that suggests that surgical rehabilitation affords new decorum. The wooden leg, furthermore, enables actions that would not seem to depend on the presence of a foot. Sitting "straight" and "behav[ing] himselfe man-like," the man using the "hollow case" secures an ideal of masculine behavior, producing a body capable of performing sexually in "Bed" and socially at "Boord," and rendering "good service" for the country. These texts envision a social norm, a qualitative expression of prostheticized appearance to which the lame soldier's body might be restored. The surgeon aims to undo the deformations of identity that result from the "defect" of a lame leg, demonstrating that a disabling encompasses how a body appears as much as what a body can do. These influential surgery texts emphasize the aesthetic power of the prosthetic to mask even the perception of disability.

Embedded within the most ambitious proclamation of the surgeon's aims, however, is a tacit recognition of the cycle that lands a soldier on the operating table. The final surgical "case" that Woodall puts before his reader in the section on dismembering is speculative: "I will suppose or suggest a valiant well-deserving Souldier, for the honour of his King and Country, pressing forward in fight, should receive a wound by a shot upon his legge" (sig. 3N4r). This conjecture allows Woodall to detail three surgical modes—immediate, delayed, and deferred amputation—that a new practitioner might consider in treating the wounded leg. The putative patient is the best possible recipient of surgical restoration, for "valiant," "well-deserving," and "pressing forward in fight" for king and country, the soldier is exemplary in his military service.

Yet this martial labor makes him the most obvious candidate for the amputations Woodall's pupils will need to perform. What is more, the text heralds newfound possibilities for fixing the wounded soldier so that he may "doe good service" again, returning to the battlefield once more. The supposed soldier is an imaginative template for a looping dystopian future of wounding, supported by the very technological innovation the surgeon practices. This fictional example, in a surgical manual that aims to rehabilitate the wounded soldier, lets slip the political mechanism ("for the honour of his King and Country") that sends the citizen to fight, rendering the battlefield a recursive site of human injury.

"Enter Ralph, Being Lame": Civic Bodies and Theatrical Futures

Against these assertions of surgical confidence, the stage direction in *The Shoemaker's Holiday* that identifies Ralph as lame foregrounds the uncertainty of prosthetic attachment. Alanna Skuse has argued convincingly that the play's preoccupation with the *stuff* of London, from workshop materials to market commodities, contrasts with Ralph's bodily lack and "troubles the always-tremulous distinction between props and prosthetics."[68] Yet *"being lame"* (10.52) refracts an unstable collection of descriptions. "Lame" does not describe a body as much as it demands an actor's choice. He could assume a prosthetic, like the one that Paré pictures, strapped around the able leg; tie up one leg to rest it on a wooden stump, suggesting amputation at the knee; suspend a bent leg from a shoulder strap and hobble around the stage using crutches; or perhaps simply exaggerate an irregular gait that favors one leg. Discussing the property of Kent's wooden leg, Nardizzi speculates that an actor "conscripted an abled leg to perform the 'stump' that is the sign of amputation," a performance that "exacerbates the indeterminacy located at the site of prosthesis, for it exploits the tension between illusion and realism in such a way that could have persuaded audiences not to see things that were visible there."[69] Ralph's lame (missing? wooden?) leg remains a prominent ambiguity as the stage direction recasts him in terms of his wounded body, the inescapable sign of his service in England's war. To review: on his immediate return, Ralph says that he "wants limbs," suggesting that perhaps he has lost both legs; Margery specifies his "left leg" as "not well"; and Ralph himself later refers to his "lame leg" as the reason for Jane's misrecognition. Rather than celebrate the repair a wooden leg can offer, the play instead underscores the injury that Ralph's movements disclose. Refusing to bear out the restorative possibilities of the surgeon's craft, Dekker's play amplifies instead the uncertainty of the citizen-veteran's relation to labor and the permanently unsettling loss that service in war inscribes. The stage direction in the printed text is inaccessible to an audience in the theater but demands a performance choice about the limp, stilt, or wooden leg, offering a glimpse into the process of acting that every role entails.

In the final scene, the play visually differentiates Ralph's body by putting him into motion. When the pancake bell brings the shoemakers to the hall for holiday breakfast, Eyre commands his journeymen to serve with an order that singles out what Ralph cannot do: "Avoid, Hodge; run, Ralph; frisk about, my nimble Firk! Carouse me fathom healths to the honour of the shoemakers!" (20.14–16). The imperatives capture the gleeful abandon of Eyre's festive proclamation and underscore Ralph's limited movement; even if Ralph can "carouse," he presumably does not "run" and "frisk about" like the others. In folk tradition, as Elizabeth Rivlin has discussed, the "merry shoemaker" is a stock character who engages in song and dance and is associated with "intellectualism," signified by "physical weakness, often taking the form of lameness."[70] If the final scenes of Dekker's play accent the merry figure, no one else shares Ralph's lameness; in fact, the displays of cheer demarcate Ralph from the others by accentuating his gait. At rest, lined up behind Eyre awaiting the banquet, or working on shoes in the shop, the journeyman who limps may appear indistinguishable. Ralph's limp becomes visibly detectable, even prominent, when he is compelled to join the other men in the song and dance routines of the concluding feast and the shoemakers are actually moving across the stage. The theatrical delineation of movement requires the crucial liveness of the actor's body and highlights the citizen-veteran in the midst of a civic feast, an emblem of the irreparable loss that war produces.

If "being lame" is available only to the reader on the page, the discursive work of the dramatic fiction turns the adjective into an epithet. Ralph is called "lame Ralph" repeatedly throughout the rest of the play, renaming his character and reminding spectators of his maimed body.[71] The opening scene defines him as the "Ralph" pressed into service by the City of London, and Hammon claims to have a letter that records the death of a "Ralph Damport" (12.83); yet on Ralph's return, the other shoemakers seize instantly on "lame," referring to him as "my fellow lame Ralph" (16.146) and to Jane as "lame Ralph's wife" (16.150). Later, as Eyre commands, "Firk, Hodge, lame Ralph, run, my tall men, beleaguer the shambles, beggar all Eastcheap" (20.21–22), his hyperbolic charge to the journeymen affirms a fantasy of harmony that includes Ralph, but distinguishes him by his war injury. A version of this many-as-one problem permeates the play, since even the title demands that an editor choose between the individual and the collective, between *The Shoemaker's*

Holiday and *The Shoemakers' Holiday*. The dilemma of apostrophe placement succinctly captures the problem of the disabled journeyman's relation to the corporate body of his craft. With "fellow," the play invokes the guild's collective; with "lame," that composite body atomizes into parts, as Ralph is visually and discursively distinguished from the others.

The final scene of *The Shoemaker's Holiday* offers a much darker formulation of the relation between the individual and corporate body. Early critical readings of the play's ending as a "concluding harmony and festival" gave way to those that emphasize the shaky foundations of communal celebration; as Jeremy Lopez puts it, Dekker only "achieves a sense of holiday by cheerfully pretending, like his characters, that the fissures in the edifice are not there."[72] I trace these fissures in the scene's emphasis on the king's plans for war in France, as a gesture to the comedy's tragic future. All of the shoemakers in London assemble for a banquet, and they enter as the king strategizes with Lincoln about the future of the war:

> With the old troop which there we keep in pay
> We will incorporate a new supply.
> Before one summer more pass o'er my head,
> France shall repent England was injured.
>
> (21.137–40)

England's retribution for metaphorical "injury" demands physical "incorporation," the replenishing of a figural body of soldiers that requires the prosthetic supply of new soldiers. And then the king asks, "What are all those?"—presumably referring to the citizens gathered before him. Lacy completes his line with the answer, "All shoemakers, my liege" (21.141), perhaps cueing a gesture of obeisance from the assembled company, a collective demonstration of their loyalty. Oddly, however, the king repeats his question as if incredulous at the sheer number of men before him: "My mad Lord Mayor, are all these shoemakers?" (21.144). This repeated query prompts Eyre's affirmation of their devotion: "All shoemakers, my liege, all gentlemen of the Gentle Craft, true Trojans, courageous cordwainers" (145–46), to which the shoemakers collectively respond: "God save your Majesty!" (148). The play's ending thus affirms the corporate body of the shoemakers and advances their capacity for artisanal labor when the king permits them to sell leather on two market days of each week. It is easy to see why this scene upholds citizen hospitality: Eyre invites the king to "add more honour to the Gentle Trade: / Taste of Eyre's banquet" (183–84), constituting the London guild as the court's ideal of beneficence. Bonds of labor triumph over cosseted inheritances of title.

I return, however, to the king's reiterated question. Why ask twice whether every man he sees is a shoemaker? The play closes with the shoemakers arrayed before the king who has just proclaimed the need for a "new supply" of bodies at the front. Turner insightfully observes that this gesture of incorporation "can be read either as the final comic fulfillment of a collective idea—a celebration of corporate *communitas* in which even the king becomes a member, rather than its head—or, more cynically, as a call to arms that Lacy will again evade and from which Ralph will only suffer more injury."[73] My reading, if cynical, is just as collective in its tragic force: Ralph's distinctive loss is precursor to the potential future of *every* shoemaker. I cannot perceive the play's concluding couplet, "When all our sports and banquetings are done, / Wars must right wrongs which Frenchman have begun" (21.190–91), as anything less than a gesture to the guild system that incorporates labor and furnishes new bodies to be incorporated into the old troops. The king's repeated question indicates his dawning awareness of the bodies arrayed at his disposal. If the play's final line suggests that "wars" follow "banquetings," the visual tableau of the final scene underscores the potential for every citizen to be converted into a soldier, and then into a citizen-veteran. The guild structure churns in concert with the state's military aims. Ralph's lamed body is not a singular form to be reincorporated into the civic body, but the future of every citizen powerless to escape the sanctioned shuttle from workshop to battlefield.

* * *

Closing this chapter on the corporate spectacle of bodies poised on the brink of disabling injury, I want to underscore the early modern theater's refusal to celebrate the aims of undetectable restoration. Plays return repeatedly to the problem of compensation, imagining the soldier left without enough money for a prosthetic device, and still less with profitable labor. In *The Life of Sir John Oldcastle* (1600), by Anthony Munday, Michael Drayton, Robert Wilson, and Richard Hathway, characters who are former soldiers rue their lack of official license to beg on their return to England: a soldier identified only as "2" observes that they have no identification as beggars, "but what we beare uppon our bodies, our maimed limbs, God help us," while another, "4," avows, "And yet, as lame as I am, Ile with the king into France, if I can crawle but a shipboorde, I hadde rather be slaine in France, than starve in England."[74] Thomas Dekker's *The Wonder of a Kingdom* (c. 1622) features a *"lame-legg'd Souldier"* nearly forced to surrender his wooden leg to a broker when he cannot pay his debts, who complains that the broker demanded that he "Laid downe my stumpe here, for the Interest, / And so hop home."[75] Such glimpses of war's future are commonplace in drama across the period, even setting aside the many examples of wounded soldiers who turn out to be faking their disabilities. Even hypothetically—from Boult's offhand exclamation in William Shakespeare and George Wilson's *Pericles, Prince of Tyre* (1607), "What would you have me do? go to the wars, would you? where a man may serve seven years for the loss of a leg, and have not money enough in the end to buy him a wooden one?" to Jasper Mayne's play *The Amorous Warre* (1648), when Artops exclaims, "I feele my selfe, already / Partly compos'd of Flesh, partly of Wood"—plays equate martial service with bodily loss, envisioning wounded soldiers with wooden legs and limping strides.[76] Representative in the very offhandedness with which they define uncompensated bodily loss as a nexus of labor and profit, these examples assume that bodily impairment, reshaped as disability through economic and social relations, is war's inevitable result.

These lame soldiers also counter the surgeon's claim that a wooden leg is "not easily discovered" because the theatrical prosthetic renders the body ostentatious. As a formal constraint, if not intentional polemic, "lame" must be shown in order to become the defining feature of a dramatic character. Ralph's character is likely played by an able-bodied actor who performs lameness on his character's return from war, but other characters, like Stump and Bowyer, counter any simple equation of skilled action with able-bodied actor. Characters such as Champernell in John Fletcher and Philip Massinger's *The Little French Lawyer* (c. 1620; described in the second Folio dramatis personae as "a lame old Gentleman") and Don Sanchio in Francis Beaumont and Fletcher's *Love's Pilgrimage* (c. 1616; described in the dramatis personae as "an old lame angry soldier") enter the stage already marked as lame and exit the same way.[77] Champernell avers, "I have one leg shot, / One arme disabled, and am honour'd more, / By loosing them" (1.1.274–76), affirming injury as "honour" despite disabling lack of function. The play is replete with jokes that linger on his lameness ("My Lord limpes toward you" [3.1.112]), even from Champernell himself ("You that have legs says so, / I put my one to too much stresse" [4.5.1–2]). Although Don Sanchio is the butt of mockery when he enters his scenes *"carried"* (s.d. in 3.4, 5.4), his lameness even temporarily extends to his opponent in a duel, Alphonso, who consents to be equally restricted: "Come bind me in a chaire" (5.6. 86). These lame soldiers with prominent prosthetics do not foreground rehabilitative fixing but defiant persistence, effectively reordering the terms by which bravery is articulated in the fiction, while the play points at their lameness.

I conclude this chapter, then, with a hypothetical that complicates our reading of these visibly disabled characters as only ever "cripping up"—the critique, as I noted in the introduction, of an able-bodied actor who plays a disabled character. These examples hint at a scripting that may derive from the actor's body rather than the character's body. They demand that we ask, for example, whether the many "lame" soldiers that appear across Thomas

Dekker's plays may be not only a fictional reflection of England's history of war in the 1590s or a metaphor for the wounded body of the state, but also possible evidence of scripting roles for specific actors, one of whom had some form of limb difference.[78] If, as Martin Wiggins observes, the King's Men "apparently had an actor able to perform one-legged parts," since the actor would play Claus in *Beggars' Bush* (discussed in chapter 3), Champernell in *The Little French Lawyer*, and possibly, if the actor "was a very long-standing member of the company, he might also have played Stump in *A Larum for London*," what might this suggest about plays written for the company?[79] I entertain this speculative theater history—to which I will return in the coda—in order to underscore the possibility that these plays record an actor's distinctive embodiment rather than metaphorize a character's fiction of disability.

Ultimately, the theater's formal work with the actor's body does not—indeed, will not—plot a teleology that accords with the celebration of medical innovation by disappearing the lameness of the soldier. While the surgical manuals narrate their technological achievements as an improvement on inherited classical medical knowledge, and as they anticipate refining such techniques to render soldiers' war injuries undetectable, the dramatic archive magnifies lameness by exploiting it as an effect of theatrical prosthetics. The lame soldier of the opening anecdotes asserts a disability exceptionalism to encourage martial labor, but the missing or wooden leg exposes the injury that follows, inevitably, from service in the wars. Read against the celebratory sense of the prosthesis, these plays end up scrutinizing the loss the soldier suffers, activating the "lame" body through movement that is transformed into disability by social significance. Such scrutiny exposes the problems of recompense and loss, bringing into sharp relief the bodies most vulnerable to the state's exercise of power. They reveal the lame soldier as a dramatic character stuck in transformation, stranded between categories, unknowable as a citizen and suspect as a veteran. The state can never fully compensate the wounded soldier for the sacrifice of his body—but these plays also suggest that the state is always looking "askance" at the body of the wounded soldier and trying to look away from the war to which his body bears witness.

Far from being erased, the lame body becomes prominent through theatrical practice—not the victorious wounds of a soldier-hero, but the lingering loss of a shoemaker's body disabled by the very structure of citizenship itself. The next chapter returns to the worry that disability is only feigned, considering cultural concerns about disguise and the replicability of disability signifiers in the stock character of the crippled beggar. But in Cripple, a character whose multiple theatrical prosthetics are a virtuosic site of capacity, we find that disability grounds a circuit of exchange on which the theater thrives.

Chapter 3

Performing Cripple in Theatrical Exchange

> One saying to a crook-back'd person that it was a great default to be crook-back'd: hee answered: Rather is it an over-plus.
>
> —Anthony Copley, "Of Crookednes and Lamenesse"

The epigraph to this chapter comes from Anthony Copley's *Wits fittes and fancies* (1595), a collection of jests that features, as I have noted in the previous chapter, a section titled "Of Crookednes and Lamenesse." Focused on embodiment, like other sections in the collection—"Of Noses," "Of Drunkards," "Of Face and Skarres," "Of Blindnes," "Of Talnes," "Of Fat and Grosse," "Of Leannes," "Of Age," "Of Garrulity," and "Of Littlenes"—this section takes bodily appearance as the basis for humor. "Crookednes" collapses a person into an adjective, and the jests typically privilege the scrutinizing spectator rather than the object of the gaze. Here are two of the jests that Copley collects: "One that was a litle crooked fellow and verie craftie withall: an other compar'd him to the common law," and "A crook-back'd Plaintiffe besought a Judge to doe him right, and the Judge answered: Well may I heare you, but right I can not doe ye."[1] The "crooked" body is like the "common law"; the man who is "crook-back'd" cannot be set to rights even if the judge were fair. Joking about the impossibility of getting an honest judgment in a court of law, the wordplay circles around a body's literal crookedness to mean moral crookedness. When the literal meaning is restored to the figure of speech, however, the jest doubles back on the person himself, who is assessed as "very craftie" or undermined in his plea for justice. These ableist jests, David M. Turner has taught us to understand, are a commonplace form, expressions of the "comedy of corporeality" that is everywhere in early modern texts.[2] Grouped by their target for humor, these anecdotes reinforce the idea that a "crooked" person's value consists in the opportunity he offers for an onlooker's show of wit.

Yet, in the midst of casually cruel barbs about physical difference, two editions of Copley's volume feature a "crook-back'd person" who speaks back, and he gets the last word about his form. The jest goes like this:

> One saying to a crook-back'd person that it was a great default to be crook-back'd: hee answered: Rather is it an over-plus.[3]

Overlapping literal, figural, and metaphorical interpretations of being "crook-back'd," the jest speaker wrenches disability into the financial realm with "default." This definition suggests too much rather than too little: addition, not subtraction, plenitude, not lack. Total the value of the bent body, and this form comes up short. Within the stricture of these lines, however, something else happens. The jest proposes an alternative understanding of crookedness too, an answer offered by the crook-back'd person himself. His riposte—"Rather is it an over-plus"—reverses the governing economic assumptions. Overplus defines the crook-back'd body by "surplus" or "excess."[4] The body is still the target for humor and social critique in a predictably threadbare punch line, and the jest is thirdhand repartee, spoken by an unnamed person reduced to his form's adjective. Yet the shift to dialogue embeds resistance to the onlooker's perception of the "crook-back'd" man and to the onlooker's assumption that a "crook-back'd" form is obviously negative and merely deficient. The crook-back'd man marshals a rejoinder to that perception. The undecidability of "overplus" creatively reconfigures a relation to the world driven by bodily appearance. The jest marks the illusory, glancingly elusive interpretive possibility of the crooked shape and insists on apprehending that shape—and that *person*—otherwise.

This chapter begins from the anecdote's claim that disability may be a kind of generative overplus. I focus on one play in particular, the unattributed *The Fair Maid of the Exchange* (c. 1602, printed 1607), whose central character, Cripple, defies a concept of disability reducible to either commonplace impairment or wondrous difference.[5] Distinguished by his "crutches" (1.1.107) and his "crooked habit" (4.1.31), Cripple works in his shop drawing patterns, moonlighting as a supplier of verse to would-be suitors, and reengineering the romantic preferences of the female characters.[6] Never identified by any other name, Cripple is individuated by his disability, though his impairment is far from disabling. Although modern readers rightly recoil from the slur of the epithet "cripple," the range of affective responses that attach to Cripple in the play complicate uniform judgment about his character.[7] Desired by Phyllis, sought for counsel because of his "wit and policy" (2.3.253), and denigrated as "halting rascal" (4.2.245), "this paltry crutch" (2.2.133), and "crooked knave"

(5.1.228), Cripple is central to economic productivity and comic sociability in the play.

The title announces the play's generic affiliation as a city comedy, or exchange comedy, set in London's Royal Exchange and energized by the competing logics of "commerce and celebration" that drive the genre.[8] Preoccupied with emerging capitalism and economic productivity as well as the relationship between marketable goods and the marriage market, the play uses Cripple to think through the commercial value of successful impersonation. Cripple is marked, to recall one definition of character, as singularly "deformed" through distinctive theatrical prostheses. These very prostheses render his shape reproducible by other characters. Like the "lame" soldier of the previous chapter, the "crippled" beggar is ubiquitous in early modern plays, a type character that sparks theatrical expectations for a plot that exposes feigned disability. Paired with rogues and vagabonds in contemporary prescriptions against begging that sought to root out wandering imposters, the crippled beggar mobilizes visible disability as a plea for charity. But if the official gaze looks awry from the lame soldier, the crippled body compels suspicious scrutiny. This drama of verification is often played for laughs, with a predictable character arc when the disability is revealed to be fraudulent. If, as Bert O. States observes, comedy "requires the stereotype as the basic material out of which it builds a world that, above all else, is instantly recognizable," the trope of the disabled beggar trades on this recognition.[9]

Cripple, however, challenges this pattern of comic expectation by shifting from type into character, for he never reveals himself to be nondisabled and never begs, although the play pointedly associates him with such rhetorics of appeal.[10] Disability does not consist in visible bodily anomaly, in appearing crippled, in using crutches, or in having a crooked habit. Instead, I argue, Cripple's character reveals disability as a fundamental inability to impersonate in a world that demands the transformation it claims to punish. In the play's centerpiece scene of imitation, Frank Golding impersonates Cripple, borrowing his distinctive prosthetics as theatrical properties in order to court Phyllis Flower, the "Fair Maid," to great success. Building on Genevieve Love's dazzling reading of Cripple as a "figuration of theatrical movement-between, in which actor's body and character's being compete and collaborate," I understand Cripple as a model for the theater's iterative work of imitation.[11] In Lindsey Row-Heyveld's insightful reading of feigned disability in the play, Cripple is "required to perform his own disability in order to paradoxically prove his honesty."[12] In the reading that follows, I track how Cripple's distinctive form is fixed by social perception into disability, and how his form's unfixing makes social exchanges possible.[13] Cripple's disabling has the force of a plot twist—or, more precisely, a plot's refusal to twist into predictable shape—when *Fair Maid* ends with a crippled character who does not throw off his disguise, dwelling instead in the overplus of his "crooked" form.

Fair Maid demonstrates the value of broadening the field of inquiry for disability in early modern drama, for Cripple elevates the problem of feigning associated with disability to the very condition of theatricality itself. Cripple is the only character who appears intrinsically fixed in the theatrical economy, guaranteed by virtue of his singularly crooked shape. Yet if Cripple appears to be part of the exchanges that render identity endlessly fluid, he is still excluded from this circulation, the unfair made of exchange.[14] Ultimately, the balked exchange suggests that success in the financial and social negotiations that drive early modern city comedy depends on duplicitous impersonation carried out by an able body, rather than on productive labor such as Cripple performs. Cripple's deformed body is not intrinsically disqualified from acts of financial exchange, but rather disabled by perceived immobility in a dramatic world of shifting shapes and impersonating bodies.

Fantasies of Type: Feigning the Beggar

The type character of the crippled beggar makes disability the site of virtuosic display, for the beggar's association with theatrical techniques of feigned disability undermines a clear distinction between able and disabled bodies. I noted in chapter 2 that the capacity for labor is the primary criterion for ability in early modern England; disability distinguishes those who are unable to work. Alongside surgical accounts of rehabilitation, sixteenth-century French surgeon Ambroise Paré also offers advice for surgeons on how to unmask the beggar's pretense. Paré catalogues examples of "imposture," such as a woman pretending to have a canker on her breast and a man counterfeiting a leper.[15] The examples repeat a familiar assertion: fraudulent beggars play on the compassion of a public audience to compel pity through the ostentatious display of impairment or illness. For Paré, the beggar's pretense may skillfully amplify an existing condition or adopt a full-body disguise as an infectious disease results in an ostracized social identity. A stolen limb from a corpse may become a putrid prop to hide a healthy arm, or an ulcer may be composed of an elaborate arrangement of cloth and paint.[16]

Against these theatrical ruses, Paré celebrates the perception that medical scrutiny affords. The physician notices that the gruesome canker is at odds with the woman's otherwise healthy appearance, and he exposes her deceit, to be punished by civic authorities. Of one beggar who boasts "that he knew how to counterfeit several illnesses, and that he had never found greater profit in it than when he counterfeited the leper," Paré reports that the man is condemned to "get the whip on three successive Saturdays" and then banished. Even so, Paré concludes: "When it came to the last Saturday, the people shouted at the top of their voices to the executioner: 'Strike, strike, officer! He can't feel anything; he's a leper!' wherefore at the voice of the people the executioner was cruelly bent on whipping him so hard that shortly afterward he died, both because of the last whipping and because of having opened up his wounds again three different times: a thing which didn't amount to any great loss for the country" (77). Spectators at the scene of public punishment encourage violence by pretending to take the deception literally, citing leprosy as a justification for cruelty. Feigned disability is the pretext for feigned ignorance, a record of public approval to which the surgeon lends his expert credibility. Yet these accounts worry that the hideous body of the beggar, effective for solicitation, may be fictive and—like the best ambition for a theatrical prosthetic—impossible to distinguish from reality.

Paré's anecdotal description of the imposture reflects the legal instrument that puts beggars and actors in the same category. Paola Puggliati has argued that laws clamping down on itinerant and contingent labor associate players and beggars because of their shared "practices founded on simulation, disguise and self-transformations."[17] The Elizabethan "Acte for Punyshment of Rogues Vagabondes and Sturdy Beggars" included unlicensed actors among the populations of those punished for vagrancy, and fourteenth-century statutes governing vagrancy inflected the 1598 and 1601 major statutes of Elizabethan poor relief, ratified well into the seventeenth century.[18] As the mechanism of charitable support shifted from the medieval practice of almsgiving and parish funds to poor relief administered by the state, such relief included measures to ensure that people feigning disability were barred from financial assistance. Indeed, Linda Woodbridge observes that this suspicion extended so far that Robert Allen's *A Treatise of Christian Beneficence* (1600) labels the proper recipients of charity the "'uncounterfeit impotent,'" thus "assum[ing] 'counterfeit' as the default setting for impotence," and Deborah Stone argues that "the very category of disability was developed to incorporate a mechanism for distinguishing the genuine from the artificial."[19]

Disability emerges as a fault line for a concept of productivity that depends on identifying people who are temporarily or permanently unable to labor and require assistance from the state. The legal preoccupation with disqualification begins by assuming that a beggar feigns disability in order to avoid working, preferring charity to wages.[20] Split between official proclamations that decreed state relief for those unable to labor and social practices of charitable giving in response to begging, the cultural discourse on disability heightened scrutiny of the disabled body. Within the "shift between almsgiving-as-aid to government-controlled social assistance," Row-Heyveld argues, "physical impairment became the primary attribute deserving of charity and, simultaneously, the primary characteristic to invite suspicion about the need for such charity."[21] The act of witnessing invited by the beggar's display is meant to compel charitable relief from an onlooker. Official state policy that constituted disability as a category for relief did not map evenly onto social customs, to be sure. As Stone notes, an exception remained for alms given to people who were blind and lame even after almsgiving was forbidden, and Robert Henke demonstrates the ongoing practice of "individual, voluntarist charity" well into the seventeenth century, even beyond the allowance of donations to the poor law's category of the "lame, blind, or sick, aged, or impotent people."[22]

Yet this demand for veracity of a beggar's impairment appears to be no less fervent in the corpus of proliferating fictions that claimed to expose the coordinated frauds that beggars and rogues were imagined to undertake. Influential popular texts from the mid to late sixteenth century, such as Thomas Harman's *Caveat for Common Cursetors* (c. 1566), John Awdeley's *The Fraternity of Vagabonds* (ca. 1561), and Robert Greene's cony-catching pamphlets (1591–1592), insisted on the pervasive threat of beggars faking disability, purported to offer a glossary of cant language and an anatomy of rogue types, and even imagined an organized criminal underworld.[23] The prevalence of this material reminds us how attractive such fictions were, prefiguring a social "fantasy of identification," in Ellen Samuels's term, an attempt to ensure that "embodied social identities . . . are fixed, legible, and categorizable."[24] In rhetoric that William C. Carroll terms the "histrionics of poverty," which he associates with the early modern theater, fictions of beggars who feign disability to shirk labor "inscribed the beggar's body both as a potentially valuable commodity and as a site of lawlessness and subversion."[25] Patricia Fumerton has cautioned scholars of early modern literature to "resist the push toward theatricality" that would move from historical conditions of vagrancy to dramatic texts and substitute Shakespeare's characters—Tom o'Bedlam in *King Lear* or returning soldiers in *Henry V*—for actual "unsettled" laborers.[26] Dramatic representations export concepts of disability too, as Row-Heyveld has demonstrated, firming up the link between feigned impairment and the figure of the beggar. Even as medical, legal, and fictional texts provoke suspicion about disability, offloading epistemological authentication of disability onto witnesses, theatrical performances of beggary may also put the body of the actor on view as he strips down to the impoverished, hungry form of a supplicant. Henke, in a wide-ranging reading of continental and English traditions of theatrical performance, perceptively observes that "we might consider the representation of a beggar to be the ur-role, or ground fiction, of the actor himself."[27] If the actor's body grounds the figure of the beggar, the dramatic fictions to which I now turn celebrate the beggar's visible anomaly as the product of theatrical properties and skill.

In what follows, I briefly examine plays that feature disabled beggars and advertise the "humors" of a character to frame *Fair Maid*'s deployment of Cripple. *Fair Maid*'s subtitle, *With The pleasaunt Humours of the Cripple of Fanchurch*, bills Cripple alongside the "Fair Maid" with a claim that the play will delight an audience.[28] I find that *Fair Maid* is a hinge between the disguise expectations of a humor comedy and the theatrical proficiency of beggar communities in tragicomedies that follow. Larding plots with feigned disability, these plays link the trope of the disabled beggar with skilled action. The paratactic stress on Cripple's "Humours" recalls the "extremely popular" play by George Chapman, *The Blinde Begger of Alexandria most pleasantly discoursing his variable humours in disguised shapes full of conceite and pleasure* (1598), which hails a character marked by bodily impairment.[29] Invoking humors, the play constellates several meanings: predominantly associated with Galenic medical discourse, the four humors are fluids that form the physiological basis of the self, determining sickness or health and also, as they vary in concentration and balance, shaping the material basis of emotion and personality.[30] In Ben Jonson's *Every Man in His Humour* (1598) and *Every Man Out of His Humour* (1599), and George Chapman's *An Humorous Day's Mirth* (1597, printed 1599), humors individuate characters in a comedy by gripping them in particular obsessions. The prologue to Jonson's *The Alchemist* (1610) expresses humors as key to personation, announcing that "Bawd, squire, imposter, many persons more, / Whose manners, now called humours, feed the stage," delineating each character by something like psychological compulsion.[31] Taking the insight that a humor drives idiosyncratic characterization into a discussion of theatrical personation, Alexander Paulsson Lash has convincingly argued that the introduction of "humors," first associated with a character on the title pages of extant playbooks from 1598, heralds new practices of writing for actors. Advertising humors, plays signal plots that demand quick changes of costume and shifts in passion, demonstrating the skill of the actor who "has mastered his own bodily disposition" and can move effortlessly between disguises.[32]

Chapman's play packs many roles into the title's "blind beggar," and his astonishingly popular play—performed twenty-two times between 1595 and

1597 before its printing in 1598—starred the famed actor Edward Alleyn.[33] Reveling in Alleyn's talent, *Blind Beggar* underscores the humorous variability the title advertises, for the "pleasure" of these "shapes" is actually the actor's movement between "blind Irus" (the beggar, neither blind nor an actual beggar), "Duke Cleanthes," "Count Hermes," and "Leon," a "wealthie usurer."[34] Although readings of *Blind Beggar* typically affirm the title character as a base identity—so that, as Victor O. Freeburg writes, "the 'Beggar' leads a quadruple life which requires a constant shifting of costume"—the variances of role and disguise are so swift and stark that the actor's form is the only continuity from which these characters proceed.[35] Entering first as Irus, the titular beggar, he announces, "I am Cleanthes and blind Irus too / And more than these, as you shall soone perceive" (sig. A3v). This string of conjunctions does not rest in stable characterization for even the space of a line. In the play, the multiple roles deceive an onstage audience, and the fun of the disguise is the big reveal at the conclusion. Expounding these humors, Lash suggests that Chapman goes so far that he has "sublimated the moral threat of deception into a comedic celebration of his star actor's capacity for transformation."[36] Foregrounding the characterization shifts within the dramatic fiction, the play rewrites acts of feigned disability, especially the "Blind Beggar," as spectacular displays as much as untruths.

Following *Blind Beggar*, other plays that announce a titular beggar incorporate disability disguise into the structure of plot revelation. The Admiral's Men played Henry Chettle and John Day's *The Blind Beggar of Bethnal Green* (1600, printed 1659), which advertises "the merry humor of Tom Strowd the Norfolk yeoman" in its subtitle; William Haughton and Day appear to have followed with *The Second Part of The Blind Beggar of Bethnal Green* (1601), also known as *The Second Part of Tom Strowd*.[37] Following Chapman, Chettle and Day's play uses feigned disability to disorient status. Momford is a noble wrongfully charged a traitor; he assumes the identity of a blind beggar and attempts to clear his name, right his daughter's wrongful dispossession, and regain his wealth. The play's dramatis personae, before Momford announces in the play that he is "pretending my self blind" (sig. C3v), names him "*Momford* the Blindbeggar" (and his daughter "*Bess* the Blind-beggars Daughter" [sig. A1v]) even though he has not yet adopted the disguise.[38] To defuse the political charge of falsehood in his disguise plot, the play underscores Momford's unjust disenfranchisement and cues laughter through scenes in which even his daughter fails to recognize him. This *Blind Beggar* play fuses impairment and beggary into a single identity that is maintained until the conclusion. When "*Momford discovers himself*" (sig. K2v), in the stage direction at the end of the play, the king immediately names him his high treasurer. This figure of the beggar adopts signifiers of disability as a prosthetic addition, and the play concludes with a familiar plot of revelation that displays the shedding of the disguise.

Further iterations of the disabled beggar spin the singular character out into an imagined commonwealth of feigners who are skilled in specific portrayals of physical difference. In John Fletcher and Philip Massinger's play *Beggars' Bush* (c. 1616, printed 1647) disability is reducible to disguise. Well versed in the trope of "noble disguised as a beggar," key characters trade the court for the beggars' commonwealth, assuming beggary, only to jettison it at the end of the play.[39] The scene that revolves around the problem of kingship ends up reviewing theatrical conventions of disguise when Prig, one of the candidates for the title of beggar king, boasts that he will be "a very tyrant" (2.1.16), enumerating the "priviledges, / Places, revenues, offices" he will take "as forfeit" (24–25).[40] He threatens to confiscate the very theatrical accoutrements with which the beggars have staged their appeals for charitable aid; he will, he tells them, "call in your crutches, wooden legs, false bellyes, / Forc'd eyes and teeth, with your dead arms" (26–27). This assertion of tyrannical power sounds like the recitation of a company's list of stage properties—he will seize everything from the "old rag" (29) and "birdlime, blood, and creame" (30) used to "make you an old sore" (31) to the "sope / As you may fome with i'th Falling-sicknesse" (31–32)—and the catalogue of technologies enumerate a range of visual special effects. What looks like foaming at the mouth from an epileptic fit is traceable to soap. Among the play's repeated displays of feigning, this scene's lengthy digression on the kind of bodily counterfeiting that Paré aims to deconstruct is especially notable because most of the scene is extraneous to the plot. The title of beggar king has already been determined, since another beggar, Clause (who is really Gerrard, a noble in disguise), has prearranged his own apparently random nomination for ruler, enlisting the aid of a passerby he has planted. Though irrelevant to narrative logic, the scene invites the audience into the conspiratorial pleasure of disclosing how disability may be adopted as a disguise.

Having called out the theatrical counterfeiting required to play the beggar, the scene in *Beggars' Bush* fantasizes that such displays may be codified in a master text that prescribes the method of acting. Recounting the laws of the beggars' commonwealth, the beggars refer to a "table / That doth command all these things" (2.1.131–32), as if a compilation of disability impostures made explicit. Clause, now nominated king, pledges to enforce the rule that governs economic distribution by ensuring that each beggar keeps to "his own path and circuite" (124), and prescribes that all beggars observe to the "table" of possible feignings. As another beggar explains, this text

> enjoyns 'em
> Be perfect in their crutches, their fain'd plaisters,
> And their torne pas-ports, with the ways to stammer,
> And to be dumb, and deafe, and blind, and lame,
> There, all the halting paces are set downe,
> I'th learned language.
>
> (2.1.132–37)

In the manner of a travel phrasebook or instruction manual (or the fictions of cony-catching pamphlets), the beggars' book collects the "learned language" of disability counterfeiting—theatrical techniques to enact impairments of gait, speech, sight, sound, and appearance. The impulse to classify the range of skill displayed by these beggars-as-actors lumps many forms of difference together, putting stammering with limping, and "fain'd plaisters" with "crutches." Directed to "be perfect" in the performance of disability—which is to say, to make their feigned disability indistinguishable from real disability— the beggars evince actorly prowess. The rest of the scene indulges in the valorized quick changes such a book forecasts, for when passersby enter, the beggars leap into action with "postures" (165) to appear "Blinde, and lame" (169). Begging for charity, the beggars enact visible impairment complemented by a soundscape of linguistic difference, from a vocalization ("Ao, ao, ao, ao" [191]) by a character who "signes" (192) and another character who stammers, a specificity the text preserves ("He is de-de-de-de-de-de-de-deafe, and du-du-du-du-dumb [194]).[41] The scene first announces and then enacts the performative appeal of bodily difference, demonstrating how disability is feigned while underscoring the virtuosic range of the actor.

Clause is extracted from the play, furthermore, to become one of the most recognizable dramatic characters of the early modern theater. The scene of feigned disability (2.1) in *Beggars' Bush* is reproduced in the late seventeenth century as a "Droll-Humour" called "The Lame Common-wealth" for the collection *The Wits* (attributed to Francis Kirkman), printed in 1662.[42] Clause appears in the frontispiece (figure 3.1), alongside other characters such as "Sir J. Falstaff" and "Chang[e]ling," who populate the playhouse stage while spectators look on from above, below, and beside. The characters appear in motion— gesturing, dancing, hobbling—and each is labeled with a name or identity. Clause is shown as a lame beggar, wearing tattered clothing and employing a cane, with his leg tied up and suspended behind him. The frontispiece is a visual prosthetic to the text, and the panoramic array of characters builds a tableau from many different plays. Henry Marsh's note on the compilation calls the volume "a *Miscellany* of all Humours which our Fam'd Comedies have

Figure 3.1. [Francis Kirkman?], *The Wits, Part 1* (London, 1662). Call#: ART Box L847t1 R1 no.1 (size S). Used by permission of the Folger Shakespeare Library under a Creative Commons Attribution-ShareAlike 4.0 International License.

exquisitely and aptly represented in the becoming dress of the Stage," and identifies the text as a *"Body of Humours"* that assembles parts of many plays to compose one "entire *consistencie,* the making of a *fluid* a *solid* Body."[43] A droll-humor may be a single character or scene, a chunk of a play. Marsh imagines the work of extraction as the exercise of formal wisdom, for "he that knows a Play, knows that Humours have no such *fixedness* and indissoluble *connexion* to the Design, but that without *injury* or *forcible revulsion* they may be *removed* to an *advantage.*"[44] The compilation unfixes each example from a plot's "fixedness" in order to pursue the "exquisite" work of the stage at the expense of linear narrative. The droll is part and whole at the same time, for a single droll acts as a synecdoche for the "Fam'd Comed[y]" from which it is drawn. Cobbled together into one text, however, they collect an array of theatrical humors, producing a new form. Figuring the play as a body, Marsh imagines each humor as a part amputated without injury to the whole, removed on the grounds of detachability because it is least intrinsic to the plot. The scene from *Beggars' Bush* meditates on the assemblage of properties and skilled actions that make disguise possible, and it operates as a theatrical prosthetic that enables the miscellany to survey what "the Stage" can do.

Most of all, the frontispiece reminds us that the figure who appears instantly recognizable as the disabled beggar type character is, in the play, simply the character most skilled in feigning disability. Though Clause shakes free of the other beggars in the end, the frontispiece freezes him in his pose of pretended impairment. In keeping with Mitchell and Snyder's identification of disability as a narrative prosthesis that inspires a story but must be cured or finally removed from view, in *Beggars' Bush,* Clause's disability turns out to be a politically expedient ruse—and, because such a deception ensures his safety from the usurping ruler, his act is gratefully forgiven. This narrative orientation to plot, however, cannot account for the frontispiece's depiction of characters cramming the stage in recognizable poses and postures. The droll's method of synecdoche, rather than linear development, reproduces Clause as shorthand for the delights of theatrical practice itself, a display in which it is impossible to know whether he is feigning. Itinerantly unfixed but reproducing hierarchical political order, and mobilizing bodily injury as a spectacular plea, the character compresses theatrical practice into the display of disabled exigency. He presents a figure formally extricable from the play yet intrinsic to its theatrical appeal.

Indeed, "beggar" plays that follow *Fair Maid* in the seventeenth century extrapolate the association of actors and beggars into interchangeability. The final act of Richard Brome's *A Jovial Crew, or, The Merry Beggars* (c. 1641, printed 1652) reinstates feigning nobles revealed to be idealized beggars. The play concludes with a play-within-the-play that judges social kinds, offering a class parable that gets interrupted by state judgment in the form of court officials. Breaking up the beggars' play, Oldrents, the gentleman landowner, dissolves the anarchic community, dividing the actors into two groups: real beggars, who flee, and nobles, who have only been posing as beggars. Newly reconciled, the nobles return to society, and Oldrent declares, "Here are no *Beggars* . . . no *Rogues*, nor *Players*."[45] As dramatic catastrophe in the technical sense, these words are literally true: everyone left onstage has a place in this society. Less humorous is the rhetoric he employs, lifted directly from the legal association of rogues and unlicensed actors. *A Jovial Crew*, Brome claims in the dedication, was the final play staged before Parliament ordered the closure of theaters in 1642, having *"the luck to tumble last of all in the* Epidemicall *ruine of the Scene; and now* limps *hither with a* wooden Leg, *to beg an Alms at your hands"* (sig. A2v). Printed a decade after its performance, the play figures itself as a beggar, cut off from viable labor, turning to charity because the theatrical scene has disappeared. The note collapses the equivalence asserted by "no *Rogues*, nor *Players*" into a category that allows for no demarcation at all. The ruin of the theater as an institution is expressed in the proliferation of disabled plays it produces. Beggar, player, rogue, and play: they are all the same thing.

A Cripple / the Cripple in *The Fair Maid of the Exchange*

I offer this brief survey of conventions signaled by "humours," and associated with disability in "beggar," in order to adumbrate the theatrical traditions that shape disability into metatheatrical comment on an actor's skill. Apparent impairment proves to be a useful disguise, doffed as easily as it was donned, once a character has achieved his purpose. Set against these examples of extant plays that promise "humors" and make disability central to characterization, *Fair Maid* turns the formula of adjective plus noun—"blind beggar"—into a character, Cripple, distinguished on the basis of visible bodily difference. Since *Fair Maid*'s title singles out Cripple for the "humors" he will offer, spectators tutored by the prevalence of beggar plays might well assume that they are about to enjoy yet another comic stereotype of the disabled beggar who fakes impairment as a disguise to further his own ends and easily dissembles. *Fair Maid* disorients expectations, however, by making Cripple the fixed center around which a world of impersonation orbits. Turning Cripple into a character rather than a type, the play anatomizes expectations about disability feigning in a setting of volatile exchange.

Early critics emphasized Cripple's dynamism and centrality, despite the marginal position his lack of a proper name might imply. Barron Field, editing the 1845 Malone Society volume, calls Cripple "a very original character," and Charles Lamb names him "the hero of the comedy," while Edmund Gosse describes Cripple as a "delightful creation."[46] Yet critics also puzzled over Cripple because his originality seemed at odds with the telos of a disabled character, who surely could never play the hero of a romantic comedy. Lamb notes regretfully that Cripple's efforts to help Frank display his "heroic qualities of mind and body," since he "procur[es] for [Phyllis] a husband, in the person of his friend Golding, more worthy of her beauty than he could conceive his own maimed and halting limbs to be."[47] The play's substitution of Frank for Cripple was understood as a necessary result in a period when "physical as well as mental perfection was demanded of the hero of the age," for, in Felix Schelling's estimation, an "Elizabethan could not accept the logic of the situation and marry 'the fair maid' to a cripple."[48] Nonetheless, Gosse observes that "the notion of making the tall and handsome Frank personate the Cripple so perfectly as to deceive the girl who loves the latter, and win away her heart, is incredible and unnatural."[49] Theatrical personation is the problem at the core of the nineteenth-century critical assessments of *Fair Maid*. While Cripple is delightful to read, he is uncomfortable to watch. Lamb laments that it would be difficult to find an actor who would choose to "personate the infirmities" of Cripple because "these personal deformities, however consistent with heroism in the reading of works of fiction, cannot be embodied by an actor without ridicule."[50] This reading of Cripple's disability as unquestionably diminishing persists well into the twentieth century. As a scholarly edition in 1980 observes, although Cripple remains "the most interesting character of the play," the ending reflects commonsense judgment: "To have Phyllis waste herself on Cripple would violate a romantic sense present in the average person."[51]

These readings locate Cripple's centrality to the theatrical economy of the play in the very disability that also disqualifies him. Recent critics have illuminated the play's economic concerns and its representation of women's labor, exploring the Exchange location as a site of fervor for new concepts of the market.[52] Cripple, however, is no longer the "most interesting" dramatic character in the social world of the play. He is called "the prime mover of the plot," though an "outsider and somewhat monstrous"; he is the "market personified, the activity of exchange," who is "still more a force, or a function, than an individual"; and although Cripple "determines how erotic energy should flow" by directing the marriages, he occupies a "singular position—he is both part and not-part of the community."[53] Identifying Cripple as a character that exceeds the frame of the plot, turning him into something like the play's playwright, these readings figure Cripple through abstractions of force and flow. In these accounts, Cripple is distinctive because of his capacity to exceed the limitations that individuate him, not because of discomfort with his apparent disability. Cripple oscillates in critical thought between being the play's most memorable character and being barely a character at all.

Cripple, that is, poses both a theoretical problem and a theatrical problem. The prologue to *Fair Maid* invites expectations about Cripple by conjuring a kind of stereotypical beggar—definitely crippled and possibly fraudulent—before the play has even begun. In the form of a sonnet, the prologue promises that the play will be a comedy, its muse appearing in the "humble sock that true comedians wear" (Prologue, 1–2), and "borrowing no colors from a quaint disguise" (3–4). The octave announces the genre and the sestet implores the audience to "shore up our tender pamping twig" (9) by glossing over any deficiencies of the newly sprouted play, their "favor's sunshine gilding once this sprig" (11). The image of applause as sustaining appreciation turns sunlight into gold, a recompense that reconfigures the exchange between actors and spectators as coined approval. The couplet concludes by wrenching this economy of attention into a beggar's plea: "Though our invention lame imperfect be, / Yet give the cripple alms for charity" (13–14). As if preoccupied with the central character in the play that follows, the verse employs a crippled beggar to imagine itself as a flawed work, punning on alms poised between donation and applause. Although "invention lame" is a modesty trope about literary production, gesturing to a generic hierarchy that regards comedy as less accomplished than tragedy, the appeal to charity goes beyond the depreciation of poetic labor. Rewriting performance as a plea for aid, the play cements the association between actors and beggars.

Though no performance records remain for *Fair Maid*, the prologue's doubling registers very differently depending on who speaks it. If Cripple, the character who is called "the cripple" in the play, speaks the prologue, the prologue radically undermines the play's emphasis on his work and economic independence by collapsing the distinction between Cripple as dramatic character and the figure of a begging "cripple" in the cultural imagination. If Frank, who impersonates Cripple later in the play, speaks the prologue, the play gestures toward contemporary suspicions of the beggar's potential deceit. Before Cripple himself has officially entered the stage, the dramatic fiction evokes an ambiguous, rhetorically charged double who engages the audience to consider the value of the theater's ability to counterfeit for entertainment.

The bid for "charity" in the prologue resolves into the opening scene's work with Cripple, which challenges a straightforward interpretation of Cripple's crutches as a sign of incapacity. Opening with a scene of attempted assault on

Phyllis (the "Fair Maid") and Ursula as they deliver handworked cloth to a customer, *Fair Maid* introduces Cripple, who comes to their rescue despite his self-described "huge deformity" (1.1.77), exhorting himself to "now stir thee, Cripple, and of thy four legs / Make use of one to do a virgin good" (86–87). Counting his "four legs," as if his crutches are limbs, with a bawdy pun that associates his distinctive body with eroticized heroism, Cripple rescues the women and redirects the play toward comedy rather than tragedy. When Cripple intervenes, beating off the attackers with his crutches, Bobbington, one of the villains, hails him as "thou that hast more legs than nature gave thee" (114). Cripple's crutches are unnatural bodily excess rewritten as superhuman hypertrophy. This brief victory, however, is quickly undone when the villains return to "snatch away his crutches" (107) and Frank Golding enters, his aid required for the women and Cripple himself, who "came in rescue of virginity" (123) but now needs his own deliverance. Even Phyllis, who praises Cripple for having "freed us once from thrall" (124), concedes, "but now the second time they wrought his fall" (125), a couplet that parodies Cripple's heroism when the second line rhymes on his botched attempt at rescue. In the space of a scene, by making Cripple first the character endowed with virtuosic excess and then the butt of a joke, the play establishes him as singular and as actually impaired, vulnerable to disabling encounters in his environment.

The taunts lobbed at Cripple throughout the play echo the pratfalls of the opening scene and recast him as a type character, as if he were on loan from one of the beggar plays I discussed earlier. Bowdler, a young impoverished gentleman, insults Cripple as a "filthy dog" (2.2.6) and "lame rogue" (4.2.241), derogatory terms that yoke animality, antisemitism, and ableism.[54] Although Bowdler regards Cripple with some sense of companionship, his vitriolic compilation of stereotypes addresses Cripple as if he is exactly the "rogue" stock character who deserves punishment. Cripple himself at times even seems complicit with these expectations of type; his own syntax establishes the tension between the particular name and the general type that vie throughout the play. After his self-exhortation to "Cripple" (1.1.85), he thanks Frank, saying, "May but the cripple be / Of power to gratify this courtesy" (130–31). Phyllis likewise shifts between apostrophe that addresses him as if "Cripple" is his proper name ("cripple, my heart is thine, and shall be still" [1.3.217–18]) and references to "the Cripple" that reduce him to his distinctive embodiment ("Instruct the cripple to find out my love" [2.2.209] and "Say what they will, / I'll love the Cripple, and will hate them still" [4.1.156–57]). The twin forces of specificity and abstraction pervade the printed text: "Cripple" is capitalized in the printed text of the quarto, and the definite article is echoed in some textual features (such as the stage direction that reads, *"Enter the Cripple"* [s.d. at 1.1.74]) but not others (such as the casting table in the 1607 text that marks him simply as "Cripple" or the stage direction *"Enter Cripple in his shop"* [s.d. at 4.2.0]). These inconsistencies heighten the tension between character and type: Is he "Cripple" or "the Cripple"? Simply deciding what to call Cripple poses the problem of determining whether and how his distinctive body individuates his identity through visible difference.

As the play unfolds, however, Cripple proves to be an astonishing departure from the stereotypical beggar who receives charitable aid obtained by faking disability. Though deformed, Cripple works. Although his physical anomaly associates him with appeals for aid, he does not beg. Instead, Cripple is an artisan who draws embroidery designs in his shop (he is called "master drawer" [2.2.41]) and also serves as a scrivener, writing letters and dispensing poems to suitors who require verse for the courtships they pursue. The play emphasizes his labor in his interactions with a client ("I have been mindful of your work" [2.2.42]) and in a stage direction (*"The Cripple at work"* [s.d. at 3.2.0]), a phrase echoed by Frank's announcement that "the cripple is at work" (3.2.2). His labor sets him apart from the other male characters in the play—impecunious young gentlemen and gullible, greedy patriarchs—who default on loans, accuse each other of fraud, and profit from underhanded business deals. Some of these financial transactions are obviously specious: Bobbington, the assailant from the opening scene, returns with a stolen diamond to swindle Master Flower, Phyllis's father, who eagerly accepts suspicious collateral if he stands to gain. Other spendthrifts are simply profligate: Bernard, a young gentleman "indebted a hundred pound" (2.2.199) and "not worth a hundred pence" (201), goes out dancing at his friend's admonition to "tickle it tonight, for tomorrow thy heels may be too heavy" (191–92). Despite the heavy-heeled future of ankle fetters in debtors' prison, Bernard and other gentlemen make merry, undeterred by the consequences of ruin. Cripple, instead, eschews invitations with the plea, "My business stays me here" (196), and exclaims, "I'll now turn provident. I'll to my shop / And fall to work" (205–6). Cripple's labor differentiates him from the recipient of charity for whom the poor laws might stipulate relief. This depiction of a disabled craftsman in his shop confounds the historical stereotype of the beggar who shirks work as well as the dramatic stereotype of the beggar revealed to be an aristocrat in disguise.

Cripple's emphasis on "business" gestures to the most obvious expression of a dramatic world structured by economic calculation. The title's allusion to London's Royal Exchange situates the play's financial transactions and artisanal labor within important historical developments of the early modern period, such as emerging forms of capitalism and trade, international commerce, and controversies over domestic production of goods.[55] The Royal Exchange, London's central site of civic commerce, was founded by Sir Thomas Gresham in 1566, modeled on Antwerp's bourse, and officially opened in 1571 by Queen Elizabeth. Jean E. Howard has demonstrated how the Exchange "entered the culture's imaginative life as a densely coded site speaking to the dangers and pleasures of new kinds of commercial practice," figuring in "complex and contradictory" theatrical representations.[56] In cultural convention, Howard notes, the ground floor of the Exchange, "the place of big financial transactions," was regularly imagined as a "male space"; by contrast, "the pawn, site of everyday consumption, is insistently connected with women who sell or who buy in its shops."[57] Cripple himself recalls a past in which he strolled through the ground floor of the Exchange in the company of the men who now enter his shop. Addressing Bowdler, he reminisces, "In th' Exchange! I have walked with thee there, before the visitation of my legs, and my expense in timber, at the least a hundred times" (2.2.53–54). Although neither Cripple nor the play seem interested in the origin of his impairment beyond this exclamation, his "visitation" reassigns his character to his shop near the pawn, now stripped of the proper name he presumably possessed before becoming "Cripple."

The Exchange's gendered distinction of space inflects critical readings of Cripple's physical deformity, furthermore, since he works near the shop where Phyllis Flower and Moll Berry labor as seamstresses. In this pairing, Juana Green suggests that the play offers a possible way to explain his limp, because "from an early modern perspective, effeminization results from associating too closely with women."[58] This association between deformity and femininity follows from Aristotelian theories of generation, which understand the female body as one defect removed from the male body; Rosemarie Garland-Thomson suggests, similarly, that "the non-normate status accorded disability feminizes all disabled figures."[59] Cripple's readiness to engage in plots that discipline female desire complicates this affiliation with the women, however, for Cripple does not exactly fit in at the pawn. He frustrates the wishes of Phyllis and Moll, organizing Frank's substitution when Phyllis intends to marry Cripple himself and steering Moll, the daughter of a wealthy merchant, away from Bowdler to marry Bernard, another impoverished gentleman indebted to her father. Cripple's rejection of Phyllis, furthermore, does not reflect bodily incapacity as much as a wholesale refusal of marriage as an institution. When Phyllis visits his shop to profess her love, Cripple admits that "Phyllis bears me true affection" (2.2.240), and then he defends his response:

> But I detest the humor of fond love.
> Yet am I hourly solicited
> As you now see, and fain she would make known
> The true perplexion of her wounded heart.
>
> (241–44)

Cripple will not subject himself to the "humor of fond love"; he is not unfit for marriage but irritated by Phyllis's "hourly" flirtations. Proclaiming that "fancy shall never marry me to woe" (251), he asserts: "Take this of me: a young man's never marred, / Till he by marriage from all joy be barred" (252–53). Cripple expounds on the "marring" effect of marrying with an expression that sounds like proverbial wisdom. Later, when Cripple offers Frank the opportunity to woo Phyllis, he acknowledges himself "too foul for such a beauty, and too base / To match in brightness with that sacred comet" (4.2.25–26), but this refusal is notable for its metaphorical abstraction. Cripple himself does not understand his refusal of Phyllis's affection as the necessary consequence of his deformed shape.

Although the shift in Cripple's mobility prevents him from engaging in the social performances that the ground floor of the Exchange facilitates, Cripple proves more than able to direct the young gentlemen who seek to make their fortunes through marriage. Cripple's labor to advise other men in impersonation exposes the conceptual framework of exchange that permeates the dramatic world. Subterfuge and deceit are necessary strategies; characters transform themselves according to the moment's need, pretending to be other than who they are to get what they desire. The stress on exchange in this exchange comedy concentrates a generic trend for city comedies that stage the thrill and uncertainty of a moment when the concept of value was "coming to be conceived as being created in the process of exchange itself," reimagined as the result of fluctuating cultural practices.[60] The early modern theater was both a part of the market, the result of "forces which shaped dramatic commodities to answer the various manifestations of social desire," and also a cultural institution that was invested in representing, among other things, the "ethical, epistemological, and affective freight" of the nascent market's complexity.[61] Jean-Christophe Agnew has shown how the "formless, qualityless, characterless nature of the money form" posed a conceptual challenge to representing the emerging market economy and the acts of exchange it entails. *Fair Maid* derives energy from engaging what Agnew describes as the "coherent and repeated pattern of problems or questions about the nature of social identity, intentionality, accountability, transparency, and reciprocity in commodity transactions—the who, what, when, where, and why of exchange."[62] If the emerging market economy ushers in a new sense of transactional possibility, the money form facilitates newfound opportunities for exchange across literal and metaphorical registers. Cripple is confined to labor in his shop, cut off from the Exchange and the exchanges that are the heart and soul of London, but his generative excess offers the surplus on which such an exchange is founded.

Theatrical Prosthetics and Feats of Impersonation

Fair Maid thematizes this novel sense of exchange as a relay between fixed identities and the market constraints that unfix social roles. The play centers Cripple as the character whose theatrical prostheses both fix and unfix his identity. Cripple's "crutches" and "crooked habit," the stage properties associated with his character, produce his conspicuous singularity and multiply the possibilities for imitation. Cripple's "crutches" distinguish him from the very first scene as the character whose bodily supplement alters and amplifies his natural form. There is no extant performance history of the play: the actor who performs Cripple may not actually require crutches, though it is also possible that the role trades on the embodied knowledge of an actor who employs crutches. Within the fiction, Cripple's prostheses differentiate his body as singularly in need of support. The "crutches" verify his character's impairment when Cripple requires them to move around. Bobbington's address to Cripple as "thou, that has more legs than nature gave thee!" (1.1.114) imagines the crutches as substitute for and addition to legs at the same time, as "more than" limbs that are quantitatively excessive and qualitatively different. Cripple's prosthetic objects obtain what Will Fisher identifies as the "peculiar status" of being detachable from yet crucial to the body's materiality.[63] The concept of prosthesis elaborated in early modern surgical texts and rhetorical manuals designates the supplement as "that which presents itself as a supplementary operation, designed to remedy the imperfections of nature, [which] must at the same time admit of the artificial as unnatural."[64] The prosthetic remedy may supplement, I noted earlier, what is missing but it points to the very lack it strives to conceal. Alternatively, the prosthetic remedy may advance, implicitly or explicitly, a fantasy of wholeness that transforms the original body. The prosthetic capacity to exceed the status of supplement, as Lynn Festa shows, thus "suggests that the body's boundaries furnish no calculable limit as to what humanity might be or do."[65] Cripple's crutches accomplish the function of legs, yet they expand to imitate his person too, turning his prosthetic devices into stage properties.

I have suggested throughout this book that the theatrical frame for thinking about disability in performance challenges conceptions of literary disability as a form of prosthesis. In the generative concept of narrative prosthesis expounded by Mitchell and Snyder, disability "alleviates discomfort by removing the unsightly from view."[66] Although *Fair Maid* does end with a decided rejection of Cripple's deformed shape, this account of narrative is too limited to explain the play's complex work with material prosthetics that circulate in the act of impersonation. *Fair Maid* foregrounds Cripple's disability not as narrative provocation but as theatrical experimentation. Rather than remove Cripple's "unsightly" body from view, the play stresses the generative capacity of Cripple's character. Cripple is crucial to a theatrical economy of exchange in which he cannot participate because he funds the act of impersonation. *Fair Maid* mobilizes the kaleidoscopic potential of theatrical prosthesis through Cripple, transforming properties extrinsic to the actor into a body apparently intrinsic to the character.

Cripple's "crutch" rescales and compresses his dramatic character. The crutches are routinely identified with Cripple himself. In one scene, Bowdler names him accordingly:

> Bow.: Come, Crutch, thou shalt with us.
> Crip.: Not I.
> Bow.: Down, dog! I'll have thy company.
> Crip.: I have business.
> Bow.: By this hand, thou shalt go with us.
> Crip.: By this leg, I will not.
> Bow.: A lame oath! Never stand to that.
> Crip.: By this crutch, but I will.
>
> (2.2.86–93)

When Bowdler reduces Cripple to "crutch," the synecdoche of the object stands in for his person. The repartee turns on the idea of substitution, from Bowdler's threat of physical force ("by this hand") to Cripple's distinctively unforceful leg ("by this leg"). Bowdler's double pun, on the "lame" oath and the impossibility of taking a "stand," prompts Cripple's contradictory response, "By this crutch but I will," which substitutes the wooden support for the body part of his previous line. In this progression of bodily based oaths, Bowdler constructs the rhetorical figure from Cripple's body, mapping onto the stage property the lame leg, the wooden support that substitutes for the leg, and the nickname for Cripple himself. The crutch ends their verbal play, yoking theatrical and conceptual prosthesis to become the overriding, irreducible marker of Cripple's identity.

This prosthetic conjunction of shape and support is even more conspicuous in Cripple's second prosthesis, his "crooked habit." Cripple's "habit" may be either a cloak that covers—and defines—his shape, or simply the distinctive posture of his body. The multiple definitions of "habit" in the period range from "bodily apparel or attire" to "bearing, demeanour, deportment, behaviour" and "bodily condition or constitution," perforating any clear distinction between the exterior and interior of the body.[67] As Ann Rosalind Jones and Peter Stallybrass have shown, this doubled sense of "habit" as both clothing and person, in the sense of that which is "habitual," is especially generative for the stage.[68] The adjective "crooked" echoes this boundary-crossing multiplicity. One definition of "crooked" means "bent," and, when applied to the body, having "limbs bent out of shape, deformed"; in a second, metaphorical sense, "crooked" is that which is "dishonest, wrong, perverse; perverted, out of order, awry."[69] Like "habit," "crooked" forks into figural and literal meanings, combining moral judgment and distinctive shape—and implicating both in the process. The term's ethical charge, like the jests about a crooked body's falsehood, calls attention to the ease with which a body's shape may be read for significance. As both material object and metaphorical sign—for unlike the visually apprehended "crutch," the "habit" must also be established as "crooked" rhetorically—Cripple's "crooked habit" denotes the contours of the body beneath and seems to connote the crippled beggar's deceit.

Yet, in keeping with the "overplus" insisted on by the crooked figure with whom I began, "habit" also blurs the distinction between that which is extrinsic and intrinsic to the body. Cloak or (and?) shape, Cripple's "habit" may be a matter of costume or of personation. While Peter Hyland maintains that "the requirement for a change in posture demanded by Frank Golding's disguise as the Cripple needs no explanation," the play's stress on "habit" as a garment undercuts this assurance that the disguise is limited to embodied posture.[70] In act 2, Frank assumes a "porter's habit" (2.3.141) at the plea of his brother Ferdinand (who wants him to thwart their other brother, Anthony, by intercepting a love letter to Phyllis). Ferdinand suggests the "base attire" (143) as a disguise and commands Frank: "Here is a porter's habit. On with it, brother" (165). Once he has donned the theatrical property, Frank compares himself to Jove, exulting that his "habit may prove mighty in love's power" (183). Before Frank adopts Cripple's habit, then, the play employs a habit as a costume to transform identity, successfully disguising the body beneath. My point is not to settle this distinction but to highlight the strange opacity of Cripple's "crooked habit," even when the play explicitly points at it. *Fair Maid* provokes, rather than answers, the question of whether "habit" is a property of the body or a property on the body. This uncertainty, in turn, troubles the distinction between where Cripple's "crooked habit" ends and where a "crooked" body might begin.

This energetic ambiguity about whether disability resides in the property or in the body recasts the central act of exchange in the play as an unequal distinction between prosthesis and property. Metaphorizing exchange as figurative, and then making it literal, the play emphasizes the ease with which certain bodies may feign disability. In act 4, Frank appeals to Cripple to assist him in securing marriage to Phyllis, citing his obligation from the play's opening scene. Cripple responds by offering a "gracious opportunity" (4.2.23) to Frank; when Phyllis returns to his shop, Cripple promises to "resign the same / To you, my friend" (24–25), and continues:

> Wherefore I will immediately you take
> My crooked habit, and in that disguise
> Court her, yea, win her, for she will be won.
> This will I do to pleasure you, my friend.
>
> (30–33)

Whether "crooked habit" is garment or body here, Cripple proposes it as identity marker, a stage property that will enable Frank's impersonation. While all theatrical representation invites the viewer's gaze, this scene intensifies the pleasures of diagnostic spectatorship when Cripple offers his "crooked habit" to Frank, indulging the spectator's desire to see the (presumably) crippled body beneath the prosthesis. Without his habit and crutches, is Cripple still recognizable as "the cripple" when he transfers the stage properties to Frank? The multiple prosthetics are technical excess, but they are also theatrical necessity. The "crutch" operates as a synecdoche that substitutes for Cripple himself, while the "crooked habit" enables a mode of metonymic replication that allows Frank to stand in for Cripple. Cripple may retain one crutch while Frank uses the other, but the habit's crossing between garment, bodily shape, and person requires a second body to duplicate a character.

The dramatic fiction reifies the conventional association between crippled figure and moral deceit by inviting the audience to watch an actor readying himself for the part of "Cripple." After Cripple leaves, Frank discloses his motive: "Now, brothers, have amongst you for a third part, / Nay, for the whole" (4.2.47–48). He envisions Phyllis as the alternative to his lack of inheritance as the youngest son. Addressing his brothers in apostrophe, he explains that "though my father did bequeath his lands / To you, my elder brethren" (49–50), he desires a different prize, for "the moveables I sue for / Were none of his" (50–51). Phyllis is a property, like land, and since she may be won, marriage is yet another competitive financial transaction; Frank therefore disguises himself as Cripple in order to reap the economic gains enabled by this shape. As he waits for Phyllis to arrive at Cripple's shop, he exclaims:

> Am I not like myself in this disguise?
> Crooked in shape, and crooked in my thoughts?
> Then am I a cripple right. Come, wench, away!
> Thy absence breeds a terror to my stay.
>
> (53–56)

Pretending to be "crooked in shape" by appropriating Cripple's form, Frank suggests that the disguise matches his true intention to deceive Phyllis. He is not physically crooked, but he is morally crooked. Frank's disguise exposes a fault line between metaphor and body, using the literal sense of the term to cross into the figural.[71] Regurgitating the skimpiest moralizing shorthand for the form he assumes, Frank posits a causative association between his "crooked . . . thoughts" and anyone's "crooked . . . shape." He works from the outside in, only to find that he is "like" himself. Calling himself a "Cripple right," Frank generalizes from the character whose prostheses he has borrowed, relying on the stereotype to produce a pun that works like one of Copley's jests.

The hazard of Frank's impersonation weighs on him, for this correlation of inner thought and outer shape concedes the vulnerability of his own body in the mimetic enterprise. His "terror" discloses the stakes of theatrical transformation's deforming effects, which go beyond the sumptuary. The form he personates may be a "stay," bringing him uncomfortably close to a similitude he is "like" only in thought. This potential to take effect is both characteristic of performance more generally—as Erika T. Lin puts it, "the only material medium that is also simultaneously the act of becoming"—and, as I have discussed in the introduction, historically specific to the early modern period's fear that acting a part might stick.[72] Frank's worry about feigning this "counterfeited shape" (5.1.103) signals the fear of acting's consequences, given how the "counterfeit" is already bound up with feigned bodily impairment in the period. Yet Frank never considers the cost of impersonation in any other disguise. Dressed as the porter, Frank exclaims, "How strangely am I metamorphosèd!" (2.3.177) and remarks on his "strange disguise" (181). This reflection on metamorphosis yields no speculation about the threat of transformation, however, for the porter's "habit" is clearly a costume, in keeping with the prevalence of disguise in early modern theatrical fictions.[73] Frank's meditation on his feigning lets slip the possibility that an imposture that evinces "thoughts" takes hold in a "shape" that threatens a stable identity. The labor required to counterfeit Cripple demands Frank's submission to the semiotics of stage properties or embodied posture that, though adopted temporarily, may unpredictably alter Frank's own form. *Fair Maid* distinguishes between the "porter's habit" that may be assumed and then discarded, and the temporal threat of materializing a "crooked" habit's "stay."

Despite these ontological risks, however, the performance of disability is both spectacularly lucrative and stunningly easy. Frank's impersonation of Cripple turns out to require very little from the actor, since the sturdy theatrical conventions of feigned impairment dictate his appearance. His attempt to counterfeit Cripple at work is clearly bad (he exclaims, "Now frame thy hands to draw: / A worser workman never any saw" [4.2.57–58]), a lack of success that ratifies Cripple's skill as a craftsman. As Row-Heyveld notes, Frank "conspicuously botches" his feigning of Cripple.[74] Beyond simply indicting bad acting, however, the play demonstrates how easy it is to recycle tropes about crippled beggars. Frank cannot believably reproduce a drawer at the workbench, but having assumed the theatrical signifiers of a crippled beggar, he does not need to work. Little else is required for a successful interpretation because the social perception of disability moves so predictably from appearance of the body to assumptions about the person. The play lingers on Frank's preparation to play the role, and his opening lines emphasize spectatorship that depends not on lines of sight but on habits of thought. Frank's rhetoric and behavior are manifestly unlike Cripple's, but they do not have to be, so easily is this type character communicated. The scene is less invested in convincing offstage spectators than in checking the boxes of disability stereotypes, exposing just how ill equipped his spectators are to look beyond such conventions.

Frank profits, furthermore, when Phyllis takes his disguise for truth. Phyllis encounters Frank-as-Cripple, and the play makes a point of spectatorial inattention, for she does not appear to notice the absence of skill in the craftsman she loves. Encountering Frank-as-Cripple, Phyllis exclaims, "Yea, yonder sits the wonder of mine eye" (4.2.59), and intends to confront him with her desire. Frank begins by putting on a long show of protest before he finally appears to have a change of heart and concludes:

CRIP.: I am too base.
PHIL.: My wealth shall raise thee up.
CRIP.: I am deformed.

PHIL.:	Tut, I will bear with that.
CRIP.:	Your friends' dislike brings all this out of frame.
PHIL.:	By humble suit, I will redress the same.
FRANK:	[*Aside*] Now to employ the virtue of my shape!

(106–10)

Frank imagines Cripple's "shape" only as a detriment to marriageability, enumerating all the objections that he can muster, which Phyllis counters with her own resources in stichomythic response. Her wealth will account for his baseness and she will "bear with" his deformity because value depends on individual perception. To Frank, disability is an automatic disqualification, and so he presses Phyllis on the affront that he presumes such an appearance must spark. Frank-as-Cripple announces "I am deformed" as an impediment to marriage, the obvious consequence of disability. The scene reproduces Frank's imagination of what it is like to be crippled as if the lines are Cripple's revelation of his own experience.

In the printed text (figure 3.2), the play imitates this theatrical transformation. The speech prefixes in this portion of the scene change briefly from "Frank"

> For to be short, I cannot fancy thee.
>   *Phil.* For to be short, you cannot fancie me:
> Oh cruell word, more hatefull then pale death,
> Oh, would to God it would conclude my breath.
>   *Frank.* Forbeare, forbeare, admit that I should yield:
> Thinke you, your father would applaud your choice.
>   *Phil.* Doubt not thereof, or if he doe not, alls one,
> So you but grant to my affection.
>   *Crip.* I am too base. *Phil.* My wealth shall raise thee vp.
>   *Crip.* I am deform'd. *Phil.* Tut, I will beare with that.
>   *Crip.* Your friends dislike brings all this out of frame.
>   *Phil.* By humble sute I will redresse the same.
>   *Frank.* Now to employ the vertue of my shape:
> Faire mistresse,
> If heretofore I haue remorseleffe beene,
> And not esteemd your vndeserued loue,

FIGURE 3.2. Unattributed, *The Fayre Mayde of the Exchange* (London, 1625), sig. H4r. Call#: STC 13318. Used by permission of the Folger Shakespeare Library under a Creative Commons Attribution-ShareAlike 4.0 International License.

to "Crip," as if ratifying Frank's impersonation of Cripple. Perhaps the anomaly is a printer's slip; indeed, one editor reassures readers there is "no need to suspect corruption" because the text simply reflects Frank's performative identity.[75] Understood through Keir Elam's generative distinction between performance text as that which is "produced *in* the theatre" and dramatic text as that which is "composed *for* the theatre," the printed text of *Fair Maid* unexpectedly charts an ideal perception of stage business in the performance text.[76] This textual accident, replicated in all three extant seventeenth-century editions of the quarto, effaces the gap between actor and character at the key moment of Frank's disguise. As Frank ventriloquizes the reservations he imagines Phyllis might harbor about Cripple's person, the printed text attributes them to the speech prefix of Cripple himself. Frank's speech prefixes revert to his own name when he reanimates Cripple's persona with his own desires and begins to woo Phyllis instead of deflecting her assertions. The printed text confirms the value of Cripple's singular form for Frank's appeal, and the speech prefixes uncannily reflect the moment he stops playing Cripple and starts playing himself.

Frank's ability to impersonate Cripple results in a successful suit, the most pointed example of the power of seeming to be what one is not. For the duration of the impersonation scene, the play lingers on a deformed body as an object of intense desire. When the other Golding brothers enter, Phyllis asserts her choice of Cripple in a parody of wedding vows, insisting that

> even in sight of both you here present,
> I give my hand, and, with my hand, my heart,
> Myself, and all to him! And with this ring
> I'll wed myself.
>
> (4.2.183–86)

The expression of fullest independence—"I'll wed myself"—uttered by the play's titular character is undercut by the feigning to which Phyllis is not privy. To Phyllis's pledge, Frank completes the line with "I take thy offering" (186), then gives her a ring, and declares: "Let us seal affection with a kiss" (188). When this public demonstration of affection sparks Ferdinand's exclamation, "Oh, sight intolerable!" (189) and Anthony's proclamation of a "spectacle worse than death!" (190), Frank-as-Cripple drives home his victory over his brothers: "Now, gentlemen, please you draw near and listen to the cripple" (191). The disgust of the Golding brothers perhaps prefigures the legacy of critical revulsion at the idea of pairing Cripple and Phyllis in marriage.

What is clear, however, is Frank's admission of his own form as a liability in the economic pursuit of Phyllis and her fortunes. To Master Flower, Frank later confesses: "If I had wooed her in my proper shape, / I do believe she never would have liked me" (5.1.95–96). He pleads to return again as Cripple, letting Master Flower in on the plan so that he will see through the appearance Frank presents: "Therefore since I shall have her, give me leave / To come and court her in my borrowed shape" (97–98). Frank's sense of his "proper shape" as deficiency reasserts the temporality of the impersonation, as if the demands of courtship were subject to the power of illusion, and his need for Cripple's theatrical prosthetics. To carry out his hopes of gain, Frank's body must be dissembled because his figure is less desirable, at least momentarily, than Cripple's distinctive frame.

Associating Cripple's social value specifically with his disability, the play's complicated scene of disguise heightens attention to the skilled display required of the actor. For Frank, Cripple's prostheses are only theatrical properties, a costume that he can put on and take off again. After Phyllis leaves, Frank reestablishes the difference between Cripple's body and his own, calling for Cripple as "the substance of this borrowed shape" (4.2.212). When Cripple enters, Frank thanks him ("Poor in the well-framed limbs of nature, but / Rich in kindness beyond comparison" [214–15]) and proffers the disguise, saying, "Here I resign thy habit back again" (217). Their exchange does not clarify the question of whether Cripple's habit is a garment or a posture, since "substance" may be both body and prosthesis, but it reminds us that Frank has merely borrowed Cripple's habit. His "imitation of disability," as Love observes, "enjoys a privileged relationship with theatricality."[77] When Cripple, earlier in the scene, urges Frank to "assume this shape of mine; / Take what I have, for all I have is thine!" (35–36), he describes the transaction as an exchange, saying, "Supply my place, to gain thy heart's desire" (37). In another play, the moment when Frank supplants Cripple might be a simple swap of theatrical properties, underlining the ease of assuming and discarding the items that mark a role.

The key thing to see here is that, in a play that has so relentlessly marked exchange as a reciprocal action, this exchange is never equal. Cripple supplies theatrical prosthetics that are uniquely individual, and therefore make his identity particularly available for imitation, but the play marks his body as specifically unable to adopt another form or play another role. Frank can impersonate Cripple, but Cripple cannot impersonate Frank. Imitation is the secret to Frank's marital success, which is also financial success, even though the social world of the play—like the laws disciplining vagrants—appears to valorize the stable identity of the laboring artisan at work. Cripple's distinctive body (as Paul Menzer puts it in a different context) "makes him easy to mimic but renders him incapable of mimicry" and therefore confers on him "an extraordinary stability of identity."[78] Cripple's position within the circuit of performance illuminates an unacknowledged investment in a body with a capacity for disguise, a capacity that the play identifies with the protean fantasy of the actor. Distinguishing between prop and prosthesis at the level of character, *Fair Maid* differentiates between bodies that appear to be whole, self-sufficient, and capable of impersonating other bodies, and those bodies that are not.

"An Overplus": Comedy and the End(s) of Disability

In *Fair Maid*, disability does not depend on how a body looks but on what a body can or cannot do, and the crucial doing is not labor but impersonation. An able body, in this early modern city comedy, is defined by the ability to engage in endless iterations of performance, by borrowing a prop rather than depending on a prosthetic device. The end of the play underscores this definition when Cripple cannot assume a temporary role and impersonate a nondeformed subject—when, that is, he cannot perform a shape other than the one he possesses. Although Phyllis's expressions of desire for Cripple propel the plot, *Fair Maid* finally denigrates Cripple's figure through social exclusion, as it simultaneously articulates the rewards of impersonation through the prospect of advancement by marriage.

The play's disavowal of Cripple in the final scene shatters the illusion of his singularity through the onstage doubling of his character. Impersonating Cripple again, Frank proclaims his love for Phyllis. Master Flower pretends to prevent Frank's suit, but Phyllis swoons until Master Flower consents to the marriage: "Wed thee, Phyllis, to thine own content. / Here, take my daughter, Cripple; love her well" (5.1.273–74). At this point, Cripple enters with Frank's brothers and Bowdler, uttering what will be his final lines in the play: "Gentlemen, sweet bloods, or brethren of familiarity, / I would speak with Phyllis. Shall I have audience?" (282–83). No one answers his question, for Phyllis, at the sight of this second Cripple, exclaims: "Help me, dear father! Oh, help me, gentlemen! / This is some spirit! Drive him from my sight!" (284–85). When Frank-as-Cripple protests, "Were he the devil, thou shalt not budge a foot" (286), Phyllis answers both "Cripples" by adopting the negative rhetoric directed at Cripple throughout the play:

> Hence, foul deformity!
> Nor thou, nor he shall my companion be.
> If cripples dead the living seem to haunt,
> I'll neither of either. Therefore, I say, avaunt!
> (288–91)

Phyllis rejects both Cripple and Frank-as-Cripple as "foul deformity," collapsing disability and theatrical action in the character's transformed shape. Her declaration "Nor thou, nor he" suggests either that the Cripple who enters is the "dead" Cripple that "haunts" the Cripple who is "living" (Frank), or that both ("Nor thou, nor he") are "Cripples dead" that haunt her in their doubled presence. Love reads Cripple's "prosthetic doubleness" as "origin and model for the coexistent excess and deficiency of impersonation," as an uncanny doubling of a character who is already double; at the end of *Fair Maid*, Cripple possesses "not just four legs instead of two, but eight legs instead of four."[79] Phyllis dismisses both of them, and her language ("I'll neither of either") reproduces the multiplicative logic of metonymic reproduction. In the pair of crutches and the crooked habit, the play has staged an excess of prosthetic parts for Cripple. Phyllis's strangely plural exclamation, "cripples dead," encodes the figure's capacity for excessive impersonation. From the synecdochical excess of properties, the final scene produces a metonymic excess of Cripples, staging Cripple as the performative double of himself.

By making Cripple the doubled figure, furthermore, the scene effectively redefines him as duplicitous. While the text does not clarify whether Cripple is aware of the disguised Frank when he enters, Bowdler's assessment of this onstage doubling is the laughing promise of the title's "pleasing humours." On seeing the doubled figures, Bowdler exclaims: "Zounds, two cripples! Two dogs, two curs! 'Tis wonderful!" (5.1.287). In response to this pejorative doubling, Frank casts off his disguise, as if to show that there is only one "foul deformity":

> Dear heart, revoke these words.
> Here are no spirits, nor deformities.
> I am a counterfeit cripple now no more,
> But young Frank Golding, as I was before.
> Amaze not, love, nor seem not discontent;
> Nor thee, nor him, shall ever this repent.
>
> (292–97)

Frank distances himself from Cripple's shape once he finds the frame no longer useful, believing that his self-revelation will compel Phyllis to choose him. In rhetoric that recalls the worry over the potentially fraudulent crippled beggar of the play's prologue, Frank emphasizes the visual evidence of his form ("as I was before") against the disguise he now sheds. Here he employs the distinction between prop and prosthesis to produce knowledge of his seemingly unprostheticized body; undeformed, Frank is newly desirable and definitively ideal. This disguise as the "false" Cripple undoes the real Cripple, since only Frank is able to remove his assumed props. Frank's reference to himself underlines the sonic association between his name, "Frank," and the quality of frankness as honesty. His revelation positions Cripple, now the sole deformed figure, as the expected stereotype, a "counterfeit cripple." Type overrides character in this scene, as if to prompt the question, aren't all Cripples inescapably counterfeit?

Over the rest of the scene, Phyllis dispatches the suits of the other Golding brothers to settle on Frank, while Cripple remains silent. Although Phyllis had vowed that neither "the beauty of the fairest one" (5.1.218) nor the "golden Golding" (215) is worth a "higher price or value unto me / Than is a lump of poor deformity" (220), the end of the play does not preserve this choice. Critics first read the startling shift in Phyllis's affections as evidence for lack of authorial skill, as the playwright makes Phyllis "most unaccountably transfer her affections at last, for the mere purpose of letting the curtain fall upon her marriage with somebody."[80] For others, the shift is still more evidence of market operations that structure the play, since, as Richard Waswo points out, "the desire that counts, in the material economy and the comedic one, is collective, not individual," and "switches of affection," like exchanges of value, "are perfectly acceptable."[81] More recently, Row-Heyveld understands Cripple's silence as an extension (and complication) of the play's ableism, for he "dissembles his disability, crafting it into a very particular ableist type," and this craft is evident to the audience.[82] Building on Love's insight that the play offers a "prosthetic version of theatrical being," and Naomi Baker's argument that the play foregrounds a "fundamentally prosthetic" mode of identity, however, I see the ending of this play less as a moral judgment of Cripple's character than as a destabilization of type altogether.[83] Cripple does not throw off his habit to reveal hidden nobility, nor does he prove to be a nondisabled figure in disguise. Cripple's silence, a textual lacuna that has proven difficult for critics to parse, thwarts a final judgment: Does Phyllis choose Frank because she has been expecting the stereotypical reversal, in which Cripple would reveal that his disability is feigned? Does Cripple, who has resisted Phyllis's affections, welcome the marriage plot from which he has escaped, surveying the matches he has engineered? Or does his silence reinforce his central but marginalized position in exchange, as the figure whose dynamic overplus is crucial to theatrical doing but superfluous to the comedy's punishing end?

To be sure, the play has staged the problem of the "counterfeit" as socially pervasive and economically disruptive, and Cripple is the only figure explicitly rejected at the end of the play. Fittingly for a comedy with a plot that centers disguising, double-crossing, and swindling, the play ends with the threat of punishment. Instead of the wedding we might expect from the genre, the play concludes with the arrest of Master Flower, whose illegitimate business dealings have finally caught up with him. Flower speaks the last words of the play, exclaiming,

> Words here are little worth. Wife, and friends, all
> Go with me to my trial. You shall see
> A good conceit now brought to infamy.
>
> (5.1.373–75)

Flower's "good conceit" is the catchphrase with which he endorsed Frank's disguised courtship and accepted a stolen jewel as collateral. Unlike other city comedies that conclude with a trial—notably Ben Jonson's plays, which are preoccupied with moral and legal consequences—*Fair Maid*, having raised the prospect of collective justice, defers the judgment.

Read alongside Copley's jest at the outset of this chapter, we notice that even if Cripple's form is socially disabling, the comedy's remarkably clunky final scene destabilizes judgments about the presumed deficiency of any "crooked shape." The play unfixes the predictable correlation between value and function to reveal that what looked like lack might be generative excess. Although Frank's body was initially the norm—recall critical assumptions about "tall and handsome Frank"—the fiction invests Cripple with desire and theatrical potential, and the overplus that accrues to his figure finally troubles the rhetoric of unveiling that Frank seeks to reinscribe. Requiring Cripple to be the spectacle of difference against which Frank can be defined, the play risks Frank's comparison to prosthetic plenitude. Frank underestimates the evacuation of his character through participation in the dramatic economy of exchange, reclaiming his "proper" shape as superior to Cripple's because he can doff the disguise. By the final scene, however, he has spent most of his time on stage performing Cripple, unsettling the idea that there is a clear "I" to be reclaimed—or at least, failing to motivate Phyllis's choice of his character. Once he borrows Cripple's prostheses, Frank never really exits the economy of disguise. As the play essentializes Cripple's body through prostheses, it also marks Cripple as the original, the "truth" behind Frank's impersonation, in light of which Frank is merely a copy. *Fair Maid* stages a demand for impersonation that implicitly defines the body most able to navigate the exchanges that preoccupy this comedy.

* * *

The theatrical practice of performing disability in this play teaches us to question how disablings function through encounter—asking *who* is disabled, and by *what*, exactly?—rather than to assume the legibility of bodily difference.

Fair Maid transfers the ethical consequences of fraudulent deception onto the character of Cripple, whose agency and identity do not finally remain in his own hands. Cripple shoulders the cost of the play's attempt to distinguish between permissible and illegitimate forms of imaginative self-representation. Cripple has emerged in the play as uniquely individuated figure—the undisclosed gold standard that generates the value from which theatrical counterfeiting proceeds. In return, the play turns him back into a stereotype, that flexible, recognizable avatar of fraudulence, one that is infinitely, even most easily, replicable. The material prostheses—the props that become the "crutches" and "crooked habit"—index Cripple's deformity, and Cripple's shape draws attention to the possibilities and instabilities of theatrical form. *Fair Maid* complicates retrospective characterizations of early modern disability as putatively stable, while also demarcating the essentializing mechanism of the crippled beggar stereotype. Disability names the condition by which Cripple cannot participate fully in an economy of performative exchange. In a historical moment rife with representations of fraudulent disabled beggars, disability is, paradoxically, performed as the utter impossibility of disguise.

Cripple's generative overplus challenges the surety of the surgical treatises and laws that punish the "counterfeit impotent," and the theater uses Cripple to work out the limits of impersonation. Punished for fraudulence, Cripple points us back to the very conditions of playing that imagine performance as a material art of making. The play trades on impersonation, the prominence of disguise echoing theatrical practice in which one actor often plays multiple roles, at the very moment when early modern English culture was concerned to identify and punish counterfeiting bodies, and when antitheatrical writers were quick to dismiss acting as lying.[84] The actor, however, is the only person who cannot mislead, because he announces the feigning in advance.[85] As Samuel Butler puts it in his character sketch of "A Liar": "No man is a lyar, that does not pretend to tell truth, as a player deceives nobody, because he professes to do it, and he deserves best when he does most."[86] The player can be trusted for verity because his verisimilitude is no truth claim from the start. The actor's work "deserves best" applause when he "does most" the feigning with which he is tasked. Yet, as the end of the comedy suggests, the figure with the most capacity for transformation bears a judgment for feigning from which he ought to be manifestly exempt. Cripple's unique position in the circuit of imitation formally resembles the actor, whose power to feign is celebrated and, at the same time, denounced for unsettling stable social hierarchies. *Fair Maid* reveals the stakes of the exchanges that depend on distinguishing between disability and imitation, turning a disability aesthetic into theatrical form.

In this chapter, I have traced how the play unfixes a type character through his generative overplus and then fixes him back into type as Cripple suffers the burden of punishment for feigning. The play employs disability as something like a shock absorber for the formal exchanges of imitation on which successful market negotiations rely. In the next chapter, I explore what happens to judgments about appearance when a character extravagantly marked as ugly refuses to comply with those judgments. Taking scrutiny into the realm of the aesthetic, disability's formal undoing troubles the logic of surface reading.

CHAPTER 4

Changing the Ugly Body

> A Description is only a shadow received by the eare but not perceived by the eye: so lively portrature is merely a forme seene by the eye, but can neither shew action, passion, motion, or any other gesture, to moove the spirits of the beholder to admiration.
>
> —Thomas Heywood, *An Apology for Actors*

> It is not out of most men's observation, that one most admirable Mimicke in our late Stage, so lively and corporally personated a Changeling, that he could never compose his Face to the figure it had, before he undertook that part.
>
> —Edmund Gayton, *Pleasant Notes Upon Don Quixot*

Beginning with an overview of "prodigious births" that ranges across historical periods, species, and geographies, the unattributed pamphlet *A certaine relation of the hog-faced gentlewoman called Mistris Tannakin Skinker* (1640) arrives at a "domesticke" scene in Holland in 1618, when the titular character's mother gives birth:

> But whether they were unthankful for such an unexpected blessing, or what other thing was the cause, I am not able to determine: but so it hapned, that in the yeere 1618, she was safely delivered of a Daughter, all the limbes and lineaments of her body, well featur'd and proportioned, only her face, which is the ornament and beauty of all the rest, had the Nose of a Hog, or Swine: which was not only a stain and blemish, but a deformed uglinesse, making all the rest lothsome, contemptible and odious to all that lookt upon her in her infancie.[1]

The gaspingly long sentence concludes with a whiplash revelation that reorients the description of this child's entire appearance. Although the rest of her body is "well featur'd and proportioned," the face, the "ornament and beauty of all the rest"—and not even her entire face but the nose, specifically—transforms her whole person through a ruinous detail. Warping the body out of shape, the "Nose of a Hog" grafts an animal part onto the human form. The nose stops being a nose when it becomes a "deformed uglinesse." The adjective "deformed" stabilizes "ugly" into a noun, as if ugliness is an uncontestable property of this body, and the phrase that follows, "lothsome, contemptible and odious," traces the affective circuitry of response. Spectators who "lookt upon" this sight feel loathing and contempt, as if they could not respond otherwise. The "stain" or "blemish" is manifestly obvious as a departure from an ideal of beauty, and the narrator presumes this fact as collective consensus. Everyone thinks her face is ugly—and you would think so too.

The title page foregrounds this feature, making the face a focal point that converts her person to mere backdrop. The image (figure 4.1) depicts Mistress Skinker interacting with a suitor, since the pamphlet emphasizes that her nose will not be changed to that of a human—or as the title puts it, "can never recover her true shape"—until she is married. To the reader, her misshapen nose resembles a mask in the shape of a pig's snout, like the property an actor assumes to signify the "Nose of a Hog." The gentleman refuses even the aversive sight the narrator projects; perhaps he is caught in mid-bow, or bends to kiss her hand. One thing is certain: he does not look at her face.

The account and image trouble cause and effect, part and whole, and singularity and abstraction, and they prompt a series of questions. What is the relation between the anomalous feature and the body? How does the bodily property define the person? What rubric of difference can distinguish between a "stain," a "blemish," and (the worst) a "deformed uglinesse"? What is the relation between the perceiving viewer and the presumed offense of the feature, signaled by terms such as "lothsome" and "contemptible"? And the pamphlet prompts a new question, doubling back to a familiar word: What does "deformed uglinesse" convey that mere "deformity" or "uglinesse" would not? Why, that is, does this account need two terms to register the fullest intensity of aesthetic judgment?

Considering the "ugly" body, I propose to move our study of early modern disability firmly into aesthetic categories. In early modern usage, "ugliness" and "deformity" are cognates, sometimes amplifying each other (as in "deformed uglinesse") and sometimes yoked in reciprocity. In his influential dictionary, Edward Phillips models this association when he defines "deformity" as "ugglinesse."[2] Margaret Cavendish echoes the mutual explication in "Of Monsters," asserting: "That which is ugly, is that which is deformed, and that is deformed that is mishapen, and that is mishapen that is made crooked, or awry, or one part bigger or less than another."[3] The relay of "that is" in the parison's chain of equation gives way to a sequence of possibilities, linked by "or," that climaxes to a comparative measure, "bigger or less than." Ugliness

122 CHAPTER 4

FIGURE 4.1. Mistress Tannakin Skinker, hog-faced woman, 1640. Credit: Wellcome Collection. CC BY.

is a concept crammed into an adjective, gobbling up new terms, from "mishapen" to "awry" to (as we will see) "ill-favored." The proliferation renders distinctions unstable: an ugly thing both is and is made, as if posing a threat of becoming ugly at any moment. This insistently negative array evokes the moral interpretation that equates deformity with evil, the model of early modern disability it is this book's project to complicate. Ugliness slides into deformity, which slides into misshapenness, which slides into crookedness. These categories are never neutral. They are indecorous, contravening the Renaissance concept of *decorum* that associates ruled order with moral and aesthetic value.⁴ Decorum is a vexed concept in the period: in Ellen MacKay's incisive formulation, "decorum is an aesthetic judgement that retrospectively affixes its formal justification onto a supposedly intrinsic but in fact unspecified and unspecifiable trait."⁵ Slippery to define, the concept of ugliness partakes of a basic uncertainty about the object deemed ugly, even when it appeals to a judgment that appears fixed. The anomaly is both the part that secures generalizing to the person (you know an ugly body when you see her "deformed uglinesse") and the part that escapes categorization altogether (her "deformed uglinesse" is no longer a recognizably human nose). Ugliness, I suggest in this chapter, reorients the concept of disability from what a body can do to how a body looks. And how a body looks becomes who a person *is*, a transformation that exposes ugliness as a disabling that is social to the core.

Rather than subsuming "ugly" into the broader category of "deformity," therefore, this chapter pulls the terms apart from their knotty conjunction to consider how ugliness troubles a logic of reading bodily appearance and disables spectatorship in the process. I draw on the notion of the "gifts of the body," less familiar from our modern perspective on disability. In early modern philosophical and medical discourses, the three "gifts of the body" are strength, health, and beauty—each an essential, though mutable, bodily property. Citing Galen and Aristotle, surgeon Alexander Read explains that "there be three gifts of the body, to wit, Health, Strength, and Beauty, all which medicine is to direct."⁶ Understood both as attributes of and ambitions for a body, these three properties appear together consistently, occasionally amplified by a fourth "gift." Barnabe Googe's translation of a poem by Marcello Palingenio extends them: "Strength, beauty, health, activity / these foure the body oweth."⁷ John Higgins's translation of Richard Huloet's *Dictionarie* labels these the "Endowements" of the body, "called the giftes of nature," or *"dotes corporales,"* which he lists as "beauty, health, riches, strength."⁸ Thomas Rogers, discussing "the goodes of Nature," explains, "By this worde Nature is understoode the vertue, force, and property of every thing. In this place the goodes of Nature be also understoode, all such thinges as are in the body of man, as health, strength, beauty and bignesse."⁹ Health, strength, and beauty: we can understand "strength" as the capacity for labor, the coordinate for ability that I have traced in prior chapters. In this chapter on the "ugly" body (and in the next chapter, on the "sick" body), I turn to aesthetic and medical discourses that appear to be far afield of our modern concept of disability but highlight the temporal contingency of the "gifts of the body" in early modern thought.

Furthermore, while it may seem counterintuitive to consider ugliness within the scope of disability, a long tradition of so-called ugly laws barred people with visible impairments—"unsightly beggars" and "diseased," "maimed," "mutilated," "disgusting," and "improper" persons—from appearing in public, especially when soliciting charity.[10] Susan M. Schweik's magisterial study of these legal codes in the nineteenth and twentieth centuries observes that such laws evince "a startling indeterminacy of scope," for the definition of offending appearance "cannot find one term to settle the question of its own object."[11] In the final instance of a charge under the code (in Nebraska in 1974), Schweik notes that the judge's question—"What's the standard of ugliness?"—evinces "a deep conflation of 'disease, maiming and deformity' with the word 'ugly.'"[12] Attempting to discipline the action of begging, these laws construct the very appearance of disabled beggars as a visible offense. Documenting the policing of disability in public, Schweik's study discerns how appeals to ugliness shroud an arbitrary judgment under the naturalizing veneer of affective response. In earlier chapters, I noted how disability evokes a stare that, as Rosemarie Garland-Thomson observes, "enlists curiosity to telescope looking toward diagnosing impairment."[13] Ugliness, on the contrary, prompts no such diagnostic scan or concern about feigning. Fully apparent, the ugly face is recognizable by the affective response it seems, as if inevitably, to compel.[14]

The presumption of shared norms of appearance—even if they may be unspecifiable—aligns concepts of aesthetic decorum with what Robert McRuer identifies as "compulsory able-bodiedness," an unquestioned demand for able bodies and able minds. Compulsory able-bodiedness, McRuer writes, "assumes in advance that we all agree: able-bodied identities, able-bodied perspectives are preferable and what we all, collectively, are aiming for." I build on this key insight: compulsory able-bodiedness "repeatedly demands that people with disabilities embody for others an affirmative answer to the unspoken question, 'Yes, but in the end, wouldn't you rather be more like me?'"[15] At the heart of a crip perspective on disability is the possibility of answering no to that question. The norm centers the able-bodied person, for whom the answer to the question ("Wouldn't you rather be more like me?") appears so obvious that it barely feels like a question. A crip dissent, by contrast, revolts against a standard of ability for bodies and minds that such a norm assumes. In a world where appearance is everything, the refusal to affirm able-bodied preference is a refusal to subscribe to the hierarchy that prioritizes able bodies over disabled bodies, and able minds over disabled minds.

In this chapter, I locate a surprising dissent from normative judgments of appearance in the early modern theater's work with the "ugly" character. Ugliness incites an epistemological crisis of witnessing that exposes the naturalizing moves of aesthetic discourse and troubles theatrical seeing.[16] I begin by considering ugliness in early modern philosophical discourse and then turn to Beaumont and Fletcher's play *The Captain* (1612), which recruits spectators to the gaze of desire at the character with distinctive appeal and reaps comic fruit for the marriage plot. I then turn to Thomas Middleton and William Rowley's 1622 tragedy *The Changeling* and the troubling example expressed by the character De Flores, whose ugliness is registered in persistent contrast to beauty. While De Flores acknowledges the specificity of his "bad face" (2.2.151) and "foul chops" (2.1.85), he refuses to understand this judgment as social disqualification.[17] De Flores, to be sure, appears to bear out the starkest moral equation of ugliness with evil, and my reading does not recuperate De Flores at the cost of diminishing the sexual violence and murder he perpetrates.[18] Rather, I am interested in how *The Changeling* employs ugliness to shape dramatic character and then conscripts spectators into De Flores's perspective on normative aesthetic judgments.[19] The surface illegibility such ugliness evinces, furthermore, constellates the character of the changeling, the tragedy of *The Changeling*, and the "Artificiall Changling," the title figure of John Bulwer's proto-anthropological treatise *Anthropometamorphosis* (1653). Against the grain of Bulwer's condemnation, I read the "artificial deformities" that he identifies with theatrical experimentation as the register of an aesthetic of particularity that engenders new forms. A chaos agent for the theater, ugliness unfixes the relation between signifier and signified, only to fix the relation again, but differently, foregrounding the witnessing by which disabling social judgments proceed.

Loathing the "Bad" Face: Physiognomic Reading and *The Captain*

After he rehearses strength, health, and beauty as the three gifts of the body, the surgeon Alexander Read defends medicine's corrective work. Read asks: "Seeing by reason of the face, a man is called beautifull or ugly, who can deny that they deserve the care of a Physitian, and Chirurgean?"[20] The contrast between a face that is "beautifull" and a face that is "ugly" justifies the labor of medical arts to preserve and correct the gift of beauty. This exercise is what physician Bulwer calls "Cosmeticall physic," or "the exornatorie part of Physick," medical knowledge "whose office is that whatsoever is according to

Nature, that it is to preserve in the Body, and so consequently to cherish and maintaine the native Beautie thereof."[21] Cosmetical physic exceeds the beautifying work of cosmetics in our modern sense, to encompass the efforts of physicians and surgeon to care for—to "preserve" and "cherish" and "maintain"—the surface of the body.[22] With a particular focus on the face, Read's discussion of beauty and ugliness inherits a slippage between definitions of physiognomy as the practice of reading the signs of the body and physiognomy as an anatomical term that refers to the face.[23] Collapsing a reading of the face into judgment of the person, Read expresses the episteme associated with predictive looking, yet he admits that the verdict depends on the gaze of others. Paradoxically, ugliness is both intrinsic, since a face may be corrected by the surgeon's skill, and epiphenomenal, a shifting judgment of what is seen that depends on who is doing the looking.

Other discussions of physiognomy find it likewise difficult to clarify exactly what ugliness is and what ugliness can mean. In John Florio's 1603 translation of Michel de Montaigne's essays, the essay "Of Phisiognomy" praises beauty, describing it as a "potent and advantageous quality" that is "within two fingers' breadth of goodness."[24] Two fingers' breadth: within the space of a human hand, according to Montaigne's metaphor, beauty slides into moral value. If beauty hovers near to goodness, however, the relation between ugliness and evil is harder to discern. Montaigne first links ugliness and deformity with a conjunction, "an unnaturall ill-favouredness, and membrall deformitie," and then explains that ugliness (or "what we call ill-favouredness") is "a kinde of unseemelinesse at the first sight which chiefly lodgeth in the face; and by the colour worketh a dislike in us" (sig. 3G5v). This definition underscores the disproportionate reaction to ugliness on "very slight grounds" that are nonetheless immediately perceptible, at "first sight." What prompts this "dislike"? The list of cues to such an impulse are indeed slight: "a freckle, a blemmish, a rude countenaunce, a sower looke, proceeding often of some inexplicable cause, may be in well ordered, comely and compleate limmes" (sig. 3G5v). The marring effect scales up from mark to complexion to countenance, encompassing a momentary grimace, even if there is no apparent reason for the sour look. Whether the face is working against the body or the spot is working against the face, ugliness is always public because it is always a matter of perception. As a mechanism for moral prediction, however, this example of physiognomic evidence hedges its bets. "This superficiall ill-favourdnesse," Montaigne explains, "which is notwithstanding the most imperious, is of lesse prejudice unto the state of the minde: and hath small certaintie in mens opinion" (sig. 3G6v). The marks betray their lack of consequence in the limited reactions they provoke. Provoke they do—for encounter prompts response, as if ugliness cannot be resisted—but the pimpled face and blemished complexion that strike a viewer as ugly do not finally produce predictive "certainty" about the person.

Montaigne explicitly contrasts this superficial appearance with a depth model that sutures moral interpretation to deformity. He distinguishes the "other, by a more proper name called a more substantiall deformitie," as that which "beareth commonly a deeper inward stroke" (sig. 3G6v). Unlike the "freckle" or "blemish" of surface ugliness, there is no instantly recognizable example of this "more substantiall" departure from an idealized form. Drawing on Cicero, Montaigne explicates the category of moral deformity with a metaphor meant to clarify, one that descends from face to foot: *"Not every shooe of smooth-shining leather, but everie well-shapen and hansome made shooe, sheweth the inward and right shape of the foot"* (sig. 3G5v). Like worn leather, the unwelcome appearance of the marred face is inconsequential. What matters is the shoe's shape, rather than its surface. Yet if the shoe is the body and the foot is the soul, and the "deeper" deformity is more than a scuff mark on leather, is this substantial "stroke" a misshapen shoe, or a wrongly shaped foot (or both)? Does the encasing shoe disclose the shape of the foot, or remake it? Appealing to a deformity that goes beyond appearance, the metaphor does not resolve into a stable distinction between surface and depth, or between that which is fixed and that which is accidental.[25] This lack of clarity results from the quandary at the heart of scrutinizing predictions: the surface of a body may never be revelatory enough. Although "there is nothing more probable than the conformity and relation of the body to the soul," Montaigne concedes that "those Features and Moulds of face, and those Lineaments, by which men guess at our internal Complexions and our fortunes to come, is a thing that does not very directly and simply lye under the Chapter of Beauty and Deformity" (sig. 3G6v). Probable but never certain, the practice of physiognomy, despite the best effort to summon authoritative judgments, hesitates over legibility. The distinction between superficial and deeper deformity never conforms to a scale of blemish, and physiognomy cannot quite detect how far below the skin resides the truth of a person.

The idea that even pronounced ugliness offers only a "guess" at a person finds its polemical end point in the claim that judgments about bodies may be sheer social construction. In the introduction, I noted that Robert Burton exhorts his reader to dispute the moral determinism of the physical form. "Thou art lame of body, deformed to the eye," he writes, "yet this hinders not but that thou mayst be a good, a wise, upright, honest man."[26] Burton's "deformed to the eye" concedes that appearances are constructed by another's gaze. Suggesting that scrutiny turns variation into negative constraint, Burton offers a catalogue that ranges from kings and emperors, to philosophers and orators, to soldiers and statesmen, whose physical defects reveal nothing about their persons and prevent none of their accomplishments. As Naomi Baker's illuminating reading of ugliness explores, Burton is committed to the idea that "the body does not make the man."[27] In his chapter, "Deformity of Body, Sickness, Baseness of Birth, Peculiar Discontents" Burton cuts across categories to discuss the social effects of biographical facts that seem predetermined. The frame of the chapter sets "deformity of body" alongside "sickness" and "baseness of birth"; juxtaposing misliked appearance and lowly status, he denaturalizes the fantasy of innate aristocracy. If the disabling vicissitudes of the body do not determine a man's moral possibility, the accident of birth need not determine worth. The implication is that rank, like disability, is an unelective disqualification from a social hierarchy founded on the value that Burton calls "parchment nobility."[28] By the end of the section, Burton retreats from the political implications of such a claim, insisting that "innate rusticity" will reveal itself no matter the discipline imposed on a body, for "a cur will be a cur, a clown will be a clown."[29] Yet this effort to decouple bodily contingencies from natural distinctions has no hard stop: if commonplace assumptions about impairment are contested, value defined by blood and status goes too. Invoked to ground other social distinctions, a concept of disability as manifest disqualification is, in turn, unmoored as a naturalizing force.

The judgment that characterizes physiognomic interpretations turns out to be situational despite the ease with which such interpretations masquerade as description. Neoplatonic conceptions of form prized ordered regularity, and Stephen Greenblatt has suggested that "featurelessness is for Elizabethan culture the ideal form of human beauty."[30] Blankness is a moral and social value that carries normative judgments about how a body should look.[31] This idealization of blankness inflects early modern discourses of gender differently, as Baker demonstrates: ugly women are assumed to be evil; and beautiful women are presumptively evil because beauty is "an artificial cover for a deformity whose moral and physical referents are inextricably linked"; but "the meanings of male ugliness are opaque."[32] Even without the ministrations of cosmetical physic, a man's ugliness is undecidable because his outer appearance may be qualified by the goodness of that within which passes show.[33] This opacity is valuable to the theater, which must signify visible difference. In a play, ugliness may require a theatrical prosthetic, such as a painted scar or plastered mark to denote distinctiveness, and because the link between disfiguration and negative moral interpretation is so familiar as a visual shortcut to character, ugliness seems like a foregone conclusion. Because the correlation between outer appearance and inner person is never stable, however, the theater flummoxes and confounds spectators who try to figure out what exactly a character's ugliness means.

I trace one such pleasurable instance of the unstable correlation between appearance and character in Francis Beaumont and John Fletcher's *The Captain* (1612). In their play, the ugliness of the titular captain, Jacomo, appears at first a referendum on his character, one in which the audience participates, only to find this moral judgment upended by the marriage plot. Jacomo enters the play feeling touchy about his appearance, which has "no vertue" (2.1.96) and makes him fit only for the antisocial disposition that soldierly life requires.[34] Asking "What can my face / That is no better then a ragged Map now / Of where I have marcht and traveled profit me?" (87–89), Jacomo locates his deficiencies in a face that, "spoil'd" (91) as a child, now bears the scars of his past while also locking him into a soldierly future. As he admits, his face is a "true prognostication / Of what man must be" (92–93). Jacomo refuses a physiognomic reading, because it would be pointless: his appearance, unlike that of his "young and handsome" friend (71), clearly proclaims that he is suited only for a soldier's life of fighting and drinking. His complaint is bolstered by considering his equally disconcerting body, with legs that look as if an artisan "clap[ped] a paire of cat-sticks to my knees, / For which I am indebted to two School-boyes" (99–100). Jacomo's skinny legs emerge as prosthetic caricatures, sticks that are children's playthings. His similes are comparative judgments, verdicts on his appearance shared by nearly everyone who meets him, who agree that his nose should be "shorter" (2.2.41) for an "ill-mounted face" (42) and compare his body to a "long walking-bottle" (47). His skin is especially apparent, for other men that he meets insist his "hide (for sure he is a beast) is ranker / Then the Muscovy leather: and grain'd like it" (48–49) and remark that he "looks / Of a more rusty swarth complexion / Than an old arming doublet" (2.2.37–39). Leathery hide, not skin; worn cloth, not complexion. These descriptions racialize his appearance—perhaps they are a gesture to the theatrical technique of producing difference in skin color through fabric; perhaps they refer to velvet patches on his face, a practice to hide scars from the pox.[35] The comparisons to beast and arming doublet compose the ugly body as simultaneously inhuman and archaic. Taking stock of his appearance, the lexicon of ugliness expands to deforming comparisons that range far beyond the human as they seek similitude with which to express contempt.

If this fixed reading of the ugly appearance denigrates the character, however, the comic plot undercuts the predictability of response to such a face. The logic of *The Captain*, in a modern idiom, runs something like this: chicks dig scars.[36] Frank, one of the prominent female characters in the play, declares that she loves Jacomo and finds his appearance exemplary of the soldier's profession, that "of all the old world, only left to keepe / Man as he was, valiant and vertuous" (1.2.123–24). Frank's invocation of a glorious past reframes Jacomo's weathered looks; they are a badge of honor. Calling her "bewitched, or mad, or blinde" (2.2.35), Frank's companions marvel that "she would never have taken such a scar-crow else / Into protection" (36–37). Frank's friends imagine her judgment has been incapacitated, for her besotted response of love at first sight is so far from the norm of reaction to his appearance that they suggest that she no longer possesses the faculties of reason and perception. Against these interpretations, Frank herself subscribes to the view that ugliness is in the eye of the beholder. When Clora, her friend, harps on the captain's unattractiveness—as in the comment that Jacomo's body "can promise nothing / But laziness and long strides" (3.3.30–31)—Frank refuses to accept Clora's perception of his figure. Distinguishing Clora's assessment ("These are your eyes" [31]), Frank asks, "Where were they *Clora*, when you fell in love / With the old foot-man, for singing of Queen *Dido*?" (32–33). Any person in the right costume, wearing "old velvet trunks" (34) and a "slyc't Spanish Jerkin, like *Don John*" (35), might attract attention as the object of love. Desire is shaped by seeing, a perception of appearance that is inherently theatrical because the contingency of the spectacle sparks response.

The Captain initially validates a link between person and appearance by substantiating the moral deficiency that Jacomo's crudely formed exterior suggests. He turns out to be uncivil, unmannerly, deeply misogynistic, and given to bouts of drunkenness and brawling. This referendum on his person only heightens the comic tension of the play, which pushes Frank's devotion to extremes before Jacomo moves from defiance to humility. The play reconciles Frank's desire and Jacomo's roughness by turning his ugliness into apt evidence of his need for moral reformation and then—finally, barely—duly reforming him. Drenching Jacomo in urine poured from Frank's window, in a parody of a preparation from cosmetical physic or an ignoble baptism, the women tie him to a chair and force him to witness Frank's sorrow at his refusal of her love. Finally, convinced that she sheds real tears, he accepts the prospect of a different verdict on his appearance, marveling, "I did not thinke it possible any woman / Could have lik'd this face, it's good for nothing, is't?" (5.4.81–82). The plot answers this rhetorical question with a "yes" and "no" at the same time. The conclusion preserves the sense that women desire according to individual liking, expressed competitively as a comparative judgment. As Frank tells Clora, Jacomo's face is "better then your *Julio's*" (85). Suggesting that there is no accounting for the individualistic character of desire, the play indulges her expression of unreasonable desire and then couches it in respectability. Jacomo knows that he is, unaccountably, marrying up—and the play's spectators, aligned with Frank, participate in the aesthetic pleasure of distinctiveness. Marking the ugly character through a barrage of invective, the play nevertheless undercuts the predictive mechanism of ugliness, because it is not entirely clear whether the match will succeed or whether Frank's choice of a husband will be disciplined back into the confines of typically handsome masculinity.

The end of the play therefore exemplifies what the prologue asserts in its opening lines, "For all men's eyes, / Ears, faiths, and judgements are not of one size" (3–4). The ugly character is the linchpin of this refusal of a one-size-fits-all policy. Desire trumps physiognomy, and it is difficult to tell what the reading of this body means. The domestic comedy concludes with the news that wars have begun again, and Jacomo's final line in the play promises his new wife, "I'le teach thee presently to be a Souldier" (5.5.130). The ending underscores perhaps how little this character has changed, though the play hooks the audience into a structure of formal involvement in the heroine's pleasure. In *The Captain*, the ugly character points us to the theater's experiments with collective witnessing, experiments that test the epistemological resources of sight by demonstrating the appeal of specificity. Ugliness may contravene beauty, but still prompts surprise and even love. Affirming the character's singularity, the dramatic fiction foregrounds the capacity of theatrical form to reorient aesthetic judgments.

The Changeling's Instruments of Theater

The Changeling concentrates the affective power of ugliness in the character of De Flores, the character with a "bad face." This focus on his distinctive appearance implicates every element of the drama—including *The Changeling*'s many "changelings," to which I turn at the end of this chapter—in the act of scrutinizing bodies. The play is preoccupied with "harrowingly claustrophobic" representation of private spaces of masculine knowledge and power, and with "views missed, prospects misread," incessant references to what is not seen.[37] But *The Changeling* also projects the sense that the surface of the body is simultaneously manifest and illegible. Surfaces may be feigned, but feigning also appears inscrutable, from Alsemero's virginity test designed to exhume intimate experience to the bed trick's structural assumption that women's bodies are interchangeable. In the world of the play, "ugliness is excess; it is what stands out, what marks (unwished-for) difference," Gordon McMullan insightfully suggests; and through this extravagant excess, *The Changeling* marks "the spread of social pollution manifest as *ugliness*," in turn exemplifying the genre of tragedy itself, since the play (with its double plots) is itself "hybrid, multiple, grotesque."[38]

Building on this reading, I argue that what makes De Flores distinctive is that, in a play world and Jacobean culture that understands ugliness as a manifest pollutant, *he* does not understand his ugliness as "unwished-for" aesthetic disqualification. *The Changeling* individuates De Flores through ugliness that resists erasure and confers on him the unsettling power of anatomizing a normative gaze. To be clear, my reading hinges on the unflinching disgust with which the play treats De Flores; as I noted above, I part from critics who argue that Beatrice-Joanna capitulates to De Flores's assurance of his desirability and I do not seek to recuperate him here. Unlike Frank, who openly avers her desire for Jacomo despite his ugliness, Beatrice-Joanna is not won over. Instead, I track how the play demonstrates divergent logics of ugliness: as legibly predictive, in Beatrice-Joanna's assessment, and as dynamically particular, in De Flores's. Rather than simply confirming a physiognomic reading, in which physical appearance predicts evil inclinations, or reversing the polarities—to reveal that, in fact, he is good!—the play unsettles the normative frame of bodily interpretation. Presumed by others to accept the disqualifying limits of his bodily deficiency, De Flores refuses to concur. Conferring on De Flores the scrutiny of Beatrice-Joanna, into which he draws spectators too, the play troubles the very basis for reading bodily appearance.

From the beginning of the play, Beatrice-Joanna reacts to De Flores with loathing, calling him an "ominous, ill-faced fellow" (2.1.53) and a "villain" (57) and comparing him to a "basilisk" (1.1.115), a "serpent" (229), and a "standing toad-pool" (2.1.58). Trained to look at the body in order to evaluate the person, she understands De Flores's features to display the innate baseness of his being. She has "not spared to tell him" (1.1.133) of her dislike, as if she expects him to agree with her verdict on the offense his face produces. When Beatrice-Joanna puzzles over extricating herself from her impending marriage to Piracquo, she muses that "blood-guiltiness becomes a fouler visage" (2.2.40), only to be struck by the possibility of such a face. In the middle of conversation with Alsemero, Beatrice-Joanna breaks off into an aside:

> And now I think on one. I was to blame:
> I ha' marred so good a market with my scorn;
> 'T'ad been done questionless! The ugliest creature
> Creation framed for some use, yet to see
> I could not mark so much where it should be!
>
> (41–45)

Beatrice-Joanna correlates De Flores's face with "blood-guiltiness"; this equation, in turn, sparks her inspiration for tasking De Flores with the murder of Piracquo. She conceives the act as inappropriate for a man of Alsemero's status—and looks. On the basis of De Flores's appearance, she predicts his moral evil and then naturalizes this judgment as divinely created order. Beatrice-Joanna understands De Flores's "fouler visage" as automatic disqualification that registers his baseness, and her self-reproach for mistreating him extends only to worrying that she missed her opportunity for "use." Turning De Flores into an instrument, Beatrice-Joanna tacitly invokes a scale of aesthetic pleasure. The "ugliest creature," having no value in being seen, may at least accrue value through usefulness to the purposes of others.

If the logic of disqualification undergirds social hierarchy by correlating visible appearance and status, Beatrice-Joanna's affective response to De Flores naturalizes this correlation. De Flores "disturbs" (2.1.52) Beatrice-Joanna more than any "other passions" (53), and after encountering him, she can "scarce leave trembling" (92). She calls this physical response an inexplicable "infirmity" (1.1.109), a response that Alsemero chalks up to the contingency of individual desire. Every object may be "both loved and loathed" (125), he insists, because of natural affinities and antipathies that exist independent of a person's will.[39] Yet this model of revulsion as whimsy does not account for Beatrice-Joanna's reduction of De Flores to the bad feeling he prompts in her. Her address to De Flores as "thou thing most loathed" (2.1.72), and her imaginative example—"put case I loathed him / As much as youth and beauty hates a sepulchre" (2.2.66–67)—develops into the conviction that she will "rid" herself of "two inveterate loathings at one time: / Piracquo and his dog-face" (2.2.146–48). She turns "loathing" into a noun that objectifies both the suitor she detests and De Flores, reduced to an epithet of appearance rather than a name. Even in the final act of the play, Beatrice-Joanna, destroyed by her contract with De Flores, asserts: "His face loathes one" (5.1.69). This formulation reframes a subjective judgment as a collective verdict, a reasonable response that any "one" else might likewise express.[40]

Whereas Beatrice-Joanna's interpretation braids together aesthetic judgment, moral principle, and physiognomic scrutiny, De Flores understands his appearance as particularity rather than incapacity, and he resolutely sources his own value. Against Beatrice-Joanna's readings of his figure, De Flores advances his own interpretation of ugliness, in which appearance amplifies, rather than impedes, desire and agency. Despite Beatrice-Joanna's rejection, De Flores insists his face may spark a different response in the future:

> I must confess my face is bad enough,
> But I know far worse has better fortune,
> And not endured alone, but doted on;
> And yet such pig-haired faces, chins like witches',

> Here and there five hairs, whispering in a corner,
> As if they grew in fear one of another,
> Wrinkles like troughs, where swine-deformity swills
> The tears of perjury that lie there like wash
> Fallen from the slimy and dishonest eye—
> Yet such a one plucked sweets without restraint,
> And has the grace of beauty to his sweet.
>
> (2.1.37–47)

Other people who have whiskery chins, wrinkles, and watering eyes are De Flores's index of the individuated character of desire rather than proof of inevitable rejection. These "bad" faces fit the bill for Montaigne's account of surface ugliness, and they invite moral judgment. Chins and wrinkles and eyes are not only marred; they are like those of witches, like piggish troughs, like slimy pus. Yet the recitation only heightens De Flores's conviction, since these faces, "far worse" than his own, are not merely "endured" but "doted on" as the object of attraction. De Flores does not revalue ugliness as beautiful but insists that desire transforms perception. By the end of the scene, citing "daily precedents of bad faces / Beloved beyond all reason" (2.1.84–85), De Flores believes that his own "foul chops" (86) may likewise trigger a counterintuitive response of "favour" (86). Though ugliness tends to blurring, De Flores will not let himself be dismissed from view, bragging that he imposes on Beatrice-Joanna "twenty times a day—nay, not so little—" (2.1.29), finding "ways and excuses / To come into her sight" (30–31). In this creepy scopic regime, De Flores watches Beatrice-Joanna, places his own appearance in front of her, and insists on the possibility that *his* body could be the object of desire.

These contradictory assumptions about ugliness set in motion the interpretive conflict of their first lengthy exchange. Beatrice-Joanna believes that De Flores shares her moral framework for interpreting his ugly face, while De Flores counters the idea that his ugliness is fixed, or that his face predicts response to his person. In their dialogue, Beatrice-Joanna assumes that De Flores understands his bad face as his greatest liability, while De Flores believes that the content of her speech reveals her change of heart:

> BEATRICE: What ha' you done
> To your face o' late? You've met with some good physician;
> You've pruned yourself, methinks.
> You were not wont to look so amorously.
> DE FLORES: Not I;
> 'Tis the same phys'nomy to a hair and pimple,

	Which she called scurvy scarce an hour ago:
	How is this?
BEATRICE:	Come hither. Nearer, man.
DE FLORES:	I'm up to the chin in heaven!
BEATRICE:	Turn, let me see.
	Faugh, 'tis but the heat of the liver, I perceive't.
	I thought it had been worse.

(2.2.72–81)

Although the two characters complete each other's lines *metrically*, Beatrice-Joanna talks to De Flores and De Flores talks to the audience.[41] What would be a stichomythic exchange between a pair of lovers in a comedy takes the tragic form of a dialogic misfire, a set of observations ("You've met with some good physician," "I thought it had been worse") and commands ("Come hither," "Turn, let me see") from Beatrice-Joanna and a series of asides from De Flores.[42]

The logics of ugliness collide, but neither character recognizes this conflict because each takes the other to confirm a prior position. When Beatrice-Joanna concludes that being "used / To a hard face, 'tis not so unpleasing" (87–88) and affirms that an appearance "mends still in opinion, hourly mends" (89), De Flores understands her to mean that her perception of him has changed: exactly as he suspected, familiarity breeds affection. By contrast, as Beatrice-Joanna enlists De Flores to commit the murder she intends, she beckons him to proximity with her person, dissembling her revulsion to reassure him that his face is not as bad as it appears. As the scene progresses, her imagination of him remains limited; she thinks he only wants money ("Belike his wants are greedy, and to such / Gold tastes like angels' food" [2.2.126–27]) and extrapolates from his presumed poverty to his inferior person. Her limited asides clarify her belief that De Flores also understands his ugly appearance as evidence of social and moral disqualification. She understands his "bad face" to invite repulsion, which moves inexorably into a judgment of the whole person as ugly. Crucially, the play implicates spectators in De Flores's perspective on the encounter, though he is no less mistaken in his reading of Beatrice-Joanna's actions. De Flores maintains his channel to the audience throughout the scene, confiding his glee in the spectators. The offstage audience observes the interaction while aligned, even unwillingly, with De Flores, judging Beatrice-Joanna's misinterpretation of his ugliness from his perspective.

For De Flores, the interaction has confirmed his conviction that his specific features are desirable to Beatrice-Joanna, that she is attracted to him not despite how he looks, but because of it. At the end of the scene, he exclaims:

> O my blood!
> Methinks I feel her in mine arms already,
> Her wanton fingers combing out this beard,
> And being pleased, praising this bad face.
> Hunger and pleasure: they'll commend sometimes
> Slovenly dishes, and feed heartily on 'em;
> Nay, which is stranger, refuse daintier for 'em.
> Some women are odd feeders!
>
> (2.2.148–55)

De Flores imagines the erotic possibility of Beatrice-Joanna's "wanton" desire as intensified response to his face. He rehearses her caress as the act of stroking his beard, as if she lingers on the pleasure of his "bad face" rather than averting her eyes. This image of intimacy culminates in generalizing about the unpredictability of female desire. Frank Whigham argues that the "vocabulary of odd feeding," which De Flores evokes in his fantasy of Beatrice-Joanna's response, "repeatedly presents itself to Renaissance dramatists as a language for inappropriate desire."[43] Yet the grounds on which *The Changeling* asks the audience to interpret this desire as "inappropriate" keep shifting. Rehearsing this casually misogynist commonplace, De Flores turns the mirror admiringly on himself. Beatrice-Joanna and De Flores have struck a bargain on misapprehension, for she thinks their interaction confirms De Flores's proclivity for evil because of his disadvantaging face, but he believes that she has begun to find him desirable because of that face. It is as if Beatrice-Joanna has been reading Montaigne, and De Flores has been reading Burton.

The play casts their opposed understandings into relief in volatile conflict a few scenes later. De Flores commits the murder Beatrice-Joanna commissioned and returns brandishing Piracquo's finger, and where she sees a contract, he sees a pledge. De Flores's affront at the proffered payment, "Do you place me in the rank of verminous fellows / To destroy things for wages?" (3.4.66–67), accurately describes Beatrice-Joanna's correlation of appearance with worth. Based on his face and his service, she employs his "rank" as a tool to accomplish her aims and refuses to acknowledge his insistence on speaking back. Her responses ("I understand thee not" [70] and "I'll double the sum, sir" [75]) miss the point because they presume the transactional basis of their interaction. Not until she begs him to "make away with all speed possible" (79) and "take thy flight" (83), to which De Flores responds, "You must fly too, then" (83), does she begin to comprehend their perspectives. Her response—"I?" (84)—signals her dawning awareness of her complicity, though she still assumes natural hierarchy divides her own self from the "ugliest creature" (2.2.43) to which she had earlier likened De Flores. When she protests, "Think but upon the distance that creation / Set 'twixt thy blood and mine, and keep thee there" (3.4. 133–34), the imperatives imply that a natural order is intrinsic to the body, and that distance in status ("blood") may be marked in the appearance. But De Flores rejects the idea that a natural distinction divides them, commanding her to "Look but into your conscience; read me there. / 'Tis a true book; you'll find me there your equal" (135–36) and "settle you / In what the act has made you" (137–38). As he insists that Beatrice-Joanna identify herself as the "deed's creature" (140), the image of the monstrous birth undoes her assumptions about surface ugliness by locating evil within her instead.[44] Beatrice-Joanna is confronted with the revelation that De Flores has been looking back at her. This scene, which concludes in sexual violence, upends social status at the cost of reaffirming the misogynist logic of female subjection; as Cristina Malcolmson has observed, in "the play's most radical moment about the class hierarchy, it is also most traditional about the sexual hierarchy."[45] Forced to confront De Flores as subject rather than as caricature of disgust, Beatrice-Joanna understands, with shock, that she is complicit in the deed she outsourced, and that the body that she had believed was so interpretable is, in fact, no more so than her own.

The Triumphs of Ugliness

Making a point of his ugliness, *The Changeling* scripts an importance for De Flores that far outstrips the source material. John Reynolds's extremely popular volume *The Triumphs of God's Revenge, Against the crying, and execrable Sinne of Murther* (1621), from which Middleton and Rowley draw their plot, records a series of "tragical histories" that end with clear resolutions.[46] In the source, Reynolds begins by cautioning his readers about the sins of adultery and murder, the "shortest way to ride poast to hell" (sig. Q1v). His account begins and ends with Alsemero, and the misogynistic lessons are clear: beauty deceives, and women's eyes send "invisible lances" (sig. Q3r) of love to lead men astray. The source upholds this consequence of beauty by permitting no character to deviate from it. Without any hint of a repulsive appearance, De Flores is described only as "a Gallant young Gentleman, of the Garison of the Castle" (sig. S4r). Beatrice-Joana "approves him to be a fit instrument to execute her will," and she "with many flattering smiles, and sugered speeches, acquaints him with her purpose and desire" (sig. S4r), convincing him to kill Piracquo. De Flores, "having a long time loved *Beatrice-Joana*" is "so caught and intangled in the snares of her beautie" (sig. S4v) that he instantly agrees.

De Flores is an "instrument," purely responsive, whose role in the narrative is defined by Beatrice-Joana's requests and advances. Most importantly, he is a blank: an unremarkable gallant whose only defining feature is his unrequited love. Once the deed is done, *"De Flores* (like a gracelesse villaine) having dispatched this sorrowfull businesse, speedily acquaints *Beatrice-Joana* heerewith who (miserable wretch) doth heereat infinitly rejoyce, and thankes him with many kisses" (sig. T1v). Even if the parenthetical descriptions condemn De Flores, there is no suggestion of Beatrice-Joana's revulsion, nor—in the crucial difference from the play—does this courtly service lead to sexual violence.

What is surprising, to a reader who comes to the source text after *The Changeling*, is how smoothly the plan proceeds. His rival gone, Alsemero marries Beatrice-Joana, and all seems well. Three months later, Alsemero becomes jealous and "hee curbes and restraynes her of her libertie" (sig. T2v), and in turn, Beatrice-Joana "looks no longer on her husband with affection, but with disdayne and envy" (sig. T3r). When Alsemero is away, De Flores arrives with a letter for Beatrice-Joana, and "with many amorous embracings and dalliances, (which modestie holds unworthy of relation:) shee acquaints him with her husbands ingratitude" (sig. T3r). He joyfully "revives his old sute, and redoubleth his newe Kisses," and she "not onely ingageth herselfe to him for the time present, but for the future, and bids him visite her often" (sig. T3v). This is a relationship that Beatrice-Joana gladly initiates, and their mutual delight is only slightly marred when Beatrice-Joana confesses the murder to Alsemero, who forgives her and charges her to avoid De Flores in the future. However, Beatrice-Joana and De Flores cannot halt their relationship, and they resume meeting in secret whenever Alsemero is abroad. The narrative catastrophe offers a reversed image of the way that Alsemero's closet will function at the conclusion of Middleton and Rowley's play. Tipped off by a servant about the affair, Alsemero pretends to leave, only to hide secretly "in his Studie" and eavesdrop on the bedchamber ("*Alsemero* heares all, but doth neither speake, cough, [s]neeze, nor spit"), while De Flores arrives at Beatrice-Joana's request and "they fall to their kisses and embracings." When he can hold back no longer, Alsemero "throwes off the dore, and violently rusheth foorth." In a scene that the narrative does not hesitate to replay in gory detail, Alsemero finds them "on his bed, in the middest of their adultery," and shoots them, then runs them through with a sword, and then finally "stabs them with so many deepe and wide wounds, that they have not so much power, or time to speake a word, but there lye weltring and wallowing in their blood" (sig. V1r). United in an affair prompted by Beatrice-Joana's lust, the pair is punished with violence that piles up an excess of brutal weapons. Though Alsemero will eventually be sentenced for his own misdeeds, the story of Beatrice-Joana and De Flores ends here, curtailed of final death speeches but left "wallowing" in their judgment. Despite the promise of speedy didactic "triumphs" at the outset of the story, this road to hell is neither short nor swift.

The Changeling begins by marking De Flores's face as blatantly, transparently, repulsively ugly. Visually reorienting him as a figure of particularity, theatrical form explodes the narrative limitations of the source. Yet in this environment of intensified scrutiny, the play refuses to dramatize the ocular proof of Beatrice-Joanna's collaboration with De Flores. There is no scene of Alsemero's discovery that the source primes a reader to expect; he is not hiding in his closet, stifling a sneeze.[47] Rather than offering a scene of eavesdropping, the final scene of the play begins with Alsemero and his friend Jasperino, who wait for Beatrice-Joanna and reference an event they (or perhaps only Jasperino) witnessed. When Jasperino notes that the "prospect from the garden has showed enough / For deep suspicion" (5.3.2–3), Alsemero responds:

> The black mask
> That so continually was worn upon't
> Condemns the face for ugly ere't be seen.
> Her dèspite to him, and so seeming bottomless.
>
> (3–6)

This "black mask" covers, and also paradoxically reveals, a face severed from the person, in a platitude about a face judged ugly without even coming into view. Rendering ostentatious the fault it was intended to hide, the mask suggests that a spectator need not even see the face to know that it is "ugly." Alsemero's image collapses surface and depth as the "black mask" becomes the face itself; appearance is both manifest evidence and that which cannot be perceived.[48] Comparing the artificial covering to Beatrice-Joanna's supposed dislike of De Flores, which is "seeming bottomless," the metaphor suggests that there is no limit to dissembling of the surface.

Without a scene that corroborates a definitive revelation of Beatrice-Joanna's unfaithfulness, the play confers the power of foregone judgment on Alsemero. Although the source emphasizes the speed with which Alsemero kills the lovers after he spies on them (they have "not so much power, or time to speak a word"), *The Changeling* slows down the scene to elaborate Beatrice-Joanna's condemnation. At Alsemero's accusation, "You are a whore" (5.3.31), Beatrice-Joanna laments the "horrid sound" of the word, which

> blasts a beauty to deformity.
> Upon what face soever that breath falls,
> It strikes it ugly. O, you have ruined
> What you can ne'er repair again.
>
> (31–34)

The term evokes seismic transformation, irrevocably recasting Beatrice-Joanna as morally corrupt and therefore ugly. The image of miasmic "breath" that turns "beauty to deformity" is later echoed in Alsemero's exclamation, "O, thou art all deformed!" (77). Deformity is expressed in the face and "strikes it ugly," reducing appearance entirely to another's perception. Equating this ugliness with irreparable ruin, Beatrice-Joanna rues the permanence of this judgment. Baker has argued that the play begins with "conventional" frameworks for the "significance of physical appearance," but then distinguishes between ugliness and deformity on the basis of gender. She summarizes: "Beatrice-Joanna cannot define her identity in her own terms and is instead constructed by others as deformed," while De Flores, "despite his ugly face, demonstrates a shocking ability to manipulate the terms of his own identity."[49] Although this construction of the contrast between beauty and deformity is evident, I do not think that the shock is only in De Flores's manipulation of these terms. Rather than hitching moral truth to literal appearance, as if he is physically ugly and she is morally ugly, the play undoes any easy equivalence. While Beatrice-Joanna talks about his ugliness in the play as if it transparently telegraphs both status and murderous potential, De Flores challenges the very basis of appearance on which this judgment proceeds.

Even when the final scene pairs Beatrice-Joanna and De Flores in a shared tableau of death, De Flores refuses to be accommodated into a normative interpretation that would parallel his physical deformity to Beatrice-Joanna's moral deformity and ratify a clear moral interpretation of ugliness. Alsemero locks Beatrice-Joanna and De Flores into his closet and choreographs a grand reveal for the other men in the play. When he opens the closet doors, De Flores has fatally wounded Beatrice-Joanna. She exclaims, "My loathing / Was prophet to the rest, but ne'er believed" (5.3.156–57), an admission that fits the didactic expectations of a tragic punishment, but this retrospective judgment does not clarify the causative lesson of ugliness. While Beatrice-Joanna asks that her blood be "cast . . . to the ground regardlessly; / Let the common sewer take it from distinction" (152–53), De Flores revels in the final triumphs of singular possession and self-regard.[50] Proclaiming that he has "drunk up all, left none behind / For any man to pledge me" (170–71), De

Flores refuses social relations through total consumption. Fulfilling his desire, he rejects even the patriarchy's bond; no man will pledge him because there is nothing left. De Flores maintains the distinction that sets him apart, the sole character who gets exactly what he wants in the course of the play—and fails to repent for his actions.

Once De Flores and Beatrice-Joanna are safely dead, the final scene obscures, rather than clarifies, the signifying power of ugliness in the play. Alsemero instates the long-awaited moral judgment, rehearsing the changes that other characters have undergone:

> Here's beauty changed
> To ugly whoredom; here, servant-obedience
> To a master-sin: imperious murder!
> I, a supposèd husband, changed embraces
> With wantonness, but that was paid before.
> [*To Tomazo*] Your change is come too: from an ignorant wrath
> To knowing friendship.—Are there any more on's?
>
> (5.3.197–203)

This summation shifts the tragedy into an excerpt from a commonplace book, abstracting dramatic characters into moral emblems (and notably letting Alsemero off the hook). Alsemero's choice of verb tense chimes with the tragedy's conclusion: "changed" reveals what has been there all along.[51] Beatrice-Joanna is accorded the "beauty" that becomes "ugly," while the punning "master-sin" aligns De Flores's obligation with his insurrection rather than making his appearance the sign of deserved loathing. Alsemero's rehearsal of the changes undergone by each character adds depth to the surface reading the figure of the changeling—and *The Changeling*—demands, as what was within erupts to identification. This recitation is followed immediately by confessions from Antonio and Franciscus, whose changes are revealed as the punishment of disguise, and by Alibius, whose change from jealous husband is promised as a future beyond the play. What made De Flores distinctive in performance is reduced to plot, a notion of sin that quietly restores hierarchy while sidestepping the question of what can be read, and what can be known, from a body. The final scene disorients any didactic interpretation, a nightmare apparition for defenses of the theater that firm up the link between seeing and doing.

De Flores's ugliness enables the theater to marshal attention to the structure of scrutiny that produces aesthetic judgments in the first place. Rather than dismissing the social effects of De Flores's face, the play asks us to take seriously a character who refuses to absorb the catastrophic burden of his unattractiveness. In his discussion of *The Changeling*, Algernon Charles Swinburne identifies De Flores as a "strangely original tragic figure," remarking that he "is so horribly human, so fearfully and wonderfully natural, in his single-hearted brutality of devotion, his absolute absorption of soul and body by one consuming force of passionately cynical desire."[52] De Flores is "strangely original" because he is like *us*: "horribly human," his "single-hearted" focus locates the originality of the figure—that slide from character to "man"—in the psychological domain of desire. For William Empson, by contrast, De Flores is the "real changeling from which the play 'derives its title,'" and the definition of change that Empson identifies is "madness," that which separates the self from the world.[53] For subsequent critics, the symptom of this madness is De Flores's idea that Beatrice-Joanna may eventually fall in love with him, despite his face. This argument, importantly, depends on the difference between print and performance. "A person merely reading the text might subscribe to De Flores' superficial logic that concludes it is possible that a delicately-reared woman might chide herself to bed with him," A. L. Kistner and M. K. Kistner suggest, "but faced on stage by the hideous malignity that De Flores is supposed to be, he might realize that only utter irrationality could expect such an outcome and only in madness could it come to pass."[54] Premising social norms on the visual perception of audiences in the theater, they argue that De Flores's ugliness drives a wedge between spectator and reader.

This strand of critical history reprises aesthetic judgment in the key of character, calling De Flores the changeling because he refuses to comply with the obvious consequence of his ugliness. De Flores's distinctive particularity sparks our interest (he is "like us"), but he is a changeling and evinces madness because he refuses to accept what everyone else knows: Beatrice-Joanna could never love an ugly man. The reading of De Flores's "hideous malignity" maps a normative aesthetic judgment that understands ugliness as disabling, but I find that the play uses his "superficial logic"—what I would call the illegibility of surface reading—to confound such a conclusion. The play aligns spectators with De Flores's defiant gaze and desire to expose how disabling social judgments work. Staging ugliness, the play reveals the stakes of theatrical form. A character's vantage is never confined to one perspective, and *The Changeling* makes spectators witness to De Flores's critique of Beatrice-Joanna's reduction of him to an object of loathing. Validating De Flores's audacious refusal to stick to the script of innate disqualification, the play corrodes the moral grounds of bodily interpretation.

Deforming the Artificial Changeling

The identification of De Flores as the changeling that I have just noted associates the play's epistemology of ugliness in the castle plot with the hospital plot too. A "changeling" has multiple definitions in the early modern period, from a fickle person, to a person changed for another, to an intellectually disabled person. Although the final scene of *The Changeling* rehearses many possible candidates for "changeling," the dramatis personae at the beginning of the printed playbook assigns the character to Antonio. He enters in *The Changeling* with the stage direction *"like an idiot"* (s.d. at 1.2.81); later he removes the "shape of folly" (3.3.133), telling Isabella to "cast no amazing eye upon this change" (3.3.131); and finally, he is exposed as one of the "counterfeits slipped into these disguises" (5.2.73) in the "hospital of fools and madmen" (72). The patients confined in the hospital offer early modern representations of what we would today identify with mental illness or intellectual disability. *The Changeling* does not document historical realities; dramatic depictions of Bedlam, or London's Bethlem Hospital, as Carol Thomas Neely has shown, "foreground theatre's core elements: bodies and illusion, costumes and props, disguise and role-shifting."[55] In fact, the play's most sustained representations of "fool" and "madman" characters turn out in the end to be counterfeiting. The changeling is another dramatic character depicted in the frontispiece of *The Wits* (figure 3.1 in chapter 3), which perhaps even refers specifically to the character of Antonio in Middleton and Rowley's play. In the engraving, the type character "Changling" has a schoolbook from which he is incapable of learning, as both the book and his hands dangle from his wrists in a gesture that physician John Bulwer, in his *Chironomia*, associates with despair or "abasement of mind."[56] Bulwer, a physician best known for his work on gesture, and treatises on sign language and lip reading, translates bodily particularities into semiotic units. Enacting this "iconic gesture," in Farah Karim-Cooper's generative phrase, the dramatic character of the changeling extrapolates from hands to mind to self.[57] The role depicts "a spiritless vacancy of mind and limp flexibility of body," Joseph R. Roach notes, and requires the actor to enact a kind of blankness, given "how pliantly the outward shape was thought to conform to the actor's inward state of mind."[58] The changeling's incapacity surfaces as fixity, a shape that is legible as stuckness, the impossibility of change, development, or growth.

The concept of the changeling cuts across medical, theological, moral, and social terrains and is invoked to explain perceived deficiencies, or changes, in a person that cannot be attributed to a clear cause or recruited to a stable effect. Bulwer relates the folklore, or "old Tradition" that "some Children that have been surreptitiously taken away, and others put in their roome, which have been deformed Innocents, which we commonly call Changlings" (sig. 3Z1v). The changeling myth of fairy replacement for human child accounts for a child who is inscrutable, according to normative protocols of sociality, by positing that, appearances to the contrary, this child may not actually be human. Bulwer's discussion of the changeling arrives more than five hundred pages into *Anthropometamorphosis*, which employs the figure of the "Artificiall Changling" as a problem for artifice that transforms the body.[59] Bulwer's text—excessive, anxious, finicky, voluminous—deserves far more attention than I have space to discuss, but I highlight here his concern about how the body's manifold transformations produce an ugliness that sticks.

Although the first edition of the text, in 1650, featured no images, the second edition, printed in 1653—the same year *The Changeling* quarto was printed—added engravings to illustrate the array of possible modifications of the human body. The additive style of Bulwer's massive tome is best conveyed by reproducing the piled clauses of the text's full title:

> *Man Transform'd: OR, THE ARTIFICIALL CHANGLING: Historically presented, In the mad and cruell Gallantry, foolish Bravery, ridiculous Beauty, filthy Finenesse, and loathsome Loveliness of most NATIONS, fashioning and altering their Bodies from the mould intended by NATURE; with figures of those Transfigurations. To which artificiall and affected Deformations are added, all the Native and Nationall Monstrosities that have appeared to disfigure the Humane Fabrick. With a VINDICATION of the Regular Beauty and Honesty of NATURE.*[60]

The "Artificiall Changling" is a figure who is both in the process of transformation—"fashioning and altering"—and already "Transform'd," with manifold "Deformations" and "Monstrosities" already evident on the body. Transgressing the aesthetic ideal of ruled proportion, the changeling revolts against the "Beauty" of nature. The subtitle's compendium of bodies that depart "from the mould intended by NATURE" is rife with admonitory adjectives about the list of "Transfigurations" from which nature's originary form may be extracted. The metaphor of the changeling is echoed in the theatrical language—verbs of presentation, of deformation, of fashioning—with which he registers the transformational powers of artifice. Conjured as doings that warp the body, and as things done, these "Deformations" evince the exercise of fashion and will while they overpower the very bodies that adopt them.

I turn to this volume to consider how, as Bulwer attempts to catalogue these deformations, inviting readers to look at and learn from the changeling's artificial ugliness, he produces a gaze that escapes didactic control. On the page

FIGURE 4.2. John Bulwer, *Anthropometamorphosis: man transform'd: or, the artificiall changling* (London, 1653), sig. A1r, title page. Call#: B5461. Used by permission of the Folger Shakespeare Library under a Creative Commons Attribution-ShareAlike 4.0 International License.

facing the title, an image puts many different deformations on view (figure 4.2). The scene is trial and pageant, curtains pulled back to disclose judge and audience, while figures of medical knowledge prosecute bodily transformation and the subjects of their protest are arrayed at the bar. Above and outside the scene of judgment, divine revelation splits the heavens in a shaft of light that proffers both the *Magna Charta Natura* and the crown and scepter, labeled *"Per Leges Natura,"* while animals appeal to humanity, an angel announces that God made humans erect, and a devil cackles with glee to imagine such transformations. Rejecting the "rule" of the body, the changeling's microcosm of disorder unsettles other divinely ordered hierarchies. A lengthy explanation, "The intent of the Frontispiece unfolded," details each element of the image as a scene of judgment on "all *abusers of their Bodies*, who have new-made and deformed themselves" (sig. A1r).

The frontispiece affords the reader the opportunity to view these bodies in full-length renderings, as accused persons and spectators themselves, awaiting the judgment that follows. Some figures stand in profile, disclosing extended ears, a hyperlong nose, a face embossed with beauty marks; others, hands raised to swear an oath of testimony, stand with their backs turned, to offer a full-length rendering that emphasizes hirsute and tattooed bodies. This image flattens the difference between offending part and whole, between ear gauged to extreme length and scarified body covered in long vertical stripes. Reducing each figure to one example of deformation, the scene individuates bodies according to their defects, distributing the changeling's artifice before the opening poem amalgamates the frontispiece back into a single figure. The poem summons to account "Changling *Proteus*," whose "abusive shapes" disclose the violence enacted "on thy Forme" (sig. A3r). The "Changling" is both self-defacing subject and the object of formal violence, borrowing the actor's shape-shifting transformations but halted in print long enough to enumerate the range of deformities. Castigating "Nature-scoffing art" that challenges "wise Nature's plastique hand" by "eradicating" features or, by contrast, making them "Art-augmented" (sigs. A3r–v), the poem cites specific examples—horns implanted in the head, noses pierced or cut off, cheeks bored through—depicted in the frontispiece. Analyzing the figures arrayed in the trial scene, the poem combines them into a single protean form, both the limit of transformation and array of every conceivable possibility.

The text channels the theatrical form into its structure, organized as twenty-four "Scenes of Man's *Transformation*," a unit of dramatic composition keyed to each part of the transformed body (sig. 5*1r). Each scene, such as "Certaine fashions of the Head," "Monstrous conformations, properties, colours, proportions, and Fashionable affectations of eyes," and "Cruell and fantasticall inventions of men, practiced upon their Bodies" (sigs. 5*1r–v), orients the reader to dismissive commentary on cultural practices of other nations. Caught between blazon, physic manual, and theatrical script, the volume progresses from the top of the body downward, from head to feet, focusing on a specific feature. Each scene pairs descriptions of elective bodily modifications, matched to different cultures, with engravings that illustrate these features. The examples move between bodily comportments produced by disciplining the body, such as binding hands or feet from infancy to elongate the shape, to temporary adornments, such as painting or staining the body, to modifications that extend a natural habit, such as overly long fingernails. Ultimately, the difficulty is where to draw the line on the "vertue of ornamentall Decorum" (sig. 2Q2v). Bulwer inherits "cosmeticall physick" (sig. B2v), the art of repairing ugliness, from classical authorities, but there is no clear line between changes that redress accidental defect and preserve the bodily gift of beauty, and changes that corrupt nature by art. As the constant invocations of theatrical form suggest, nature is not so easily distinguished from artifice. The "Artificiall Changling" the title condemns is simultaneously the figure for elective body modifications gone too far beyond "cosmeticall physic" and an amalgam of transformational practices that have already taken effect.

If the ugly face should, in physiognomic discourse, teach the viewer about the person, Bulwer's scenes find the real horror in a reader who cannot tell where the natural defect ends and artificial defect begins. The reader who has "well viewed the Scenes and Devillish shapes of this Practical Metamorphosis," the narrative promises, "will clearely see" (sig. *2v) the "corporall Apostacy" of "Monstrosities" that are "Native" rather than "Naturall" (sig. *2v). We might imagine that Bulwer would link explicitly to antitheatrical critiques of actors' transformations, wary of the effects of visual display. Instead, he doubles down on the possibility that seeing might reroute the artificing reader. Bulwer's didactic method depends on spectatorship, as if the theater slowed down in the act of performance, stabilizing into scenes and shapes that allow the reader to pore over them. The "Hint of the *Use* of the Treatise," the final moment of paratext that detains the reader before the scenes commence, describes the book's intent to "serve as a Glasse for the pernitiously-affected Gallants of our time to looke in, and see the deformity of their Minds" (sig. 3*4v). Fun house mirror rather than looking glass, the text transforms the educable reader by offering a reflection for gallants. Look at the illustration, the direction insists, and anatomize the "deformity" of mind in outward appearance; what is more, see your own mind in another's fashion and recognize how ridiculous you look. For Bulwer, the matter of this scrutiny is nothing less than the human being himself, for reformation occurs when "men descending into themselves, may know themselves *to be men and not beasts*" (sig. 3*4v). This scrutiny that produces self-knowledge occurs in the register of depth—"descending into themselves"—to define the essential core of humanness from which their exteriors have strayed.

The artificial changeling's threat is transformation, but more specifically, a transformation so absorbing that it is, Bulwer says, "as if man consisted meerely of an outside" (sig. 4C4v). Nothing but surface, this body has no stable form beyond what is perceptible. This verdict arrives in the appendix to *Anthropometamorphosis*, "Exhibiting the Pedigree of the English Gallant," which surveys the "transformation and deformity of Apparell" (sig. 3Z2r) donned by Bulwer's English readers, whose clothing is not cut "according to the naturall shape and proportion of the body" (sig. 3C4v). The end of the volume thus recapitulates the opening poem's equation of "Monstrosities of Art" with "Forme-Transforming Garbes": when a man tries to "translate" himself into "a Changeling, or some ougly Elfe" (sig. *4v), it may be impossible to tell the difference between body and clothing. Matching English fashions with the body modifications practiced elsewhere, the appendix reenacts the recursive instability of the work that the text has already done, by reusing some of the engravings from earlier scenes for comparative illustrations. One image (figure 4.3) depicts two men who appear to regard each other on the page. The man on the left displays the garb and hat of a gallant, wearing a suit with trim and buttons, a cloak, and long shoes that split into prongs at the toe, carrying a walking stick.[61] The man on the right, an image that appeared earlier in the volume in the scene of "foot-fashions" (sig. 3I1v), is bare chested, wearing a split loincloth, cloak, and round hat, carrying a spear. He has extremely long feet. The page juxtaposes these two figures, rendering their bodies in full length although the point of the example is the difference in their feet.

The opposition of the two figures complicates Bulwer's critique of artifice, however, by threatening to collapse into similitude. Bulwer laments the English "fashion" that has prioritized appearance over function: wearing "our forked shooes almost as long againe as our feet, not a little to the hinderance of the action of the foot, and not only so, but they prove an impediment to reverentiall devotions; for, as one notes, our boots and shooes are so long snouted, that we can hardly kneele in Gods house" (sig. 3B3v). The gallant wears "long snouted" shoes patterned on the "feet of a monstrous bignesse" (sig. 3B3v), such as the figure on the right is understood to display. Examining the "pedestrall vanity" (sig. 3B4r) that gives the gallant a "mind to imitate" this shape, Bulwer cannot point to a natural English foot. He reminisces about an earlier moment when a "short foot" was thought "more handsome and fashionable," and before that, "square Toes were grown in Fashion," and before

FIGURE 4.3. John Bulwer, *Anthropometamorphosis: man transform'd: or, the artificiall changling* (London, 1653), sig. 4B3v, p. 548. Call#: B5461. Used by permission of the Folger Shakespeare Library under a Creative Commons Attribution-ShareAlike 4.0 International License.

that fashion, "sharpe piquant Toes were altogether in request" (sig. 3B3v). To be sure, the strategy of comparison reproduces a hierarchy that prioritizes the shod English man, since Bulwer is uninterested in whether the barefoot Indian man evinces the same experiment with fashion. However, the diatribe that accompanies the image never establishes the natural size and shape of the foot he is so concerned to retrieve from the hindrances of fashion.[62] The English gallant models his shoes on the foot fashions of others; and, as a result, the English foot becomes what the surface of the shoe displays. The image enacts the text's guiding theatrical metaphor of surface in the form of a shoe. Spinning out into discussion of shoe fashions, Bulwer can only set the boundary of the natural by positing that, "were it not for the sence of paine," men would enact a Procrustean bargain, cutting their feet "to the length of their

Phansies" (sig. 3B4r). Pain is the only curb to artificiality, when the body itself flags the endpoint of transformation.

Even this apparent limit, however, gives way to the irresistible pull of artifice that may permanently transform the body. Consolidating ugliness around the mutability of the self, Bulwer returns to the changeling as a figure for the deforming power of imitation. He condemns the fashionable open-breasted cut of women's gowns, noting that "some Ladies who by this inconvenient Garbe of nakednesse have lost the use of their hands, which have been resolved and hung Changeling-like, through a refrigeration of the originall of the Nerves, which from the Neck send those Nerves to the Hands which enable them with motion" (sig. 4B2r). Bulwer's immediate target of critique is immodesty, of course, but the immobilizing effect on the body is of as much concern to the physician. Deforming vestures produce an involuntary transformation. The garment transforms the English body beneath because the gown's cut enforces a pose that cuts off the circulation of the nerves running to the hands. Bulwer's diagnosis conflates the resulting posture with the theatrical character of the changeling, whose hands hang loose and immovable. Theatrical similitude—"Changeling-like"—expresses the body that has been fixed into a position from which it cannot escape. Taken literally as well as figuratively, the changeling is a figure for the destructive transformation of the body, as if the labor to fashion the self has no limits. Artifice becomes surface.

The argument's final swerve into the theatrical problem of metamorphosis implicates the reader in the encounter with unforeseen deforming bodily change. Structuring the didactic power of the text around the visual effect of theatrical form, from the "scenes" of bodily change that Bulwer promises to the "Theatre of the World" he invokes, the *"Artificiall Changeling"* cannot shake the interactive experience of co-embodiment that the text's guiding theatrical metaphor hails. If, in Stephen Gosson's antitheatrical screed, the theater's danger is the form's enactment beyond the fictional content—so that Gosson concedes that *some* plays may be *read* with profit—for Bulwer, the act of reading is prematurely unsettled by the performance that erupts in the text's very production.[63] For, where readers might expect to find a list of errata in the opening pages, the text offers instead a peremptory justification of print's indefensibility against powerful artifice. The prefatory "Note" insists that "the Errata's are not to be charged upon the Presse, but upon the Transforming Argument of the Book, which being nothing but artificiall Errata's, and affected Deformities, drew in literall blemishes and misprisions of sense, by way of Analogy, insomuch as when they appear'd inevitable, it was conceived they might passe for a new Elegancy with the Pedantique Quixots of the Pen, who (indeed) are most concern'd in it" (sig. 4*4v). Errors in the printed texts are the fault not of the printer, but of the "affected Deformities" represented, which infect and mar the printed book. The book not only illustrates deformities; unaccountably, the volume itself impersonates the "artificial Errata's" of the bodies it treats. Even the fixity of print yields to the unfixing power of such "blemishes."

How is a reader to construe the self-reproducing mistakes that follow from a text that has swallowed the theater, scene by scene? On "cursory perusall," the passive narrative voice concedes, "these mistakes appeared, which may thus be corrected. The others being many, are referred from the indifferency of the Corrector to the humanity of the Reader, with an *Humanum est Errare*" (sig. 4*4v). To err is only human, but these "literal blemishes" disclose the possibility that the book's unfixing power dismantles the text's didactic aims in advance. In fact, these errors, introduced into the text by the very "affected Deformities" they portray, may tip into a "new Elegancy." Theatrical transformation is both the engine for and supreme fulfillment of Bulwer's worries about artifice, for deformities make new forms possible. "Blemishes" or other particularities, rather than formal perfection, drive aesthetic innovation. In an insight that returns us to the claims of disability aesthetics with which this chapter began, Bulwer admits that deformity unfixes any stable norm and may even produce unforeseen possibilities.

* * *

I have argued in this chapter that ugliness is a contingent disabling that pushes surface readings of the body to their impossible conclusion. *The Changeling* withholds the satisfaction of seeing De Flores either resentful or apologetic about his appearance, dramatizing a lack of penitence that Bulwer fears the "Artificiall Changling" will embrace. Bulwer's didactic program employs a moralizing gaze in the theater of bodily modification, yet this collective witnessing spirals out of control, the logical consequence of a feigning that undermines fixed values. The problems of distinguishing between face and form, of discerning between "surface" and "deeper" deformity, and of accounting for the discrepancy between natural shape and artful self-fashioning are nowhere more pressing than on the stage. I have noted the danger of this conformation between inward state and outward shape in the stickiness of acting. The changeling is another part, like Richard III, that may irreversibly deform the actor. Writing in the mid-seventeenth century, in the observation that is my second epigraph to this chapter, Edmund Gayton recalls that "it is not out of most men's observation, that one most admirable Mimicke in our late Stage, so lively and corporally personated a Changeling, that he could never compose his Face to the figure it had, before he undertook that part."[64] Playing the part of the changeling decomposes the actor. Newly out of "figure," the actor lives with the result of a one-way metamorphosis that is the effect of his great success. In Gayton's account, it is precisely the talent of "lively" bodily skill that fixes this actor in his part.

Yet the theatrical invocation of the figure of the changeling captures the other end of the spectrum of transformation too. The changeling also demonstrates the actor's skilled capacity for deformation. In Ford, Dekker, Middleton, and Rowley's *The Spanish Gypsy*, composed around the time of *The Changeling* and acted at court by the same company, Pretiosa summons the figure of the changeling as the pinnacle of skill:

> Yes, father, I will play the changeling:
> I'll change myself into a thousand shapes
> To court our brave spectators; I'll change my postures
> Into a thousand different variations
> To draw even ladies' eyes to follow mine;
> I'll change my voice into a thousand tones
> To chain attention. Not a changeling, father?
> None but myself shall play the changeling.
>
> (2.1.106–13)[65]

The changeling is both a specific character and a general figure for the actor's craft. The actor changes "postures" in both embodied "shapes" and presentational "tones" to "chain attention" of witnesses and auditors. The changeling's skill translates into showstopping command: those "thousand different variations" compel even the most inattentive spectator to follow her figure. Pretiosa forecasts this role and, with every "change" of shape, posture, and voice, surely enacts the part as she promises what she will do. This speech is strange because, as the play continues, Pretiosa never appears to nominate herself a "changeling"; she remains in the equally stereotypical (and equally prejudicial) role of a "gypsy" until her own noble birth is revealed at the end of the play. Critics have suggested that perhaps the same actor who played Antonio in *The Changeling* takes the part of Pretiosa here, accounting for the eruption of a meditation on—and performance of—the changeling in a play where none is enacted. Winking at the virtuosic shifts, the play foregrounds the actor's skill.

The phrase "play the changeling" thus returns us to the twin pistons of singularity and reproducibility that drive theatrical practice and entangle disability in theatrical witnessing. In Gayton's anecdote, the changeling is the limit of theater, the actor who, having deformed his shape, cannot play another part. In Pretiosa's account, the changeling is the theater's most extreme example of virtuosic possibility, the figure most able to move among any parts she adopts. The personation that may disable the actor's capacity or (in Bulwer's account) transform a woman through her fashionable dress, permanently fixing a body in a role, simultaneously evokes the thrill of the fullest spectrum of unfixing transformations. The changeling is both fixed shape and expression of unfixing, governed by the surface logic that renders ugliness illegible. De Flores's insistence on his particularity, the thing that makes him a figurative changeling in critical history, jams the circuit of interpretation that reads from body to the heart of a person. Anatomizing the act of perceiving ugliness, the theater experiments with dissolving the boundary between natural and artificial, between what can be seen and what can be feigned. In the process, the theater implicates spectators in the thrill of witnessing performance's deformations.

In the next chapter, as we will see, the problem of cause and effect posed by surface reading gives way to symptomatic effects that will not be reduced to a cause. In the act of performance, the "sick" body highlights the relationship between the body of the actor and the body of the character. Under public scrutiny that attempts to discern between that which is real and that which is feigned, the performance of disability may also become permanent. Foregrounding the problem of unelective immobility that overtakes the body, moments of disabling become flash points for the temporality of theatrical representation.

Chapter 5

Playing Time, or Sick of Feigning

> Palsie. Trembling, shaking, quavering, quivering, unjointed, unsteadie, fainting, numme.
>
> —Joshua Poole, *The English Parnassus*
>
> I have considered our whole life is like a play: wherein every man, forgetful of himself, is in travail with expression of another. Nay, we so insist in imitating others, as we cannot (when it is necessary) return to ourselves; like children, that imitate the vices of stammerers so long, till at last they become such, and make the habit to another nature, as it is never forgotten.
>
> —Ben Jonson, *Timber: or, Discoveries*

Philip Barrough's *The Methode of Phisicke* (1583) enumerates diseases of the brain characterized by loss of voluntary control over the body. One cluster of illnesses of the head—including madness, melancholy, tremors, apoplexy, palsy, and epilepsy—shares symptoms identified by their immobilizing effect. For example, apoplexy is a "stopping of the brain" wherein the body loses sensation and mobility; palsy is when either side of the body, or sometimes a single part or "member" ("the hand, the legge, or the tongue"), becomes insensible and immobile; the falling sickness, or epilepsy, is a "convulsion" of the body that happens "not continually, but that which chaunceth at sundrie times"; and in a "crampe," the sinews "are drawen, and pluckt up against ones will."[1] Barrough's influential volume, which went through at least seven more editions by the 1650s, distinguishes these diseases by the symptoms that overtake the body, and he emphasizes the temporal fluctuations of these involuntary responses. Nearly a century after Barrough, William Salmon's exhaustive physic compendium, *Synopsis Medicinae* (1671), similarly ranges across examples from epilepsy (or "falling sickness") to stupefaction in explicating diseases that are marked either by a loss of voluntary motion or by uncontrollable movement, with uncertain duration of effect.

He defines palsy as *"a Disease in which the whole Body, or the one half, as the right or the left side, or else a particular Member, doth lose Sense or Motion, or both*, according as all, or some of the Nerves be obstructed"; and he classifies it as one of the "Diseases Universal" because the symptoms affect the entire body.[2] Salmon follows Lazare Rivière, who understands palsy as an example of a chronic disease, distinguished from acute diseases because they "are of long continuance, being oft-times great, as Gouts, Palsies, Dropsies, Consumptions, &tc."[3] Differentiated by their duration, these diseases shift in and out of perceptibility, becoming apparent as they affect the body—temporarily or permanently. Grouped symptomatically by intermittent effect, this cluster of diseases was linked in English medical discourse of the sixteenth and seventeenth centuries and understood in terms of sickness. Today, we typically identify such diseases as periodic or acquired disabilities, without necessarily likening the intermittent tremors of cerebral palsy, punctuated episodes of epileptic seizures, or immobilizing effects of a stroke.

I begin with these examples to foreground why my account of early modern disability engages the "sick" body, an investigation that may appear far afield of our modern concept of disability as an identity. The "gifts of the body," as I noted in chapter 4, yoke health, strength, and beauty as signature properties of the human form in early modern thought. Renaissance conceptions of sickness repeatedly blur the line between disease and disability through this slippery sense of the body's susceptibility; health is impermanent, briefly sustained against time's ravaging effects. While the examples I treat in this chapter are limited to a cluster of diseases linked by the effects they produce, I hope this argument gestures to the importance of considering early modern texts at the intersection of medical history and disability studies. The critical account of health, ever since Michel Foucault's analysis of the "normal" body, highlights the medical model of disability, which prioritizes attempts to cure and fix the deviant body, bringing it into line with quantifiable norms of appearance, shape, or function.[4] Disability theory, as I discuss below, qualifies a celebratory account of medical progress by critiquing the ideology of cure that results from this drive to normality. Precisely because cure is not yet quantified in a modern sense, and because the structures of classification and institutionalization that Foucault describes are inchoate, early modern texts offer alternative conceptions of health and disease that speak to the medical model as it emerges in modernity and can productively extend our disability analysis.

Early work in disability theory distinguished between disease and disability etiologies in order to value disability as a minority identity, an expression of human variation rather than a condition to be corrected.[5] Building on this foundation, recent work locates resistance to the medical model in a critique of what Alison Kafer calls the "curative imaginary," a concept of disability that "not only *expects* and *assumes* intervention but also cannot imagine or comprehend anything other than intervention."[6] The curative imaginary understands a disabled person as moving, unquestioningly, toward a future of cure. Such a future imports nostalgia for a nondisabled past (though such a past may never have existed) and strands the disabled person in an unwished-for present.[7] The logic of cure operates on indefinite deferral, bolstered by the fantasy that derives, in Eli Clare's words, from "an imagination of what I should be like, from some definition of *normal* and *natural*."[8] Early modern concepts of cure are not yet tethered to a defined norm, but the felt force of that subjunctive—"what I should be," in Clare's formulation—is a recognizable aspiration. Furthermore, as Kafer observes, "familiar categories of illness and disability—congenital and acquired, diagnosis and prognosis, remission and relapse, temporarily able-bodied and 'illness, age, or accident'—are temporal; they are orientations in and to time, even though we rarely recognize or discuss them as such."[9] As a fixed future, cure imposes a linear narrative of progress on bodies and minds. The temporality of the early modern diseases that I trace here, which shift into visibility through symptoms of intermittent and uncertain duration, puts their disabling effects on view. Understanding disease as that which temporarily incapacitates or permanently alters a body, early modern concepts of sickness foreground the contingency of health.

This chapter considers what the "sick" body accomplishes on the stage, signifying through unelective movement such as a spasm or fit, or involuntary immobility such as a dead palsy. Engaging sickness, my argument works alongside important scholarship that has traced the preoccupation with the early modern theater as a site of infection. London's rhetorics of infection linked plague threats to theaters in diverse public texts such as edicts that prohibited playing and playgoing during plague outbreaks, civic reports of body counts, and jeremiads of divine punishment.[10] In Ellen MacKay's incisive reading, the early modern theater is fascinated by the "sudden, gripping, sickening, and ineradicable affliction that symptomizes the materiality of performance," which infects through "causeless efficacity."[11] Here, however, I take up uninfectious conditions that are decidedly happening to someone else. Beginning with medical discourse on epilepsy that demonstrates the difficulty of reading from symptomatic display back to cause, I then turn to theatrical staging. Across the texts I consider in this chapter—from physic discourse to Reginald Scot's work on witchcraft to brief examples from plays such as *The Woman Hater, Othello,* and *Hengist, King of Kent*—symptoms of sickness demonstrate how the early modern theater depends on disability to traffic in the bodily indistinguishability that constitutes the very limit of performance. The sick body that most self-evidently aligns disease and disability with the threatening power of theatrical action is the title character of Ben Jonson's *Volpone* (1606). Feigning throughout the play, Volpone suddenly experiences a fit of palsy in the trial scene; the actor who plays a role becomes vulnerable to an experience he thought he was feigning. Like the reported spectacle of Julius Caesar's epileptic fit, the example with which this book began, the theatrical doing of disability complicates theatrical seeing. *Volpone* troubles the distinction between a cramp and the imitation of a cramp.

This problem of witnessing reminds us that, in the theater, an actor's body is the very basis of theatrical signification. In a dramatic fiction, a gesture is legible within a semiotic system that refers the actor's movements to the character's action. Discussing the signifying work of the actor's body, Keir Elam observes that "even purely contingent factors, such as physiologically determined reflexes, are accepted as signifying units." As an example of this contingent signification, Elam quotes Groucho Marx's anecdote about noticing scratches on an actor's leg in a performance and then converting these marks into significant details about the character ("'at first we thought this had something to do with the plot and we waited for these scratches to come to life'"). The liveliness of the actor's body, Elam posits, means that "the audience starts with the assumption that every detail is an intentional sign and whatever cannot be related to the representation as such is converted into a sign of the actor's very reality—it is not, in any case, excluded from semiosis."[12] Any eccentricity of the actor's body, in other words, is understood to refer back to the character and is perceived as a meaningful feature in the dramatic fiction until proven otherwise. This emphasis on what the actor's body brings to dramatic character is at the heart of a disability critique of modern theatrical practice. Disabled actors are rarely cast for parts that do not specifically script disability, Carrie Sandahl argues, because modern Western theories of acting prize an actor's body that can be "neutral." This presumption of neutrality means that actors distinguished by physical difference are not cast because (it is claimed) "their impairments would detract from the playwright's or director's intent for a nondisabled character."[13] Disability oversignifies, and the disabled actor's "very reality" accrues to the dramatic character. When a disabled actor's distinctive body evinces involuntary movement or loss of control, the semiosis of the actor's body has the potential to scramble the distinction between what is happening to the actor and what is happening to the character. Involuntary actions, such as a shake or quiver, raise the question of *when* a movement becomes a gesture.

To be sure, the symptoms of tremors, palsies, and fits could also be considered textbook examples of "cripping up," when a nondisabled actor plays a disabled character.[14] The theater borrows signifiers that are the properties of certain bodies, facts of embodied particularity—which have historically resulted in disabled people being ostracized and excluded. In performance, a hyper-able actor employs the visible distinctiveness of these bodies, adopting a limp, using crutches, or donning a prosthetic hump, in order to exploit these signifiers as a special effect without regard for the embodied knowledge of people with disabilities. If, as M. Remi perceptively observes in a study of autistic rhetoric, "involuntarity is a project of dehumanization," the criterion of voluntarity is also at stake in performance.[15] The theater's demand for the actor's virtuosic action of epileptic fit or trembling body only accrues to the dramatic character if the actor can stop—if she can control the time of the fit.[16] Yet this important insight into modern acting does not fully comport with the early modern theater's conviction that the actor's body is never stable and that performance is a form of making with unpredictable results. As I have been arguing throughout this book, the early modern theater insists that performance is an "act executed," to borrow Gosson's phrase; in this chapter I consider how disabling performance operates as a fixing mechanism as much as an unfixing iterability.[17] Exposing a curative imaginary that demands voluntary control of the body, the early modern theater also calls into question the spectator's capacity to distinguish signifying actions. By formally illuminating the vulnerability of the actor to that which he performs, I suggest at the end of this chapter, the theater may even provoke the spectator to an unexpected recall of her own vulnerable self.

Diseases to Commodity: Recognizing Cause and Effect

The early modern theater's forays into staging a character with palsy, epilepsy, convulsions, or other states of uncontrollable bodily movement borrow from medical scrutiny. I open this section by first considering medical discourse focused on palsy and epilepsy, diseases defined by the uncertain temporality of their effects, and diseases in which the relation between cause and symptom appears especially contestable. Joshua Poole's entry on "Palsie" in his manual for English poets (my first epigraph to this chapter) elaborates effects ("trembling, shaking, quavering, quivering, unjointed, unsteadie, fainting, numme"), indexing a body that cannot be consciously governed.[18] Extraordinarily visible, these symptoms prompt questions about agency over the body.[19] Renaissance physicians inherit a mixed discourse from classical medical theory, which refers to epilepsy as the "divine malady" because the sudden unpredictability of the fit suggests a supernatural cause. The Hippocratic treatise on the falling sickness painstakingly debunks this view, noting that the "disease styled sacred comes from the same causes as others . . . so that there is no need to put the disease in a special class and to consider it more divine than the others; they are all divine and all human. Each has a nature and power of its own; none is hopeless or incapable of treatment. Most are cured by the same thing that caused them."[20] Epilepsy is just as subject to the application of medical knowledge as any other disease, an episteme that insists on natural rather than supernatural cause to regard the symptom as treatable. Epilepsy is a spectacular case, but its cause is like that of all diseases; it is a spectacular example of the rule, not the exception.

Renaissance medical discourse similarly explains such bodily symptoms by tracing the effects of such diseases back to their causes. Barrough, for instance, lists three possible causes for epilepsy: a "disease in the braine" related to humoral imbalance; "vapours and humors" that ascend to the brain from the stomach; and "a thing like unto a cold ayer, comming from some member, and creeping up to the braine," a rare effect of the environment (sig. C3r). Whether internal to the brain, internal to the body, or external to the body, all these causes result in effects that overtake the body, though they differ in frequency and duration. Patients "fall downe," are "plucked up," "snort," "tremble," and "turn round about," and the "peculiar signe of this disease is foming at the mouth" (sig. C3r). The symptoms are beyond the patient's control. The rest of his chapter, like the rest of his volume and the broader physic discourse, offers directives for cure that include bloodletting, diet restrictions, and purgatives. While these cures may help the patient to amend voluntary behavior, physic discourse also links symptomatic signification of the broader class of diseases to causes not as easily ameliorated. Palsy, further distinguished by "member" or "body," is often linked with gout, traceable to rich diet and overconsumption, as when Thomas Cogan finds "some that bee of a sound constitution by nature, doe yet through intemperancy so corrupt their complexion, that either they live not untill they be old, or else their old age is most fulsome and lothsome," a corruption that he connects specifically to court customs: "In this number chiefly be Courtiers, Lords, Ladies, Gentlemen, and Gentlewomen . . . for these commonly live not so long as the inferior sort."[21] Brought on by "intemperancy" and bad diet, the disease has unexpected coordinates, for the most vulnerable bodies are those whose wealth ensures access to epicurean luxury that renders them sicklier. Cure outstrips the medical domain, entering into the realm of social judgments that understand disease as a consequence that reveals a person's action. Palsy and gout offer an opportunity to critique the patient's choices for ill health—like syphilis jokes that read a missing nose as an encounter with the French pox, or find in the velvet patch of the courtier a useful cover for an unsightly lesion as well as a fashionable accessory.

Another thread runs through discussions of these diseases, too: irritation at public disregard for professional diagnosis. A sermon by John Trapp on a biblical account of healing, which dwells on the ill effects of leprosy, interprets "the palsy, or as some say, the Epilepsy," as evidence for divine power. Trapp embeds a distinctly Protestant dig in commentary on a biblical verse: "For the Priests," he writes, "to enrich themselves, perswaded the superstitious people, that this disease, as being suddain, hidden, and for most part incurable, was an immediate hand of God, and could be cured by none but Priests."[22] In the scriptural context, "Priest" is a Jewish religious figure, but Trapp's next line considers the dubious value of verse charms prescribed by a "French Mountebank," a Catholic resonance that allows him to critique the practice of magical healing. Using "palsy" interchangeably with "epilepsy," Trapp pauses in the exposition of divine healing to condemn the self-interest of those who claim that a cure requires supernatural rather than medical treatment. In the causative imaginary of early modern medicine, to adapt Kafer's phrase, these diseases prompt suspicion that the cure may not be referred to medical knowledge. Physician John Webster's discussion of "the efficacy of Words or Charms" for healing laments that "the common people, if they chance to have any sort of the Epilepsie, Palsie, Convulsions or the like, do presently perswade themselves that they are bewitched, fore-spoken, blasted, fairy-taken, or haunted with some evil spirit."[23] "Epilepsie, Palsie, Convulsions," he suggests, are especially liable to suspicion of "suddain" and "hidden" causes, because the symptoms suggest a powerful external force acts on the body of the patient. With "or the like," the sentence trails off into similitude, gesturing to other diseases equally defined by temporal fluctuation and loss of control.

These highly visible symptoms are a contested object for medical knowledge that attempts to assert authority over the phenomenological experience of the patient. It might be surprising to hear Webster, better known for his ardent (and controversial) embrace of natural magic and Paracelsian medicine, disavow the assertion of occult causes. Yet when he discusses the common attribution of epilepsy to divine cause, he is firmly in the camp of the unmagical, fuming that "if you should by plain reasons shew them, that they are deceived, and that there is no such matter, but that it is a natural disease, say what you can they shall not believe you, but account you a Physician of small or no value, and whatsoever you do to them, it shall hardly do any good at all, because of the fixedness of their depraved and prepossessed imagination" (sigs. 2T2r–v). Rejecting the "natural" origin of the disease, the patient's "imagination" attributes the symptom to a cause impervious to medical intervention. The "fixedness" of the patient's mind is the impediment to the physician's practice. Thus, Webster recommends making use of a placebo effect, instructing the reader to "indulge" the patient's "fancy" and "seem to concur" with their worries, to "hang any insignificant thing about their necks" with an assurance that it is a magical charm, and then finally to "give them that which is proper to eradicate the cause of their disease." This practice, he asserts from experience, will "cure" patients in "great numbers" (sig. 2T2v). This response underscores the stakes of the epistemological uncertainty of the sudden and public effects of such a disease.[24] The association with occult forces—like Richard Gloucester's accusation of witchcraft in chapter 1, or the narrator's hesitation over the curse that binds the hog-faced infant in chapter 4—attributes physical anomaly to an unknown cause. Symptoms of epileptic fits and dead palsies prompt a similar concern about involuntary loss of agency and individual will.

Webster's discussion of "supposed witchcraft" gestures to the broader discourse that expounded medical knowledge to contest certain beliefs about occult causality. Influential texts such as Reginald Scot's *The Discoverie of Witchcraft* (1584), Samuel Harsnett's *A Declaration of Egregious Popish Impostures* (1603), and Edward Jorden's *A Briefe Discourse of a Disease Called the Suffocation of the Mother* (1603)—the last written by a physician after testifying at a witchcraft trial—foregrounded medical expertise to diagnose madness, hysteria, and other diseases, epilepsy among them, so as to convince readers that such conditions could be treated and cured.[25] Inheriting classical models of medical knowledge, and leaning heavily on gender stereotypes about women, these texts nonetheless attempt to discredit the attribution of inexplicable illness to the exercise of malevolent supernatural power. Scot notes, for example, that communities presume witchcraft when "children are visited with diseases that vex them strangely: as apoplexies, epilepsies, convulsions, hot fevers, wormes, &c."[26] While the end of the sentence makes space for any number of vexing diseases, the first few examples should not surprise us: apoplexy, epilepsy, and convulsions are all diseases whose symptoms grip the body in volatile display. Scot blames both "unskillful Physitians" and "ignorant Parents" (sig. C4v) who leap to the conclusion that one of these immobilizing diseases is the effect of a witch's exertion of voluntary control, a power indexed by the ability to incapacitate others.

Scot devotes most of the volume to debunking misperceptions about the agency witches are presumed to possess over the bodies of others, and he pinpoints spectatorship as the faulty instrument of ill reason. Book 13 of *Discoverie of Witchcraft* associates the text's professed topic with dozens of examples of apparent magic, in order to demonstrate the fallibility of a gaze that cannot be trusted to decipher bodily action. Alongside healing stones and perspective glasses, Scot considers "illusions" that "proceedeth of fraud and deception of sight" but turn out to be "counterfeit actions" (sig. 2B2r) and "miracles wrought by Juglers" (sig. 2C1r) rather than magical cures. Scot demonstrates that what looks like the exercise of occult force is actually an expression of a different temporality of cause and effect. "To make one dance naked," he explains, requires making a "poor Boy confederate with you," who will unclothe and "seem" to "shake, stamp, and cry"—or at least "begin" to do so, "if you can procure none to go so far" (sig. 2D2r). Scot demystifies the appearance of magical power by disclosing the loophole of imperceptible cause. You may think you perceive a possessed body that trembles and convulses, Scot tells his readers, but this spectacle resolves into a poor boy hired in advance to perform a fit that only seems spontaneous.

As a "most notable execution by this art" (sig. 2D7r), Scot describes a framing device that turns an actor's body into the illusion of a dead body, a spectacle that turns out to be a combination of actors' bodies and a property that transforms them. After discussing displays that hinge on the perception of grievous bodily harm, with examples from knife eating to eye gouging (and the theatrical properties that make such tricks possible), he explains the "decollation of John Baptist," in which the performer appears "to cut off ones Head, and to lay it in a Platter" (sig. 2D7r). The full-page plate that follows reveals the frame that transforms the bodies of two boys into the single character of John the Baptist, with his head on a platter at one end of the table, and headless body at the other end (figure 5.1). The plate depicts the "forme of the planks," the wooden board made of two planks with a hole at either end (in an overhead view that would not be visible to spectators), and then "the order of the action, as it is to be shewed" (sig. 2D8v), depicting the trick in progress: one performer sits under the board with his head through one hole, as if on a platter, while the other boy lies on the board, with his head hidden under the table. Fixed into place by the form of the table, the two bodies create the spectacle of a single beheaded body.

Scot's account explains the cause of such a bodily effect, capturing the framing device and the "order of the action" that converts the actors into the tableau. To "make the sight more dreadful," he notes special effects including smoke in the nostrils and blood sprinkled on the face of the boy whose head is visible, so that "the head presently will appear stark dead; if the boie set his countenance accordingly" and the display will "astonish the beholders" (sig. 2D7r). The property transforms the bodies of performers into the end point of the display, one that is temporary (indeed, Scot notes that they must not

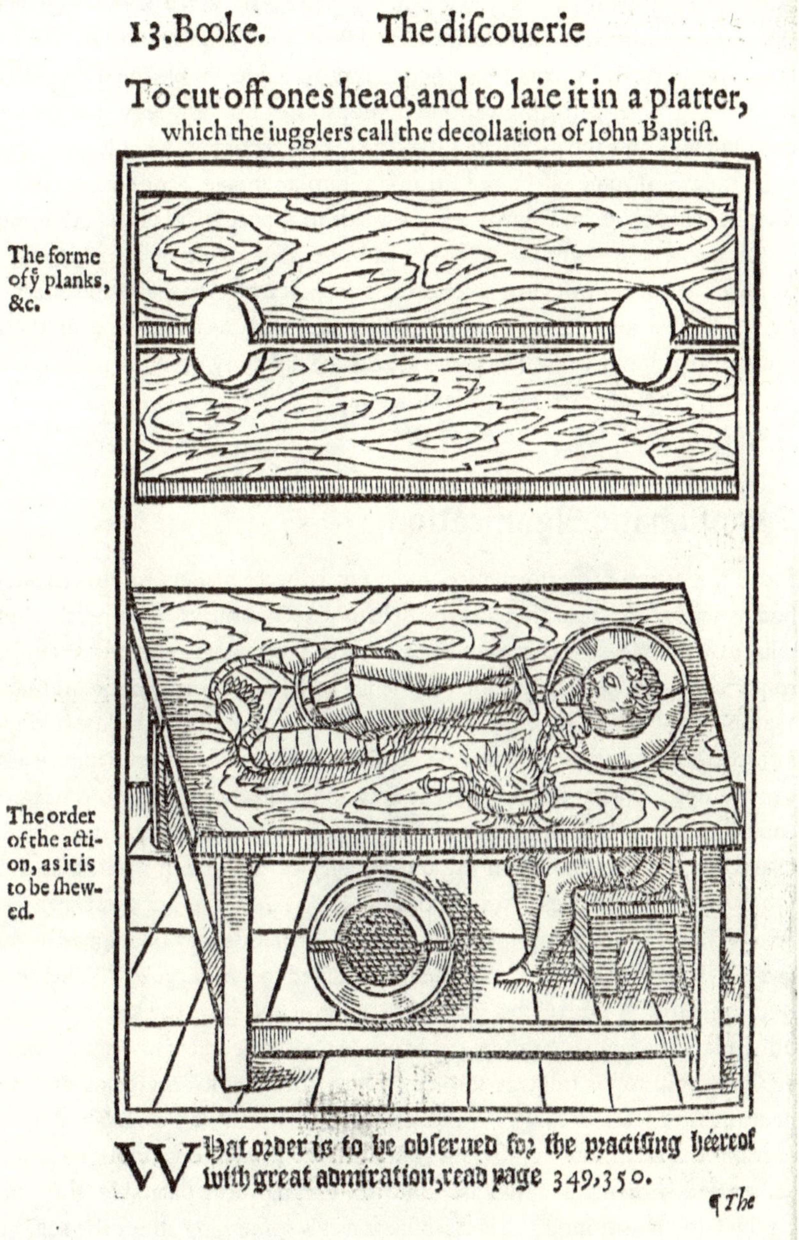

13.Booke.   The discouerie

To cut off ones head, and to laie it in a platter,
which the iugglers call the decollation of Iohn Baptist.

The forme of y̌ planks, &c.

The order of the action, as it is to be shewed.

What order is to be obserued for the practising héereof with great admiration, read page 349, 350.

¶ The

FIGURE 5.1. Reginald Scot, *The Discouerie of Witchcraft . . . verie necessarie to be knowne* (London, 1584), illustration facing p. 353. Call#: STC 21864, copy 1. Used by permission of the Folger Shakespeare Library under a Creative Commons Attribution-ShareAlike 4.0 International License.

"suffer the company to staie too long in the place" [sig. 2D7v]). Flinging open the curtain to reveal the actors in the middle of their representation, Scot extracts the spectacle from its enactment in time to render visible the show otherwise inaccessible to the viewer. He demonstrates not only how the trick is done but also how the prosthetics stabilize the perception of what is seen. Taking a theatrical stage effect and turning it into an image, Scot comments on the ease with which bodies may even be made to appear "stark dead." Although this example may seem like a far cry from the debunking of a supernatural cause for an epileptic fit, Scot associates them on the basis of cause and effect—the thing that appears true may be explained with recourse to a different cause or temporality of effect—and asserts the difficulty, even the pleasurable difficulty, of reading the spectacle of a body.

Symptomatic Signification

Scot's discussion of performance, meant to educate readers to discern such bodily illusions as tricks, hints at the deligh of such displays. The theater capitalizes on the pleasure that Scot's text attempts to foreclose: astonishment in response to a spectacle without knowledge of its mechanics. In the dramatic examples to which I now turn, I consider how symptoms of sickness hinge interpretation on the spectator's perception, foregrounding performance as a site of unpredictable signification. As durational effects, such symptoms both complicate theatrical meaning within a play, as they are exploited by dramatic characters, and comment on the temporality of the fiction itself. Like Falstaff's intent to "turn diseases to commodity" (1.2.242) in Shakespeare's *The Second Part of King Henry the Fourth*, such impairments may be feigned at the level of the character or, if unfeigned, resignified to a new cause.[27] When Falstaff exclaims, "A pox of this gout! Or a gout of this pox! For the one or the other plays the rogue with my great toe" (237–39), he refers his injury not to an illness, but to his military service ("I have the wars for my color, and my pension shall seem the more reasonable" [240–41]). Falstaff's explanation re-narrates the limp, sourced to gout (associated with overconsumption) or pox (associated with venereal disease), into something more palatable. Working on the basic presumption that disability reveals something about the self, his offers a different fiction for cause. Reverse engineering the reading from body to symptom, Falstaff posits an etiology for his disabling that works to his advantage.

A palsy suggests that the effects of aging are out of a character's control, but does not map straightfowardly onto a character's volition or agency. When

Lucio stands in for the duke in Beaumont and Fletcher's *The Woman Hater* (1607), he reviews the trappings of authority he must assume before his petitioners arrive and finds that the "things there are to be observ'd" (5.1.12) comprise "gownes and caps" (37) and "new made words to scatter" (34–35) and also new techniques of corporeality. He has "learn'd to write a bad hand, that the Readers may take paines for it" (39–40) and orders that his servants "give out I have the palsie" (41), an explanation of the shaky handwriting that substantiates his age.[28] The rumor of palsy confirms the seniority expected of a duke and the diet associated with such status, and Lucio's mention of palsy allows the gentleman a disparaging aside ("'twere better though, if you had [42]). When his gentleman inquires whether "your Lordship hath no hope of the gout?" (48) and Lucio disappoints with "Uh, little sir, since the paine in my right foote left me" (49), the gentleman warns him: "'T will be some scandale to your wisdome" (50). Palsy and gout are signs of age and the conspicuous consumption wealth affords, a characterization strategy that conflates the physical process of decay with a chosen lifestyle of overconsumption.

For the aged character, time's degrading effects may betray the self, a comic possibility that works against the character's own assertions. Thomas Tomkis's *Albumazar* (1615) jokes about the sexagenarian Pandolfo, "amorous as youthfull May, / and gray as January" (sig. B2v), who intends to marry Flavia, who is sixteen.[29] Tossing away his cane, the "poore prop of feeblenesse and age," Pandolfo claims no need to:

> walke with such sires
> As with cold palsies shake away their strength,
> And loose their legges with curelesse gouts.
>
> (sig. B3r)

Separating himself from the palsies and gouts of his peers, Pandolfo refuses to accept the "curelesse" physical state at which he has in fact arrived. No new young love could recover him—and the young woman he woos in the play would not wish to. The extreme age gap makes his passion laughable as a gulf between the character's sense of himself and his actual physical state. Pandolfo's state invites risibility when his body (predictably) betrays him with tremoring weakness despite his protestation. And, beyond the dramatic fiction, theatrical enactment of the role offers a comic invitation for the boy actor who may heighten his imitation of the tremors and incapacity.

However, even when the play is sympathetic to a palsy caused by aging, the formal illegibility of the symptom is up for debate. For example, when Jack Cade and his rebels confront Lord Saye in Shakespeare's *The Second Part of Henry the Sixth*, Saye contends that "long sitting to determine poor men's causes / Hath made me full of sickness and diseases" (4.7.86–87), and then, when Dick the Butcher asks why he "quiver[s]" (90), Saye responds, "The palsy, and not fear, provokes me" (91), a defense premised on the impairment age entails.[30] Saye avers that such movements—trembling, quivering, nodding, and jerking of his head—are involuntary. He is not afraid; he simply cannot help his motions. Cade, however, interprets them as signifiers of voluntary rebellion: "Nay, he nods at us as who should say 'I'll be even with you.' I'll see if his head will stand steadier on a pole or no. Take him away, and behead him" (4.7.92–94). The cruel joke that takes Saye's shudders for pretense, as if his body speaks louder than any discursive appeal, helps to doom Cade's rebellion in the arc of audience sympathy. Saye's disabling demonstrates the power relations in the scene rather than clarifying whether his trembling is caused by fear or age or refusal. The exchange underscores the ease with which Cade's judgment makes bodily evidence signify any way he pleases, for even the interpretation of his own body does not belong to Saye himself. This moment participates in the play's broader examination of bodily scrutiny, from the discovery of Simpcox's feigned disability to the scrutiny of Gloucester's corpse; here, the shaking arm or quaking body appears to disclose a character's internal state without his volition.[31] Paradoxically, the play employs Saye's symptom as both the truest sign of the self and the absolute expression of his lack of agency.

These examples use palsy to experiment with apparently involuntary movement—shaky hand, gouty foot, or nodding head—that prompts debates about cause. A display of epilepsy elevates the signification of the part to total incapacitation of the character's body, and the fit that overtakes a dramatic character stops the clock of plot. Thomas Middleton's *Hengist, King of Kent; or, The Mayor of Queenborough* (1620), one of Middleton's two "most popular, most noted, most quoted works," features a brief episode of incapacitation, a male character's epileptic fit.[32] This event could almost be a blip in the play, were it not for the fit's duration, which extends the scene. The Saxons have just arrived in Britain under the command of Hengist, and Hersus, a Saxon lord, reveals in an aside that he is love with Roxena, Hengist's daughter. Learning that Roxena has followed them from Germany and that the Britons' king, Vortiger, is smitten, Hersus foresees this news as the end of his secret affair with Roxena. When Hengist inquires of Hersus what troubles him, Hersus responds:

> A kind of grief about these times o'th'moon still.
> I feel a pain like a convulsion,
> A cramp at heart, I know not what name fits it.
>
> (2.4.194–96)[33]

Symptom of both anatomy and passion, the "cramp" becomes a physical expression of grief and pain that Hersus cannot name. And "fits" turns out to be a pun; when Vortiger and Roxena enter, arms intertwined, Hersus believes that Hengist will give Roxena to Vortiger and after he exclaims, "O that will do't, 'twill do't" (221), something happens. While editors typically insert a stage direction (in the Oxford edition: "[*He faints*]"), Hersus's action is more ambiguous, for Vortiger's response ("What ails our friend? Look to him" [222]) does not clarify the details of the spectacle. This presentational action—whatever it may be—suspends plot development, stalling the progress of political negotiations since all the characters react to Hersus. Suddenly apparent to spectators onstage and offstage, the disabling fit is more like a theatrical event than a discrete property of the character.

Furthermore, the scene requires a quick-witted spectator to narrate the uncertain display as a recognizable medical condition. Roxena transforms the event through diagnosis, explaining:

> O, 'tis his epilepsy, I know it well,
> I helped him once in Germany. Comes't again?
> A virgin's right hand stroked upon his heart
> Gives him ease straight, but't must be a pure virgin,
> Or else it brings no comfort.
>
> (222–26)

Identifying Hersus's "ail[ing]" as an epileptic fit, Roxena turns his presentational action into a narrative that forms the history of this character ("Comes't again?"). Diagnosing him, Roxena appeals to a distinctly nonmedical cure: stroking him with her "virgin's right hand," she can "ease" his condition. The erotic possibility of this cure for epilepsy produces a virginity test for herself (lost on none of her onstage spectators, for Vortiger completes her line, marveling, "What a task / She puts upon herself unurged for purity" [226–27]). This venture, however, draws her into a joint performance from which she cannot escape. Hersus's fit is feigned, and having implicated herself in the cure, she is enmeshed in the disabling action. The rest of the scene splits Hersus and Roxena from the rest of the onstage audience, as the lovers accuse and plead with each other, while it appears that Hersus experiences the fit and Roxena labors to effect a cure. Hersus refuses to stop feigning epilepsy ("I will not stand on purpose, though I could, / But fall still to disgrace thee" [236–37] and "All this art shall not make me find my legs" [243]) even though Roxena now depends on his recovery to appear a virgin ("I prithee, wilt thou willfully confound me?" [244]). Their exchange is often marked by editors as asides, but no one else speaks in this part of the scene; even the most powerful figures are stuck, waiting out the fit that has immobilized Hersus. After uttering a final threat that yokes dissembled disability with sexual violence ("But if thou ever fail'st me, I will fall, / And thou shalt never get me up again" [247–48]), Hersus regains his feet and Roxena concludes, "See, my lord, / A poor maid's work. The man may pass for health now" (249–50). Executing epilepsy's show as a disabling event, Hersus creates the opportunity to hold private conference with Roxena in front of the governing patriarchal authorities. He turns Roxena's exercise of cure into his own power to signify, an opportunity available because he feigns, rather than experiences, the fit. The character as actor can "fall still" out of volition, controlling the timing of his act of feigning. Yet even the feigned fit introduces a split between the laboring actor and the apparently insensible character and requires a narrative of diagnosis to transform the display into recognizable sickness.

When the epileptic fit is not feigned by a character, though it is feigned by an actor, the play subjects the dramatic character to an event that he cannot perceive. In Shakespeare's *Othello*, Othello's epileptic fit accomplishes both an apparent revelation of character and a horrifying demonstration of the spectator's diagnostic power to narrate the incapacitated figure. In the opening scene of act 4, after Iago has provoked him, Othello responds with a long speech act that concludes:

> I tremble at it. Nature would not invest herself in such shadowing passion without some instruction. It is not words that shakes me thus—Pish! Noses, ears, and lips? Is't possible?—Confess?—Handkerchief?—O devil!
> [*He*] *falls in a trance.*
>
> (4.1.39–43)[34]

Othello's language repeats, splinters, unspools. His exclamations fragment into single words that reflect Iago's prompting ("handkerchief," "confess," "lips") and into verbs that reflect his physical state ("I tremble" and "shakes me thus"), culminating in a stage description that reflects the actor's presentational work: he "falls in a trance." Iago waits onstage, exulting to himself, "My medicine works!" (45). The fit—whether Othello is still trembling, or writhing, or otherwise shaking—continues through the entrance of Cassio, who presumably gestures to the prone figure, for Iago responds that Othello experiences "epilepsy" (50), and suggests that Iago "rub him about the temples" (53). Iago deploys medical knowledge to authenticate the fit, explaining that this is a "second fit" (51), which must take its course, or else "he foams at mouth, and by and by / Breaks out to savage madness" (54–55). When Othello recovers, Iago narrates this fit back to him as a "passion" (77) and an "ecstasy" (79), a temporary absence from the self. Othello himself cites the "shadowing passion" induced by Nature, arising from his suppositions about Desdemona's guilt. He understands his own trembling as somatic proof of Iago's claim and reads this effect back to a cause. Meanwhile, Iago has turned the "trance" into a series of diagnoses that convert the disabling into a truth about Othello's person. Disability accrues social significance far beyond medical contexts as the structure of the scene encourages the audience to understand the fit as evidence of Othello's incapacitation.

Critics have typically taken this scene to index Othello's disintegrating mental state, arguing that the play prompts sympathy for the character's vulnerability.[35] Or, by contrast, they read this fit as a metaphor for subjection, emphasizing Iago's exercise of power in the scene.[36] In Justin Shaw's perceptive reading of this scene, "coupled with Iago's interpretation, Cassio's surveillance of Othello's trance disables and racializes him."[37] I note how the scene's scripted indignity employs the Othello actor himself, in the labor of actively engaging in the character's fit, to ratify Iago's racist narrative. Making Othello subject to a bodily vulnerability he can neither choose nor control, the play both marginalizes the titular character while he remains onstage and compels visible effort from the actor. And the "trance" goes on for a long time, far beyond the printed stage direction. Such an event is like other presentational actions that foreground the actor's body—a dance, a fight, a song, a kiss—except for the fact that the epileptic fit is about who a character is, not just what a character does. Let me underscore the double-edged work of this theatrical display, which splits character from actor: the epileptic fit allows the theater to produce an experience inaccessible to the *character* in the dramatic fiction, who has no awareness during the fit, while it simultaneously demands the *actor*'s virtuosic display of skill.

At first glance, the range of examples I have just offered appear to accord with Peter Womack's generative formulation of theatrical signification, in which "acting the text—or, better, *playing* it—randomizes the relationship of verbal or visual signs to their expected referents," producing both "a corrupting inauthenticity" as well as "a euphoric liberation of the signifier."[38] Womack reads Volpone's performance of sickness (to which I will turn shortly) as the example of this display: his "representation" is a lie and his "performance" is a carnivalesque celebration of the capacity to play at anything he wishes.[39] Sickness, Womack continues, is an example of theatrical signification at its most dynamic: "On the stage there is no necessary difference between the symptoms of a 'real' disease and those of a simulated one. The one is worth the other—carrying the same meanings and producing the same effects."[40] In his compelling account, acting unyokes the actor's bodily properties, to (temporarily) replace them with other properties, and the imitation of sickness, like any other performed bodily state, signifies as much as the actual state of sickness. I want to suggest, however, that in the early modern conceptions, sickness is precisely a problem for the distinction between real and simulated bodily experience. The logic of theatricality that Womack spells out so clearly is challenged by the early modern conviction that imitation cannot simply be concluded at will.

In earlier chapters I noted the antitheatrical polemics and theatrical anecdotes that worry over the role's deformation of the actor's body. Here I turn briefly to Michel de Montaigne's essay "How a Man Should Not Counterfeit to be Sicke." Montaigne assembles an exhibit of counterfeiters who adopt poses of bodily infirmity and are then unpleasantly surprised when they get stuck in the pretense. He cites Martial's relation of a courtier who (as John Florio puts it in his 1603 translation of Montaigne's work) "fained to be troubled with the goute" and so "caused his legges to bee ointed and swathed, and lively counterfeted the behaviour and countenance of a goutie man." He then remembers a story from Appian of a man who, fleeing Rome, disguises himself and "counterfet[s] blindnes in one eye" with "plaister" that acts as a "maske" over his eye.[41] What these examples have in common is the strangely transformative effect of the thing feigned. The faker of gout learns that "in the end fortune did him the favour to make him goutie indeede," and the counterfeiter "found that under that maske he had altogether lost the sight" (sig. 2L6v) of his eye. Toward the end of the essay he adduces the example that "*Plinie* reports of one, who dreaming in his sleepe, that he was blinde, awaking the next morning, was found to be starke blinde, having never had any precedent sickenes," which Montaigne credits to how "the power of imagination may very well further such things" (sig. 2M1r). In addition to "fortune" as a cause that makes the feigner experience a real effect, Montaigne offers several other explanations for why these transformations of the body might occur: in the first instance, "idlenes, together with the warmth of the medicaments and swathing, might very well drawe some goutie humor into the legge of *Martials* goutie fellow" (sig. 2M1r), and in the second, "it may be the action of his sight was weakned, having so long continued without exercise and the visuall vertue was wholy converted into the other eie" (sig. 2L6v). Enumerating possible causes for transformation that range from the material properties required for feigning to imagination's power, Montaigne emphasizes this point: feigned effects may become real ones.

Notably, these examples are of ordinary people who find it expedient to counterfeit a disability, only to be overtaken later by unexpected results. Montaigne therefore lands on a general principle: avoid feigning bodily difference.

He affirms that "mothers have great reason to chide their children when they counterfet to be blind with one eye, crompt-backt, squint eyed, or lame, and such other deformities of the body; for, besides that the body thus tender may easily receive some ill custome, I knowe not how, it seemeth that fortune is glad to take us at our word; And I have heard divers examples of some who have fallne sicke in very deede, because they had purposed to faine sickenes" (sig. 2M1r). This catalogue of disability collates many "deformities" alongside sickness, and each of the examples threatens to mar the body permanently. Falling "sicke in very deed" becomes the fit punishment for choosing "to faine sickenes"; the body's "tender" materiality responds to the formal shaping of such a "counterfeit" experience, and the result fixes the body in the very falsehood it adopts. To counterfeit being *sick*—the essay's title heading, under which Montaigne includes gout and blindness, as well as the general category of deformity—is different from counterfeiting other properties of the self. The blindness sticks to the man fleeing Rome, although the more general disguise of clothing does not. Feigned sickness produces an effect without a cause, a valuable ruse if you want a believable excuse for avoiding court, but a stunt that entails immense risk. In Montaigne's examples, the effect may reverse engineer a cause that, in turn, produces a different temporality of transformation. Even if you are not a professional actor, he suggests, counterfeiting may hold for a longer duration than you wish, becoming a truth of embodied experience. As Jonson himself observes (in the excerpt that is the second epigraph to this chapter), the distinctive speech that begins as imitation may become a "habit" and then second "nature."[42]

This principle of imitation is fuzzy on how long it takes before counterfeiting grips the body. Yet the reproducibility of theatrical performance may be vulnerable to the temporality of theatrical action, and, in the reading of *Volpone* to which I now turn, the play experiments with this distinction between actor and character. Ultimately, I am suggesting that the early modern stage's ventures with "simulated" diseases derive their ontological charge from the possibility of collapsing such a distinction between real and imitated diseases and—conversely—from the possibility of snapping the actor out of the thing he imitates. One theatrical risk, to follow Montaigne, is that the counterfeiting transforms the actor, beyond the point of volition. At the other extreme, the theatrical risk (or delight) of counterfeiting sickness, especially in the physically demanding examples I have surveyed, is equally possible and far more likely: the gap between what the actor is doing and what the character is experiencing becomes so pronounced that the spectator starts observing the actor who is shaking on the stage as a body, not a character.[43] Either the thing imitated takes effect, or the fiction of imitation disappears from view altogether. These moments of disabling, in the form of spectacular displays of the sick body, offer high dividends for the early modern theater even as—or perhaps, precisely because—they threaten to yank the curtain from the whole edifice of the theater's formal relay between actor and character, and between script and personation.

Feigning Sickness in *Volpone*

Ben Jonson's *Volpone* appears to be a sustained exercise in the lucrative performance of faked disability. The play's opening acrostic tells us that Volpone "feigns sick" (line 1), and we watch him appear to be deathly ill in order to trick the stream of "clients" (1.1.76) who, hoping to inherit his wealth, parade to his sickbed with extravagant gifts.[44] Volpone's delight in the theatrics of the scam inspired one early strand of criticism to interpret his exuberant performance as evidence for the play's moral lesson condemning greed.[45] Since Jonas Barish's magisterial argument for Jonson's stage loathing, *Volpone* has looked like a condemnation of acting, of a piece with Jonson's embrace of print as an alternative to the fleeting delights of the theater's scrum of incapable actors and inattentive audiences.[46] A second strand of criticism observed that Volpone's relish for acting new and impossible parts is entirely the point, since his self-imposed impostures go far beyond the wealth he accrues.[47] Volpone's "glory" (1.1.30) is in the joy of ongoing deception, not in the gifts but the gulling, "more in the cunning purchase of my wealth, / Than in the glad possession" (31–32). His motivation for this elaborate personation is proof of either Jonson's resistance to or revelry in the theatrical pleasure of an actor's skilled transformations.

Volpone's obvious counterfeiting of illness has also been understood as a kind of cripping up. Drawing on Tobin Siebers's explication of "disability drag," Lauren Coker calls Volpone's performance a "metatheatrical staging of disability drag" and argues that "Volpone's lack of legitimate disability at the play's outset—alongside the overt performance of an ailing body—undercuts the perception of disability as a material and lived bodily condition."[48] I share the ethical impulse of this critique of the actor whose resulting performance diminishes the embodied knowledge of disability as a lived identity. Understood from the perspective of early modern theatrical practice, however, the invocation of legitimacy is complicated by the materiality of theatrical representation. Rather than upholding a theory of the theater as only ever interpretive, understanding performance as the mere reconstruction of a script, *Volpone* suggests that performance may grip the actor's body in unexpected effects that go far beyond a single cause. To put it differently, the play demonstrates that the criterion of authenticity cannot account for the intermittent temporality of effect associated with diseases known by their uncertain symptoms or for the susceptibility of the actor's own vulnerable form. When Volpone is put on display as legal proof in the play's first trial scene, when he is all body and no language, he is suddenly unable to control the terms of his feigning. Reorienting the witnessing of feigned illness from within the dramatic fiction, theatrical performance returns to the spectator's own embodiment and awareness of her body's volatility in time.

From the opening of the play, Jonson aligns us with Volpone's feigning, as we watch the title character rush to assume the properties that his act requires. When Voltore, the first visitor, arrives, Volpone commands Mosca, his servant and co-conspirator, "Fetch me my gown, / My furs, and night-caps" (1.2.84–85), assembling his costume at a furious pace. He repeats these demands in the effort to prepare for the role ("Give me my furs" [97] and "My caps, my caps, good Mosca" [114]). After Volpone has donned these items, Mosca reminds him that the disguise requires further prosthetics ("Stay, sir, your ointment for your eyes" [115]), before Volpone settles into his performance:

'Tis well. My pillow now, and let him enter.
Now, my feigned cough, my phthisic, and my gout,
My apoplexy, palsy, and catarrh,
Help, with your forcèd functions, this my posture,
Wherein this three year I have milked their hopes.
He comes; I hear him. Uh! uh! uh! uh! Oh—
(123–28)

Volpone's "Now" invokes the illnesses and their "forcèd functions," or faked symptoms, that are required for his "posture," the term that comprises both the gesture of illness he adopts and the scheme of artifice he runs from his sickbed. Volpone's enumeration as he prepares for his first visitor turns "sick" from one thing into many: cough, phthisic, gout, apoplexy, palsy, catarrh. This catalogue of performed recrudescence is neither a single illness nor an indeterminate malaise, but a range of symptoms, from the shakiness of palsy to the hacking cough of phthisic, or tuberculosis. Volpone's "sick" body is not an abstraction but a bundling of specificities, not merely additive but exponential. Each term of diagnosis proves just as specific as the stage properties that he employs, from the ointment for his eyes to his "sick pillow," with different symptoms, ranging from chronic to acute, that work at different speeds. His performance requires verbal utterances, for the repeated "Uh, uh, uh" and drawn-out "Oh"—each perhaps a cough, a wheeze, a groan—equivocate between speech acts and stage directions. These sonic effects are presentational actions that accrue to representation; like a hiccup, they trouble the line between voluntary action and involuntary reflex. Volpone's "posture," that is, adds up to more than the sum of stage properties and actor's body.

These scenes, furthermore, test Volpone's capacity to counterfeit loss of vitality over time and require a confederate to narrate and corroborate his intensifying symptoms as his posture of illness progresses to debilitation. Mosca stage-manages the interactions between Volpone and his visitors. For his first visitor, Voltore, Volpone demonstrates his condition through sonic punctuation: "I feel me going—uh! uh! uh! uh! / I am sailing to my port—uh! uh! uh! uh!" (1.3.28–29). The next scene's gull, Corbaccio, requires only the show of illness, because the aging Corbaccio's own deafness and palsy (as if he is *Albumazar*'s Pandolfo recast) demonstrate a self-deception born not of love but of desire for profit. Volpone draws the audience into his performance, confiding through an aside that Corbaccio is "indeed more impotent, / Than this [Volpone] can feign to be" (1.4.2–3). Mosca narrates Volpone's condition, expounding on Corbaccio's query about "apoplex" (35) with vivid descriptions of Volpone's physical state ("His speech is broken, and his eyes are set" [38], "His mouth / Is ever gaping" [41–42]; "A freezing numbness stiffens all his joints" [43]). Each scene is a new opportunity to improve the show of impotence. By the time Corvino, the final suitor, arrives, Mosca has reapplied Volpone's makeup ("Another bout, sir, with your eyes" [1.4.162]) and ratcheted up the verbal production of his illness. Mosca describes Volpone as bereft of every sensation but the crudest touch: "Not dead, sir, but as good" (1.5.4); "He cannot understand, his hearing's gone" (15); "Put it into his hand; 'tis only there / He apprehends. He has his feeling yet" (18–19). This acting is inaction, for Volpone must not respond as Mosca's description grows more derogatory with every phrase, urging Corvino to join him in denouncing the insensible figure. With further scrutiny of his body, Volpone's acting—what Maggie Vinter incisively discusses as the "posture of inactivity" by which he "put[s] on a spectacle of the unspectacular"—requires increasing immobility.[49] Unlike the previous examples of immobilizing illness I have noted, Volpone willingly submits to being put on view, his symptoms described by Mosca as he performs. For Volpone, being "sick" is a form of theatrical making, a series of actions that are each more demanding than the previous enactment.

The play, which devotes a significant portion of the fourth act to Volpone's trial, prompts the question: Can legal protocols for witnessing a sick body detect feigning? Volpone takes his sickbed imposture public before Venice's court, where Jonson has transformed the Avocatori from attorneys to judges. Bonario, the son of one of Volpone's suitors, seeks justice for Volpone's attempted rape of Celia, Corvino's wife, and he turns to the Avocatori, who are charged to determine the truth of Volpone's "strange impostures" (4.5.18). Against critics who read the Avocatori as compromised from the outset—"corrupt" and "obtuse magistrates"—Frances Teague convincingly argues that playgoers would have expected them to be "sound judges" who determine the trial's outcome on the virtues of the evidence.[50] In Lorna Hutson's virtuosic reading of Jonson's plotting, his trial scenes involve the audience by revealing the logic that shapes "accidents" into judgments. As Hutson writes: "The audience *has seen everything*" and is therefore ethically implicated in the judgment too.[51] The trial scene distills the processes of shaping evidence into competing narratives, as Voltore (acting as Volpone's lawyer) and Bonario both appeal to the court to judge the capacity of Volpone's body. In Katharine Eisaman Maus's brilliant discussion of impotence trials, material evidence of bodily dysfunction literally cannot be shown and therefore the body offers an "unstable limit beyond which an intense, imperfect scrutiny, whether theatrical or juridical, cannot proceed."[52] The trial scene, in other words, invites confidence in the legal authorities, foregrounds the problem of discriminating insight, and withholds full visual confirmation of Volpone's body. My reading draws on these insights but roots the shock of the trial scene's judgment—the inability to determine Volpone's feigning—in the problem of perception. While the legal procedure demands a fixed "now," this limited spectatorship cannot account for diseases that shift in and out of visibility, or for the duration of performance when the character never moves out of the act. *Volpone*'s cynical take on witnessing renders the claim of ability unfalsifiable, for the trial suggests that even skilled judges cannot, in the time-limited space of legal judgment, comprehend for the temporal logic of illness. Nor can they fail to be implicated in their interpretation of ability and embodiment.

The court transforms Volpone's appearance into legal evidence to determine whether or not he is feigning this physical state. Bonario "beseech[es]" (4.5.16) the court that the absent Volpone "may be forced to come, that your grave eyes / May bear strong witness of his strange impostures" (17–18). Bonario's plea presumes the self-evidence of Volpone's body, as if appearance is its own testimony, and he convinces the Avocatori of the necessity of scrutiny. Even though Voltore protests that Volpone "is not able to endure the air" (20), the Avocatori demand his presence, with "Bring him" and "We will see him" (21). In the following scene, when Volpone is carried into the courtroom, the mere sight of this body is more effective than its description, but the evidence does not work in the way Bonario expects. A stage direction added to the Folio text reads, "*Volpone is brought in, as impotent*" (s.d. at 4.6.20), and modern editors typically gloss "impotent" as "wholly disabled."[53] Voltore hails Volpone's entrance:

> Here, here,
> The testimony comes that will convince,
> And put to utter dumbness their bold tongues.
> See here, grave fathers, here's the ravisher,
> The rider on men's wives, the great imposter,
> The grand voluptuary! Do you not think,
> These limbs should affect venery? Or these eyes
> Covet a concubine? Pray you, mark these hands:
> Are they not fit to stroke a lady's breasts?
> Perhaps he doth dissemble?
>
> (20–29)

Voltore's narration reconstructs Volpone's inert form as negative proof. He turns feigning into being in order to demonstrate his client's incapacity—in order to confirm, that is, what the "sick" body cannot do. Redirecting the legal gaze ("See here" and "mark") to Volpone's "limbs," "eyes," and "hands," Voltore cites them as visual evidence that Volpone is unable to perform the acts of which he is accused ("affect venery," "covet," and "stroke"). Volpone never speaks, replicating the "utter dumbness" that Voltore claims this appearance demands from his spectators. The opening questions ask the judges to read Volpone's bodily capacity for erotic action, but the final question conjures an alternative possibility. "Perhaps he doth dissemble?" ventriloquizes Bonario's objection but renders his assent impossible.

Volpone's form reorients all the other bodies on the stage as the Avocatori gather around him to peer at the sight in a collective act of witnessing. Bonario's call for ocular proof has backfired because their gaze produces a judgment about bodily capacity in the static time of the present. The judges rule on what this immobilized body cannot do, rather than on whether or not this disabling is an act of seeming. Cutting into Voltore's line, Bonario attempts to break through the spectacle by requesting that Volpone be further tried. Demanding, "I would have him proved" (4.6.30), Bonario attempts to jolt Volpone's form into action, in order to establish that there is no cause for the feigned effect. But Bonario fails to comprehend the power of the wish to cordon off another's sickness from any experience of the self. When Voltore invites the Avocatori to punish Volpone, to "try him, then, with goads or burning irons" (31), for he has "heard / The rack hath cured the gout" (32–33), he turns this "cure" of Volpone's impotence back on the Avocatori themselves. Acceding to Bonario's request, he inquires:

> Which of you
> Are safe, my honoured fathers? I would ask,
> With leave of Your grave Fatherhoods, if their plot
> Have any face or colour like to truth?
>
> (42–45)

Reinscribing Volpone's feigned present as the prospective future of the Avocatori themselves, Voltore shifts the Avocatori's attention to their own aging bodies. While the object of legal evidence can never be fully separated from its perceivers, this general principle of subjective witnessing narrows the gaze of the judges. Bonario's misguided faith that the sick body speaks for itself underestimates how strenuously the Avocatori refuse to recognize their own vulnerability. Here, the sick body constitutes *apparently* uncontestable evidence of disability as limitation, but this future of unelective incapacity is one that may become true for the judges too.

Unsurprisingly, the court's second trial punishes Volpone with a future that distances their own implicated witnessing. The sentence attempts to restore accuracy to public perception that has been warped by Volpone's playacting. Addressing Volpone, they pronounce that:

> judgment on thee
> Is that thy substance all be straight confiscate
> To the hospital of the *Incurabili*;
> And since the most was gotten by imposture,
> By feigning lame, gout, palsy, and such diseases,
> Thou art to lie in prison, cramped with irons,
> Till thou be'st sick and lame indeed.
>
> (5.12.118–24)

The decree strips Volpone of the health that he has risked and the gold that he has collected from his visitors; the judges condemn him to reenact his "imposture" until he is "sick and lame indeed."[54] The pun "to lie" compresses Volpone's con game into a speech act, making Volpone's body sick in the deed of representation. The hospital's name, "Incurabili," pronounces cure impossible: this future arrests time by sealing off the possibility of change. The court's sentence asserts incurable stasis, not a present-deferring "curative imaginary" but an equally final causative imaginary. Striving to convert performance into reality, the sentence finalizes the "now" of feigning in order to cut off the character from any opportunity to experience something other than the sickness he has performed. By extending the present imitation into the future, the legal judgment forcibly concludes Volpone's experiment with theatrical doing. The punishment fits the crime by collapsing the experience of feigning into the thing feigned.

One of the commendatory poems on the play, printed at the beginning of the 1607 quarto, appears to respond to this sentence in advance. The poet meditates on the play in performance and print when he announces:

> VOLPONE now is dead indeed, and lies
> Exposèd to the censure of all eyes
> And mouths; now he hath run his train and shown
> His subtle body where he best was known.
> In both Minerva's cities, he doth yield
> His well-formed limbs upon this open field;
> Who, if they now appear so fair in sight,
> How did they when they were endued with sprite
> Of action?[55]

Here is quarto text as corpse: exposed, immobile, impotent against naysayers. The enjambed pun on "lies" converts feigned imposture to full exposure. The "subtle body" is presumably the life of the play's performance at the universities to which the epistle is dedicated, a contrast heightened by the strangely proleptic "dead indeed" that names the suggested end of Volpone's judgment in the final scene. Critics such as James Bednarz and Richard Dutton have urged us to attend to how the quarto publication of the play emphasizes acting.[56] This priority for performance challenges the repeated "now" that identifies the end of Volpone's life with a revelation the play itself cannot produce. The final "sprite of action" equivocates between performances of the play and a sense of the actor as the formal cause of the play, for the concluding question positions its readers alongside the Avocatori at the trial, prompting us to ask what it is that we think we perceive in a fixed body's "well-formed limbs."

Something of this sprightliness sticks, even when the court aims at a hard stop. In the epilogue, Volpone, the Fox in this beast fable, wriggles free of his captors to address the audience with an appeal:

> The seasoning of a play is the applause.
> Now, though the Fox be punished by the laws,
> He yet doth hope there is no suff'ring due
> For any fact which he hath done 'gainst you;
> If there be, censure him: here he doubtful stands.
> If not, fare jovially, and clap your hands.
> (5.12.152–57)

The epilogue unmoors the actor–character relationship, because it does not quite end the fiction of the play, nor does it quite restore the actor to himself again as he seeks the audience's responsive applause. Is this Burbage or Volpone? It is not exactly Volpone, because the character exits with the others, headed toward his imprisoning fate. Nor, however, is it entirely the actor who returns, since he appears as the Fox ("here he doubtful stands"). Coker argues that in this scene the actor "affirms detachment" and "the speaker fails to link materially to the body he enacts."[57] I am far less certain about this detachment, however, given that the speech never settles on any distinction between the material presence of the actor and the fiction of character. Rather than severing personator from thing personated, *Volpone* displays the blurring of fictional boundaries, deferring the punishment of Volpone's fixing cure.

"A Dead Palsy": Involuntary Action and the Limits of Performance

I have been suggesting that the early modern theater's staging of sickness discloses a fault line between the body of the actor and the body of the character as embodied displays, such as palsies and fits, trouble spectatorial perception. The final section of this chapter argues that *Volpone*'s unsettling temporality of the "sick" body takes effect and, by putting the disabling stakes of performance on view, redirects attention to the body's susceptibility to time. Volpone's sustained enactment of the sick body in the trial scene of act 4 is also the play's apparent ending. Famously, John Dryden observed that "there appear two actions in the play; the first naturally ending with the fourth act; the second forced from it in the fifth."[58] Vindicated by the court, Volpone pushes the imposture further by pretending to be dead, and crucially errs when he invests Mosca with the power to supplant him. This final feigning becomes a problem of plotting that implicates characterization, since Volpone's action seems out of keeping with the shrewd scheming he demonstrates earlier. Anne Barton contends that Volpone's improvisational technique goes awry because he is "a man who makes the fatal mistake he does in the fifth act because he is trying to repair a newly shattered sense of vitality, self-confidence and control over his circumstances."[59] Stephen Greenblatt argues that this structure of false conclusion is necessary for the moral education of the audience because what comes after the trial scene is *"deadness"*; if the play is about Volpone's "fashioning of this theatrical self," the "lull" after the trial scene reveals the "yawning emptiness" of a successful deception.[60] These modern assessments of *Volpone*'s final act echo the late seventeenth-century judgment of literary critic John Dennis. In a letter to William Congreve,

CHAPTER 5

Dennis identifies the problem of character as a matter of causation. For Dennis, "the Character of *Volpone* is Inconsistent with it self" because Volpone's rash and "Giddy" behavior in the final act marks a turn from the "Craftily" managed affair of the first four acts, and this turn produces "the greatest alteration in the World, in the space of twenty-four hours, without any apparent cause."[61] From the beginning of the play's reception, Volpone's causeless and swift change in behavior in the final act of the play is inexplicable.

More than a lull, a preamble to new action, or an inconsistency in character, however, I understand the opening scene of act 5 to reorient the play's entire view on the limitations of an actor's body in performance. Far from splitting the fifth act from the prior four acts, Volpone's soliloquy discloses the trial scene from his perspective. Fortified with a bowl of wine, Volpone reflects:

> Well, I am here, and all this brunt is past.
> I ne'er was in dislike with my disguise
> Till this fled moment. Here 'twas good, in private,
> But in your public—*cavè*, whilst I breathe.
> 'Fore God, my left leg 'gan to have the cramp,
> And I appre'nded straight some power had struck me
> With a dead palsy. Well, I must be merry
> And shake it off. A many of these fears
> Would put me into some villainous disease,
> Should they come thick upon me; I'll prevent 'em.
> Give me a bowl of lusty wine to fright
> This humour from my heart: Hum, hum, hum.
> 'Tis almost gone already; I shall conquer.
>
> (5.1.1–13)

In this soliloquy, Volpone speaks to himself as an actor, reflecting on the representational action that has taken effect with unpredictable force. Real incapacity—the cramp, the dead palsy—overtook Volpone. His "left leg 'gan to have the cramp" and the humors aroused by his feigning produced a "dead palsy"; he goes on to imagine that, in the future, such "villainous diseases" may take effect unexpectedly. The stage direction *"as impotent"* turns out not to have been a simile; the body in the trial scene was not representing a palsy but experiencing one. The antitheatricalist's concern that the actor will not be able to extricate himself from the character he is feigning comes true within the fictional world of the play. To put it in the terms of theatrical form that I discussed in the introduction and have been using throughout this book, Volpone has not realized that his "doing" of disability is also a "thing done."

Volpone reveals that such transformations are consequences of what acting is: a making that happens in and through the actor's body and therefore may transform it. Volpone has never doubted that his sickness is a sheddable ruse, another "disguise" (5.1.2) that he assumes as one of many roles. Early in the play, as he turns out an exuberant act as Scoto of Mantua, Volpone's only worry is how to double-cast himself in both places, how to play both mountebank and sick magnifico ("I must / Maintain mine own shape, still, the same: we'll think" [1.5.128–29]). When his attempt to rape Celia is thwarted by Bonario's intervention, he exclaims, "I am unmasked, unspirited, undone" (3.7.277), but his "own shape" remains securely distinct from the sick similitude he enacts. By contrast, his posttrial soliloquy expounds the danger of impersonation as clearly as Philip Stubbes, Stephen Gosson, or William Prynne avow that theatrical pretending threatens bodily transformation. Outside of his "private" house, Volpone cannot control the scrutiny that the trial effects on his bodily feigning in public. Sickness becomes disabling when it no longer operates on his chosen timetable of pretense, when he comes up against the limits of voluntary command of his body. Volpone has been casing the boundary between actor and character throughout the play, winking to Mosca (and us) as he carries out his scheme. His notion of performance is confined to stage-managing properties and skill in counterfeiting bedridden impotence. *Volpone* demonstrates that disability tests the very limits of performance, rerouting feigning into startling constraint; Volpone the character-turned-actor finds that sickness cannot be reduced merely to external signs but may, instead, make real the thing that was only feigned. Volpone thinks that disability is a semiotic; *Volpone* finds that disability is a logic.

Volpone's counterfeiting palsy is not the only place we might have turned to look for disability in the play. Dennis also faults Jonson for mocking Corbaccio's deafness, the effect of age, when Volpone and Mosca trade asides at Corbaccio's expense and deride his inability to perceive the truth of his aging body.[62] Volpone and Mosca observe that Corbaccio's desire for gain means that he:

> Feels not his gout, nor palsy, feigns himself
> Younger by scores of years, flatters his age
> With confident belying it; hopes he may
> With charms, like Aeson, have his youth restored.
> (1.4.153–56)

Actually experiencing some of the illnesses Volpone feigns, Corbaccio has become the yardstick against which Volpone's own feigning may be laughed off. For Dennis, such humor "is contrary to the end of Comedy Instruction" because "Personal Defects cannot be amended; and the exposing such, can never Divert any but half-witted Men."[63] Jokes at the expense of Corbaccio's disability fail because he cannot voluntarily "amend" his physical faults. Dennis's comment on the didactic aims of the theater hearkens back to Philip Sidney's discussion of comedy as "an imitation of the common errors of our life" that teaches by negative example, "so as it is impossible that any beholder can be content to be such a one."[64] For Sidney, when the educable beholder laughs, she learns from the play. Laughing *at* something divides a spectator from what she sees on the stage and asks her to recognize herself at the same time, an identification that produces the lesson of avoidance. (Fools look ridiculous; don't be one.) Notably, Dennis does not resist the laughter that the play scripts at the expense of some of the characters who are marked out by physical difference. Nor would Sidney, who writes that "we laugh at deformed creatures, wherein certainly we cannot delight."[65] Volpone's command to "call forth my dwarf, my eunuch, and my fool, / And let 'em make me sport" (1.1.69–70) demonstrates how the comedy uses Nano, Castrone, and Androgyno to prompt laughter simply by being themselves.[66] With names that collapse difference into person, like Cripple in *The Fair Maid of the Exchange*, the play proposes that we laugh along with Volpone in his "sport" of entertainment.[67]

Congreve, Dennis's interlocutor, agrees that the play's mockery of Corbaccio is a fault. He clarifies that "sometimes *Personal Defects are misrepresented for Humours*, I mean, sometimes Characters are barbarously exposed on the Stage, ridiculing Natural Deformities, Casual Defects in the Senses, and Infirmities of Age."[68] Dennis's resistance to mocking a character's disability is a formal objection rather than an ethical identification. To magnify physical comedy and encourage laughter at such characters demonstrates defective plotting, since "Natural Deformities," "Casual Defects," and especially "Infirmities of Age" cannot be helped. These features of a character are not a motive or "Humour," because there is no cause-and-effect relationship the spectator may decipher for a lesson. Barish, reflecting on this seventeenth-century exchange about the play, thinks that Dennis takes the impairment too literally, positing that "what makes Corbaccio ridiculous is not his deafness as such but the fact that this never interferes with his avarice." For Barish, "the deafness itself takes on the quality of a moral failing; it is no more a simple physical defect than Falstaff's fatness."[69] Working with a concept of disability as metaphor, Barish identifies the power of a distinctive body for characterization, but I would suggest that the problem is one of witnessing rather than morality. The play's "barbarous" display of Corbaccio, ridiculing features that are out of his control, exposes how little control may be exerted over a body in the first place.

Such "Personal defects," Dennis observes, "cannot fail to bring a thinking Man to reflect upon the Misery of Human Nature; and into what he may fall himself without any fault of his own."[70] Harping on a character's fault of age that is impossible to correct, theatrical action jolts a spectator out of the play's artifice and into the awareness of his own bodily vulnerability. Corbaccio's "deformities," his palsy and deafness, work at the expense of the dramatic fiction by unsettling how, whether, and—importantly—when the body's vulnerability can be codified into a lesson. Watching Mosca and Volpone deliver asides at Corbaccio's expense, the "thinking Man" begins to reflect on the process of aging and to see the future to which his own body inexorably proceeds "without any fault of his own." The spectator may be reminded that health is a temporal gift of the body, one that is never fully secure. Linger too long in the play, mocking Corbaccio for the impotence and infirmity of age, and the fiction points back at the spectator too.

* * *

Refusing to isolate *Volpone*'s fifth act as mere corrective to the ending that arrives too soon, therefore, we understand the play's revelation that the body is subject to unelective changes. Volpone the character, as actor, may be unable to extricate himself from the ploy of feigning that fixes him involuntarily in what he has feigned. Yet the problem of involuntarity is not left on the stage. Montaigne's essay "Of the force of imagination" (1.20) meditates on this illusory sense of control over the body through a series of questions:

> How often doe the forced motions and changes of our faces, witnesse the secretest and most lurking thoughts we have, and bewray them to by-standers? The same cause that dooth animate this member, doth also, unwitting to us, embolden our hart, our lungs, and our pulses.... Is there nought besides these muscles and veines, that rise and fall without the consent, not onely of our will, but also of our thought? We cannot commaunde our haire to stand on end, nor our skinne to startle for desire or feare. Our hands are often carried where we direct them not.
>
> (sig. E4r)

Muscles contract, veins rise and fall, but not by conscious choice, underscoring the lack of command over the most intimate operations of our own bodies. Even a limb, such as the arm, that appears voluntarily controlled may jump without apparent stimulus. The hair that stands on end, the startle reflex, the churn of the stomach: such movements are "besides our intent, and against our meaning" (sig. E4r). Isolating involuntary actions that move between physiology and affect, Montaigne shows how every human body depends on processes that are unaccountable to "consent," "will," or even "thought." Any body's repertoire of unelective corporeal responses goes far beyond conscious control. A reflexive movement may be translated into a gesture, and a fleeting expression may betray an undisclosed thought or suggest an intention despite unconscious action.

At the outset of this chapter, I noted Yergeau's insight that the criteria of voluntariness, applied to signifying acts, has been used to consign autistic rhetoric to the realm of stimulus response and diminish the humanity of autistic people. Yergeau revalues autistic rhetoric as an expression of "the interbodily potentials, desires, and moments that structure an autistic life, or any life."[71] I take Yergeau's argument to underscore the damage done by assuming that voluntary control is normative and imposing the judgment of involuntariness on autistic people. Yet the early modern examples I have noted here—from the actor who is overtaken by that which he has feigned, to the spectator who becomes unexpectedly aware of time's ravaging effect on his body, to the philosopher whose pulse throbs without his consent—admit no easy presumption of voluntariness. The bodily display that sources disability's special effects in the early modern theater demands that an audience member recognize how limited is the command of their (our!) own corporeal repertoires and how thin are any normative claims to willed control over the body. (Haven't I been irritated when a twitch or shudder has been converted by my interlocutor into meaningful motion? And haven't I transformed someone else's jump or shiver into significant expression, to their own great irritation?) Leaping between the precincts of action and communication, the unstable circuitry of the human body moves in excess of signification, a fact that the theater puts on view because it works with the actor's body as device of semiotic transfer. This excess troubles the tenuous distinction between meaningless and meaningful gestures—and exposes how normative concepts of bodily signification express power relations rather than inherent truths of communication.

We may easily assent to this proposition in theory, but I want to stress how deeply this claim cuts to the heart of theatrical form, which depends on distinguishing the actor's gesture as a clue to character, and mapping intention onto action in order to make sense of the dramatic character in the fictional world of the play. Staging the sick body, theatrical form relies on disability to unfix theatrical signification. Doing so, it discloses the fixing mechanisms that draw the line on human difference. In palsy, epilepsy, and other diseases characterized by involuntary movements, the theater complicates a clear distinction between seeming and being, risking the actor's body and the unexpected affective responses it may prompt as a mechanism for productively disabling signification. Disability pulls spectators into the time that is happening to the bodies on the stage, into the theater's insistence on running out the clock on feigning, and into the effects that time is wreaking even on their own embodied selves. The early modern theater's work with the contingency of the actor's body, taken to its logical conclusion, sounds the universalizing note of human vulnerability common to every body.

If witnessing is the mechanism for producing unexpected affinities between spectator and dramatic fiction, the next chapter takes the unfixing power of performance to the concept of the monster, the dominant early modern analogue for disability. Against the distanced gawking that the monster's prodigious appearance invites, I trace the theatrical production of wonder through the form of the actor. The theater constructs the monstrous body out of stage properties. Militating against an ideology of absolute otherness that drives the concept of the monster, the human body of the actor unfixes the presumption of alterity.

Chapter 6

Making the Monster

> The character of Caliban is generally thought (and justly so) to be one of the author's masterpieces. It is not indeed pleasant to see this character on the stage any more than it is to see the God Pan personated there. But in itself it is one of the wildest and most abstracted of all Shakespear's characters, whose deformity whether of body or mind is redeemed by the power and truth of the imagination displayed in it.
>
> —William Hazlitt, *Characters of Shakespear's Plays*

This monster. Some monster of the isle. A most delicate monster. A very shallow monster. A very weak monster. A most poor credulous monster. Monster. A most perfidious and drunken monster. This puppy-headed monster. A most scurvy monster. Poor monster. An abominable monster. A most ridiculous monster. A howling monster. A drunken monster. O brave monster.[1]

Encountering Caliban for the first time, Stephano and Trinculo turn to the word "monster" to describe his figure. The term resounds nearly fifty times in Shakespeare's *The Tempest*, though the lines above record its usage just in act 2, scene 2. Taken together, these examples compound the term in a litany of address that feels increasingly like parody as the play proceeds. Like "deformed," and "ugly," keywords in earlier chapters of this book, "monstrous" suggests a shared judgment about a body that departs from expected form—without ever quite specifying what that body looks like. *The Tempest* pointedly underscores the sense that the "monster" is both fixed and amorphous, for Stephano and Trinculo qualify the label with other terms, from "strange fish" (2.2.27) to "mooncalf" (105), that constellate nonhuman figures with bodily difference. Yet they return insistently to "monster," an abstraction that presents as description, throughout the scenes they share with Caliban. Conceptually, monstrosity is expansive enough to include "four legs and two voices" (88), when Stephano believes Trinculo and Caliban are a composite creature, and limited enough to enforce distinction—"this is a devil, and no monster" (96)—when that body calls Stephano by name in Trinculo's voice. The concept of monstrosity precedes the individual instance, even as each iteration changes the object called a monster. I will return to Shakespeare's play at the end of this chapter, but I begin by noting that the monster is apparently recognizable at first glance yet unable to be pinned down in any stable description. When Stephano and Trinculo train their gaze on Caliban, they perceive a monster. Their relentless invocation of monstrosity prompts us to ask, though: What, exactly, does a monster look like?

I open with this act of witnessing that turns into meaning-making as a provocation for this chapter's argument that the theater's formal making unfixes the legibility of monstrosity. My account of early modern disability in this book, which began by considering how Richard III's proclamation that he is "deformed" points us to the presentational work of the actor's body, concludes with a chapter in which the "monstrous" body highlights the representational work of performance. Theatrical characters described as monstrous—like the bodies described as deformed, lame, crippled, ugly, and sick that I have taken up in earlier chapters—depend on the signifying instrument of the actor's body. Monstrosity snaps into focus on the stage when read against the overwhelming scrutiny of the monstrous body in early modern cultural discourse. Put in the terms of theatrical form I have been tracing so far, performance's "doing" pushes back on the "thing done" of cultural signification to which the logic of monstrosity aspires.[2] I read this generative unfixing in relation to the etymologies of the word "monstrous"—"to show" and "to warn"—which point not to a specific bodily referent but to the act of showing itself. When the theater invokes the trope ("here is a monstrous character"), the unstable medium of the actor's body unfixes what monstrosity can mean. The monster is never wholly other, as I will demonstrate, for the monstrous character is the most extreme version of the theater's habitual attempt to make a character out of an actor's body. The formal construction of the monstrous character drags acting into an epistemological crisis of witnessing.

Over the past two decades, scholars have demonstrated that monstrosity is a key framework for early modern political, religious, and scientific discourse. Early modern texts summon monsters to inscribe reading practices, demarcate the limits of the human, prompt natural philosophy, account moral transgression, and inspire wonder.[3] The concept is ubiquitous in literature of the period; for every text that treats a body described as monstrous, we could identify scores that employ monstrosity as metaphor, with rhetoric marshalled to figure invisible inner evil.[4] Renaissance inheritances of classical models of monstrosity are vexed, multiple, and contradictory: in the Aristotelian inheritance, the monster is defined by bodily defect or excess, whereas in an

Augustinian tradition, the monster is a divine sign of formal diversity. As Elizabeth B. Bearden summarizes, "Attitudes toward monstrosity have been uniform in their diversity."[5] In texts that range from widely circulating pamphlets of monstrous birth narratives with bespoke woodcuts to travel narratives to medical treatises, the significance of monstrosity extends far beyond a single register of interpretation, posing the difficulty of determining how far a body can go before it departs from human resemblance. The monster is both "religious sign" and "social metaphor," for monstrosity's "figurative utility" toggles between description and interpretation, and between the singular body and the abstract category.[6]

Disability studies has understood monstrosity as a distinctly early modern conceptual frame for human variation that is nonetheless part of the historical continuum of attitudes toward bodily anomaly.[7] In the trajectory that Rosemarie Garland-Thomson discusses as a "movement from a narrative of the marvelous to a narrative of the deviant," a narrative in which "wonder becomes error," monstrosity defines what is early about early modern disability.[8] The horror and awe that monstrosity provokes comprise archaic responses to physical abnormality that we would identify today as congenital deformity, and the product of a distinctively premodern epistemology that gives way to systematic classification of monsters as part of the realm of the human sciences by the nineteenth century.[9] Lest we idealize this sense of "wonder," important scholarly work has restored our attention to the people who were designated monsters, the "real bodies of so-called freaks, [who] were put on display in parlors, taverns, churches, and cabinets," and to Bartholomew Fair's apparatus of exhibition, in which "monsters were normal and their extraordinary form became part of a spectacle of the unnatural, the grotesque, and the lewd."[10]

Analyzing such spectacles in modernity, critical work has elaborated the concept of the "freak," juxtaposed with and embodying disability as the performative spectacle of ostentatious physical distinctiveness. The freak—understood in Robert Bogdan's account as the effect of "a set of practices," or as an "identity realized through gesture, costume, and staging," in Rachel Adams's generative reworking of the term—is a spectacle that is made, not born.[11] In this chapter, I work from the insight that this spectacle of freakishness is always produced for spectators. Rather than charting a direct line from the early modern monster to modernity's sideshow exhibitions, however, I take up the monster through the practices of theatrical form, which unsettles the very concept of the monster by implicating spectators in the process of making and witnessing monstrosity. After considering how plays such as *The City Match* and *The Birth of Merlin* designate the monstrous character through theatrical properties and manage the speech that may challenge a monstrous spectacle, I then turn back to *The Tempest*, to consider how the monster is made up wholesale.

Stressing the ideological incoherence of monstrosity, I build on scholarly work that has challenged a teleological orientation to modernity. As Katharine Park and Lorraine Daston have shown, the range of meanings assigned to early modern monsters includes "portents signifying divine wrath and imminent catastrophe," "violations of both the natural and moral orders," "marvels" that "reflect[ed] an aesthetic of variety and ingenuity in nature as well as art," and "deformities or natural errors" that were "the occasional price to be paid for the very simplicity and regularity in nature from which they so shockingly deviated."[12] Their account complicates the critical narrative in which monstrosity moves from supernatural to pathological, expressed in Michel Foucault's formulation of monstrosity as "a juridical-natural complex" in the eighteenth century that would contribute to the "principle of both qualification and correction" that define the norm.[13] Stephen Pender has argued that the monster is a key early modern site for exploring how "personhood is subject to embodiment," and as Bearden powerfully demonstrates, early modern examples of discourses on monstrosity offer a "copious" history of representation of "society's oscillations between sanctification of and discrimination against people with disabilities."[14] Rather than consigning monstrosity to a distinctive early modern phenomenon, we can perceive the back-formation of a cultural process that converts human difference into disqualification.

Furthermore, even if the rhetoric of monstrosity displays a "flight into metaphor" in the fixed print of narrative accounts, theatrical form affords no such dematerialization.[15] The legacy of monstrosity's discursive construction stretches back to Aristotle's conception of the monster as a second-order deviation of the paradigmatic body of the human.[16] This inheritance raises the stakes on theatrical form. *Script* a monster, and the dramatic fiction evokes a ready-to-hand set of associations with portent, punishment, and prodigality. Monstrosity is a fixing carapace of trope, figurative resources drawn from a thick concept of alterity, as I have noted in the many variations of "monster" that the clowns attempt to attach to Caliban.[17] *Stage* a monster, and the actor's body is asked to veer as far into the territory of absolute difference as it can possibly go. In the theater, the actor plays the role of (inhuman, nonhuman, subhuman) monster with all the resources of prosthetics, costume, paint, and properties such a character requires. The monstrous character is sheer representation. To put it another way, the monster's unnatural artificiality, a staple of early modern treatises and sermons, is something the stage recognizes as the end point of performance's material practice.

While the promise of viewing a monstrous body at the fairground depends on a claim to singularity ("pay to see what you've never seen before"), by necessity, every monstrous character is also replicable. This repetition is true of dramatic character more broadly. The stage formally refuses an original, and the theater builds iteration into its practice—every performance is another night, another actor, another production. The monstrous body tests the limits of the theater by yoking opposed protocols of spectacle, beyond simply showcasing a player's ability to play a role or counterfeit a shape. When a body is described as "monstrous," the logic of repetition that underpins theatrical representation is at odds with the logic of singularity (this body, born in this place, with these specific deformed features) that gives the rhetoric of monstrosity its force in early modern print culture and in the fair's display. When the theater stages monsters, the fact of the role's reproducibility hollows out the claim to authenticity that makes the monster so appealing. At the same time, because no performance ever happens the same way twice, the theater offers a monster that is uniquely singular because it is temporary, produced at the intersection of actor's body and monstriferous properties. The iterative work that constitutes early modern theatrical practice demonstrates that the monster is always made up, fixing an actor's body through the power of theatrical prosthetics, and unfixing the monster's alterity in the process.

I find, therefore, that the early modern theater contests the very concept of monstrosity it evokes. Theatrical performance of monstrosity renders an actor's recognizably human body wondrous—by which I mean produced by stage properties and projected as an illusory effect of performance—but only in exactly the way that every character's body is wondrous. More than an early modern analogue for disability, monstrosity offers an analytic for the protocols of witnessing that convert a body—a *person*—to anomaly. Staged monstrosity challenges the distance on which disability's othering depends, threatening to speak back across the gap between spectator and objectified form. Through the very act of mimesis that constitutes its representational practice, the theater undermines the discursive fervor the monstrous body is taken to incite and reveals the incoherence of monstrosity as a concept.

Monstrous Form: Spectacle, Theatricality, Transformation

Before moving to the plays that will be my chief concern, this section sketches conceptual frames for the "monstrous" body in the period, rubrics of thinking evident in medical texts, monstrous birth pamphlets, and antitheatrical treatises. Each example that follows is representative of the problems posed by the very acts of looking that such texts aim to solicit. Building on Bearden's insight that the "iteration of monstrous bodies . . . results in an unnatural narratology that ironically naturalizes the prevalence of monstrosity as the human experience of disability," my work with the following examples extends the stakes of monstrosity's iterability, ultimately turning to theatrical performance.[18] Reproducing the tension between image and description, the texts I explore in this section worry plainly about the fixed silence of the object they treat. Announcing constitutive tenets of monstrosity, their ideological commitments are remarkably explicit. These documents ask readers to look with them at the monstrous bodies they survey; they ask us to perceive "monsters" fixed by textual description and woodcut depiction, objects of an interpretation imposed from without by a viewer.

In early modern medical discourse, the body deemed monstrous often relies on a comparison between the static monster and the dynamic human form. One such example may be observed in Thomas Johnson's 1634 English translation of Ambroise Paré's 1573 volume *Des monstres et des prodiges* (*Of Monsters and Marvels*), where one plate depicts the images of man and monster (figure 6.1). One figure is a subject capable of action and one figure is an object on view as spectacle. The caption for the top image reads, "The effigies of a man without armes, doing all that is usually done with hands," while the bottom caption reads, "The effigies of a monster with two heads, two legs, and but one arme."[19] Johnson condenses the examples visually, equivocating between man and monster within the framing device of the page.[20] This conjunction amplifies their contrast in capacity. The body of the "man without armes" is astonishingly mobile, clothes fluttering from the action he has just completed; the caption maintains that he is extraordinarily capable of compensating for his missing arms. The whip balanced on his shoulder is still cracking.

This emphasis on doing as an illustration of human capacity recurs in discussions of monstrosity. In *Anthropometamorphosis*, John Bulwer pauses during a long disquisition on what he calls "Monstrosities and depraved conformations" (sig. 2R3r) of the body, to marvel at John Simons: "Born without Armes, Hands, Thighs, or Knees," Bulwer writes, yet "from the wast upward as proportionable a body as any ordinary man wanting his Armes" (sig. 2R4v). Simons's skill is evident in all the things he can do: "He writeth with his mouth, he tyeth a knot upon thread or haire, though it be never so small, with his mouth, he feedeth himself with spoon-meate, he Shuffels, Cuts, and Dealeth a pack of Cards with his mouth" (sig. 2R4v). The account elaborates

LIB. 25.   *Of Monsters and Prodigies.*   977

The effigies of a man without armes, doing all that is usually done with hands.

The effigies of a monster with two heads, two legs, and but one arme.

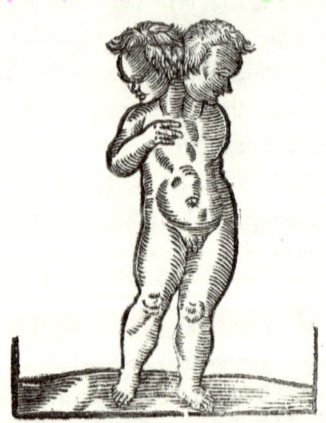

Nnnn3

FIGURE 6.1. Ambroise Paré, *The Workes of that famous Chirurgion Ambrose Parey* (London, 1634), 977. Call#: STC 19189. Used by permission of the Folger Shakespeare Library under a Creative Commons Attribution-ShareAlike 4.0 International License.

on his ability to go beyond basic sustenance and communication. Tying miniscule knots, shuffling, cutting, and dealing cards, Simons reproduces with his mouth what hands do—and then demonstrates his capacity to perform such tasks even more proficiently. Bulwer recurs to the language of compensatory function to explain what Simons can do in "recompence of this error (as they call it) of Nature." He praises the "wonderful dexterity of men of distorted, lamed, or dibilitated members, or who are altogether deprived of them," who skillfully substitute "other members besides their offices they were ordained for" (sig. 2S1r). Celebrating the possibility of conscripting a mouth or feet to do the work of hands, Bulwer insists that a person whose body is "distorted" or "lame" may still attain unexpected function.

By contrast, lacking such signs of human dexterity, the body labeled a "monster" remains poised in statuesque nudity. The monster is not a figure in motion, demonstrating dexterous capacity and skill; the monster is not "doing," but being. The body's features are evident in outline and detail, so that readers may contemplate its departures from the human form. The description fixes the image by recapitulating those features, described as simultaneously excessive ("two heads") and deficient ("but one arme"). Juxtaposing the two bodies, the page models contrasting versions of bodily difference. In the first, ordinary objects (a whip, an axe, a pair of dice) become prosthetic devices through which the person demonstrates his supplemented agency. In the second, monstrous appearance renders the figure inert, encouraging the reader to quantify the lack of limbs and the excess of heads rather than imagine this body accommodated. The prodigious man recruits mouth and legs to do the work "usually done" by hands, a virtuosic repurposing of other body parts for unexpected functions. The monster is a done object, flattened to the page for scrutiny of how far the form departs from the normative human body.

This two-dimensional rendering is typical of monster "newes" reportage—pamphlets and broadsides announcing anomalous births. These texts promise to reward careful attention to the features of the monstrous body and typically split the burden of proof between the description and accompanying image. The print medium facilitates the act of looking for a reading audience that can pore over the details at leisure. One of the most familiar examples from the period, the 1617 pamphlet *A Wonder Woorth the Reading*, promises "A True and faithfull Relation of a Woman" who "was delivered of a prodigious and Monstrous, *Child, in the presence of divers honest, and religious women to their wonderfull feare and astonishment*."[21] The depiction of this "prodigious and Monstrous" body (figure 6.2) appears under the subtitle as if to corroborate the truth of the account by offering a visual referent for the "Relation" that follows, and the subtitle emphasizes specificity, offering the details of day ("Thursday,

A WONDER, WOORTH THE READING,

OR

A Tr... nd faithfull Relation of a Woman, now dwelling ...entstreet, who, vpon Thursday, being the 21. of Augu... last, was deliuered of a prodigious and Monstrous, Chil..., in the presence of diuers honest, and religious women to their wonderfull feare and astonishment.

LONDON
Imprinted by *William Iones* dwelling in Red-crosse-streete 1617.

FIGURE 6.2. © The British Library Board. *A Wonder Woorth the Reading* (London, 1617), C.127.g.17 Title page.

being the 21 of August last"), place ("now dwelling [on] Kentstreet"), and year ("1617") as grounding facts on which to build the political, moral, and theological interpretations in the account that follows.[22]

Yet this appeal to the singularity of one birth yields immediately to a genealogy of other such figures as if the particular monster also stands in for the general category of monster. The narrative conscripts the reader as witness in a series of questions that culminates: "What miraculous, Monstrous, and Prodigious births have beene presented to our eyes, as hideous spectators of deformitie?" (sig. A3r). Proliferating terms of difference—miracle, monster, prodigy—the question invites spectators to a collective gaze ("our eyes") that remembers "deformitie" as a site of scrutiny. An account of a monster prompts the memory of other such singularities, as if the image invites readers to conjure a wonder cabinet in their minds in which to place the newest exhibit. Affiliated by the responses they invite, encapsulated by the adjectives "miraculous," "monstrous," and "prodigious," a child deemed a monster evokes other monsters even if they share none of the specific features that make this body monstrous. The sticky collation of other monsters attending the "strange newes" of each successive birth multiplies the monstrous discourse and, in the process, reduces the form to yet another discernible spectacle of strangeness.[23]

Although the title suggests the appeal of attending to this news, the account only arrives at the description of this child after enjoining readers to repent upon witnessing this "most strange and mo[n]strous accident in nature" (sig. A3r). The pamphlet proclaims a "monstrous Message *sent from the* King of Glorie" (sig. A1v) that requires a lengthy account of the body's features to detail such a proclamation. The narrative describes the body as:

> a Female child with a halfe forehead, without any scull, having a faire proportioned body from the brest downward: the said child had its mouth & eyez miraculously placed in the sayd halfe forhead neere upon the breast, upon the said halfe fore-head lay a peece of flesh of two fingers thicke round about, the flesh being wonderfully curled like Gentle womens attire: being of a very blew coullour like a turcke Cocke, the eyes being very bigg staring and very firy red. . . . Beholding agayne the Child, they saw the eares of it fastened to the halfe forhead, not being like to Christians eares, but stood pricking up, behind each eare, was two little bones standing up overgrowne with flesh, and having very long heaire.
>
> (sigs. A3r–v)

Highlighting the "faire proportioned body" before zeroing in on the features that are "miraculously placed," the narrative compares the monstrous excrescences of the child's face to things that are not human, from an ornament on a gentlewoman's dress to the blue color of a turkey. Describing the "Female child," the similes nonetheless assert her inhumanity, emphasizing the strangeness of this wonder with every comparison. Likewise, the example of dissimilitude ("not being like to Christians eares"), a judgment introduced after the midwife and other women attending the birth see the countenance of the child and begin to pray, presupposes that the monstrous body is legible from birth. Even unexpected features of this body may be drawn into the lesson, for ears turn out to be religiously distinguished—a designation of "Christian" that perhaps encodes "English" and "human" too.

Readers educated in this monstrous appearance may then turn back to the frontispiece, to match these details with the features illustrated there, for the printed codex form enables a reader to flip between description and image. Implicating the readers in interpretive practice, the narrative narrows into scrutiny of detail, focusing on the "peece of flesh" that is "two fingers thicke round about." As a unit of measurement, "two fingers" invokes a shared human form only to defamiliarize the body as a measuring stick. The injunction simulates new knowledge by asking the reader to perform the cognitive work of comparison: look to your own hand, reader, reperform such an encounter with altered flesh by recognizing two fingers, and then imagine that what you are seeing is the scale of curled flesh on a forehead. The reader who flexes her fingers may feel as if she has learned something new about the bodily alterity of this monstrous form. Like the spectators gathered around this child, who perceive more details of her features by "beholding agayne," the reader turns to the text to look, and look again, at that proof of prodigiousness that overwrites even her own hand. The pamphlet offers only the illusion of interpretation because the text projects its own verdict onto the reader. This circuit of meaning-making, the shuttle between description and image, reinforces the ideological fixity of monstrous meaning.

This fixed interpretation, however, also recognizes the threat that feigning poses to the monster's ideological work. Before introducing the child, the pamphlet cautions: "Therefore, lest any should meet my discourse with a scoffe, and smilingly say? This is an usuall tricke put upon the world for profit; and that this monstrous Childe birth (whereon my present subject is chiefly grounded) was begotten in some monster hatching brayne; produced for a Bartlemew faire babie; and sent at this time (for order sake) to be nurced at the common charge of the newes affecting multitude; let them know, that not one syllable shall be added to the making up of an untrueth" (sig. A3r). Preemptively positing a skeptic who scoffs and smiles, the pamphlet anticipates the claim that this birth is a "usuall tricke" carried out "for profit"—that the monstrous body is simply "produced" for display at London's Bartholomew

Fair. In the pivot to the fairground, the narrative addresses itself to a reader aware of how rarely spectacles can be taken for certainty.[24] Presuming a reader who is skeptical of commercial aims, the pamphlet's defensive prolixity charts a knowing audience that expects to be entertained by a fake. Haunted by the fair's coffers, the printed text distinguishes between the monstrous birth it claims for truth and the spectacle that emerges from a "monster hatching brayne" that solicits the price of admission. The "monstrous Childe birth" and the "Bartlemew faire baby" are two sides of the same spectacular coin because the economics of spectacle dictate the figure's market value in the entertainment business.

In antitheatrical texts, the monster is a common pejorative for the actor engaged in the labor of transformation. Like the pamphlet's fear of the conjunction of natural and artificial monster making, early modern polemics against the theater use monstrosity to figure performance's dangers. In *A Mirrour of Monsters* (1587), an early contribution to antitheatrical discourse, William Rankins explains his choice of "monsters" in the title. He observes, "Some terme them Comedians, othersome Players, manie Pleasers, but I Monsters, and whie Monsters? Bicause under colour of humanitie, they present nothing but prodigious vanitie."[25] The page includes marginal glosses that distill these insights: "They are Monsters," "They colour their vanitie with humanitie," and "Plaiers transforme their bodies which is the image of Christ into the shape of brute beasts" (sig. B2v). Rankins redefines acting from occupation to transgression; while actors are called "Comedians" and "Players" by others, he reverses the ontological poles. A player treads the boundaries of humanity; more precisely, humanity is a varnish on a form that has already become feral. Rankins employs the language of monstrosity to figure multiplicity, also frequently employed in connection with the doubleness of disguise in the theater. Perceptively discussing Rankins's condemnation of acting, Mark Thornton Burnett observes that the actor is not so much "a prodigy portending the end of the world" but rather "a 'monster' in a double sense—'monstrous' in constantly changing his attire and 'monstrous' in the commercial profit that he reaped from making a spectacle of his own body."[26] I would contend, however, that the spectacle of the actor's body is far from stable, for as monstrosity grips the body through attire, it unsettles the markers of that body altogether. When Rankins indicts the actor as "seem[ing] . . . the limbs, proportion, and members of Sathan" (sig. B2v), the muddle of seeming and being underscores monstrosity's hold on the body itself, never as reversible as a neat distinction between actor's body and character's attire. Imagining an actor engaged in the act of personation, Rankins insists that "the temple of our bodies . . . is made a stage of stinking stuff, a den for theeves, and an habitation for insatiate monsters" (sig. B2v). Transmuted in miniature into the space it occupies in performance, the actor's body is not sacred "temple" but blasphemous "stage"; the "monsters" are something like dramatic characters, the actor's body a "habitation" that harbors all possible transformations. The player's artifice reveals a natural state that has already been transformed.

This view of performance uses the monster as a vehicle for charting the theater's ontological unsettling of the human body. In prior chapters, I have noted the worry that the actor—feigning, deforming, changeling—may fail to extricate himself from the character. In Rankins's account, we can observe another implication, echoed with much dismay by early modern writers: the transformation that characterizes the actor's work may be practiced by anyone, a porous threat beyond the theater's doors. Thus, when Robert Burton, writing in the seventeenth century, indicts the changeable man, he laments the person who may "turn himself into all shapes like a Chameleon, or as Proteus *omnia transformans sese in miracula rerum*; to act twenty parts & persons at once for his advantage, to temporize & vary like Mercury the Planet, good with good, bad with bad; having a several face, garb, & character, for everyone he meets."[27] The modern edition translates Burton's Latin phrase to "who transformed himself into every possible shape," but *miracula* more sharply rendered is "monstrosity." Slipping from an object that is monstrous to the verb of transforming, Burton invokes the actor as Proteus. The actor commands "all shapes," but Burton's account extends this protean power to any man who, having understood how to exchange his shape for another, may prove a changeling. This language returns us to antitheatrical insistence that acting is functionally a lie, but the real threat here is the simultaneity. The man may act all the "parts & persons at once," recharacterizing himself at will in order to assume unfixable variance according to his "advantage." The actor's monstrous capacity for transformation now defines social relations and reorders human relationships at every scale. Taken to the limit, theatricality is indistinguishable from monstrosity, permeating everyday life beyond the temporal and spatial limits of the stage.

"So Foul a Monster": *The City Match* and *The Birth of Merlin*

In what follows, this chapter turns to several plays to consider how the theater fixes and unfixes the "monstrous" body. Monstrous characters speak back, hastening wonder and a slew of other affective responses, perhaps even the risibility that the monstrous birth pamphlet fears its account may prompt. My turn to early modern plays suggests that, making monstrous alterity concrete through the human form of the actor, the theater does not "ultimately confirm" that alterity.[28] In performance, the monstrous character does exactly the opposite. Theatrical displays of monstrosity reshape the working cultural definition the theater imports from texts and images we have encountered here. Identified as monstrous, the characters I study forge new inscriptions, however partial and incomplete, that reconfigure the category. Staging a "monstrous" character, these plays probe the incoherence at the heart of the discourse of monstrosity itself.

Jasper Mayne's 1639 comedy *The Citye Match* makes a monstrous figure through theatrical techniques, producing the spectacle of a monstrous fish that indexes profit rather than portent. Plotwell, an impecunious young gentleman, finds a potential victim in the naïve Timothy Seathrift and decides to turn him into an unwitting actor before a gullible crowd. Plotwell asks Captain Quartfield, "But hark you, Captaine, / What think you of a *Fish* now?"[29] His friends all agree that they can use Seathrift to dupe spectators who will pay to see a wonder: "Rich *Seathrifts* sonne, he'l make a rare sea-Monster" (sig. G2r). The play gives over the entire third act to this well-practiced scam. The conspirators pair the aquatic production with a musical setting ("*Salewit* shal make / A song upon him" [sig. G2r]) and frame the spectacle through commercial advertisement, as Bright, Newcut, Plotwell, and Roseclap begin by "*hanging out the picture of a strange fish*" (sig. H1r) to solicit customers for their show. Questioned by the others about whether the fish they advertise will be profitable, Salewit notes that he owns the theatrical prosthetics required for the performance ("the properties of the last fish" [sig. G2r]), and Roseclap attests to the Captain's prior success, for he "is used to it: this is the fift[h] fish now / That he hath showne thus" (sig. H1r). The iterations of this performance are extremely profitable, if they also tenuously depend on the fortitude of the human actor; notably, one performance took in "twentie pound" when the victim was especially inebriated, allowing for a longer run ("the Captain kept him, Sir, / A whole weeke drunk, and showd him twice a day" [sig. H1r]). The verb of spectacle ("show[e]d") simultaneously encapsulates the performance (Timothy is being shown) and the produced nature of this sign (to be shown is also to be narrated into a wonder). When Bright announces that the Captain has ensure that Timothy is fully inebriated (he has "foxt him rarely"), he admonishes the others to sculpt Timothy into a fishy shape with speed: "Bid the Captaine hasten, / Or hee'l recover and spoile all" (sig. H1r). The spectacle incapacitates the actor in order to reduce him to a body positioned for immobilized display. The time-sensitive monstrous production depends on how long Timothy's drunkenness will keep him slumbering, silent, and viewable.

200   CHAPTER 6

As they prepare the sign advertising the exotic fish, Newcut marvels at the visual representation, wondering how one picture suffices to depict multiple productions and declaring the spectacle of Timothy's body "could not be like this" (sig. H1r). Plotwell insists that the image they post is merely the precursor to the commercial possibilities to come:

> ROSECLAP: Faith I doe grant
>   This is the strangest fish. Yon I have hung
>   His other picture into th'fields, where some
>   Say tis an oregrowne Porcpisce; others say
>   Tis the fish caught in the Cheshire; one to whom
>   The rest agree, said 'twas a Mermaid.
> PLOTWELL: S'light,
>   *Roseclap*, shalt have a patent of him. The *Birds*
>   Brought from *Peru*, the hairy *Wench*, the *Camel*,
>   The *Elephant*, *Dromedaries*, or *Winsor Castle*.
>   The *Woman* with dead flesh, or *She* that washes,
>   Threds needles, writes, dresses her children, playes
>   Oth' Virginalls with her feet, could never draw
>   People like this.
>
>   (sig. H1r)

Plotwell knows as well as *The Citye Match* does that people will pay to see the marvels they desire, and the "strangest fish" is his oft-repeated staging of such a wonder. His list ranges from bodies notable for size, impairment, and extraordinary talent to objects highlighted for geographical difference and architectural feat. The hyperability of "She" who threads, writes, dresses, and plucks strings with her feet recalls the image of the performer without arms from Paré's book on monsters, who manages properties with ease, "doing all that is usually done with hands." Plotwell's assessment of these other wonders as merely less successful commodities proves true in *The Citye Match* when a crowd arrives to see the sea creature. Mrs. Holland and Mrs. Seathrift—Timothy's mother—turn up, protest the price ("We gave but a groat / To see the last fish"), marvel at the social status of the audience ("here be Gentlemen / Sure tis a rare Fish"), betray eager desire for spectacle ("I long to see this fish"), and demonstrate practiced evaluation when they encounter the promotional picture ("Look M[r]s *Seathrift*, / What clawes he has" and "Nay marke his feet too" [sig. H1v]). While the play makes hay of their claim to sophistication—both of Timothy's parents see their son as the monstrous fish and they do not recognize him, though Mr. Seathrift is suspiciously resistant and Mrs. Seathrift is admiringly engaged—the scene overrides the familial with the financial. The spectators who wait impatiently for entrance are customers well accustomed to the protocols that attend the exchange of money for the sight of a rare object.

Their response to the moment of discovery converts the stage direction, *"Drawes a Curtain behind it Timothy a sleepe like a strange fish"* (sig. H2r), from a simile into a linked chain of associations:

> QUARTFIELD: And Gentlewomen, you now shall see a sight,
> Europe nere show'd the like; behold this fish.
> MRS. HOLLAND: O strange looke how it sleeps
> BRIGHT: Just like a Salmon
> Upon a stall in fishstreet,
> MRS. SEATHRIFT: How it snorts too,
> Just like my husband
> WAREHOUSE: 'Tis very like a man.
> SEATHRIFT: 'T has such a nose and eyes.
> SALEWIT: Why tis a Man fish;
> An Ocean Centaure, begot between a Syren
> And a he stockfish.
>
> (sig. H2r)

Like a salmon, like my husband, like a man. Quartfield's claim for the singularity of "this fish" demands that the exhibitors improvise an increasingly outlandish story to explain away the affective likeness of the similes. Their narrative reinforces the audience's investment in the thing that needs to be more nearly piscine than human. Taking the role of exhibitors, Quartfield and Salewit present the fish and detail the circumstances of capture, describing how "the States of Holland would have bought him of us / Out of a great designe" to the tune of "a thousand dollars," in order to use the fish for military action against Spain, to "doe service / Unto the state" (sig. H2v). Their narration relies on all the tropes associated with the display of wonders, yoking together the disruption of a strange object in the London viewing space, the political significance of Holland's military strategem, and the spectatorial desire to marvel at the fish that lives up to this tale. Importantly, the exhibitors must produce the ontological difference at once visually apprehensible, evidently monstrous, and epistemologically inaccessible, requiring a story that explains what is special about *this* monstrous fish. In a script that is part carnival barker and part travelogue, Quartfield recounts how the fish's language has improved in the nearly five years of exhibition, as they "have shown him in most Courts / in Christendome" (sig. I1r). The monstrous figure entangles national politics and hierarchies of status in the fiction he prompts. The men who are gathered as spectators exchange skeptical asides, while the women beg to "trie him with some questions" in order to "see what Creatures may be brought to" (sig. I1r). The spectators become more dubious as the fish's tale becomes more improbable, but the play is not invested in deconstructing the theatrical creation of monstrosity to reveal the sum total of stage properties thickly layered onto Timothy's body. On the contrary, the scene demonstrates how to make a monster and how lucrative that making can be.

Yet the success of the spectacle depends on managing the actor's body, which threatens to erupt uncontrollably through the properties that render him unnatural. Timothy is subject to the human demands of a hangover. Woken by the song that describes him as a monstrous fish, Timothy laments his state ("Oh, Captaine—pox—take—you—Captaine" and "O—God—my—head—"), groans of protest that must be explained away at perilous length by his exhibitors ("Hee'l imitate a man" and "he has heard me / Calld Captaine, and my fellow curse sometimes" [sig. I1r]). Timothy's unwitting response threatens the show because it risks destroying the spectacle. The exhibitors offer increasingly unwieldy justifications for the fish's language until Quartfield ends by announcing that they "doe show no more to day; if you desire / To see, come to us in *Kings-street* tomorrow," with the stage direction, *"They draw the Curtaine before him"* (sig. I1r). The plot pivots as soon as this risky venture is contained, but only after the scene dwells on the elaborate experiment with theatrical embodiment, layering actor as incapacitated character as monstrous fish. An unwitting party to his own exhibition, Timothy returns to full consciousness and registers belatedly the duress of display:

> How's this? my hands
> Transmuted into Clawes? my feet made flownders?
> Arrayd in Finnes, and Scales? arn't you
> Ashamd to make me such a Monster? pray
> Help to undresse me.
>
> (sig. I2v)

Transmuting hands, remaking feet, and arraying a body, the exhibitors have dressed up a man to make a monster. Although Timothy's appeal for help suggests some worry about extricating himself from the act, the play evades the antitheatrical concern that the performance of monstrosity might permanently transform the body of the actor. Instead, the production undoes the premise of monstrous signification as overt marker of difference by deconstructing the display. Hitting all the notes of spectacle—claws, fins, scales—the display requires nothing but theatrical prosthetics. Monstrosity is a kind of quantitative celebration of the transformational power of stage properties. All that is needed for a monstrous body is a body.

The ease with which the conspirators construct a successful spectacle out of a human body requires us to rethink assumptions about the self-evident alterity of the monstrous—or marvelous, or wondrous, or prodigious—body. Timothy nearly shatters the ruse with his undocile laments. The formal intrusion of his speech risks the spectacle's collapse, beyond even the content of his nauseated exclamations. The show depends on the audience remaining inattentive to the human actor, perceiving only the character-as-object, reduced to the inhuman materiality of the monstrous fish's properties. Speech threatens to interrupt this fixed image. A sideshow's spectacle, Susan Stewart observes, depends on "the tableaulike silence of the freak's display" and the discursive mechanism of the barker's pitch; "dialogue across that silence is forbidden, for it is necessary that, like the aberration, the normal be confined to the surface, or appearance, of things."[30] The monster's conceptual entity ("this is a monster") requires a split between the spectacle and interpretation, imposing a frame narrated by another voice, whether that is exhibitor or pamphlet author.[31] Stewart argues that the freak's "anomalous status is articulated by the process of the spectacle as it distances the viewer, and thereby it 'normalizes' the viewer as much as it marks the freak as an aberration."[32] The speech of the spectacle would destroy the objectification of the monster *and* the putative normality of the spectator. The conceptual category of the monster enacts a fundamental bait and switch: a claim that is based on comparison, a body that appears exceptionally tall or short or malformed, becomes the basis for asserting absolute difference. The viewer looks at the freak and thinks, "I am not that thing." The monster's speech is an act of response that endangers the spectacle of absolute difference by returning to a comparative frame. Looking back—still more, speaking back—the monstrous form calls the act of witnessing into question. Unveiling a backstage scam and refracting the vexed interpretations of a monstrous form, the theater exposes the spectacle as production.

I emphasize the point that speech ruptures the perception of the monster as I turn to Merlin, a monstrous character whose appearance prompts multiple and conflicting judgments when he finally arrives in the play that bears his name. Printed in quarto in 1662 but performed in 1622, William Rowley's *The Birth of Merlin, or, The Child Hath Found his Father* begins with a war between the Saxons and the Britons and ends with the founding of Uther (Uter in the play) Pendragon's rule.[33] Merlin, known as a wizard and prophet, was a fixture in Britain's origin stories: versions of his political prophecies, recorded in chronicle histories, were retailed and debated throughout the seventeenth century.[34] Although we may rule out the title page's pronouncement that Shakespeare coauthored the play, *Birth of Merlin* was believed, for a time, to be part of the Shakespearean apocrypha.[35] In Rowley's play, Merlin links the main plot's epic history of Aurelius, king of Britain, with a comic plot of a clown (never named in the text) and his pregnant sister Joan, who seek the unknown father of her child, Merlin, and are both caught up in the political and cosmological stakes of Merlin's prophetic gifts.[36] Described as "the Prophet" in the dramatis personae, Merlin does not appear until the third act of the play. After being born offstage and apparently growing into a figure that is both adult and child in the space of a scene, he enters, anomalously hirsute, castigated as a "Childe born with a beard on his face" (3.4.37) and "bearded abortive" (4.1.182).[37] Drawing on the myths that emphasize Merlin's supernatural conception by the devil, the play proposes a conspicuous appearance for the title character that lines up with the tropes of monstrous births. Merlin's extraordinary hairiness reads just like a woodcut's depiction of a monster might.[38]

Historical accounts of Merlin rarely conjure him as extraordinarily hairy, even as they stress the significance of his parentage to national history. Thomas Heywood's prose account, *The Life of Merlin* (1641), hesitates over the question of whether Merlin is a "Prophet," a "Predicter," or a "Seer" (sig. C1r); Heywood focuses on Merlin's royal blood in the account of his parentage and offers no hint that Merlin's appearance distinguishes him.[39] According to Heywood, Merlin's mother is "a Royall Virgin the daughter of King *Demetius*" (sig. C1v), whose answer to the question of Merlin's paternity ("that shee never had the societie of any one mortall or humane, only a spirit assuming the shape of a beautifull young man, had many times appeared unto her") is supported by the "modestie and constancie" (sig. E3r) of her nobility. The servants of the king track Merlin down when they encounter children playing by the gate, "who amongst other breathing words cast into *Merlins* teeth, that hee was but some Moon-calfe, as born of a mother who knew not his father" (sig. E2v). The insult "Moon-calfe" names Merlin's ancestry, rather than his appearance; it is a condition of paternal influence that has no bearing on his form. Indeed, Heywood's history emphasizes instead how well Merlin looks the part of the sage, with "strange promising things in his aspect, as having a quick and piercing eye, an ingenious and gracious countenance, and in his youthfull face a kinde of austeritie and supercilious gravity" (sig. E3r). Merlin's appearance, though youthful, accords him trust about his wisdom and insight, while it also certifies his nobility.

By contrast, Rowley's play makes much of Merlin's anomalous features. The play's subtitle, *"The Child Hath Found his Father,"* resounds through the first half of the play in the clown's incessant variants on the phrase. Hunting for the man who has impregnated and abandoned his sister—"the Childe must have a Father" (2.1.151), "the Childe shall have a Father that's certain" (2.1.177), and "to have a childe without a father, were most unnatural" (3.1.74–75)—the clown asserts the status and wealth this claim to a father will surely make possible. When the devil appears to Joan, he proclaims that the "fatal fruit thou bear'st within thy womb / Shall here be famous till the day of doom" (3.1.155–56). By suggesting that supernatural paternity warps the "fatal fruit" out of shape, the play recalls Aristotelian concepts of generation that credit the father's forming influence. Later, during the scene in which Merlin is born offstage, the devil jubilantly forecasts the "abortive birth now coming" (3.3.5).[40] Presenting monstrosity as the product of his conception, the devil summons Lucina, the Fates, and other "spirits of infernal deeps, / Squint ey'd *Erictho*, midnight *Incubus*" (3.3.12–13) to "aid this birth prodigious" (14) and "bring this mixture of infernal seed, / To humane being" (18–19). Merlin's monstrosity appears to be confirmed when his mother contributes human matter that the devil's "infernal seed" has misshapen into a "birth prodigious." Occluding the scene of Merlin's birth with demonic blessing while the event is happening, the play underscores the unnatural and inhuman registers of the monstrous birth prior to Merlin's entrance.

However, if Merlin's demonic paternity sets up the expectation that he will materialize as terrifying portent, another set of voices in Rowley's play construe Merlin's monstrous appearance as evidence of powerful divine gift. Lucina pronounces that the Fates will give the child "all their assisting powers of Knowledge, Arts, / Learning, Wisdom, all the hidden parts / Of all-admiring Prophecy" (3.3.25–27), so that "his Art shall stand / A wall of brass to guard the *Brittain* land" (28–29), to be exercised in service of national aid. Merlin's conception is amplified by occult forces, but Lucina redefines this supernatural gift as prophetic endowment. This judgment reorients Merlin's prodigious appearance to a temporal standard, since "even from this minute, all his Arts appears / Manlike in Judgement, Person, State, and years" (30–31). In an instant, both Merlin and his art are advanced in appearance. His monstrous body displays not only the imprint of demonic conception but also supernatural power to explain a future yet incomprehensible. The preposterous appearance of a child with a beard, grown before his time, is a figure for the act of prophecy itself, an act that refuses to respect the dramatic unity of time. Indeed, Merlin's mother herself reads Merlin's abnormalities as a sign of distinctive achievement.[41] He appears "'gainst nature and our common births, / He comes thus furnisht to salute the world" (3.4.48–49). The judgment that Merlin is "'gainst nature" calls back to definitions of monstrosity as unnatural; for Joan, Merlin's exceptional figure is as much against their "common births," a distinction that renaturalizes social status.[42] Merlin himself refers the altered substance of his body to a refusal of linear chronology, insisting that he "can be but half a man at best" (3.4.18). What sounds like an admission of lack is only evidence of supernatural compensation, for his "growth and bigness" (21) are not the effect of time but a promise for the future, as he claims that his "years / Shall be more strange than yet my birth appears" (21–22). Merlin mobilizes the rhetoric of the strange birth as evidence of powerful excess. Though he is chronologically only one day old and already fully grown, his actions and abilities cannot be conceived in terms of a clock sped up. Instead, the vantage he offers is the play's refusal of the usual rubrics of time and space.

The play offers one further register for the explanatory paradigm of monstrosity, however—one that shifts in tone to the inescapably comic. In the mouth of the Clown, the supernatural forces of dark magic give way to an assessment of indecorum. When the Clown encounters Merlin, he calls him a "Moon-calf" (3.4.12), "either a witch or a conjurer" (32), "Hartichoke" (37), and "Moncky" (44), language that recasts Merlin's visage in the pejoratives of a monstrous birth. Observing to Joan that "by his beard he is more like your husband" (35–36) and asking, "a Childe born with a beard on his face?" (37), the Clown keeps returning to Merlin's hairiness as the discrepancy between person and appearance: "Hast thou a beard to hide it, wil't thou show thy self a childe, wil't thou have more hair then wit?" (4.1.86–87). Yet when the tropes of monstrosity are evoked, as they are at every turn, they prove woefully inadequate to explain the significance of the body he perceives before him. Lamenting, "I have heard of some that has been born with teeth, but never none with such a talking tongue before" (3.4.40–41), the Clown identifies Merlin with embarrassing excess. Merlin, he claims, "is worse then *Tom Thumb*, that let a fart in his Mothers belly, a Childe to speak, eat, and go the first hour of his birth, nay, such a Baby as had need of a Barber before he was born too; why sister this is monstrous, and shames all our kindred" (44–47). Merlin's "monstrous" features are not fearsome but inappropriate. Reading Merlin's features, the Clown misses the point of his gifts, mostly concerned about the public response of shame this precocity provokes. Monstrosity provides no settled register because—especially in the mouth of the Clown—these characteristic features do not add up to a clear interpretation. Instead, Merlin's hirsute appearance is another species of social impropriety, as if the monstrous fish had clambered down from his perch and walked home with Joan.

Rowley's play makes Merlin out of properties but confers on him the power to mobilize the meaning of monstrosity; he deciphers all of the prodigious spectacles in the rest of the play. In addition to Merlin's ostentatious beard, his book, and his wand, Udall notes, "as far back as 10 March, 1598, the Admiral's Men were in possession of a 'merlen gowne and cape'" that denote the character.[43] The play exploits all of these properties first by employing them to construct a figure of alterity and then by testing how speech might dissemble the reductive signifying spectacle of such a body. *The Birth of Merlin* deploys monstrosity to indict ignorance: like the Clown, you might grasp for "monster" when you are at a loss to ascertain the significance of an anomalous body you encounter. (Like the Clown, you would be wrong.) Merlin's appearance does not neatly equate to legibility at any level of social hierarchy or education, whether the spectator is a clownish dolt or a supercilious magician—and the play affords the chance to laugh at both figures.[44] While his hairiness is apparent and reviled from his entrance, Merlin's powerful language takes effect within the fiction to extend the play's purchase on history.[45] Merlin facilitates the array of the play's special effects, which work across epic and parody, valorizing the "half-demonic wizard" through his technical and pyrotechnical skill.[46] Just after the Saxon magician has mocked Merlin for his appearance, a stone falls on the magician's head, killing him; when the devil pursues Joan, Merlin's mother, she flees to the top of a rock and Merlin splits it open and traps the devil inside. Merlin closes the play by offering a final show of ghostly figures, or "visible apparitions" (5.2.88), that foretell the future of Britain's rule. History is bound up in spectacle, which must be interpreted, and Merlin concludes the play by moving from being the object of theatrical surprise to the purveyor of theatrical displays.

Saddled with the tropes of monstrosity, Merlin is nonetheless accorded agency to shape his own actions. While the monster's making depends on a split between display of spectacle and narrative account, *The Birth of Merlin* repairs this disjunction. Merlin is a crossover character who connects the plots and shifts between prose and verse—even speaking Latin when he defeats the devil. Praising "learned Merlin" (5.2.79), the play endows Merlin with the most powerful speech in the end. Making Merlin perceptible as a character who can pun as easily as he can pronounce the doom of the ruler, the play conflates multiple etymologies of monstrosity to underline Merlin's capacity both to show and *authorize* meaning. The Prince speaks the final lines of the play, gesturing to a future that becomes the past and reaches into the present, encompassing the audience of the play's performance: "All future times shall still record this Story, / Of *Merlin's* learned worth, and *Arthur's* glory" (5.2.109–10). The play embeds a monstrous body within one of the foundational stories of British history. Merlin's power makes possible the vexed origin of Englishness, which is just as contested when his figure is revived in the monarchical debates of the 1640s.[47] The character who enables the play to have its comic slapstick and its political edge at the same time, Merlin is endowed with prophetic volubility, a narrative command to which every other figure either acquiesces or is silenced (like the Clown, for example, who is magically tongue-tied in a scene that rests uneasily between humor and violence). The monstrous character, whose speech contests his appearance, gathers up England's future in the threads of prophecy and spins them back out into spectacle.

I have been suggesting that the play constructs Merlin as monstrous and then undercuts this assurance, turning his portentous features into a comic spectacle and remapping his prodigy as another species of ability. If this undoes the certainty that bodily indicators can be clear indices of monstrosity, the play also furnishes a very different instance of monstrosity: a monster that is pure artifice, summoned as didactic exemplum in the final scene. The explicitly named "monster" in *The Birth of Merlin*, in other words, is the figure who least looks like one. Artesia, the "*Saxon* Beauty" (1.2.81), is immediately suspect because of her beauty's captivating force. Artesia's hazard is hinted at the play's outset when she proposes a too-hasty political truce and the king of the Britons woos her at first sight, eagerly agreeing to peace with the Saxons when she arrives at his court as an ambassador; at the end, Artesia is predictably revealed as the threat the king's counselors always presumed her to be. In the final scene of the play, when her political treachery has been exposed, monstrosity is the lesson that must be made explicit by transforming a beautiful female body to a form that is something other than human. Before Prince Uter will allow himself to be crowned, he insists, "that monster first must be expel'd our eye, / Or we shall take no joy" (5.2.48–49). Edol suggests a punishment of graphic violence:

> Let my Sentence stand for all, take her hence,
> And stake her carcase in the burning Sun,
> Till it be parcht and dry, and then fley off
> Her wicked skin, and stuff the pelt with straw
> To be shown up and down at Fairs and Markets,
> Two pence a piece to see so foul a monster,
> Will be a fair Monopoly and worth the begging.
> (52–58)

Perhaps the most startlingly anachronistic moment in a play that is full of them, Edol imagines turning Uter's figurative "monster" into a literal one.[48] He knows the early modern fairground exhibition and resonates with the business acumen the monster pamphlet fears.

This sentence is a fantasy of total legibility: judgment as violence as spectacle as pure display. Edol's command would transform Artesia into nothing but appearance, the reduction of a "carcase" to stuffed "pelt." He wants Artesia's "wicked skin" to be a lesson displayed to all, a monstrosity that makes the transgression plain through punishment. The ultimate monster is reusable, desiccated and packed with straw, for the real profit is the mobile viewing it affords to spectators galore. While the play preserves Artesia's resistance to the punishment—Edol's suggestion prompts laughter from Artesia, who dismisses it as "poor invention" (60), asking, "Is there no better, torture-monger?" (61)—the proposal underlines the idea that any body may be turned into a monster, dependent on and utterly subject to public display. This vision of the female body transformed to stuffed monster extends the logic of didactic witnessing, promising that the reduction of woman to object will educate—or entertain—a crowd of spectators at the fair. The monster is the lifeless body that has been fixed in meaning, transportable to every viewer who can shell out for admittance. Staging Merlin's anomalous body, *The Birth of Merlin* admits the difference between the fantasy of punishment that relies on the static appearance of a monster and the monstrous character, whose moving, speaking power is distinctly at odds with the manifest hairiness the stage property produces. At the end of the play, the monster is not born but made.

Perceiving Caliban

The theater, I have been suggesting, unsettles the portent of monstrous alterity by making up the monster in front of the audience. Like the other figures I have examined, Caliban too is called a "strange fish" (2.2.27) and "mooncalf" (3.2.21). Caliban also participates in the array of properties that compose a dramatic character and gesture to the circuits of theatrical form's fixing and unfixing. In fact, Michael Baird Saenger has suggested that *The Tempest*'s Caliban and Ariel owe elements of their visual characterization to a pair of costumes inherited by the King's Men from a 1610 sea pageant on the Thames.[49] The pageant, Anthony Munday's *Londons Love, to the Royal Prince Henrie*, featured speeches by the characters of Corinea and Amphion, performed by King's Men actors Richard Burbage and John Rice. Records show that Burbage and Rice were given the accoutrements as part of their payment, and Saenger argues their costumes and properties might plausibly be linked to Ariel and Caliban since the actors presumably brought the properties to the company. Reading the description of Caliban in *The Tempest* as "Legged like a man! and his fins like arms!" (2.2.32–33) as something like "trousers with fins attached to them, precisely what one would imagine for Amphion," Saenger speculates that "it is possible that the costumes were one of the seeds from which the play grew."[50] From costume to character, Saenger's attention to this evidence infers a theatrical source, not in text but in property, for a play that notably does not rely on a clear single source for its plot. If Caliban is a character built from the outside in, the monstrous figure trails a performance history that exposes the monster's essential artificiality.

The suggestion that properties of costume precede *The Tempest*'s dramatic characters is rendered still weirder and richer by the full text of *Londons Love*, which slides between documentary and fictional impulses. Recounting the water pageant and describing the moment that Prince Henry's barge arrives from Richmond, the speaker evokes participation in a collaborative act of imagining: "Wherfore let us thus thinke of *Neptune*, that out of his spacious watrie wildernes, he then suddenly sent a huge Whale and a Dolphin, and by the power of his commanding Trident, had seated two of his choycest Trytons on them, altring their deformed Sea-shapes, bestowing on them the borrowed bodies of two absolute Actors, even the verie best our insta[n]t time can yeeld; & personating in them, the severall *Genii* of *Corinea*, the beautifull Queene of *Cornewall*, and *Amphion* the Father of harmonie or Musick."[51] Triton to actor to personation, the "borrowed bodies" move from other-than-human to human to mythical figure, making the "absolute Actors" a mere waypoint. Narrating this process of becoming, the speaker proposes a performance event that labors at double remove. The Tritons' "deformed Sea-shapes" precede the actors, who then "personate" allegorical characters: "deformed" registers transformation rather than negative departures from form. The personations ordered by Neptune subordinate the vehicle of the actors into distinct personations. By claiming that "in these two well-seeming and richelye appointed persons, the Dukedome of *Cornewall*, and the Principalitie of Wales . . . caried some tipe or figure, and not improperly to them so applyed" (sig. B4v), *Londons Love* defends representation as a species of typology. A parenthetical comment introduces the poet as architect of "such representations and misticall understandings" that "have always bin reputed lawfull, and are evermore allowed to holde and carrie correspondencie, with such solemne shewes and Triumphes" (sig. B4v). The actor's body, "even the verie best," is subordinated to the artistic vision that crafts the idea. Retrospectively narrating the pageant, the account decouples representation from the act of personation, shifting from the making of the actor to the making of the dramatist.

The performance conceives of representation as simultaneously iterative, in those "borrowed bodies," and transformative; acting, the pageant suggests, is a series of alterations that culminate in a distinct character. Amphion's appearance, poised on the back of a dolphin, to the crowd gathered to watch the river spectacle, is described in a block of text before his speech: *"Amp[h]ion, a grave and judicious Prophet-like personage, attyred in his apte habits, every way answerable to his state and profession, with his wreathe of Sea-shelles on his head, and his harpe hanging in fayre twine before him: personating the* Genius of Wales, *giveth the* Prince *this Farewell"* (sig. C4r). The passage dwells on attire, the "apte habits" that fit his "state and profession." Amphion's spectacle conveys the "grave and judicious" affect that has been scripted for this celebration of kingship, and Saenger associates Amphion's costume with Caliban in *The Tempest*. If we understand the costume as repurposed for Caliban's fishy construction, the "grave and judicious" elements of this personation complicate the denigration of the monster if they are recognizable as costumes from the royal spectacle. More broadly, however, the migration from public display to commercial theater replicates the logic of the monstrous character. These "borrowed bodies" produce characters through properties that signify and are resignified through reuse and reproduction. This shifting chain of signification reorients the affects that the properties are intended to evoke. This fiction of nonhuman creatures transformed to actors transformed to mythical types offers an unfamiliar account of representation, fixing Burbage into the artifice of the concept but also unfixing the past and future predicted from this display.

Speculating on Caliban's theatrical properties, I return to *The Tempest* and notice that monstrosity is the concept that Stephano and Trinculo invoke to denigrate the figure they encounter; yet by pointing at this discursive construction through repetition, the play demonstrates that "monster" manifestly fails to fix such a meaning. Caliban has long been the touchstone of a postcolonial critique that emphasizes his resistance to the subordination imposed on him.[52] Considering the sonic loop of "monster" in the play, I want to draw out the friction between the discursive concept and the theater's material practice. If Caliban's "creaturely monstrosity" is an exception that generates a new universalism, as Julia Lupton has argued, this gesture of implication occurs "not by simply reasserting that 'Caliban is human' but rather by saying that 'all humans are creatures,' that all humans constitute an exception to their own humanity."[53] For Lupton, Caliban demands we recognize our own selves in the negative exceptionality of the vulnerable creature, rather than policing the boundaries of the normal.[54] The call to understand creaturely resistance that punctures the totalizing frame of the play resonates with universalist claims for disability that press on the limits of a minoritarian perspective.[55] All bodies are unstable, changeable, and susceptible to arbitrary standards that might be drawn differently. Drawing on this insight, however, I am resistant to reclaiming the language of monstrosity because the play demonstrates not a "monster" but the imposition of "monster" as an incoherent concept. If we can understand Caliban as representative of a shared corporeal vulnerability common to all humanity, we nonetheless notice that *The Tempest* distributes this vulnerability unequally. Patricia Akhimie's reading of Caliban as "misshapen knave" illuminates Prospero's program of carceral deprivation and violence, which turns Caliban into the representative of "an uncultivatable underclass of subhuman who can labor but who cannot improve."[56] Caliban's deformity is not innate, but produced by Prospero's exercise of power that precedes the events of the play, a power that activates a genealogy of racist distinctions that remain with us today.

The insight that Caliban is framed as this figure in advance demands that we attend more closely to the repetition of "monster." Exposing the artificiality of this precondition, *The Tempest* reminds us, insistently, that the monster has to be made up as such, a formal insight that works against the assertion of absolute difference. The dramatis personae printed at the end of the play in the 1623 Folio describes Caliban as a *"salvage and deformed slave,"* and he enters the play framed by Prospero, who reasserts this description (as "most lying slave" [1.2.344]).[57] When he recounts the history of "he, that Caliban / Whom now I keep in service" (285–86), Prospero's contorted syntax leaves open the question of ontology. He claims that the island, under Sycorax's rule, was "not honored with / A human shape" (283–84) but loops Caliban back into humanity in a parenthetical exception: "(Save for the son that she did litter here, / A freckled whelp, hag-born)" (282–83). Amid the denigrating rhetoric of animality, Prospero is concerned with capacity for labor rather than spectacular appearance, announcing that Caliban "does make our fire / Fetch in our wood, and serves in offices" (1.2.311–12), a demonstration of physical ability for tasks "that profit us" (113). Prospero's emphasis on work at the beginning of the play cues spectators to note, when we first witness Caliban's delayed entrance, how he is forcibly enslaved—a form marked by physical difference, but one that does not transparently depart from the human.[58]

By contrast, Stephano and Trinculo see Caliban and immediately turn to the vocabulary of "monster." They sniff out a possibility for profit that commodifies him, recognizing Caliban as an island inhabitant that may be extracted for their own purposes. Trinculo exclaims: "A strange fish! Were I in England now, as once I was, and had but this fish painted, not a holiday fool there but would give a piece of silver. There would this monster make a man: any strange beast there makes a man. When they will not give a doit to relieve a lame beggar, they will lay out ten to see a dead Indian. Legged like a man! and his fins like arms! Warm, o' my troth! I do now let loose my opinion, hold it no longer: this is no fish, but an islander, that hath lately suffered by a thunderbolt" (2.2.26–36). Apprehending something that is "like a man," Trinculo makes humanness the simile, rather than essence, of the object he encounters. He knows that theatrical techniques produce a "monster" ("but this fish painted"), and this knowledge is bolstered by economic insight into the possibilities for an enterprising curator. Trinculo understands "make a man" as a register of financial gain, and he repeats the phrase in a chain of profit that brings out the divide between man and monster. The anticipatory force of the subjunctive forecasts the lucrative payoff of such feigning—for the exhibitor, rather than the exhibited person—when sufficient artifice scaffolds the encounter between wondering spectators who have paid for admission to a show and the object of wonder on display. Trinculo recognizes that the spectacle must be produced through a commercial apparatus, assessing the advertisement necessary to draw the requisite crowds—and he knows too that while the request for charity to living disabled people (that "lame beggar") fails to prompt sympathy from an English crowd, the allure of gazing at a contained object that is "strange" succeeds in spades. He arrives at "islander" only after moving from "fish" to "monster" to "dead Indian," and this chain of exhibition reinforces the spectacle he imagines.

While Trinculo's first response stakes out a space for Caliban in an early modern fairground, Stephano apprehends Caliban, once he is disentangled from Trinculo, as fit material for a wonder cabinet. He muses, "This is some monster of the isle, with four legs, who hath got, as I take it, an ague. Where the devil should he learn our language? I will give him some relief, if it be but for that. If I can recover him, and keep him tame, and get to Naples with him, he's a present for any emperor that ever trod on neat's leather" (2.2.64–69). Stephano emphasizes the monster's political power rather than commercial viability. Unlike Trinculo's wish to exhibit Caliban for a pay-per-view audience at the fair, Stephano's ambition apprehends the monster in relation to the political potential of a transnational gift. The monster's capacity for speech only increases his value at court; he is fit for an emperor, which is even better than a duke or a king. Stephano's language gestures to the practice of displaying exotic items in *wunderkammern*, or "cabinets of curiosities," in courts as well as medical colleges in early modern Europe, and he knows that these items include animals and people whose physical atypicality rendered them valuable.[59] Collected along with other singularities, the "monster" Stephano envisions takes his place in the viewing space as an object of exchange whose financial worth is expressed as prized rarity rather than public commodity.

Although these clown figures are well versed in what to do with a monster, the scene undoes the legibility of the "monster" they perceive as a defined body. Working against their certainty, and complicating the comic register of their perceptions, the play puts the monster on view as something that has to be made and to be made up. The speeches I have discussed above occur during a scene structured as a series of encounters that never rest on a single showing, for the monster is part of the same malleable practice with which actors do everything on the stage. Caliban enters laboring, carrying a burden of wood, and on seeing a strange creature he believes to be a devil and will go on to identify as a god, he "fall[s] flat" (2.2.16) to play dead. When Trinculo enters and encounters the object, he is never sure of what he perceives: "a man or a fish?" (24), "dead or alive?" (24–25), "a fish" (25), "a strange fish" (26–27), "fins like arms" (33), and "no fish but an islander" (34–35). With each shift around the object it looks different—like a man, like a fish—just as Timothy's marveling audience finds in *The Citye Match*. The actor's practice of making a monstrous character is a relation of similitude, a likeness that transforms the object with every change in perception.

When the storm comes again, Trinculo takes refuge in the very thing that was strange, sheltering under Caliban's cloak to share the monstrous body. The monster who was made first of one actor, with two legs and one voice, becomes what Stefano calls, when he enters the stage, the "monster of the isle, with four legs" (64–65). Burnett observes that "Caliban has shifted alarmingly in the physical particularities through which he is constituted."[60] But Caliban's shifts, in fact, reconfigure the entire conceptual frame of monstrosity. As Stefano pokes at the object and Caliban begs him to stop the torment, the monster then possesses "four legs and two voices" (88), an expansion that figures the monstrous body as compositionally infinite, capable of endless addition and subtraction. Kim F. Hall's foundational reading of this scene underscores the significance of Trinculo and Stefano's status as clowns, for their "comic entanglement" evinces the colonial imaginary's worry about the "class mobility enabled by colonial enterprise."[61] This insight into class distinction, however, cannot be easily delimited within the scene to a single body that stands apart from the monster. On the stage, these three bodies are fully entangled, even indistinguishable, in what Suparna Roychoudhury perceptively terms a "tableau of monstrosity."[62] When Stephano recognizes Trinculo, transforming the "lesser legs" of the monster to "Trinculo's legs" (102), and pulls apart the "forward voice" (89) and the "backward voice" (90) as he disentangles the two, both men attempt to distinguish Caliban through unlikeness. They turn to the vocabulary of "monster" because they know how to capitalize on a figure that they deem less than human. Yet "monster" is rendered incoherent through unrelenting repetition over the course of the scene, an inadequate description as the modifiers ("brave," "scurvy," "delicate," "drunken") fail to settle the terms of the object and to comprehend the interactive relationship that has constructed the figure. The term sounds less like a description than a manifest imposition from the clowns who have been part of the monster themselves. Monstrosity is an irreducible particularity, but this difference will never be as fixed as these figures insist.[63] There is always room under the property of the cloak for another actor's body, an extension that would recompose the monstrous body yet again.

In *The Tempest*'s theater history, much like *Richard III*'s, an adaptation of Shakespeare's text—rather than the Folio version—holds sway on the stage from the Restoration to the nineteenth century. William Davenant and John Dryden's 1670 adaptation, *The Tempest; or, The Enchanted Island*, fixes a disability stereotype into performance history by taking Caliban's monstrosity for granted. Identifying Caliban in the dramatis personae as "Monster of the Isle" (and introducing the character Sycorax, "his sister Monster of the Isle"), the adaptation changes Caliban's adjectives from the 1623 Folio: "salvage and deformed" are torqued into the noun of "monster" even before the play begins, as if a foregone conclusion.[64] For Davenant and Dryden, "monster" is a nonhuman or inhuman index for comic human follies. Caliban is repeatedly called "Brother Monster" by this play's "Trincalo," who consents to marry Sycorax. The familial terms imagine intermarriage only to set the limit of exchange at reproduction: Trincalo hopes to "geld Monster[s]" with Caliban's aid as a "rare pimp" (sigs. F3v–F4r) in order to lay claim to the island. Ultimately, *The Enchanted Island* asserts an ontological distance between monster and human. Pitting Caliban and Sycorax against each other as sidekicks to the men, the play demotes them to the point that even Ariel comments: "The Monsters *Sycorax* and *Caliban* / More monstrous grow by passions learn'd from man" (sig. K4v). Juxtaposing Caliban and Sycorax with degraded humans who lose all semblance of reasoned control, the play renders them only aspirants to humanity rather than full participants. To reiterate this point, the play strips Caliban of his soliloquy and eloquence. This influential adaptation eliminates what Hall identifies as a major affordance of *The Tempest*: Caliban's power to challenge Prospero's "imperial visions" through his speech and unfamiliar embodiment, an epistemological problem of "contradiction and contest characteristic of border spaces" rather than a clear category.[65] Shakespeare's play invests Caliban with a poetic capacity that clashes with the bodily difference the designation of "monster" appears to require. *The Enchanted Island* deprives Caliban of his linguistic power in order to more clearly delimit the monster as second-order departure from humanity.

While Caliban's descriptions of the island are commonly considered to be among the very best lines of the play, Caliban has been a character that devotees of Shakespeare have often wished only to read, not to see. William Hazlitt's assessment, in the epigraph to this chapter, praises Caliban as a "masterpiece" but refuses the pleasure of witnessing ("not indeed pleasant to see"; indeed, driving home this impersonality, Caliban is "it" rather than "he").[66] Hazlitt claims that Caliban evinces the "wildest and most abstracted" characterization in his verdict that Caliban's "deformity, whether of body or mind," is "redeemed by the power and truth of the imagination displayed in it."[67] This phrase fixes Caliban, pointing to a fantasy of difference that theatrical performance threatens. The assessment resists the contingency of personation. Prioritizing Caliban's poetry over spectacle, Hazlitt implicitly acknowledges the risk introduced by the material of the actor's body, which may interrupt the gesture of pure abstraction or fail to enact the wildness he imputes to the character. From the inverse perspective, Davenant and Dryden's adaptation ensures Caliban's alterity by cutting his imaginative speech and trimming the extended interplay with the clown figures. Presuming Caliban's legibility in advance, the adaptation streamlines the concept of monstrosity that it inherits from its Shakespearean source in order to foreground the figure's ontological difference. By curtailing the repetitions of "monster," which echo into meaninglessness in Shakespeare's play, the adaptation imports significance to the clowns' assessments, as if "monster," or the cognate "monstrous," really *could* be meaningful. There is no sheltering under the cloak together, no interactions between bodies that, in the fuzzy indistinctions they produce, draw the spectators into partaking of monstrosity too.

* * *

Rather than conclude with a play that settles Caliban firmly into position as "monster," then, I want to close this chapter with a fiction of a "monster" that dissolves into spectacle of part and whole. Twenty years after Dryden and Davenant's adaptation of *The Tempest*, another Restoration rewriting of an early modern play stages a monster, one that exposes the theater's temporal making as the monster deforms into particularity, and then reforms into another deformity. Thomas Betterton's *The Prophetess: Or, the History of Dioclesian* turns Francis Beaumont and John Fletcher's *The Prophetess* into an opera, adding music and heightening spectacle, a bid that assures the audience in the prologue that the *"Dead Stage"* will rise, *"Reviv'd by your fair eyes."*[68] In the moment of which I am thinking, the prophetess, Delphia, hovering above the stage *"in a Throne drawn by Dragons"* (s.d. at 2.3.0), orchestrates Diocles's coronation and then prevents his impending marriage to Aurelia once he attains the throne. In Beaumont and Fletcher's play, she accomplishes this by calling down special effects, *"Thunder and Lightning"* (s.d. at 2.3.129).[69] At this display, Charinus, the emperor, pronounces the moment "prodigious" (130) and "repent[s] the haste" (135) with which Diocles's marriage ceremony proceeds, and he halts the wedding until funeral rites are complete. Betterton's adaptation motivates Charinus's evocation of omen ("prodigious") by actually staging the monster, turning the exclamation into description. Extending the stage direction beyond thunder and lightning, he darkens the stage and adds the end point of this vantage: *"a dreadful Monster comes from the further end of the Scenes, and moves slowly forward"* (sig. E1v). The adaptation materializes the threatening body in a memorable stage direction that dials up the lavish display of spectacle. The monster paces toward the assembled figures who view the prodigy. Then, having made this monster, Betterton's adaptation disperses the whole form into constitutive parts: *"The Musick flourish. They who made the Monster separate in an instant, and fall into a Figure, ready to begin a Dance of Furies"* (sig. E1v). As if the variable sizing of Caliban's cloak has been used to fullest sheltering effect, the single monster turns out to be made up of Furies. The whole is made of constitutive parts, and these human bodies (*"they who made"*) recompose into a new whole, the "Figure" of a dance. They do so immediately (*"in an instant"*), making visible the theatrical temporality that constitutes the "doing" as always, simultaneously, a "thing done." Fixing the monster as form and then unfixing that monster into many different bodies, the play shows that the figure of alterity is only ever made up, wrought temporally in a medium that reduces concepts to bodies. The play's circuit of fixing and unfixing pulses between individual figures and the monstrous whole that is formally permeable and multiplicative.

I began this chapter by extracting the word "monster" from a single scene in the play and attending to how the noun is hollowed out by repetition, into a term that means everything and nothing at the same time. The theater fills this empty concept with an actor, demonstrating how to make a monster of a human through theatrical technologies that range from the properties of a "monstrous fish" to postnatal prophecies that disrupt scripted silence. Called a monster, Caliban resists the spectacle, whether it is imposed by Prospero's exercise of power or asserted by the clown figures who understand "monster" as a fixed register of difference. Monstrosity is both an artifice built from appearance-altering stage properties and a concept so incoherent that any other body may be drawn into—and therefore reshape—its parameters. And, like the masque's spirits, like the magus, like the duke and king, the figure nominated "monster" disappears when performance concludes. Monstrosity manifests as a signifying machine for the temporality of theatrical construction. Consequently, the theater's evanescence, the material instability of the body of the actor, undoes the dream of monstrosity's fixed signification.

Reading monstrosity as an early modern analogue to disability means attending to how these characters ask us to notice that bodily difference must be codified into a monstrosity that is never fixed or final. The early modern historical context for the monstrous body is one of relentless appropriation. Yet the monstrous character is also the most extreme example of what theatrical representation does. Caliban's character himself makes us look at an assemblage of costume, properties, gestures, and movement, the discourse of monstrosity laboriously materialized in theatrical practice. The monstrous character unsettles a narrative of signification by evoking unexpected attachments and unanticipated scripts. In so doing, monstrosity reveals a powerful resource for tracking disability in early modern texts. Rather than capturing a precursor to modernity's identity, disability names a contradiction between social construction and intractable materiality. The monstrous character points to a disabling charged by the fact of the actor's presence. Building the monstrous character out of properties, the process of theatrical performance does not organize a fixed showing and blatant legibility but instead reveals that the apparent self-evidence of the monstrous body is an unfixable frame.

Coda
Inviting Performance

> Because for theater one thing is as good as another, and this is the source of all comedy. Because for theater one thing is not the same as, and cannot never replace, another thing. And this is the source of all tragedy. Each of these masks, each of these faces, is wise, is wisdom incarnate. Because neither buys into the notion of what the Already known thinks is already known.
>
> —Mac Wellman, "Speculations: An Essay on the Theater"

> In art there is always a paradox involved, and here is drama's. Just because it employs this inevitably imperfect medium of humanity it must always be an imperfect art. And its strength must lie, not in logical conduct and regularity of form, but in employing to the full this rebellious human medium.
>
> —Harley Granville-Barker, *On Dramatic Method*

Both anonymous readers of this book for the press perceived an omission in the initial draft. Books in disability studies, they noted, often began with some narration about the author's own identity in relation to the field. They wondered whether this book might benefit from such a move of disclosure—a good question, for thoughtful reflection on the political commitments that follow from one's own position is a hallmark of both feminist critical analysis and disability studies. The gesture is powerful because it keeps in view disability theory's foundation in the politics of the disability rights movement and reminds us that, to borrow one reader's generative phrase, even approaches to disability that begin from form and aesthetics are political. I take their prompt, furthermore, as a corrective gesture to other modes of scholarly inquiry that, in a certain strand of historicism, would aspire to argumentation leached entirely of the author's personal investment.

I chose not to introduce the argument of my book with such a narrative. Since I began this project, I have been asked repeatedly by early modern scholars to account for my interest in disability with questions that seemed to presume that only personal experience would motivate critical attention to the topic. Such queries insist on a correspondence between an author's identity and critical project and, by confining investigations of identity to experience, troublingly establish other scholarly topics as self-justified or neutral, unmarked by subjectivity. Would they, I wondered, have assumed I was prescriptively motivated or biographically qualified to study early modern bureaucracies or liturgical practices or grammar schools? I hope this book suggests that disability reshapes our accounts of the early modern English theater, even for early modern scholars who may not identify as disabled or understand themselves (yet!) as working on disability. To put this another way, if we care about texts and bodies, about performance and witnessing—in short, if we care about the early modern theater—we should care about disability.

Yet, for the methodological and political reasons I noted above, it also feels important to say that the answer to questions about personal experience is: yes. My maternal grandparents met in the 1940s at a camp for children with cerebral palsy, an anecdotal institutional history that remains a gap in our family lore. My grandfather died before I was old enough to know him, but in my childhood memories, my grandmother employs a cane, and then a walker, and then a wheelchair, when she lived in our family home for her final years of life. I confronted questions of disability access as an undergraduate student, temporarily disabled as the result of a car accident, though it was not until later that I would read Michael Davidson's *Concerto for the Left Hand* and feel a thrill of visceral recognition. Davidson's generative insight that constraint can produce new formal possibilities recalled me to that year, learning left-hand-only compositions to perform the piano juries required for a music performance minor because my right hand was incapacitated by scar tissue. More recently, chronic pain poses the daily question of how long my body can afford to spend in the reiterative physical postures that scholarly research requires. The medical diagnosis was a forecast of future restriction even as it posited a cause: in an improbably recursive gesture to *Richard III*, reader, it is scoliosis. This condition torques my life in ways that are rarely apparent to others, though the contingency of embodied constraint shapes my day. In other words, of course I understand disability as a temporally unstable phenomenon, negotiated as lived experience but not yet as identity.

I offer these disclosures not to secure proof of my argument about the early modern theater, but to consider the implications for theorizing disability in the present. (Perhaps an additional implication is that studies of early modern bureaucracy and liturgical practices and grammar schools could also benefit from explicit articulation of critical orientations that drive their methodological practices.) Disability theory offers language for structures and concepts that have long been implicit in our assumptions about what bodies are and what they can do. In a reminder from the disability rights movement that I have repeated in this book, even an able body is only temporarily ablebodied. None of us need venture very far, once we are alert to the cultural workings that adjudicate what is "normal" and what is not, to perceive disabling structures everywhere. Disability is not only out there but always in here, woven into our daily lives. One powerful effect of working within paradigms of disability theory forged in our contemporary moment is the promise of finding recognizable antecedents for ideas—about norms, about bodies, about society, and crip reconfigurations of these ideas—that are still inchoate in the early modern period.

But in this project, I have also tried to ask: What might our current categories fail to make perceptible because we have defined in advance how disability is legible? The early modern theater's formal alterity offers a valuable resource. Documents of theatrical form, disappeared into an archive of traces and uneven preservation, produce disability knowledges that refuse predictable orderings of identity, embodiment, and experience. Rather than comply with a dictate to select in advance which differences essentialize the category of disabled identity, early modern texts demand we imagine disability otherwise. Throughout the chapters of this book, I have considered a variety of "disablings," verb-like in their orientation to theatrical process and noun-like in the fixing force of social structure or cultural proscription. From Richard III's deforming action to the monstrous character composed of properties, the staging of disability focuses attention, laser-like, on the bodies of specific characters, inviting us to read disability as a semiotic. Disability in these contexts is a kind of pointing at a body, one that is materially denoted by stage properties, costumes, and paint. Building on the social and cultural models of disability, I have traced technologies of marking that include discursive construction (those epithets and stage directions), conceptual structures such as character types, and cultural borrowings from pathologizing medical discourse, legal decrees for state assistance, and charitable appeals for aid. Just as importantly, however, disability is also a logic, a theatrical mechanism that escapes the affixing limitations of dramatic character to reorient the formal effects of an art premised on embodiment. A driver for the theater's showy stuff of corporeality, disability is fundamental to the doing of performance by scrambling the relations between part and whole, cause and effect, and particular and general. Disability is a productive glitch that interrupts the fantasy of smooth relay between form and matter, between actor and character, and between spectator and spectacle. These dramatic representations expose demands for able bodies at the heart of early modern social formations that we have not understood to require bodies, and they challenge conclusions about able bodies drawn in advance. Disability enables the early modern theater's rich and divergent discourses and practices of performance to analyze the formal problems of feigning and witnessing that are key to theatrical practice.

In the pages that follow, I trace the tension between fixing and unfixing through two late seventeenth-century texts, narrative accounts that recast the formal experiments that are the output of the early modern theater's staging of disability. In both cases, the spark of performance lights up not disabling phenomenon but the shadow of fixed disability, limning impulses that are disciplined into regularity or reduced to caricature. In 1698, when Jeremy Collier surveys the London theatrical landscape of the present and recent past, he recoils at what he encounters. In *A Short View of the Immorality, and Profaneness of the English Stage*, Collier levels many complaints against the theater, one predicated on the theater's formal cause. Like antitheatrical writers a century before, Collier relies on Aristotle's conception of the actor in relation to "Causes and Principles of Action," which he narrates as a problem of consistency.[1] Although "feign'd" characters are "formed upon the Diversities of Age, and Sex, of Fortune, Capacity, and Education," they should be scripted to act and speak what is suitably predictable to their kind, according to "Conformity of Practise, and Principle; of Nature, and Behaviour" (sig. P5v). Aligning nature and behavior, Collier worries about the relation between a character's intellectual and rhetorical capacity. Scripting characters, the author must not "let them skip from Wits to Blockheads," or, if "playing the Fool . . . never indulge them in fine Sentences" (sig. P6r). Even a cursory glance backwards finds examples, Shakespeare's *King Lear* perhaps the most obvious, that demonstrate how susceptible early modern playwrights were to the attractions of such an indulgence. Having figured the actor as the glitchy material of theater's techne, I cannot help but hear the "skip" of a character in the manner of a record scratch. Inveighing against theatrical indecorum that mismatches a character's capacity and rhetoric, Collier turns to a familiar term: "monstrous." He insists that "to manage otherwise is to desert *Nature*, and makes the *Play* appear monstrous, and Chimerical. So that instead of an *Image of life*, 'tis rather an Image of Impossibility" (sig. P6r). Leaping from a single character to the play itself, Collier consigns the whole to monstrosity. This appearance of monstrosity warps the play so that it no longer images "*life.*" Yet, in this process, the theater produces something else altogether: the "Image of Impossibility." Jeremiad or threnody, Collier's *View* finds in the problem of formal cause a threat to theatrical form. A retrospective glance at the early modern theater furnishes him with ready examples.

What is the nature of this "impossibility"? At the risk of overreading a cavil from Collier, I find this performed alternative—to "conformity," to "consistency," even to "life"—chimes with what Mac Wellman understands as the theater's formal paradox. In Wellman's formulation, my first epigraph here, every object—and here I would say "body"—is infinitely exchangeable ("one thing is as good as another"), a dream of reproducibility. At the same time, every body is also irreplaceably specific ("one thing is not the same as, and cannot [sic] never replace, another thing"), a dream of singularity.[2] Wellman aligns these impulses with experimental theater, but as my explorations show, the reach of his insight extends further back. In early modern performance, these dual currents of exchange and singularity pulse through the circuit of the play, figured most aptly in the temporary deformities of theatrical form. Still settling into representational practices that will become identified with realism's verisimilitude in the centuries that follow, the early modern theater reminds us that such mimetic norms arise unevenly. Early modern plays bear the tracks of the physical specificity of the actors for whom they were written, and they operate according to the loosest of essential conditions for mimesis. The early modern theater's traffic in disability is a tacit admission of disability's instrumentality to its formal practices, opting to "desert Nature" for the sake of a good show. Art swerves into impossibilities it will not render legible in terms of character, genre, or even play.

Scrutinizing early modern theatrical practice, therefore, we understand disability as a cultural analytic as well as an aesthetic experiment with the medium of the actor's body. Disability offers a ready set of naturalizing assumptions about a body—how it should look, what it can do, and what can be known about it from appearance. And, at the same time, disability troubles these epistemological assertions with an uncertain ontology. Performance calls into question whether a body can reliably disclose a person and suggests that the content of bodily knowledge is never stable. The early modern theater thus anticipates Harley Granville-Barker's insight (my second epigraph here) that the "rebellious human medium" of the actor is the source of the theater's "imperfect art" and its greatest "strength."[3] As we have seen throughout the preceding chapters, this paradox is irresistible to a theater that will not comply with what is, in Wellman's line, "already known."

My second example is an anonymous single-page entry in the Royal Society's *Philosophical Transactions* of 1698, sandwiched between a letter from Dr. William Musgrave about a rare palsy and a report from Isaac Newton about the effects of a poppy, and titled, "Of the Posture-Master."[4] The account describes Joseph Clark, a popular "posture-master" or contortionist, who was featured in *The Cryes of the City of London Drawne after the Life* (1688). Critics have read Clark as typical of eighteenth-century entertainment culture, a figure who assumes the visual flair of disability while being "quite able indeed to have 'normal' posture."[5] The anonymous account reports that Clark has mastered the skill of appearing "in all the Deformities that can be imagin'd, as Hunch Back'd, Pot Belly'd, Sharp Breasted; he dis-jointed his Arms, Shoulders, Legs and Thighs"; he is capable of transforming "his Face into all Shapes, so that by himself he acts all the uncouth, demure, odd Faces of a Quaker's Meeting." The body of the posture-master gathers many different forms and "Shapes" into his own; "by himself," in a feat of physical acting, he can produce an entire collectivity of differences. These poses are "deformities" because they literally change a body's form. But they are also recognizable as forms abstracted from other kinds of bodies. "Hunch Back'd" is an act of postural disjointing that adds up to a distinctly identifiable stereotype. The zenith of caricature even confounds social expectations about disabled beggars. Appearing as "an Object of Pity," Clark has "often impos'd on the same Company, where he has been just before, to give him Money as a Cripple; he looking so much unlike himself, that they could not know him." Possessing the capacity to form himself into recognizable types, Clark achieves the feat of antisimilitude—he can look "unlike himself," unrecognizable to the very crowd before whom he performed. His performance goes so far as to thwart the exercise of medical authority, for a celebrated physician ("our famous *Mullens*") "lookt on him in so miserable a Condition, that he would not undertake his Cure." The act of deforming shades into recognizable language of disease and illness, a marvel of bodily remaking good enough to fool even the most stringent medical gaze. The physician examines a body and mistakes feigning for being.

The formal problem of pinning down what a body does—indeed, what a body can do—flummoxes even the protocols of witnessing so prized by the Royal Society.[6] The correspondent admits the difficulty of reducing embodied action to narrative, noting, "I could not have conceiv'd it possible to have done what he did, unless I had seen it; and I am sensible how short I am come to a full Description of him: None certainly can describe what he does, but himself." The problem is translation between forms (how to describe in language what is perceptible visually?), and the descriptive difficulty is a register of performance's inevitable ephemerality.[7] Yet the real marvel here is how little knowledge even an encounter with this performance fails to effect. The narrator didn't know that such bodily deformations were possible, and—having seen them—he still doesn't know how to say what it is he has seen. Only the performer can give an account of his movements, but the admission suggests that even if Clark were to say what he does, the spectator would still not know *how* he does it. She would still reel at the unguessable gap between what she sees and what she thinks she knows about the limits of bodily transformation.

Clark's performance produces disability in the key of caricature, fixed in print, flattened to the page. Clark's contortions are freeze-framed abstractions, forms notable for technical prowess. Unembedded in a diegetic fiction, these bodily feints are extracted from character development and then repackaged for a witnessing public. Most of all, these temporary transformations borrow from, but never commit to, the thousand natural shocks to which an actor's flesh is heir over the course of a play. Collier's insistence that a play's excellence resides in consistent characterization and the posture-master's virtuosic compendium of deformities: both examples refuse imperfect actors and contingent interruptions. At the root, these accounts of performance aspire to polish the rough edges of mimesis into smooth predictability. Doing so, they admit in negative—by dwelling on consistency or by distilling to outline—that the theater's temporal art is bound up with the actor's risky, compelling, vulnerable body. These examples offer not a teleological end point but a dispersal. Juxtaposed, they fork into fantasies of representation and presentation.

Appealing to fixity, these accounts light up the stage as a site of formal unfixing, a space to experiment with a protean legacy. Staging disability, the early modern theater finds a resource for unfixing expectations about bodies and witnessing, one that goes far beyond merely a historicist correction to the story we have been telling about disability, to demonstrate instead how unfixable all bodies might be. The idea that these performances push disability into a new universalism draws inspiration from Madhavi Menon's articulation of a "queer universalism" as a refusal of the "line of predictability that gets drawn from the body to identity, and from desire to the self."[8] Building on Badiou, Menon finds an "anti-ontology" in the theater, "in which being can never coincide with itself. The theater text is not the same as its enacted representation, the enacted representation in turn is not reducible to the actors' ontology, and neither is the same from show to show or day to day." Above all, "the theater is witness to, indeed necessitates, the insubstantiality of identity."[9] This vision of the theater's potential to undo the constrictive lashings that hitch bodily particularity to identity is utopic, beyond even the utopian strand of theater theory that reaches for performance's "doing for and toward the future."[10] One way to concretize this utopic impulse is to return to the indeterminate histories the early modern theater holds open, before settling into paths that appear predetermined from our current vantage.

It is hard to overstate, however, the gap between this view of theater and the constraints on disabled actors in the present. As I noted in the introduction, foundational work demonstrates the discrimination that springs from insisting on the "neutral" body of the actor—with the result that certain bodies are barred from admission to classical acting programs, from casting, from receiving acclaim, when critics assume a disabled actor onstage is only being disabled, not acting.[11] This exclusion results in part from what Lennard J. Davis cogently identifies as the effect of an ableist culture's representational media, in which "disability can't just *be*—it has to *mean* something."[12] The flip side of this insistence that disability always signifies is that "possessing a functional leg is never allegorical, needs no interpretation, and is basically a degree-zero signifier without a referent."[13] This knotty complex of problems requires structural change. Classical programs should train disabled actors and learn from them how to challenge preconceptions about verse speaking and sword fighting that shape how skill is envisioned. Directors should cast disabled actors to play disabled characters—and to play characters not explicitly scripted with disabilities in order to understand what disability gain can add to a familiar text. Rather than selecting visible difference as the presentational fact that overshadows every other aspect of technique, critics should retrain their analytic faculties to attend to the many attributes that a disabled actor, like any actor, brings to characterization choices. These are structural problems that require overhaul at every level of theatrical practice; I want to stress how constrictive ableist practices have been, and how limited our critical and cultural conceptions of disability are as a result of these exclusions. At the same time, I also want to suggest that, when these changes have been achieved, such equity will still be mere preamble to a theater that learns from the radical specificity of disability's universalizing contingency to unlearn the fantasy of neutrality.

The early modern theater offers a genealogy of unfixing theatrical performance: plays as assemblages of parts, written for actors whose features sometimes generate the bodily differences of the characters. The physical idiosyncrasies that glimmer through the theater's dramatic texts do not begin as scripts that prescribe a body to be matched in casting, but as traces of the distinct bodies for whom they were composed. As Paul Menzer points out, "Textual characters took shape from the physiques of the actors. . . . Rosalind is not tall because the text says so, the text says so because Rosalind is tall—at least the boy playing her was."[14] This observation returns us to the material practices of the theater. The early modern actor's access to the part comes through the handwritten labor of the scribe, an etymology of "character" that, Menzer argues, sets up a different genealogy than that of a "'typecast' actor, with its figurative emphasis upon regularity, reproducibility and similarity."[15] Reversing the polarities by which we consider the relation between character and actor, we recognize the early modern theater's contingent challenge to modern assumptions that backfill the script. Our modern perception of theatrical process is one in which the dramatic character precedes the actor because the play precedes casting; we read discursive descriptions of characters as cues to appearance, enactment, and type. Thus, a "lame" character requires acting choices about how to signify this bodily condition, fitting a body of an actor into a character that is already there, or—more likely—prostheticizing it to produce a theatrical body. (When you are cast to play Richard Gloucester, you have to reckon with the history of that hump.)

Yet this model of character as exoskeletal frame obscures the unruly processes by which the early modern theater seems to have consumed the world and spit it back on stage. I borrow this metaphor from Bert States, who observes that theater "consumes the real in its realest forms," for its "permanent spectacle is the parade of objects and processes *in transit* from environment to imagery."[16] Rather than understand dramatic character only as the activation of preexisting metaphors, we can consider character a device that generates physical difference from the bodies of actors. What changes if, to follow Michael Bérubé's suggestion of trading "the project of encyclopedic typology" for "the affirmation of radical individuation" in our attention to disability, we read dramatic texts as the record of varied and astonishing possibilities that derive from the bodies that acted them in the first place?[17] I am not saying that early modern actors were disabled in our modern sense of the identity category; and I am certainly not saying that plays do not indulge, refract, and amplify the crassest ableism in early modern culture. Indeed, the chapters of this study have been concerned with exactly these disabling social formations that convert difference into disqualification. I am saying, rather, that the very process by which we make early modern disability legible should hold open this sense that the bodies of actors source the bodies of characters—not only the other way around. The adjectives that we now read as casting clues for visual similitude between actor and character may come not first from metaphor but from the bodies of actors.

Careful attention to the early modern theater returns us to the insight that performance originates in specificity. The fantasy in which the actor inhabits a new character, losing herself, forgets that the process of making a character sacralizes, in the literal sense of setting apart, the actor's body. No body on the stage is ever neutral—who has ever seen a tabula rasa? Typical is relative, developed by comparison to other bodies on the stage and to every other instantiation of the character. The historical conditions of the early modern theater return us to a moment when the typical has not yet settled into the normative. This history reveals that the perceived neutrality of an actor's body—as if it could be scrubbed clean for character differentiation—is a function of what has become regular, what has become predictable, what has become unremarked on in the anesthetic dulling of normative expectations. The early modern theater's aesthetic, therefore, defamiliarizes how we encounter disability on the stage. This is the analytic force of the theater's knack for rendering *as constructed* social arrangements that seem to be just "real life," when in fact they are cultural expressions rather than biological conditions. Held up to the light of mimetic practice, the stained-glass artifice of assumptions about bodily diversity become perceptible, even for a concept so apparently naturalized as disability. The story I have been telling about early modern drama insists that we recognize the power of fictions to explode the categories that an ableist culture imposes, and to contribute to the political efforts of thinking disability otherwise in the present.

The doing of theatrical practice—to return to my introductory epigraph, the idea that the actor's embodied presence is the very engine for and problem of dramatic form—challenges our fixed assumptions that seeming and being can be so easily cleaved. As a problem foregrounded by the dramatic fiction, as a demand for theatrical virtuosity, as a register of seeing and feigning, disability is a catalyst for the theater's signifying operations in the social world and a litmus test for the actor's pyrotechnical deformations. The forms of early modern disability ask us to scrutinize the oscillation of presentation and representation, to embrace possibilities that decline to close the circle of identity around a single attribute, and to submit to the theater's artful clock in order to recognize the chronologies with which our own orderings proceed. This is the gift of unfixability.

Notes

Introduction

1. William Shakespeare, *The Tragedy of Julius Caesar*, ed. William Montgomery, in *The Complete Pelican Shakespeare*, ed. Stephen Orgel and A. R. Braunmuller (London: Penguin Books, 2002), 1295–1336.

2. For a generative reading of Caesar's epilepsy as the play's engagement with emerging medical and social models of disability, see Allison P. Hobgood, "Caesar Hath the Falling Sickness: The Legibility of Early Modern Disability in Shakespearean Drama," *Disability Studies Quarterly* 29, no. 4 (2009), https://dsq-sds.org/article/view/993/1184Caesar.

3. Thus disability, Nancy J. Hirschmann observes, "is a social construction in the most obvious sense: Because of the ways that social relations, the built environment, laws, customs, and other practices are structured and organized, certain bodies are disabled, and other bodies are facilitated." Hirschmann, "Disability as a New Frontier for Feminist Intersectionality Research," *Politics and Gender* 8, no. 3 (2012): 398. The social model is widely developed in disability studies; see below for citations of the cultural model. As Petra Kuppers observes, the social model focuses on "how a society organizes itself" because—in the distinction between impairment and disabling world—disability "appears at the moment when [a] particular impairment enters the value scheme of a particular society." Kuppers, *Theatre and Disability* (London: Palgrave Macmillan, 2017), 7. Sara Hendren offers a useful overview of the distinction between medical and social models; in the social model, Hendren writes, it is "the *interaction* between the conditions of the body and the shapes of the world that makes disability into a lived experience, and therefore a matter not only for individuals but also for societies." Hendren, *What Can a Body Do? How We Meet the Built World* (New York: Riverhead Books, 2020), 15.

4. Subsequent revisions to the social model address its exclusions and weighting toward physical disability rather than intellectual or cognitive disability. The cultural model of disability observes that "impairment" is already predetermined by medical, social, and cultural norms, and that the social model cannot account for conditions, such as chronic pain, that cannot be alleviated even with accommodation. See especially David T. Mitchell and Sharon L. Snyder, *Cultural Locations of Disability* (Chicago: University of Chicago Press, 2006). Elaborating disability as a minority identity, Tobin Siebers calls disability "complex embodiment," or "a body of knowledge—a collection of skills, qualities, properties, and characteristics, among other things—both driven by the built environment and transformed by the variety and features of bodies."

Siebers, "Shakespeare Differently Disabled," in *The Oxford Handbook of Shakespeare and Embodiment*, ed. Valerie Traub (Oxford: Oxford University Press, 2016), 443.

5. I draw here on Mel Y. Chen's insight into the "collectivizing politics of nominalization" as a problem of temporality: "*Verbs* are defined as processes, that is, they are structured on some *time* relation (since things are dynamic: change is inherent to a verb)" while adjective and nouns trade this dynamism for nominalization, which "function[s] to fix, stabilize, and, most crucially, enable bounding." Chen, *Animacies: Biopolitics, Racial Mattering, and Queer Affect* (Durham, NC: Duke University Press, 2012), 73, 71, 74.

6. Michel Foucault, *Society Must Be Defended: Lectures at the Collège de France, 1975–1976 (Volume 5)*, trans. David Macey, ed. Mauro Bertani and Alessandro Fontana (New York: Picador, 2003), 28. In Foucault's account, psychiatry develops the concept of the norm as both "rule of conduct, informal law, and principle of conformity" in opposition to "irregularity, disorder, strangeness, eccentricity, unevenness, and deviation," as well as "functional regularity," which is "opposed to the pathological, morbid, disorganized, and dysfunctional." Foucault, *Abnormal: Lectures at the Collège de France, 1974–1975 (Volume 4)*, trans. Graham Burchell, ed. Valerio Marchetti and Antonella Salomoni (New York: Picador, 2003), 162. On the norm as a quantifiable standard, see Felicity A. Nussbaum, *The Limits of the Human: Fictions of Anomaly, Race, and Gender in the Long Eighteenth Century* (Cambridge: Cambridge University Press, 2003); Lennard Davis observes that the "new discursive category of disability" depends on the quantitatively "normal" body, a standard applied to diverse bodies, with the possibility of curing, surgically altering, or eliminating bodily "defects." Davis, *Bending Over Backwards: Disability, Dismodernism, and Other Difficult Positions* (New York: New York University Press, 2002), 57.

7. I discuss this critical commonplace in chapter 1; Mark Hutchings compactly expresses this formulation: "physically deformed, which for early moderns of course translated as moral deficiency, and often evil." Hutchings, "*Richard III* and *The Changeling*," *Notes and Queries* 52, no. 2 (2005): 229–30. By contrast, for a generative reading of deformity's appeal when constructed as evil, see Joel Elliot Slotkin, *Sinister Aesthetics: The Appeal of Evil in Early Modern English Literature* (Cham, Switzerland: Palgrave Macmillan / Springer Nature, 2017), esp. chap. 3.

8. Siebers, "Shakespeare Differently Disabled," 435. Work in medieval disability studies far exceeds the space of a footnote; see especially Julie Singer, introduction to the essay cluster "Disability and the Social Body" in *postmedieval: a journal of medieval cultural studies* 3, no. 2 (2012): 135–41; and Jonathan Hsy, "Disability," in *The Cambridge Companion to the Body in Literature*, ed. David Hillman and Ulrika Maude (Cambridge: Cambridge University Press, 2015), 22–40.

9. Allison P. Hobgood and David Houston Wood, "Introduction: Ethical Staring: Disabling the English Renaissance," in *Recovering Disability in Early Modern England*, ed. Allison P. Hobgood and David Houston Wood (Columbus: Ohio State University Press, 2013), 17; Sujata Iyengar, "Introduction: Shakespeare's 'Discourse of Disability,'" in *Disability, Health, and Happiness in the Shakespearean Body*, ed. Sujata Iyengar (London: Routledge, 2015), 7. See also the "Disabled Shakespeares" special section edited by Hobgood and Wood in *Disability Studies Quarterly* 29, no. 4 (2009), the first sustained attention to the intersection of disability studies and Shakespeare studies. Susan L. Anderson offers a wide-ranging overview of scholarship on disability, illumi-

nating ongoing and potential intersections with early modern drama in "Introduction: Disability in the Early Modern Theatre," *Early Theatre* 22, no. 2 (2019): 143–56.

10. Elizabeth B. Bearden, *Monstrous Kinds: Body, Space, and Narrative in Renaissance Representations of Disability* (Ann Arbor: University of Michigan Press, 2019), 7.

11. In Michael Davidson's groundbreaking reading of disability aesthetics, "disability, far from limiting possibilities of design or performance, liberates and changes the terms for composition." Davidson, *Concerto for the Left Hand: Disability and the Defamiliar Body* (Ann Arbor: University of Michigan Press, 2008), 3. A similar conviction motivates Rosemarie Garland-Thomson's "counter-eugenic arguments for conserving disability," in which disability "begins in bodily variation and the inherent dynamism of the flesh," and offers powerful aesthetic insight. Garland-Thomson, "The Case for Conserving Disability," *Journal of Bioethical Inquiry* 9, no. 3 (2012): 341, 342.

12. Genevieve Love, *Early Modern Theatre and the Figure of Disability* (London: Arden Shakespeare, 2019), 2, 22. Throughout this book, I retain italics in original text unless noted otherwise. Here I build on Allison P. Hobgood and David Houston Wood's generative account of disability "as a distinctive resource and aesthetic template." Hobgood and Wood, "Early Modern Literature and Disability Studies," in *The Cambridge Companion to Literature and Disability*, ed. Clare Barker and Stuart Murray (Cambridge: Cambridge University Press, 2018), 42.

13. See David T. Mitchell and Sharon L. Snyder, *Narrative Prosthesis: Disability and the Dependencies of Discourse* (Ann Arbor: University of Michigan Press, 2000), esp. 1–14 and 47–64.

14. Mitchell and Snyder, *Narrative Prosthesis*, 21. This orientation to disability experience founds the literary history of disability on William Hay's *Deformity: An Essay*, 2nd ed. (London: Printed for R. and J. Dodsley, 1754), which Lennard J. Davis identifies as a "watershed" event in disability self-representation because the text introduces the "disabled person in print as author and character." Davis, *Bending Over Backwards*, 55. See also Stephen Pender's foundational reading of Hay's text in "In the Bodyshop: Human Exhibition in Early Modern England," in *"Defects": Engendering the Modern Body*, ed. Helen Deutsch and Felicity Nussbaum (Ann Arbor: University of Michigan Press, 2000), 95–126. On early modern autobiographical narratives, see Encarnación Juárez-Almendros, *Disabled Bodies in Early Modern Spanish Literature: Prostitutes, Aging Women, and Saints* (Liverpool: Liverpool University Press, 2017).

15. Herbert Blau, *Take Up the Bodies: Theater at the Vanishing Point* (Urbana: University of Illinois Press, 1982), 13.

16. Or, as Petra Kuppers puts it succinctly, "non-disabled performers playing being disabled." Kuppers, *Theatre and Disability*, 37. See also Kirsty Johnston's useful account of acting and embodiment in relation to disability theater aesthetics in *Disability Theatre and Modern Drama: Recasting Modernism* (London: Bloomsbury Methuen Drama, 2016), esp. chap. 1. On disability drag, see Siebers, who notes that "the more disabled the character, the greater the ability of the actor"; critics and audiences praise performances for "accurate representation," while failing to notice that "disability appears as a facade overlaying ablebodiedness." Siebers, *Disability Theory* (Ann Arbor: University of Michigan Press, 2008), 116, 115, 116.

17. Sandahl observes, for example, that actor training textbooks routinely assert that "anything that is not neutral is the beginning of a characterization." Carrie Sandahl, "The Tyranny of Neutral: Disability and Actor Training," in *Bodies in Commotion:*

Disability and Performance, eds. Carrie Sandahl and Philip Auslander (Ann Arbor: University of Michigan Press, 2005), 261.

18. Herbert Blau observes that the words "theater" and "theory" come from the same Greek root, the word *theasthai*, "meaning to watch, contemplate, look at," so that "in the act of seeing, there is already theory." Blau, *Take Up the Bodies*, 1. The theater's orientation to spectatorship is crucial to my argument about the early modern theater in this book; I want to acknowledge, however, the important disability critique of the equation of sight with perception (expressed most explicitly, perhaps, in the ableist language of "blind" casting—now beginning to shift to terms such as "conscious" casting). Exciting new work on inclusive theater challenges our assumptions about visibility: see Jill Marie Bradbury et al., "ProTactile Shakespeare: Inclusive Theater by/for the Deaf-Blind," *Shakespeare Studies* 47 (2019): 81–99.

19. Sandahl, "Tyranny of Neutral," 262. Sandahl notes that since "outward physicality is most often used as shorthand for the character's inner psychological or emotional state," the disabled character often becomes the "work's central image" (255).

20. This selective perception exemplifies what Rosemarie Garland-Thomson calls "the normate's frequent assumption that a disability cancels out other qualities, reducing the complex person to a single attribute." Garland-Thomson, *Extraordinary Bodies: Figuring Physical Disability in American Culture and Literature* (New York: Columbia University Press, 1997), 12.

21. Petra Kuppers, "Deconstructing Images: Performing Disability," *Contemporary Theatre Review* 11, nos. 3–4 (2001): 26.

22. Both Kuppers, *Disability and Theatre*, and Johnston, *Disability Theatre*, offer useful surveys of recent work focused on disability; see also Mike Lew's reflection on the practice, with Gregg Mozgala, of adapting Shakespeare and foregrounding the virtuosity of disabled actors in *Teenage Dick* (London: Nick Hern Books, 2019), 5–8.

23. Joseph R. Roach, *The Player's Passion: Studies in the Science of Acting* (Newark: University of Delaware Press, 1985), 49.

24. On anecdotes of medieval performance as material force, see Jodie Enders, *Death by Drama and Other Medieval Urban Legends* (Chicago: University of Chicago Press, 2002). On the early modern theater's propensity for disastrous culmination, see Ellen MacKay, *Persecution, Plague, and Fire: Fugitive Histories of the Stage in Early Modern England* (Chicago: University of Chicago Press, 2011).

25. Robert Armin, *The Two Maids of Moreclack*, ed. Richard Preiss, in *The Routledge Anthology of Early Modern Drama*, ed. Jeremy Lopez (London: Routledge, 2020), esp. 743–45.

26. See Lindsey Row-Heyveld, *Dissembling Disability in Early Modern English Drama* (Cham, Switzerland: Palgrave Macmillan / Springer Nature, 2018).

27. See Love, *Figure of Disability*, 23–30.

28. Robert McRuer, "Fuck the Disabled: The Prequel," in *Shakesqueer: A Queer Companion to the Complete Works of Shakespeare*, ed. Madhavi Menon (Durham, NC: Duke University Press, 2011), 296. In McRuer's formulation, the term "crip," which disability rights activists have redefined from the slur, centers disabled people and affirms "collective crip dissent." Robert McRuer, *Crip Theory: Cultural Signs of Queerness and Disability* (New York: New York University Press, 2006), 37. I take seriously Siebers's critique of "the celebration of disability as power," which he associates with McRuer's reading of Richard as a crip figure ("Shakespeare Differently Disabled," 452). As we scrutinize the

fictions the early modern theater bequeaths, however, I suggest that we must attend to their historicity, and especially to the alterity of early modern performance. On "crip," see also Carrie Sandahl's germinal "Queering the Crip or Cripping the Queer? Intersections of Queer and Crip Identities in Solo Autobiographical Performance," *Gay and Lesbian Quarterly* 9, nos. 1–2 (2003): 25–56; Alison Kafer foregrounds the "contestatory" power and "potential expansiveness" of the term to galvanize identity politics. Kafer, *Feminist, Queer, Crip* (Bloomington: Indiana University Press, 2013), 15.

29. McRuer, *Crip Theory*, 36.

30. Tobin Siebers, *Disability Aesthetics* (Ann Arbor: University of Michigan Press, 2010), 3.

31. *Statutes of the Realm*, vol. 4, pt. 2 (London: Dawsons of Pall Mall, 1963), "An Acte for Relief of Souldiors" 1592, 35 Eliz. 1, c. 4, 847. Charles Mathew Clode notes that the act's provisions were upheld in following statutes: 39 Eliz. 1, c. 21; 43 Eliz. 1, c. 3; 1 James 1, c. 25; 21 James 1, c. 28; 3 Car. 1, c. 5. Clode, *The Military Forces of the Crown: Their Administration and Government* (London: John Murray, 1869), 1:353; *Statutes of the Realm*, vol. 4, pt. 2, "An Acte for erecting of Hospitalls or abiding and working Howses for the Poore," 39 Eliz. 1, c. 5, 905. As Steve Hindle notes, the "deserving poor" designated by the laws were "identified primarily by their *inability to labour*." Hindle, "Civility, Honesty and the Identification of the Deserving Poor in Seventeenth-Century England," in *Identity and Agency in England, 1500–1800*, ed. Henry French and Jonathan Barry (New York: Palgrave Macmillan, 2004), 38.

32. Iyengar, "Introduction: Shakespeare's 'Discourse of Disability,'" 8.

33. George Puttenham, *The Art of English Poesy*, ed. Frank Whigham and Wayne A. Rebhorn (Ithaca, NY: Cornell University Press, 2007), 304–5. See also Vin Nardizzi, "Disability Figures in Shakespeare," in Traub, *Oxford Handbook of Shakespeare and Embodiment*, 455–67.

34. Davis, *Bending Over Backwards*, 52, 58. David Turner likewise asserts that in early modernity, "the concept of disability was subsumed under other categories, notably deformity and monstrosity." Turner, "Introduction: Approaching Anomalous Bodies," in *Social Histories of Disability and Deformity*, ed. David M. Turner and Kevin Stagg (London: Routledge, 2006), 4.

35. See Katherine Schaap Williams, "Enabling Richard: The Rhetoric of Disability in *Richard III*," in *Disability Studies Quarterly* 29, no. 4 (2009), http://dsq-sds.org/article/view/997/1181. In the essay, I draw on Davis's illuminating discussion of the "dismodern subject"; although in this book I excavate the early modern concept of deformity differently than Davis does, my ideas here have been shaped by early engagement with his foundational work.

36. Irina Metzler's early work on medieval disability used "impairment" rather than "disability," for example. Metzler, *Disability in Medieval Europe: Thinking about Physical Impairment in the Middle Ages, c. 1100–1400* (London: Routledge, 2006), 5. Other scholars track specific terms for bodily difference but most now regularly use "disability" while acknowledging the complications of the terminological fit. Given the possibilities of strategic anachronism and the celebration of disability aesthetics, I refuse Jeffrey Wilson's suggestion that we should return to the limited vocabulary of "stigma," which fails to take stock of important political work forged around disability politics. Wilson, "The Trouble with Disability in Shakespeare Studies," *Disability Studies Quarterly* 37, no. 2 (2017), https://dsq-sds.org/article/view/5430/4644.

37. Martin Porter, *Windows of the Soul: The Art of Physiognomy in European Culture, 1470–1780* (Oxford: Oxford University Press, 2005), 190.

38. Thomas Bedford, *A True and Certaine Relation of a Strange-birth* (London: Anne Griffin for William Russell, 1635), sig. B2r.

39. Robert Burton, *The Anatomy of Melancholy*, ed. Holbrook Jackson (New York: Vintage Books, 1977), pt. 2, 133. On "accident" as a broader early modern phenomenon, see Michael Witmore, *Culture of Accidents: Unexpected Knowledges in Early Modern England* (Stanford, CA: Stanford University Press, 2001).

40. Burton, *Anatomy of Melancholy*, pt. 2, 133.

41. Burton, *Anatomy of Melancholy*, pt. 2, 133.

42. Burton, *Anatomy of Melancholy*, pt. 2, 134.

43. Burton, *Anatomy of Melancholy*, pt. 3, 25.

44. Work on early modern embodiment and the theater far exceeds the reach of a single citation. Foundational texts that underlined this variability include Gail Kern Paster, *The Body Embarrassed: Drama and the Disciplines of Shame in Early Modern England* (Ithaca, NY: Cornell University Press, 1993) and *Humoring the Body: Emotions and the Shakespearean Stage* (Chicago: University of Chicago Press, 2004); Kim F. Hall, *Things of Darkness: Economies of Race and Gender in Early Modern England* (Ithaca, NY: Cornell University Press, 1995), to which I return in chapter 6; Michael C. Schoenfeldt, *Bodies and Selves in Early Modern England: Physiology and Inwardness in Spenser, Shakespeare, Herbert, and Milton* (Cambridge: Cambridge University Press, 1999); Gail Kern Paster, Katherine Rowe, and Mary Floyd-Wilson, eds., *Reading the Early Modern Passions* (Philadelphia: University of Pennsylvania Press, 2004); and Katharine A. Craik and Tanya Pollard, eds., *Shakespearean Sensations: Experiencing Literature in Early Modern England* (Cambridge: Cambridge University Press, 2013).

45. John Bulwer, *Anthropometamorphosis: man transform'd: or, the artificiall changling* (London: William Hunt, 1653), sig. 3*1v.

46. Bearden notes, for example, that disability is often "voiced intersectionally with misogyny and is dependent on social constructions of female disability independent of any actual impairment" (*Monstrous Kinds*, 47). Disability thus intersects with concepts of race and gender that, as Valerie Traub observes, "become tethered to particular bodies" and also "settle into paradigmatic models for thinking about whole populations" in modernity. "Introduction: Feminist Shakespeare Studies," in Traub, *Oxford Handbook of Shakespeare and Embodiment*, 23.

47. Patricia Akhimie, *Shakespeare and the Cultivation of Difference: Race and Conduct in the Early Modern World* (London: Routledge, 2018), 8, 5.

48. Disability thus functions in the dual mode Ellen Samuels has identified: as both "*object* of identification" and a "symbolic *anchor*," the "trope of physicality" that secures other mechanisms of disqualification. Samuels, *Fantasies of Identification: Disability, Gender, Race* (New York: New York University Press, 2014), 13, 14.

49. Baldesar Castiglione, *The Book of the Courtier*, trans. and ed. George Bull (London: Penguin, 1967), 55.

50. Bearden, *Monstrous Kinds*, 54. Bearden's reading qualifies the emphasis on "self-fashioning" associated with the Renaissance; see Stephen Greenblatt, *Renaissance Self-Fashioning: From More to Shakespeare* (Chicago: University of Chicago Press, 1980).

51. Hobgood and Wood, "Early Modern Literature," 34. See Bearden, "Before Normal, There Was Natural," chap. 2 in *Monstrous Kinds*. On norms in the early mod-

ern period, see also Valerie Traub, "The Nature of Norms in Early Modern England: Anatomy, Cartography, *King Lear,*" *South Central Review* 26, nos. 1–2 (2009): 42–81; and Carla Mazzio's study of linguistic failure and rhetorical norms in *The Inarticulate Renaissance: Language Trouble in an Age of Eloquence* (Philadelphia: University of Pennsylvania Press, 2009).

52. John Bulwer, *Philocophus: or, The Deafe and Dumbe Mans Friend* (London: Printed for Humphrey Moseley, 1648), sig. A2r. The capital "D" signals Deaf identity and a minoritized language community; Bulwer's formulation here is closer to the concept of "Deaf gain," a term advanced in Deaf studies to reframe the deficit-based concept of hearing loss. On Deaf gain, see especially *Deaf Gain: Raising the Stakes for Human Diversity*, ed. H-Dirksen L. Bauman and Joseph J. Murray (Minneapolis: University of Minnesota Press, 2014); on Bulwer's interest in Deaf rights, see Bearden, *Monstrous Kinds*, chap. 2, esp. 88–89.

53. Bulwer, *Philocophus*, sig. A2v.

54. Puttenham, *Art*, 122.

55. Compare Rosemarie Garland-Thomson's generative observation that the "appearance of disability in the public sphere makes, then, for a stareable sight." Garland-Thomson, *Staring: How We Look* (Oxford: Oxford University Press, 2009), 20.

56. Foundational work in disability studies figures literary representation as a circuit; Ato Quayson describes disability as the "short-circuiting of the dominant protocols governing the text" through the affect of "aesthetic nervousness." Quayson, *Aesthetic Nervousness: Disability and the Crisis of Representation* (New York: Columbia University Press, 2007), 15. Michael Bérubé develops Quayson's image to describe disability as an on-off switch that enables some narrative functions and disables others, without resorting to "normative judgments about what a narrative ought to be." Bérubé, *The Secret Life of Stories: From Don Quixote to Harry Potter, How Understanding Intellectual Disability Transforms the Way We Read* (New York: New York University Press, 2016), 56. The account I offer here torques the circuit metaphor because—unlike the closed representational circuit of a text that disability disrupts—the temporality of performance means the theater's representational circuit is never fully closed.

57. The primary meaning of the verb "perform," in early modern usage, conveys a sense of completion; thus, as Mary Thomas Crane has shown, theatrical "feigning" expresses the accomplishment of an action rather than deception. Crane, "What Was Performance?" *Criticism* 43, no. 2 (2001): 172. John Astington notes that "counterfeit" could refer to theatrical "making," though the term "seems invested with uncertainty about what it is that is being made." Astington, *Actors and Acting in Shakespeare's Time* (Cambridge: Cambridge University Press, 2010), 14.

58. W. B. Worthen, *Shakespeare Performance Studies* (Cambridge: Cambridge University Press, 2014), 11. Critical work that takes seriously the early modern theater's power to make, not merely reflect, culture is voluminous (and exciting); for a useful overview, in addition to the works I cite below, see Henry S. Turner's introduction, "Generalization," in *Early Modern Theatricality*, ed. Henry S. Turner (Oxford: Oxford University Press, 2013), 1–23.

59. Erika T. Lin, *Shakespeare and the Materiality of Performance* (New York: Palgrave Macmillan, 2012), 9.

60. John Marston, *The History of Antonio and Mellida* (London: Printed for Mathewe Lownes and Thomas Fisher, 1602), sig. A3r.

61. Roach, *Player's Passion*, 27–28.

62. Stephen Gosson, *Playes Confuted in Five Actions* (London: Thomas Gosson, 1582), sig. E5r. Marvin Carlson notes that for Gosson, the formal cause of a play is "the manner of representation itself": the actor's feigning. Carlson, *Theories of the Theatre*, 2nd ed. (Ithaca, NY: Cornell University Press, 1995), 81.

63. William Perkins, *The Whole Treatise of the Cases of Conscience* (Cambridge: John Legat, 1608), sig. 2G7r.

64. William Prynne, *Histrio-Mastix: The players scourge, or, actors tragedie* (London: E[dward] A[llde, Augustine Mathewes, Thomas Cotes] and W[illiam] J[ones] for Michael Sparke, 1633), sigs. X3v–X4r. See also Lisa A. Freeman's study of Prynne's preoccupation with the theater in *Antitheatricality and the Body Public* (Philadelphia: University of Pennsylvania Press, 2017), chap. 1.

65. Prynne, *Histrio-Mastix*, sig. 5X4v.

66. John Rainolds, *Th'overthrow of Stage Playes* (Middelburg, NL: Printed by Richard Schilders, 1599), sig. D2r.

67. Richard Jones, "To the Gentlemen Readers and others that take pleasure in reading Histories," in *Tamburlaine the Great*, by Christopher Marlowe (London: Richard Jones, 1590), sigs. A2r–v. I thank Andrew Bozio for reminding me of this reference.

68. *Oxford English Dictionary*, s.v. "deform (v.)," definition v.1, esp. 1a and 2; definition v.2.

69. Colleen Ruth Rosenfeld, *Indecorous Thinking: Figures of Speech in Early Modern Poetics* (New York: Fordham University Press, 2018), 75.

70. William N. West, "What's the Matter with Shakespeare? Physics, Identity, Playing," *South Central Review* 26, nos. 1–2 (Spring–Summer 2009): 113.

71. Rosenfeld, *Indecorous Thinking*, 4. See also Henry S. Turner's compelling injunction to understand form "as a verb rather than as a noun." Turner, "Lessons from Literature for the Historian of Science (and Vice Versa): Reflections on 'Form'" *ISIS* 101 (2010): 582. Thus, as "an *ontological* category that is simultaneously structural and temporal," form enables reproducibility. Jenny C. Mann and Debapriya Sarkar, "Introduction: Capturing Proteus," *Philological Quarterly* 98, no. 1–2 (2019): 3.

72. Rosenfeld, *Indecorous Thinking*, 4.

73. Ben Jonson, *Timber: Or, Discoveries*, ed. Lorna Hutson, in *The Cambridge Edition of the Works of Ben Jonson*, ed. David Bevington, Martin Butler, and Ian Donaldson (Cambridge: Cambridge University Press, 2012), 7: 579.

74. Elin Diamond, introduction to *Performance and Cultural Politics*, ed. Elin Diamond (London: Routledge, 1996), 1.

75. Diamond, *Cultural Politics*, 5.

76. As Keir Elam writes, "The actor's body acquires its mimetic and representational power by becoming something other than itself, more and less than individual." Elam, *The Semiotics of Theatre and Drama*, 2nd ed. (London: Methuen, 1980; New York: Routledge, 2002), 7. Citations refer to the Routledge edition. Elam draws here on Jiří Veltruský's characterization of the actor's body as "the dynamic unity of an entire set of signs" (7).

77. Or, as Erika Fischer-Lichte puts it, since "the body of the dramatic character as brought forth by means of language will be reproduced by means of the actor's body," the actor's body is symbolized, or "made significant," and language is desymbolized:

"The significance of language is partly canceled and extinguished by the nature of the actor's body." Fischer-Lichte, "Signs of Identity: The Dramatic Character as 'Name' and 'Body,'" in *The Show and the Gaze of Theatre: A European Perspective* (Iowa City: University of Iowa Press, 1997), 294.

78. In his foundational work, Robert Weimann associates representational action with the *locus* and presentational (or "nonrepresentational") action with the *platea* to account for theatrical power. Weimann, *Shakespeare and the Popular Tradition in the Theater: Studies in the Social Dimension of Dramatic Form and Function*, ed. Robert Schwartz (Baltimore: Johns Hopkins University Press, 1978), esp. 1–11, 73–84, 151–60. Erika Lin cogently reformulates Weimann's insight to argue that early modern plays privilege characters "who articulate the most awareness of this theatrical semiotics and who showcase their ability to manipulate such signifiers." Lin, *Materiality of Performance*, 37. Critical work on character in the theatrical environment underscores the vitality of the actor in the role. See, for example, Worthen's discussion of the affordances of the role in *Shakespeare Performance Studies*, esp. chap. 3; Andrew James Hartley's account of the "degree of familiarity" that an actor brings to a role in "Character, Agency and the Familiar Actor," in *Shakespeare and Character: Theatre, History, Performance, and Theatrical Persons*, ed. Paul Yachnin and Jessica Slights (New York: Palgrave Macmillan, 2009), 159; and David Mann's discussion of the "dual apprehension, which the spectator is able to have, of actor and role as two distinct entities." Mann, *The Elizabethan Player: Contemporary Stage Representation* (London: Routledge, 1991), 3. For an illuminating account of the actor's "skill," see Evelyn Tribble, *Early Modern Actors and Shakespeare's Theatre: Thinking with the Body* (London: Bloomsbury Arden Shakespeare, 2017).

79. Or, as Love puts it "Theatrical personation is decisively figured by prosthetic disabled characters." Love, *Figure of Disability*, 22.

80. Thomas Overbury, *New and Choice Characters* (London: Thomas Creede for Laurence Lisle, 1615), sigs. M5v–M6r.

81. Philip Henslowe, *Henslowe's Diary*, ed. R. A. Foakes, 2nd ed. (Cambridge: Cambridge University Press, 1961; 2002), 320. Citations refer to the 2002 edition. Following William N. West's injunction to think intertheatrically, an approach that understands "performance as its own archive," we could trace how theatrical properties that signal bodily difference, such as the wooden leg, affiliate actors, characters, plots, and plays in surprising ways. William N. West, "Intertheatricality," in Turner, *Early Modern Theatricality*, 155.

82. On stage properties, see Jonathan Gil Harris and Natasha Korda, "Introduction: Towards a Materialist Account of Stage Properties," in *Staged Properties in Early Modern English Drama*, ed. Jonathan Gil Harris and Natasha Korda (Cambridge: Cambridge University Press, 2002); Andrew Sofer, *The Stage Life of Props* (Ann Arbor: University of Michigan Press, 2003); and Andrew Sofer, "Properties," in *The Oxford Handbook of Early Modern Theatre*, ed. Richard Dutton (Oxford: Oxford University Press, 2009), 560–74. On property use, see Frances Teague, *Shakespeare's Speaking Properties* (Lewisburg, PA: Bucknell University Press, 1991); and Tiffany Stern, *Making Shakespeare: From Stage to Page* (London: Routledge, 2004), esp. 91–112. On early modern theatrical prosthetics and the actor's body, see especially Will Fisher, *Materializing Gender in Early Modern English Literature and Culture* (Cambridge: Cambridge University Press, 2006); Andrea Ria Stevens, *Inventions of the Skin: The Painted Body in Early*

English Drama, 1400–1642 (Edinburgh: Edinburgh University Press, 2013); and Ian Smith, "The Textile Black Body: Race and 'Shadowed Livery' in *The Merchant of Venice*," in Traub, *Oxford Handbook of Shakespeare and Embodiment*, 170–85.

83. These stage directions come from *Hamlet* Q1 (G4r, 4.5.20) and *Orlando Furioso* (842); see Alan C. Dessen and Leslie Thomson, *A Dictionary of Stage Directions in English Drama, 1580–1642* (Cambridge: Cambridge University Press, 1999), 138. As Row-Heyveld notes, madness and foolishness "qualify as disability in the emerging legal definitions . . . as ailments rendering one incapable of work, grouping them with impairments like deafness, blindness, lameness, and so on." Row-Heyveld, *Dissembling Disability*, 21.

84. James Boswell, *The Life of Samuel Johnson* (London, 1791), 2:163.

85. As Love puts it, theater is "a medium always in transit," a meeting between "disabled prosthetic bodies characterized by anomalous locomotion, and the 'movement-between' of figuration itself." Love, *Figure of Disability*, 31.

86. I am thinking here of Nardizzi's insight that disability prosthetics "may be as rhetorical as they are material," and of the social model's emphasis on disabling environments. Nardizzi, "Disability Figures," 459.

87. Mitchell and Snyder, *Narrative Prosthesis*, 47, 48.

88. Mitchell and Snyder, *Narrative Prosthesis*, 55–56.

89. Mario DiGangi, *Sexual Types: Embodiment, Agency, and Dramatic Character from Shakespeare to Shirley* (Philadelphia: University of Pennsylvania Press, 2011), 5. Scholarship on dramatic character is extensive: on dramatic characters as "agents of theatrical meaning," see Jeremy Lopez, "Imagining the Actor's Body on the Early Modern Stage," *Medieval and Renaissance Drama in England* 20 (2007): 187–203, 188; on character as the "organizing principle" of a play, see Paul Yachnin and Jessica Slights, introduction to *Shakespeare and Character*, ed. Yachnin and Slights, 6; on Shakespeare's concept of character, see especially Christy Desmet, *Reading Shakespeare's Characters* (Amherst: University of Massachusetts Press, 1992), and Lorna Hutson, *Circumstantial Shakespeare* (Oxford: Oxford University Press, 2015); for a provocative account of character as a "collection of every example of a kind," see Aaron Kunin, *Character as Form* (London: Bloomsbury Arden Shakespeare, 2019), 5.

90. As Amy Cook discusses, the practice of casting depends on deciding "what makes a trait essential to a character." Cook, *Building Character: The Art and Science of Casting* (Ann Arbor: University of Michigan Press, 2018), 5. See also Johnston, *Disability Theatre*, esp. chap. 2.

91. Bérubé, *Secret Life of Stories*, 49. Bérubé's account focuses on narrative strategies, but I extend his critique of the practice of diagnosing literary characters. He observes that "disability in the relation between text and reader *need not involve any character with disabilities at all*" but can "involve *ideas about* disability, and ideas about the stigma associated with disability, regardless of whether any specific character can be pegged with a specific diagnosis" (19). As instructive contrast, see also Kuppers's reminder that, in theatrical adaptations, "the game of backdiagnosing historical figures is both rife with problems and also very good fun for minority culture members who want to create a canon for themselves." Kuppers, *Theatre and Disability*, 17.

92. Philip Sidney, *A Defence of Poetry*, ed. J. A. van Dorsten (Oxford: Oxford University Press, 1966), 36.

93. Jeremy Collier, *A Short View of the Immorality, and Profaneness of the English Stage, Together With the Sense of Antiquity upon this Argument* (London: S. Keble, R. Sare, and H. Hindmarsh, 1698), sig. T5v.

1. Deformed

1. Siebers, *Disability Theory*, 48; Quayson, *Aesthetic Nervousness*, 27.

2. Mitchell and Snyder, *Narrative Prosthesis*, 102, 105. See also Henri-Jacques Stiker's observation that the historical era of classification "neatly separates the universe of congenital *deformity* from that of inherent or acquired *disability*." Stiker, *A History of Disability*, trans. William Sayers (Ann Arbor: University of Michigan Press, 1999), 95 (emphasis in original).

3. The "new discursive category of disability," Lennard J. Davis notes, appears "continuous, running the gamut from physical impairments to deformity to monstrosity to madness," and the category requires "an institutional, medicalized apparatus to house, segregate, isolate, or fix people with disabilities." Davis, *Bending Over Backwards*, 57.

4. In addition to work cited below, classic studies include A. P. Rossiter, "Angel with Horns: The Unity of *Richard III*," in *Angel with Horns: Fifteen Lectures on Shakespeare*, ed. Graham Storey (New York: Longman, 1989); and Richard P. Wheeler, "History, Character, and Conscience in *Richard III*," *Comparative Drama* 5 (1971–1972): 301–21. On deformity as a feature of Richard's body and historiography, see Marjorie Garber, *Shakespeare's Ghost Writers: Literature as Uncanny Causality* (New York: Methuen, 1987).

5. Linda Charnes, *Notorious Identity: Materializing the Subject in Shakespeare* (Cambridge, MA: Harvard University Press, 1993), 30; John S. Wilks, *The Idea of Conscience in Renaissance Tragedy* (London: Routledge, 1990), 19.

6. Marie-Hélène Besnault and Michel Bitot, "Historical Legacy and Fiction: The Poetical Reinvention of King Richard III," in *The Cambridge Companion to Shakespeare's History Plays*, ed. Michael Hattaway (Cambridge: Cambridge University Press, 2002), 110.

7. Simon Palfrey and Tiffany Stern, *Shakespeare in Parts* (Oxford: Oxford University Press, 2007), 359.

8. Brian Gibbons, *Shakespeare and Multiplicity* (Cambridge: Cambridge University Press, 1993), 62.

9. Williams, "Enabling Richard."

10. Allison P. Hobgood, "Teeth before Eyes: Impairment and Invisibility in Shakespeare's *Richard III*," in Iyengar, *Disability, Health, and Happiness*, 28.

11. Geoffrey A. Johns, "A 'Grievous Burthen': *Richard III* and the Legacy of Monstrous Birth," in Iyengar, *Disability, Health, and Happiness*, 46.

12. Nardizzi, "Disability Figures," 466.

13. Row-Heyveld, *Dissembling Disability*, 139.

14. Love, *Figure of Disability*, 131.

15. I owe this formulation partly to Genevieve Love.

16. Abigail Elizabeth Comber, "A Medieval King 'Disabled' by an Early Modern Construct: A Contextual Examination of *Richard III*," in *Disability in the Middle Ages: Reconsiderations and Reverberations*, ed. Joshua R. Eyler (Burlington, VT: Ashgate, 2010), 186.

17. Siebers, "Shakespeare Differently Disabled," 451. Siebers queries my early formulation of the claim that Richard's deformity enables his quest for power, and suggests that "knowledge might replace power as the goal of disability interpretation" (452). I understand Siebers's generative account of embodied knowledge as one illustration of my speculation at the end of that essay: "How might we conceive of the Renaissance stage as a potential place to locate the kind of bodily contingency we associate with more contemporary literary accounts of disability?" Williams, "Enabling Richard." I would distinguish, then, between Siebers's important argument for disability identity in modernity and his reading of Shakespeare's *Richard III*, which does not account for the play's theatrical form.

18. Siebers, "Shakespeare Differently Disabled," 435.

19. Puttenham, *Art*, 335; Sidney, *Defence of Poetry*, 68; *Hic Mulier*, in *Half Humankind: Contexts and Texts of the Controversy about Women in England, 1540–1640*, ed. Katherine Usher Henderson and Barbara F. McManus (Chicago: University of Illinois Press, 1985), 268–69.

20. Robert Weimann, *Author's Pen and Actor's Voice: Playing and Writing in Shakespeare's Theatre*, ed. Helen Higbee and William West (Cambridge: Cambridge University Press, 2000), 81; West, "What's the Matter," 117.

21. Weimann, *Author's Pen*, 79. Alan C. Dessen notes that "if allusions from the 1580s through the 1600s are to be trusted, the best remembered figure from late Tudor and early Elizabethan drama was not Everyman, Mankind, or Wit but the Vice." Dessen, *Recovering Shakespeare's Theatrical Vocabulary* (Cambridge: Cambridge University Press, 1995), 110.

22. Richard Preiss, *Clowning and Authorship in Early Modern Theatre* (Cambridge: Cambridge University Press, 2014), 225.

23. West, "What's the Matter," 116.

24. Garber, *Shakespeare's Ghost Writers*, 58. This deforming action is fundamental to Robert McRuer's reading of Richard's "crip perspective" as a process. McRuer, "Fuck the Disabled," 296.

25. Martin Wiggins, *Shakespeare and the Drama of His Time* (Oxford: Oxford University Press, 2000), 23.

26. Thomas More, *The History of King Richard the Third: A Reading Edition*, ed. George M. Logan (Bloomington: Indiana University Press, 2005), 9–10.

27. *The True Tragedie of Richard the Third* (London: Thomas Creede, 1594), sig. A3v. While the only extant quarto of the play was printed in 1594, the play was performed by the Queen's Men, probably in the late 1580s or early 1590s. See Brian Walsh, *Shakespeare, the Queen's Men, and the Elizabethan Performance of History* (Cambridge: Cambridge University Press, 2009), esp. 74–103.

28. Walsh, *Queen's Men*, 77.

29. William Shakespeare, *The Third Part of Henry the Sixth*, ed. William Montgomery, in Orgel and Braunmuller, *Complete Pelican Shakespeare*, 809–57.

30. See Jonas Barish, *The Antitheatrical Prejudice* (Berkeley: University of California Press, 1981), 98–117.

31. William Shakespeare, *The Tragedy of King Richard the Third*, ed. Peter Holland, in Orgel and Braunmuller, *Complete Pelican Shakespeare*, 958–99.

32. Johns, "Grievous Burthen," 42; Marcela Kostihová, "Richard Recast: Renaissance Disability in a Postmodern Culture," in Hobgood and Wood, *Recovering Disability*, 136.

33. As Robert Weimann puts it, "Appealing to an authority that resides in the unparalleled quality of the performance, the actor/character stands back as it were and looks at his own delivery in the preceding scene." Weimann, *Author's Pen*, 91.

34. Compare insightful readings of the discourses of pity and charity in this scene, especially Mitchell and Snyder, *Narrative Prosthesis*, 103–5; Siebers, "Shakespeare Differently Disabled," 436–38; and Row-Heyveld, *Dissembling Disability*, 144–49. On the constitutive antifeminism of the play, see Jean E. Howard and Phyllis Rackin, *Engendering a Nation: A Feminist Account of Shakespeare's English Histories* (New York: Routledge, 1997), 100–118.

35. Love astutely recasts this moment around the physical evidence of Richard's remains (discovered in 2012), in which a pronounced spinal curve, from one angle, disappears from another when the spine is considered in three-dimensional image. Richard's fantasy reflects "movement—bibliographically, theatrically, spinally—between difference as definitive or as nearly inconsequential." Love, *Figure of Disability*, 141. Compare Hobgood's perceptive point that Richard's language of the shadow registers how disability "produces *invisibility*": "He is both legible and illegible; he leaves a mark, but that mark is nothing more than the absence of light." Hobgood, "Teeth before Eyes," 32.

36. Garland-Thomson, *Staring*, 95.

37. Porter, *Windows of the Soul*, 190.

38. Thomas Hill, *The Contemplation of Mankinde* (London: Henry Denham for William Seres, 1571), sig. Y1r.

39. Michael Torrey, "'The plain devil and dissembling looks': Ambivalent Physiognomy and Shakespeare's *Richard III*," *English Literary Renaissance* 30, no. 2 (Spring 2000): 123–53.

40. Mark Thornton Burnett, *Constructing "Monsters" in Shakespearean Drama and Early Modern Culture* (New York: Palgrave Macmillan, 2002), 93; Ian Frederick Moulton, "'A Monster Great Deformed': The Unruly Masculinity of *Richard III*," *Shakespeare Quarterly* 47, no. 3 (1996): 251–68, 261. I understand these generative readings of monstrosity to accord with the emphasis on social perception foregrounded in disability theory; see Bearden's foundational discussion of monstrosity in relation to disability in *Monstrous Kinds*, esp. 7–17.

41. Ambroise Paré, *On Monsters and Marvels*, trans. and ed. Janis L. Pallister (Chicago: University of Chicago Press, 1982), 42. Paré's examples of monsters include a range of congenital deformities as well as accidental illnesses. Stephen Pender trenchantly observes that "there was no clear sequence of historical development in the reception of deformed bodies; the meaning of monsters was renegotiated throughout the early modern period." Pender, "'No Monsters at the Resurrection': Inside Some Conjoined Twins," in *Monster Theory: Reading Culture*, ed. Jeffrey Jerome Cohen (Minneapolis: University of Minnesota Press, 1996), 145–46.

42. West, "What's the Matter," 121.

43. On discontinuous notions of dramatic character produced by nonstandardized speech prefixes, see Randall Macleod / Random Cloud, "'The very names of the persons': Editing and the Invention of Dramatick Character," in *Staging the Renaissance: Reinterpretations of Elizabethan and Jacobean Drama*, ed. David Scott Kastan and Peter Stallybrass (New York: Routledge, 1991), 88–96.

44. On the midline switch as a site of rhetorical power, see Palfrey and Stern, *Shakespeare in Parts*, esp. chap. 18.

45. Wheeler, "History, Character, and Conscience," 312. Put in terms of the Vice figure, Weimann argues, Richard, once crowned, must move away from presentational qualities and into a fully representational sphere, now unable to "remain outside the autonomous realm of a self-enclosed action." Weimann, *Shakespeare and Popular Tradition*, 159.

46. Charnes, *Notorious Identity*, 32.

47. Siebers, *Disability Theory*, 105.

48. See Hall's discussion of "fair" in *Things of Darkness*, esp. chap. 2. On the intersection of race and sexuality, see Urvashi Chakravarty, "'Live, and beget a happy race of kings': *Richard III*, Race and Homonationalism," in *Shakespeare / Sex: Contemporary Readings in Gender and Sexuality*, ed. Jennifer Drouin (London: Bloomsbury Arden Shakespeare, 2020), 147–67. On "fair" in relation to disability, see Katherine Schaap Williams, "Demonstrating Disability," *Early Theatre* 22, no. 2 (2019): 185–97.

49. On the significance of the "amen," see Ramie Targoff, "'Dirty' Amens: Devotion, Applause, and Consent in *Richard III*," *Renaissance Drama* 31 (2002): 61–84.

50. *The Returne from Pernassus, Or the Scourge of Simony* (London: G. Eld for John Wright, 1606). The play was likely composed between 1599 and 1602; on Kemp's characterization, see Preiss, *Clowning and Authorship*, chap. 4.

51. William Hazlitt notes that Richard III "is the character in which Garrick came out: it was the second character in which Mr. Kean appeared, and in which he acquired his fame." Hazlitt, *Characters of Shakespear's Plays* (London: Printed by C. H. Reynell, for R. Hunter and C. and J. Ollier, 1817), 226. In addition to Menzer's virtuosic reading of theatrical anecdotes of *Richard III* (cited below), see classic accounts of the play's performance history in Alice Ida Perry Wood, *The Stage History of Shakespeare's King Richard the Third* (New York: Columbia University Press, 1909) and John Scott Colley, *Richard's Himself Again: A Stage History of Richard III* (New York: Greenwood Press, 1992).

52. Antony Sher records this anecdote from Terry Hands in Sher, *Year of the King: An Actor's Diary and Sketchbook* (London: Chatto & Windus / Hogarth Press, 1985), 42.

53. Paul Menzer, *Anecdotal Shakespeare: A New Performance History* (London: Arden Shakespeare, 2015), 28. See also chap. 4.

54. See Ric Knowles, "Encoding/Decoding Shakespeare: *Richard III* at the 2002 Stratford Festival," in *A Companion to Shakespeare and Performance*, ed. Barbara Hodgdon and W. B. Worthen (New York: Wiley Blackwell, 2005); Jim Casey, "'Richard's Himself Again': The Body of Richard III on Stage and Screen," in *Shakespeare and the Middle Ages: Essays on the Performance and Adaptation of the Plays with Medieval Sources or Settings*, ed. Martha W. Driver and Sid Ray (Jefferson, NC: McFarland, 2009); and the editorial introduction to *King Richard III*, by William Shakespeare, ed. James R. Siemon (London: Arden Shakespeare, 2009).

55. Sher, *Year of the King*, 39.

56. Frederick William Hawkins, *The Life of Edmund Kean* (London: Tinsley Brothers, 1869), 1:174. On Kean's performance, see also London Green, "Edmund Kean's Richard III," *Theatre Journal* 36 (1984): 505–24.

57. Terry Coleman, *Olivier: The Authorised Biography* (New York: Bloomsbury, 2005), 209.

58. Palfrey and Stern, *Shakespeare in Parts*, 48.

59. Sher, *Year of the King*, 30. Compare Nardizzi's generative reading of Sher's performance in relation to the play's emphasis on the crutch as prosthesis and figure for genealogical futurity. Nardizzi, "Disability Figures," 462–66.

60. Sher, *Year of the King*, 30.

61. Sher, *Year of the King*, 30.

62. See especially Julia H. Fawcett's discussion of Cibber's use of deformity in *Spectacular Disappearances: Celebrity and Privacy, 1696–1801* (Ann Arbor: University of Michigan Press, 2016), esp. chap. 1; and Gillian M. Day, "Determination and Proof: Colley Cibber and the Materialization of Shakespeare's *Richard III* in the Twentieth Century," in *Shakespeare Matters: History, Teaching, Performance*, ed. Lloyd Davis (Newark: University of Delaware Press, 2003), 266–76.

63. Colley Cibber, *An Apology for the Life of Colley Cibber*, ed. B. R. S. Fone (Ann Arbor: University of Michigan Press, 1968), 77.

64. Cibber, *Apology*, 77.

65. Cibber, *Apology*, 77.

66. Cibber, *Apology*, 81.

67. Colley Cibber, *The Tragical History of King Richard III* (London: Printed for B. Lintott and A. Bettesworth, 1700), sig. B4r.

68. Fawcett, *Spectacular Disappearances*, 25.

69. Colley, *Richard's Himself Again*, 20.

70. John Philip Kemble, *Macbeth and King Richard the Third* (London: John Murray, 1817), 127.

71. Colley, *Richard's Himself Again*, xii–xiii.

72. Pauline Croft, "The Reputation of Robert Cecil: Libels, Political Opinion, and Popular Awareness in the Early Seventeenth Century," *Transactions of the Royal Historical Society* 1 (1991): 49.

73. Philip Schwyzer notes that Philip Henslowe's diary records the payment for a title that "suggests a much sharper focus on the character of Richard," but no record of completion or performance remains. Schwyzer, *Shakespeare and the Remains of Richard III* (Oxford: Oxford University Press, 2013), 208. See also Ian Donaldson's "Note on *Richard Crookback*, Lost Play (1602)," in Bevington et al., *Works of Ben Jonson*, 2:183–84.

74. Margaret Hotine maps the dates of printings and performances of *Richard III* against Cecil's career in "*Richard III* and *Macbeth*—Studies in Tudor Tyranny?," *Notes and Queries* 38, no. 4 (December 1991): 480–86. Andrew McRae notes that for Cecil, "the historical precedent provided by Richard's allegedly hunched back was particularly unfortunate." McRae, *Literature, Satire, and the Early Stuart State* (Cambridge: Cambridge University Press, 2004), 59. Peter Lake suggests *Richard III* may have been more closely linked to Cecil's representation from the beginning, for "at precisely the point at which this play was being written and produced, Robert Cecil, a seemingly godly younger son, disfigured with a hump, was emerging into prominence as the political heir of his father, Lord Burghley." Lake, *How Shakespeare Put Politics on the Stage: Power and Succession in the History Plays* (New Haven, CT: Yale University Press, 2016), 169. M. G. Aune suggests that the character of Richard III "shifted from the sphere of dramatic entertainment to become available as a tool for personal attack and political commentary." Aune, "The Uses of *Richard III*: From Robert Cecil to Richard Nixon," *Shakespeare Bulletin* 24, no. 3 (Fall 2006): 23.

75. An early articulation of this idea is found in Lily B. Campbell, *Shakespeare's "Histories": Mirrors of Elizabethan Policy* (San Marino, CA: Huntington Library, 1947), 306–34. More recently, Peter Lake develops this argument at length in *Politics on the Stage*.

76. The tropic version of this relation to Richard III is repeated in Cecil's biographies too. See P. M. Handover, *The Second Cecil: The Rise to Power, 1563–1604, of Sir Robert Cecil, late first Earl of Salisbury* (London: Eyre & Spottiswoode, 1959), 15–16; and Algernon Cecil, *A Life of Robert Cecil First Earl of Salisbury* (London: John Murray, 1915), 355–56.

77. Croft, "Reputation," 56.

78. John Day, *The Ile of Guls* (London: Printed for John Trundle, 1606), sig. A2v.

79. McRae, *Literature*, 8; Alastair Bellany, "Railing Rhymes Revisited: Libels, Scandals, and Early Stuart Politics," *History Compass* 5, no. 4 (June 2007): 1160.

80. Croft, "Reputation," 54. For full texts of extant libels, see Alastair Bellany and Andrew McRae, eds., Early Stuart Libels: An Edition of Poetry from Manuscript Sources (Early Modern Literary Studies Texts Series 1 (2005)), accessed September 20, 2020. http://purl.oclc.org/emls/texts/libels/, esp. section D.

81. Bellany and McRae, Early Stuart Libels, no. D4.

82. Bellany and McRae, Early Stuart Libels, no. D5.

83. In the vexed contradiction between the charge of corruption issued by the libels and the praise of statesmanship asserted by the defenses, Croft notes that the texts "prefigured exactly the opposing views of Robert Cecil arrived at by modern historians." Croft, "Reputation," 69.

84. Quoting Cecil's contemporary, Bellany notes that, prior to the Overbury affair, Cecil's death had occasioned the most libels. Bellany, *The Politics of Court Scandal in Early Modern England: News Culture and the Overbury Affair, 1603–1660* (Oxford: Oxford University Press, 2007), 100.

85. Pender, "In the Bodyshop," 115. See also Mitchell and Snyder's classic reading in *Narrative Prosthesis*, chap. 4, esp. 105–09; Helen Deutsch perceptively reads Bacon's essay alongside William Hay's *Deformity: An Essay* in "The Body's Moments: Visible Disability, the Essay, and the Limits of Sympathy," in *Disability and/in Prose*, ed. Brenda Brueggemann and Marian E. Lupo (London: Routledge, 2008), 1–14.

86. The chronology I am mapping here thus reverses the chronology of Davis's claim: "For Bacon, deformed people are ambitious, 'void of natural affection,' good spies, and advantaged in 'rising' in court"; thus, "Shakespeare, clearly holding to all these opinions, depicts Richard III as a crooked-back, limping sexual villain, a spying, usurping plotter." Davis, *Bending Over Backwards*, 53.

87. *The Letters of John Chamberlain*, ed. N. E. McClure (Philadelphia: American Philosophical Society, 1939), 1:397. See also Lisa Jardine and Alan Stewart, *Hostage to Fortune: The Troubled Life of Francis Bacon* (New York: Hill & Wang, 1999), 326. See also Ian Box, "Bacon's Moral Philosophy," in *The Cambridge Companion to Bacon*, ed. Markku Peltonen (Cambridge: Cambridge University Press, 1996), 273. Algernon Cecil repeats this charge in his early twentieth-century biography: "Posterity has scented in his essays on Cunning and Deformity the satisfaction for his disappointments." Cecil, *Life of Robert Cecil*, 351.

88. Francis Bacon, "Of Deformity," in *The Major Works*, by Francis Bacon, ed. Brian Vickers (Oxford: Oxford University Press, 1996), 426.

89. *The Diary of John Manningham of the Middle Temple, 1602–3*, ed. Robert Parker Sorlien (Hanover, NH: Published for the University of Rhode Island by the University Press of New England, 1976), 75. Parenthetical emendations by editor.

90. Jean E. Howard, "Stage Masculinities, National History, and the Making of London Theatrical Culture," in *Center or Margin: Revisions of the English Renaissance in Honor of Leeds Barroll*, ed. Lena Cowen Orlin (Selinsgrove, PA: Susquehanna University Press, 2006), 210.

91. Indeed, Barbara Hodgdon asks: What sparks the citizen's "fascination with Richard III, with Burbage's body (showing 'through' the character), with both?" Hodgdon, "Replicating Richard: Body Doubles, Body Politics," *Theatre Journal* 50, no. 2 (May 1998): 212.

92. Paul Menzer, introduction to *Look About You* in Lopez, *Early Modern Drama*, 267.

2. Citizen Transformed

1. Anthony Copley, *Wits fittes and fancies* (London: Richard [Jones], 1595), sig. 2B1v.

2. John Bodenham, "Examples likewise on the same," in *Bel-vedére, or, The Garden of the Muses* (London: F. K. for Hugh Astley, 1600), sig. C6r; Timothy Kendall, *Flowers of Epigrammes* (London: John Sheppard, 1577), sig. N2r.

3. Anita Silvers, "An Essay on Modeling: The Social Model of Disability," in *Philosophical Reflections on Disability*, ed. D. Christopher Ralston and Justin Ho (Dordrecht: Springer, 2010), 24. See also Irina Metzler's early suggestion that "the lack of the modern umbrella term 'disability' and the cultural implications it carries with it may also entail during the Middle Ages the lack of the entire notion of an impaired person as being disabled." Metzler, *Disability in Medieval Europe*, 5.

4. Davis, *Bending Over Backwards*, 66, 58.

5. Garland-Thomson, *Extraordinary Bodies*, 6.

6. Jasbir K. Puar, *The Right to Maim: Debility, Capacity, Disability* (Durham, NC: Duke University Press, 2017), xvii.

7. Puar, *Right to Maim*, 13.

8. Robert McRuer, *Crip Times* (New York: New York University Press, 2018), 43.

9. Linda Bradley Salamon suggests that "former soldiers who returned from battles foreign or civil were construed as a transgressive presence on the margins of public life." Salamon, "Vagabond Veterans: The Roguish Company of Martin Guerre and *Henry V*," in *Rogues and Early Modern English Culture*, ed. Craig Dionne and Steve Mentz (Ann Arbor: University of Michigan Press, 2004), 262.

10. Classic studies of dramatic representation and English warfare include Charles Greig Cruickshank, *Elizabeth's Army* (Oxford: Oxford University Press, 1946), and Paul Jorgensen, *Shakespeare's Military World* (Berkeley: University of California Press, 1956); on the practice of military impressment, see Mark Charles Fissell, *English Warfare, 1511–1642* (London: Routledge, 2001), esp. chap. 3. For a virtuosic study of military technologies and the trauma of war (from which I quote below), see Patricia A. Cahill, *Unto the Breach: Martial Formations, Historical Trauma, and the Early Modern Stage* (Oxford: Oxford University Press, 2008). Cahill argues that manuals of Elizabethan military mathematics imagine the individual as subsumed by a social form, "represent[ing] nothing less than a theory of laboring bodies, a precursor of nineteenth-century efforts

to standardize, quantify, and appropriate the productive energies of workers." Cahill, *Unto the Breach*, 7.

11. Paul E. J. Hammer notes that in addition to being at war with Spain for nearly twenty years, Elizabeth's "government also waged major campaigns in Scotland, France and Ireland before 1585, as well as conniving at 'deniable' forms of war by English 'volunteer' soldiers in France and the Low Countries and by English privateers at sea." *Elizabeth's Wars: War, Government and Society in Tudor England, 1544–1604* (London: Palgrave Macmillan, 2003), 5. Curtis C. Breight argues that the Elizabethan state's coercion and military aggression contests historiography that emphasizes England's vulnerability, in *Surveillance, Militarism, and Drama in the Elizabethan Era* (New York: St. Martin's Press, 1996).

12. *Statutes of the Realm*, "An Acte for Relief of Souldiors" 1592, 35 Eliz. 1, c. 4.

13. See Linda Woodbridge, *Vagrancy, Homelessness, and English Renaissance Literature* (Urbana: University of Illinois Press, 2001). Woodbridge demonstrates that early modern literature registered "demobilized—and often disabled—soldiers as a persistent, significant element of the destitute homeless," and that disbanded soldiers constituted a population understood as threat, noting that in 1589 "troops were called out and martial law imposed when hundreds of Drake's disbanded soldiers threatened the peace in London" (52).

14. A. L. Beier, *Masterless Men: The Vagrancy Problem in England, 1560–1640* (London: Methuen, 1985), 9.

15. *Statutes of the Realm*, vol. 4, pt. 2, "An Acte for punishment of Rogues Vagabonds and Sturdy Beggars," 39 Eliz. 1, c. 4, 899.

16. Beier, *Masterless Men*, 95. See also Salamon, "Vagabond Veterans."

17. About *A Larum for London*, Roslyn L. Knutson observes that the "appeal for audiences and readers is immediately evident in the focus of the narrative on the atrocities of war." Knutson, "Filling Fare: The Appetite for Current Issues and Traditional Forms in the Repertory of the Chamberlain's Men," *Medieval and Renaissance Drama in England* 15 (2003): 63. This topicality, Nicholas de Somogyi has argued, is evident in plays that argue for "moral reform, military readiness, and the justice of a self-defensive war." Somogyi, *Shakespeare's Theatre of War* (Aldershot, UK: Ashgate, 1998), 32.

18. *The Historie of the Tryall of Chevalry, With the life and death of Cavaliero Dicke Bowyer* (London: Simon Stafford for Nathaniel Butter, 1605).

19. On the figurations of lameness that attach to the physical body, see Susan L. Anderson, "Limping and Lameness on the Early Modern Stage," in *Performing Disability in Early Modern English Drama*, ed. Leslie Dunn (New York: Palgrave Macmillan, forthcoming).

20. References to the Low Countries associate the play with the civil wars of France, as Somogyi has discussed, and "Mahound" and "Termagent" are mistaken but no less derogatory terms associated with Islam in the period. See Somogyi, *Theatre of War*, esp. chap. 3.

21. The play was entered into the stationer's register in 1600 and printed in 1602; it was probably performed in 1599, making it roughly contemporaneous with Dekker's play, to which I will return.

22. In addition to the detailed studies of the play by Cahill and Somogyi; for a detailed discussion of Antwerp's significance and the play's topical relevance, see chap.

4 in Adam N. McKeown, *English Mercuries: Soldier Poets in the Age of Shakespeare* (Nashville, TN: Vanderbilt University Press, 2009).

23. Love, *Figure of Disability*, 72.

24. *A Larum for London, or The Siedge of Antwerpe* (London: Edward Allde for William Ferbrand, 1602).

25. Naomi Baker, "'Happy and without a name': Prosthetic Identities on the Early Modern Stage," *Textual Practice* 30, no. 7 (2016): 1310.

26. Vin Nardizzi, "The Wooden Matter of Human Bodies: Prosthesis and Stump in *A Larum for London*," in *The Indistinct Human in Renaissance Literature*, ed. Jean E. Feerick and Vin Nardizzi (New York: Palgrave Macmillan, 2012), 121, 123.

27. Love, *Figure of Disability*, 73, 85.

28. Love astutely connects the burgher and the soldier through the prosthetic contrast between Stump's missing leg and the stuffing required to turn an actor into the "Fat Burgher," which the tickle-torture scene puts on view. Love, *Figure of Disability*, 75–82.

29. See Luke Wilson, "Monetary Compensation for Injuries to the Body, A.D. 602–1697," in *Money and the Age of Shakespeare*, ed. Linda Woodbridge (New York: Palgrave Macmillan, 2003), 19–37.

30. As Somogyi notes, Stump's "wooden leg itself forms a passport between two significations, his practical peacetime neglect and his theoretical wartime role" (40).

31. Cahill points out that as "antithesis" to the "swollen-bellied" citizens, "this lame soldier is so well disciplined, the play suggests, that he is willing to fight even in an obscenely unequal contest in which virtually everyone on his side has either given up or been slain." Cahill, *Unto the Breach*, 173.

32. This idea is aligned with Sara Ahmed's insight that "labor shapes not only what bodies *do* but what bodies are assumed to be *for*," a synecdoche in which the corporate imaginary of the state translates into a hierarchy in which "some bodies become supporting limbs." Ahmed, *Willful Subjects* (Durham, NC: Duke University Press, 2014), 108, 111.

33. Alexander Leggatt, *Citizen Comedy in the Age of Shakespeare* (Toronto: University of Toronto Press, 1973), 19; Robert L. Smallwood, in his portion of the introduction to *The Shoemaker's Holiday*, by Thomas Dekker, ed. R. L. Smallwood and Stanley Wells (Manchester: Manchester University Press, 1979), 9–10.

34. Smallwood, introduction to *The Shoemaker's Holiday*, 14.

35. On the relationship between the "holiday" of the title and the dramatic economy, see especially David Scott Kastan, "Workshop and/as Playhouse: Comedy and Commerce in *The Shoemaker's Holiday*," *Studies in Philology* 84, no. 3 (1987): 324–37; David Bevington, "Theatre as Holiday," in *The Theatrical City: Culture, Theatre and Politics in London, 1576–1649*, ed. David L. Smith, Richard Strier, and David Bevington (Cambridge: Cambridge University Press, 1995); and Marta Straznicky, "The End(s) of Discord in *The Shoemaker's Holiday*," *Studies in English Literature, 1500–1900* 36, no. 2 (Spring 1996): 357–72. The "citizen history" play, Crystal Bartolovich argues, "holds the mirror up to labor in order to refuse the image as its own." Bartolovich, "Mythos of Labor: *The Shoemaker's Holiday* and the Origin of Citizen History," in *Working Subjects in Early Modern English Drama*, ed. Michelle M. Dowd and Natasha Korda (New York: Ashgate, 2011), 36.

36. The category of the citizen in the sixteenth and early seventeenth centuries has received significant scholarly attention in the past decades: John Archer demonstrates how the "status of citizen during the sixteenth and seventeenth centuries in England conferred an urban rather than a national identity." Archer, *Citizen Shakespeare: Freemen and Aliens in the Language of the Plays* (New York: Palgrave Macmillan, 2005), 6. Phil Withington shows how the "citizen" designation "signified additional public powers and responsibilities within the body politic." Withington, *The Politics of Commonwealth: Citizens and Freemen in Early Modern England* (Cambridge: Cambridge University Press, 2005), 10. See also Henry S. Turner, *The Corporate Commonwealth: Pluralism and Political Fictions in England, 1516–1651* (Chicago: University of Chicago Press, 2016), quoted below.

37. Cornelius Valerius, *The Casket of Jewels*, trans. John Charlton (London: William How for Richard Johnes, 1571), quoted in Markku Peltonen, "Rhetoric and Citizenship in the Monarchical Republic of Queen Elizabeth I," in *The Monarchical Republic of Early Modern England: Essays in Response to Patrick Collinson*, ed. John F. McDiarmid (New York: Ashgate, 2007), 110.

38. Julia Reinhard Lupton points out that "citizenship was by and large a category of municipal, not national life, naming a limited moment of self-governance and emergent capitalism within an overarching monarchic order." Lupton, *Citizen-Saints: Shakespeare and Political Theology* (Chicago: University of Chicago Press, 2005), 14.

39. As Withington notes, "in sixteenth-century London . . . [an estimated] 90 per cent of Londoners became citizens through apprenticeship." Withington, *Politics of Commonwealth*, 29.

40. John Michael Archer, "Citizens and Aliens as Working Subjects in Dekker's *The Shoemaker's Holiday*," in Dowd and Korda, *Working Subjects*, 30. As Bartolovich observes, "the major social theorists of the later sixteenth century all explicitly distinguish citizens (by which they mean wealthy merchants) from artisans, who share the attribute of laboring with noncitizens, even if they might jealously guard their own skilled status over the unskilled." Bartolovich, "Mythos of Labor," 24.

41. Thomas Dekker, *The Shoemaker's Holiday*, ed. Jonathan Gil Harris (London: Methuen Drama, 2008).

42. William Shakespeare, *The Second Part of King Henry the Fourth*, ed. Claire McEachern, in Orgel and Braunmuller, *Complete Pelican Shakespeare*, 1080–1124.

43. Smallwood, introduction to *The Shoemaker's Holiday*, 25.

44. Turner, *Corporate Commonwealth*, 132.

45. See Turner, *Corporate Commonwealth*, 136–37.

46. Thomas Deloney, *The Gentle Craft*, ed. Simon Barker (Aldershot, UK: Ashgate, 2007), 31, 33. Elizabeth Rivlin discusses the text's commercial appeal in *The Aesthetics of Service in Early Modern England* (Evanston, IL: Northwestern University Press, 2012).

47. Deloney, *Gentle Craft*, 33. See also Rivlin's extended reading of the "courtly, military, household, and commercial paradigms of service" in the presence of the shoemakers (*Aesthetics of Service*, 87).

48. Deloney, *Gentle Craft*, 34.

49. Smallwood instead identifies Crispine, Crispianus's brother, as the model for Lacy, and says that Crispianus "virtually disappears" from Dekker's play: "The return of Crispianus in glory contrasts sharply with Ralph's limping back as a cripple." Smallwood, introduction to *The Shoemaker's Holiday*, 18, 20.

50. *The Famous Victories of Henry V*, ed. Brian Walsh, in Lopez, *Early Modern Drama*, 350–81. See also Walsh, *Queen's Men*, chap. 2; and Walsh, "Performing Historicity in Dekker's *The Shoemaker's Holiday*," *Studies in English Literature* 46, no. 2 (Spring 2006): 323–48.

51. Cordwainers (shoemakers) work with new leather, while cobblers work with old; the cordwainers absorbed the cobblers into their company in the sixteenth century, but distinctions seem to persist at least in terms of status. See Paul S. Seaver, "The Artisanal World," in Smith, Strier, and Bevington, *Theatrical City*.

52. Salamon, "Vagabond Veterans," 273.

53. See Kastan's analysis of the play's "strategy of idealization" in "Workshop and/as Playhouse" (330), and Ronda Arab's discussion of masculinity and vulnerability in *Manly Mechanicals on the Early Modern English Stage* (Selinsgrove, PA: Susquehanna University Press, 2011), 55.

54. I am grateful to Kathryn Vomero Santos for this observation.

55. See Salamon's extensive discussion in "Vagabond Veterans"; see also Natalie Zemon Davis's classic account in *The Return of Martin Guerre* (Cambridge, MA: Harvard University Press, 1984).

56. I draw here on Garland-Thomson's account of the stare as a "social act that stigmatizes by designating people whose bodies or behaviors cannot be readily absorbed into the visual status quo" (*Staring*, 44).

57. See Bartolovich's observation that Ralph, "maimed in war, pays the price of history in his person" but is "still ultimately considered irrelevant to it." "Mythos of Labor," 33.

58. Nardizzi, "Wooden Matter," 127. Nardizzi's generative account stresses the prostheticized valence of the human: see also Nardizzi, "Disability Figures." As David Wills notes, "That which presents itself as a supplementary operation, designed to remedy the imperfections of nature, must at the same time admit of the artificial as unnatural, of what is counter to nature, a perversion and a monstrosity." David Wills, *Prosthesis* (Stanford, CA: Stanford University Press, 1995), 242.

59. As William Kerwin puts it, surgeons "were managers of exterior appearances and keepers of secrets about the gap between outer order and inner disorder." Kerwin, *Beyond the Body: The Boundaries of Medicine and English Renaissance Drama* (Amherst: University of Massachusetts Press, 2005), 98. On early modern barber-surgeons and the work of managing the surface of the body, see especially Margaret Pelling, "Appearance and Reality: Barber-Surgeons, the Body, and Disease," in *London 1500–1700: The Making of the Metropolis*, ed. A. L. Beier and Roger Finlay (New York: Longman, 1986); on dissection as a form of knowledge-making in English culture, see Jonathan Sawday, *The Body Emblazoned: Dissection and the Human Body in Renaissance Culture* (London: Routledge, 1995).

60. Woodall, *The Surgeons Mate, with A Treatise of Gangrena, and Sphacelos* (London: Rob. Young for Nicholas Bourne, 1639), sigs. B1v, A2v.

61. Ambroise Paré, *The Workes of that famous Chirurgion Ambrose Parey*, trans. Thomas Johnson (London: Th. Cotes and R. Young, 1634), sigs. 2R1r–v.

62. Woodall, *Treatise of Gangrena*, sig. 2C1v.

63. David Hillman and Carla Mazzio, "Introduction: Individual Parts," in *The Body in Parts: Fantasies of Corporeality in Early Modern Europe*, ed. David Hillman and Carla Mazzio (London: Routledge, 1997), xiv.

64. Nardizzi, "Wooden Matter," 123.

65. Cahill, *Unto the Breach*, 190.

66. Wills, *Prosthesis*, 242–43.

67. Wills, *Prosthesis*, 16.

68. Alanna Skuse, "Missing Parts in *The Shoemaker's Holiday*," *Renaissance Drama* 45, no. 2 (2017): 176.

69. Nardizzi, "Wooden Matter," 129, 128.

70. Rivlin, *Aesthetics of Service*, 80.

71. Thus, unlike Skuse, I do not find that Ralph's body is "so readable and yet unspeakable"; the renaming speaks of his injury constantly. Skuse, "Missing Parts," 171.

72. Smallwood, introduction to *The Shoemaker's Holiday*, 22. Jeremy Lopez, "Postmodern Gosson, or 1599 Is a Four-Letter Word," in *Thunder at a Playhouse: Essaying Shakespeare and the Early Modern Stage*, ed. Peter Kanelos and Matt Kozusko (Selinsgrove, PA: Susquehanna University Press, 2010), 137–38.

73. Turner, *Corporate Commonwealth*, 137.

74. Anthony Munday et al., *The first part of the true and honorable historie, of the life of Sir John Old-castle, the good Lord Cobham* (London: V. S. for Thomas Pavier, 1600), 1.3.339–43.

75. Thomas Dekker, *The Wonder of a Kingdom* (London: Robert Raworth for Nicholas Vavasour, 1636), sig. F1r.

76. William Shakespeare and George Wilkins, *Pericles Prince of Tyre*, ed. Stephen Orgel, in Orgel and Braunmuller, *Complete Pelican Shakespeare*, 4.6.163–66; Jasper Mayne, *The Amorous Warre* (Oxford: Printed by Henry Hall for Ric. Davis, 1659), sig. A3r.

77. John Fletcher and Philip Massinger, *The Little French Lawyer*, ed. Robert Kean Turner, in *The Dramatic Works in the Beaumont and Fletcher Canon*, edited by Fredson Bowers, 9:323–460 (Cambridge: Cambridge University Press, 1994). The play was first published in the Folio, but was likely composed between 1613 and 1625. Francis Beaumont and John Fletcher, *Love's Pilgrimage*, ed. L. A. Beaurline, in Bowers, *Dramatic Works*, 2:567–691.

78. I am grateful to Liza Blake for her insight on this point.

79. Martin Wiggins, in association with Catherine Richardson, entry for *Beggars' Bush*, in *British Drama 1533–1642: A Catalogue* (Oxford: Oxford University Press, 2015), 6:519.

3. Performing Cripple in Theatrical Exchange

1. Copley, *Wits*, sig. 2B1v.

2. Turner, "Disability Humor and the Meanings of Impairment in Early Modern England," in Hobgood and Wood, *Recovering Disability*, 60. See also Simon Dickie's comprehensive treatment of this strand of humor in eighteenth-century literature in *Cruelty and Laughter: Forgotten Comic Literature and the Unsentimental Eighteenth Century* (Chicago: University of Chicago Press, 2011).

3. Copley, *Wits*, sig. 2B1v. Copley's collection, published in 1595, 1596, and 1614 with varying subtitles, prints this jest only in the first two editions.

4. *Oxford English Dictionary*, s.v. "overplus," n., adj., and adv., Aa.

5. The play has often been attributed to Thomas Heywood, but the extant quartos of 1607, 1625, and 1637 bear no authorial designation. For the history and discussion of the authorship debate, see Laura A. Hibbard, "The Authorship and Date of the

Fayre Maide of the Exchange," Modern Philology 7, no. 3 (January 1910): 383–94; Barron Field, introduction to *The Fair Maid of the Exchange: A Comedy*, ed. Barron Field (London: Printed for the Shakespeare Society, 1846); and Karl E. Snyder, introduction to *A Critical Edition of* The Faire Maide of the Exchange *by Thomas Heywood*, ed. Karl E. Snyder (New York: Garland, 1980).

6. *The Fair Maid of the Exchange*, ed. Genevieve Love, in Lopez, *Early Modern Drama*, 816–81.

7. On the term's offense and reclamation, see Nancy Mairs, "On Being a Cripple," in *Plaintext* (Tucson: University of Arizona Press, 1986), 9–20. See also Victoria Ann Lewis, "Crip," *Keywords for Disability Studies*, ed. Rachel Adams, Benjamin Reiss, and David Serlin (New York: New York University Press, 2015), 46–48.

8. Susan Wells, "Jacobean City Comedy and the Ideology of the City," *English Literary History* 48, no. 1 (1981): 37. In addition to foundational work on city and citizen comedy cited in chapter 2, see Brian Gibbons, *Jacobean City Comedy* (Cambridge, MA: Harvard University Press, 1968); further work analyzes the historical and material conditions that comedies engage when the plays take London as their scene: see Wendy Griswold, *Renaissance Revivals: City Comedy and Revenge Tragedy in the London Theatre, 1576–1980* (Chicago: University of Chicago Press, 1986), 14–54; Theodore B. Leinwand, *The City Staged: Jacobean Comedy, 1603–13* (Madison: University of Wisconsin Press, 1986); Dieter Mehl, Angela Stock, and Anne-Julia Zwierlein, eds., *Plotting Early Modern London: New Essays on Jacobean City Comedy* (Burlington, VT: Ashgate, 2004); and Douglas Bruster, *Drama and the Market in the Age of Shakespeare* (Cambridge: Cambridge University Press, 1992), 29–46.

9. Bert O. States, *The Pleasure of the Play* (Ithaca, NY: Cornell University Press, 1994), 155. The crippled beggar thus exemplifies a character that is "a convenient marker for a conventional social type" in city comedies, allowing the playwright to "take recognition of the type for granted." Griswold, *Renaissance Revivals*, 36. Leinwand notes the generic preoccupation with "obvious types," staging "exaggerated, comic figures" that point back to offstage "stereotypes." Leinwand, *City Staged*, 12. On the persistence of this stereotype, see also Mitchell and Snyder, "Masquerades of Impairment: Charity as a Confidence Game," chap. 1 in *Cultural Locations of Disability*; and Ellen Samuels, *Fantasies of Identification*.

10. I draw here on Homi Bhabha's classic account of stereotype as a false epistemology, "a form of knowledge and identification that vacillates between what is always 'in place,' already known, and something that must be anxiously repeated." Homi K. Bhabha, "The Other Question: Stereotype, Discrimination, and the Discourse of Colonialism," in *The Location of Culture*, 2nd ed. (New York: Routledge, 2004), 94–95.

11. Love, *Figure of Disability*, 42.

12. Row-Heyveld, *Dissembling Disability*, 173.

13. Both Love and Row-Heyveld respond to an earlier version of my argument in this chapter, in Katherine Schaap Williams, "'More legs than nature gave thee': Performing the Cripple in *The Fair Maid of the Exchange*," *English Literary History* 82, no. 2 (Summer 2015): 491–519.

14. I am indebted to Paul Menzer for this pun.

15. Paré, *Monsters and Marvels*, 74. The 1573 volume *Des monstres et des prodigies* became book 25, "Of Monsters and Prodigies," in his influential *Workes*.

16. Paré, *Monsters and Marvels*, 77.

17. Paola Pugliatti, *Beggary and Theatre in Early Modern England* (Aldershot, UK: Ashgate, 2003), 1.

18. *Statutes of the Realm*, vol. 4, pt. 2, "An Acte for Punyshment of Rogues Vagabondes and Sturdy Beggars," 1598, 39 Eliz. 1, c. 4, 899. This act dates to 1598 but reflects language from earlier iterations that identified unlicensed actors in the category to be deemed rogues, vagabonds, and sturdy beggars. Paul A. Fideler points out that the Parliament sessions of 1597–1598 were especially concerned with social care: "No less than 17 bills related to poverty were considered." From this attention to the problem of poverty, Parliament passed the key statutes composing Elizabethan Poor Law, 39 Eliz. 1, c. 3 (1598) and 43 Eliz. 1, c. 2 (1601). Fideler, *Social Welfare in Preindustrial England: The Old Poor Law Tradition* (New York: Palgrave Macmillan, 2006), 99. See esp. chap. 3, "Parish, Town, and Poor Law (c.1540–1610)." In addition to Steve Hindle's work, cited in the previous chapter, see also Paul Slack's foundational work in *Poverty and Policy in Tudor and Stuart England* (London: Longman, 1988) and *The English Poor Law, 1531–1782* (Cambridge: Cambridge University Press, 1990).

19. Woodbridge, *Vagrancy*, 24; Deborah A. Stone, *The Disabled State* (Philadelphia: Temple University Press, 1984), 32. Kevin Stagg convincingly argues that "the most prominent themes in relation to the disabled evident in popular representations associated disability with fraud." Stagg, "Representing Physical Difference," in Turner and Stagg, *Social Histories of Disability and Deformity*, 22.

20. In his magisterial study, William C. Carroll points out that in the period beggars were both "a real economic and social problem" and a "symbolic or discursively created one." Carroll, *Fat King, Lean Beggar: Representations of Poverty in the Age of Shakespeare* (Ithaca, NY: Cornell University Press, 1996), 16.

21. Row-Heyveld, *Dissembling Disability*, 7, 9. See also pages 4–12 for a productively wide-ranging discussion of relevant legal documents and pamphlets about poor relief.

22. Stone, *Disabled State*, 37; see also chap. 2. Robert Henke, *Poverty and Charity in Early Modern Theater and Performance* (Iowa City: University of Iowa Press, 2015), 32.

23. On these fictions, see especially Arthur F. Kinney, *Rogues, Vagabonds, and Sturdy Beggars: A New Gallery of Tudor and Early Stuart Rogue Literature* (1973; repr., Amherst: University of Massachusetts Press, 1990), and Craig Dionne and Steve Mentz, introduction to *Rogues and Early Modern English Culture*, 1–32. Patricia Fumerton argues that Harman, along with other writers, "transform[s] the *fact* of a vagrant economy grounded on a shifting mass of itinerant labor into the *fiction* of role-playing rogues." Fumerton, "Making Vagrancy (In)visible: The Economics of Disguise in Early Modern Rogue Pamphlets," in Dionne and Mentz, *Rogues and Early Modern English Culture*, 197.

24. Samuels, *Fantasies of Identification*, 11.

25. Carroll, *Fat King*, 3, 8. See also Patricia Fumerton's trenchant discussion of historical necessities of mobility for itinerant workers in *Unsettled: The Culture of Mobility and the Working Poor in Early Modern England* (Chicago: University of Chicago Press, 2006).

26. Fumerton, *Unsettled*, 33.

27. Henke, *Poverty and Charity*, 53. Discussing Edgar's assumption of the character of Poor Tom, Henke observes that "what might be a quintessential instance of sham theatricality, of course, turns out to have immense power" in the "powerful gestic,

kinetic, and vocal features" that are nothing more than the "naked, suffering, vulnerable actor" (53). Henke's compelling study demonstrates that the performed beggar's poverty was, at times, a reflection of the actor's own poverty (a fact that the *commedia* traditions of performance underscore), and his reading usefully situates English traditions in relation to continental practices.

28. *The Fayre Mayde of the Exchange: With The pleasuant Humours of the Cripple of Fanchurch* (London: Henry Rockit, 1607).

29. Andrew Gurr, *Shakespeare's Opposites: The Admiral's Company, 1594–1625* (Cambridge: Cambridge University Press, 2009), 22.

30. On humoral theory in relation to early modern drama, see foundational work by Paster, *Humouring the Body* and *The Body Embarrassed*; Schoenfeldt, *Bodies and Selves*; and Craik and Pollard, *Shakespearean Sensations*. On the discourse of the passion in relation to acting, see Roach, *Player's Passion*, esp. chap. 1.

31. Prologue, lines 8–9. Ben Jonson, *The Alchemist*, ed. Peter Holland and William Sherman, in Bevington et al., *Works of Ben Jonson*, 3:562.

32. Alexander Paulsson Lash, "'A delightful Proteus': Humors, Disguise, and the Actor's Skill in *The Blind Beggar of Alexandria* and *1 Henry IV*," *Shakespeare Studies* 47 (2019): 205–32, 206. See also Jeremy Lopez's discussion of the frequency with which plays in the late 1590s feature an "exposure-by-disguise structure" for the pleasures of theatrical transformation. Lopez, "Imagining the Actor's Body," 197.

33. See Peter Hyland, *Disguise on the Early Modern English Stage* (Burlington, VT: Ashgate, 2011), 1–14, esp. 7; and Astington, *Actors and Acting*, esp. 110–13 on Alleyn's admired facility with disguise plots.

34. George Chapman, *The Blinde Begger of Alexandria most pleasantly discoursing his variable humours in disguised shapes full of conceite and pleasure* (London: Printed for William Jones, 1598), sig. A3v.

35. Victor O. Freeburg, *Disguise Plots in Elizabethan Drama: A Study in Stage Tradition* (New York: Columbia University Press, 1915), 127.

36. Lash, "Delightful Proteus," 211.

37. See Wiggins, *British Drama*, 4:228–32, 287–88. "The blind beggar of Bednal-Green" was also a popular ballad tune; on the ballad's representation of blindness, see Simone Chess, "Performing Blindness: Representing Disability in Early Modern Popular Performance and Print," in Hobgood and Wood, *Recovering Disability*, 105–22.

38. John Day [and Henry Chettle], *The Blind Begger of Bednal-green With the merry humor of Tom Strowd the Norfolk Yeoman* (London: Printed for R. Pollard and Tho. Dring, 1659).

39. Carroll, *Fat King*, 214.

40. Francis Beaumont and John Fletcher, *Beggars' Bush*, ed. Fredson Bowers, in Bowers, *Dramatic Works*, 3:225–362. The play likely contains revisions by Philip Massinger; see Wiggins, *British Drama*, 6:518–25.

41. Compare Hobgood and Wood's insightful observation that a printed stammer, such as that of Redcap in the unattributed play *Look About You* (1600), operates to "conserve formally an aural variation that, in performance, is ephemeral." Hobgood and Wood, "Early Modern Literature," 43. On the actor's skill, see Tribble, *Early Modern Actors*, esp. chap. 2.

42. [Francis Kirkman?], *The Wits, or, Sport upon sport* (London: Printed for Henry Marsh, 1662), sig. A3r.

43. [Kirkman?], *The Wits*, sig. A3r–v.

44. [Kirkman?], *The Wits*, sig. A3v.

45. Richard Brome, *A Jovial Crew, or The Merry Beggars* (London: Printed by J. Y. for E. D. and N. E., 1652), sig. O3v.

46. Field, introduction to *Fair Maid*, v; Edmund Gosse, *The Jacobean Poets* (London: John Murray, 1894), 135; Charles Lamb, *Specimens of English Dramatic Poets Who Lived about the Time of Shakespeare* (New York: Wiley & Putnam, 1845), 188.

47. Lamb, *Specimens*, 188. George Saintsbury calls Cripple "the real hero of the piece" but also "a very unlikely cripple." Saintsbury, *A History of Elizabethan Literature* (New York: Macmillan, 1891), 283. Arthur Melville Clark concedes, "Whether or not the genius of the author limps on and off with the Cripple, as some have supposed, is a matter of taste; personally we find him an original humor but not very likable." Clark, *Thomas Heywood: Playwright and Miscellanist* (Oxford: Basil Blackwell, 1931; repr., New York: Russell & Russell, 1967), 244.

48. Felix E. Schelling, *Elizabethan Drama, 1558–1642* (Boston: Houghton Mifflin, 1908), 1:502.

49. Gosse, *Jacobean Poets*, 135.

50. Lamb, *Specimens*, 188.

51. Snyder, introduction to *Faire Maide*, 40, 6. A. Wilson Verity suggests that the playwright "makes the cripple plead the cause of another suitor to the Fair Maid, who at the end of the play transfers her affections with a levity and a complacency that would be offensive in real life." Verity, introduction to *The Best Plays of the Old Dramatists: Thomas Heywood*, ed. A. Wilson Verity (London: Vizetelly, 1888), xv.

52. See Juana Green, "The Sempster's Wares: Merchandising and Marrying in *The Fair Maid of the Exchange* (1607)," *Renaissance Quarterly* 53, no. 4 (Winter 2000): 1084–118; Jean E. Howard, *Theater of a City: The Places of London Comedy, 1598–1642* (Philadelphia: University of Pennsylvania Press, 2007), esp. chap. 1; and Richard Waswo, "Crises of Credit: Monetary and Erotic Economies in the Jacobean Theatre," in Mehl, Stock, and Zwierlein, *Plotting Early Modern London*, 55–74.

53. Howard, *Theater of a City*, 65, 66; Waswo, "Crises of Credit," 62, 63; Green, "Sempster's Wares," 1106.

54. Howard points out that "the abusive language codes Cripple as a Jew," repeatedly associating him with dogs in a stereotypical assertion of prejudice. Howard, *Theater of a City*, 66.

55. Keith Wrightson argues that as a consequence of the emerging capitalist economy, "market relationships grew in scale, pervasiveness and power," a shift that reorganizes notions of sociality in the period. Wrightson, *Earthly Necessities: Economic Lives in Early Modern Britain* (New Haven, CT: Yale University Press, 2000), 22. See also Joyce Oldham Appleby's classic account of the conceptual impact of the "advent of the market, and the reorganization of social life through it" (22), *Economic Thought and Ideology in Seventeenth-Century England* (Princeton, NJ: Princeton University Press, 1978); and Joan Thirsk's foundational argument about the transformation of early modern society through consumer goods in *Economic Policy and Projects: The Development of a Consumer Society in Early Modern England* (Oxford: Clarendon Press, 1978).

56. Howard, *Theater of a City*, 212. Janette Dillon argues that the Exchange was both "a place *for* display" and a "place *of* display," the space a "visible marker of the power and international prominence of London's market." Dillon, *Theatre, Court,*

and City, 1595–1610: Drama and Social Space in London (Cambridge: Cambridge University Press, 2000), 61. For more on the Exchange as a place with powerful influence in the London cultural imagination, see Ian W. Archer, "Material Londoners?," in *Material London, ca. 1600*, ed. Lena Cowen Orlin (Philadelphia: University of Pennsylvania Press, 2000), 174–92; and Ann Saunders, ed., *The Royal Exchange* (London: London Topographical Society, 1997).

57. Howard, *Theater of a City*, 214.
58. Green, "Sempster's Wares," 1104.
59. Garland-Thomson, *Extraordinary Bodies*, 9.
60. Waswo, "Crises of Credit," 60. Waswo draws on Craig Muldrew's expansive study, *The Economy of Obligation: The Culture of Credit and Social Relations in Early Modern England* (Basingstoke, UK: Macmillan, 1998), which tracks the shifting notion of "credit" from social to financial obligation; see also Brian Sheerin's discussion of the credit imaginary in relation to drama in *Desires of Credit in Early Modern Theory and Drama: Commerce, Poesy, and the Profitable Imagination* (London: Routledge, 2016).
61. Bruster, *Drama and the Market*, 3; Theodore B. Leinwand, *Theatre, Finance, and Society in Early Modern England* (Cambridge: Cambridge University Press, 1999), 6. See also Bruster's discussion of the Exchange's centrality in *Drama and the Market*, 4–7.
62. Jean-Christophe Agnew, *Worlds Apart: The Market and the Theater in Anglo-American Thought, 1550–1750* (Cambridge: Cambridge University Press, 1986), 9.
63. Fisher, *Materializing Gender*, 31.
64. Wills, *Prosthesis*, 242. Wills suggests that the word itself reflects this sense of an "otherness that is the artificial" (232). See also Lochlann S. Jain, "The Prosthetic Imagination: Enabling and Disabling the Prosthesis Trope," *Science, Technology, and Human Values* 24, no. 1 (Winter 1999): 31–54.
65. Lynn Festa, *Fiction Without Humanity: Person, Animal, Thing in Early Enlightenment Literature and Culture* (Philadelphia: University of Pennsylvania Press, 2019), 103.
66. Mitchell and Snyder, *Narrative Prosthesis*, 8. I discuss this idea further in the introduction.
67. *Oxford English Dictionary*, s.v. "habit," n., 1a, 4, 5a.
68. See Ann Rosalind Jones and Peter Stallybrass, *Renaissance Clothing and the Materials of Memory* (Cambridge: Cambridge University Press, 2000). Love extends this reading: the definition of habit as "a settled practice, custom" further complicates the disability trope. Love, *Figure of Disability*, 54.
69. *Oxford English Dictionary*, s.v. "crooked," adj., 1a, 2a, 3a.
70. Hyland, *Disguise*, 37.
71. Hyland writes that Frank "sees in his disguise a negative moral actualisation of his self," although "Cripple is not crooked in his thoughts." Hyland, *Disguise*, 139.
72. Lin, *Materiality of Performance*, 9.
73. Indeed, Paul V. Kreider claims that "no single plot device is used in Elizabethan comedy more generally and more continuously than is disguise." Kreider, *Elizabethan Comic Character Conventions: As Revealed in the Comedies of George Chapman* (Ann Arbor: University of Michigan Press, 1935), 32. See Hyland's wide-ranging study for a survey of early modern plays featuring disguise.
74. Row-Heyveld, *Dissembling Disability*, 176.
75. Peter H. Davison, introduction to *Fair Maid*, ed. Peter H. Davison and Arthur Brown (Oxford: Malone Society Reprints, 1963), vii.

76. Elam, *Semiotics of Theatre*, 3.
77. Love, *Figure of Disability*, 58.
78. Menzer, introduction to *Look About You* in Lopez, *Early Modern Drama*, 268.
79. Love, *Figure of Disability*, 47, 64.
80. Field, introduction to *Fair Maid*, x.
81. Waswo, "Crises of Credit," 63.
82. Row-Heyveld, *Dissembling Disability*, 191.
83. Love, *Figure of Disability*, 67; Baker, "'Happy and without a name,'" 1324.

84. Alert to the pressures of theater as business, the casting table in the 1607 quarto asserts that "eleven may easily act this comedy" (819) and tags certain characters for possible doublings within the play. William J. Lawrence terms the boast of eleven actors a "mendacious statement." Lawrence, *Pre-Restoration Stage Studies* (Cambridge, MA: Harvard University Press, 1927), 74. Stephen Booth clarifies the table as "demonstrably impossible" because the chart puts characters and their doubles on stage at the same time. Booth, "Doubling in Shakespeare's Plays," in *Shakespeare: The Theatrical Dimension*, ed. Philip C. McGuire and David A. Samuelson (New York: AMS Press, 1979), 111.

85. I am grateful to Ellen MacKay for this insight.
86. Samuel Butler, *Characters and Passages from Note-Books*, ed. A. R. Waller (Cambridge: University of Cambridge Press, 1908), 238.

4. Changing the Ugly Body

1. *A certaine relation of the hog-faced gentlewoman called Mistris Tannakin Skinker* (London: J[ohn] O[kes] for F. Grove, 1640), sig. A3r.
2. Edward Phillips, *New World of English Words* (London: E. Tyler for Nath. Brooke, 1658), sig. L3v.
3. Margaret Cavendish, *The Worlds Olio* (London: Printed for J. Martin and J. Allestrye, 1655), sig. T4r. For a wide-ranging tour through early modern concepts of ugliness and deformity, see Naomi Baker, introduction to *Plain Ugly: The Unattractive Body in Early Modern Culture* (Manchester: Manchester University Press, 2010).
4. As Colleen Rosenfeld perceptively discusses, decorum is "an ideal of design that emphasizes harmony, proportion, measure, and rule"; by contrast, indecorum "prioritizes the member over the corpus, the part over the whole." *Indecorous Thinking*, 74, 75.
5. Ellen MacKay, "Indecorum," in Turner, *Early Modern Theatricality*, 312.
6. Alexander Read, *The Chirurgicall Lectures of Tumors and Ulcers* (London: I. H. for Francis Constable and E. B., 1635), sigs. C1r–v.
7. Marcello Palingenio Stellato, "Cancer," in *The Zodiake of Life*, trans. Barnabe Googe (London: Henry Denham for Rafe Newberye, 1565), sig. B2v.
8. Richard Huloet, *Huloets Dictionarie newelye corrected, amended, set in order and enlarged*, trans. John Higgins (London: in aedibus Thoma[s] Marshij, 1572), sig. P7v.
9. Thomas Rogers, *A Paterne of a Passionate Mind* (London: Thomas East, 1580), sig. B2v.
10. Susan M. Schweik, *The Ugly Laws: Disability in Public* (New York: New York University Press, 2009), 12. Schweik notes that "ugly" reflects "both a judgment about bodily aesthetics and the use of law to repress the visibility of human diversity in social contexts associated with disability and poverty—what we might call the sighting/

citing of the ugly." Schweik, *Ugly Laws*, 13. Rosemarie Garland-Thomson brilliantly observes that "these ordinances bar 'unsightly' citizens from public places because they are in fact too sightly"; such prohibitions aim to protect would-be starers, since "if there was no danger that one's eyes would be drawn to such sights, there would be no need for the law" (*Staring*, 73). The appeal of gazing at distinctive bodies returns us to Tobin Siebers's view of disability aesthetics as that which "prizes physical and mental difference" and "enlarges our vision of human variation." Siebers, *Disability Aesthetics*, 19, 3.

11. Schweik, *Ugly Laws*, 12.

12. Schweik, *Ugly Laws*, 6.

13. Rosemarie Garland-Thomson, "Dares to Stares: Disabled Women Performance Artists and the Dynamics of Staring," in Sandahl and Auslander, *Bodies in Commotion*, 31.

14. Here I am also thinking of Sianne Ngai's claim that the affective structure of disgust is intransitive, always "disgust *toward*" something but nonetheless "constituted by the vehement rejection or *exclusion* of its object," and "directed toward the *negation* of [its] objects." Ngai, *Ugly Feelings* (Cambridge, MA: Harvard University Press, 2005), 22.

15. McRuer, *Crip Theory*, 9.

16. Although the early modern theater does not understand the body of the actor as a stable surface, my reading builds on Ato Quayson's claim that disability "returns the aesthetic domain to an active ethical core that serves to disrupt the surface of representation." Quayson, *Aesthetic Nervousness*, 19.

17. Thomas Middleton and William Rowley, *The Changeling*, ed. Douglas Bruster, in *Thomas Middleton: The Collected Works*, ed. Gary Taylor et al. (Oxford: Clarendon Press, 2007), 1632–78.

18. The critical tendency to read De Flores's rape of Beatrice-Joanna as inaugurating sexual contact that she eventually comes to desire both reproduces the logic of rape culture and misreads the play. The notion that Beatrice-Joanna "nevertheless develops feelings" for De Flores and the tendency to use the language of consummation to describe sexual violence was a distressing feature of early criticism and unfortunately still persists. I quote, as entirely representative, Cole Jeffrey, "'Here's Beauty Changed to Ugly Whoredom': Calvinist Theology and Neoplatonic Aesthetics in *The Changeling*," *Renaissance Drama* 47, no. 1 (Spring 2019): 22; for a similar example, see Michael Slater, "'Shameless Collaboration': Mixture and the Double Plot of *The Changeling*," *Renaissance Drama* 47, no. 1 (2019): 43. Arguments in this vein ignore foundational critical readings of *The Changeling* that explicitly contested this point: see Roberta Barker and David Nicol, "Does Beatrice Joanna Have a Subtext? *The Changeling* on the London Stage," *Early Modern Literary Studies* 10, no. 1 (May 2004), 3.1–43; and Judith Haber, *Desire and Dramatic Form in Early Modern England* (Cambridge: Cambridge University Press, 2009), esp. chap. 7.

19. *The Changeling* perhaps participates in what Joel Elliott Slotkin insightfully identifies—in the context of Richard III—as an "aesthetics of deformity" that is also an "erotics of deformity." Slotkin, *Sinister Aesthetics*, 93. I do think the play leaves open the possibility of finding De Flores fascinating and attractive, an additional source of pleasure; I resist, however, the argument that Beatrice-Joanna responds to De Flores's "sinister" aesthetics in this way.

20. Read, *Chirurgicall Lectures*, sigs. C1r–v . For this claim, Read cites Aristotelian precedent from *Rhetoric*, c. 5 and Galen's *Ad Thraisbulum*.

21. Bulwer, *Anthropometamorphosis*, sig. B2v.

22. Significant scholarship has focused on cosmetics, often on the misogyny of anticosmetic treatises, such as Thomas Tuke's *A Discourse Against Painting and Tincturing of Women* (London: Printed for Edward Marchant, 1616). On whiteness as a staple of the discourse, see Hall, *Things of Darkness*, esp. chap. 2; on the mobilization of a distinction between art and nature, see Frances E. Dolan, "Taking the Pencil Out of God's Hand: Art, Nature, and the Face-Painting Debate in Early Modern England," *PMLA* 108, no. 2 (March 1993): 224–39; on the work of cosmetics in performance, see Farah Karim-Cooper, *Cosmetics in Shakespearean and Renaissance Drama* (Edinburgh: Edinburgh University Press, 2006).

23. See Martin Porter's foundational account for a full discussion of early modern practices of reading bodies through the inheritance of the classical concept of "physiognomating," the process of using the signs of the body to venture knowledge about the person. Porter, *Windows of the Soul*, 51; see esp. chap. 1. See also Julie Orlemanski's illuminating discussion of medieval physiognomic reading practices in *Symptomatic Subjects* (Philadelphia: University of Pennsylvania Press, 2019).

24. Michel de Montaigne, *The Essayes, or Morall, Politike, and Military Discourses*, trans. John Florio (London: Val. Sims for Edward Blount, 1603), sig. 3G5r.

25. And, as Mitchell and Snyder observe, "Montaigne's method of bodily interpretation continually expands the discernible range of types and, in the process, so stretches taxonomical efforts that they nearly collapse from the necessity of all-encompassing individuation." *Narrative Prosthesis*, 77.

26. Burton, *Anatomy of Melancholy*, pt. 2, 133.

27. Baker, *Plain Ugly*, 79.

28. Burton, *Anatomy of Melancholy*, pt. 2, 139.

29. Burton, *Anatomy of Melancholy*, pt. 2, 143.

30. Stephen Greenblatt, *Shakespeare's Freedom* (Chicago: University of Chicago Press, 2010), 24. For Greenblatt, Shakespeare's distinctiveness as a playwright arises in his practice of marking characters; my readings in this book situate that practice, I would suggest, within the early modern theater's formal gambits.

31. On blankness as a technology of whiteness that racializes through somatic markings, see Akhimie, *Cultivation of Difference*, esp. the introduction, and Hall, *Things of Darkness*.

32. Baker, *Plain Ugly*, 69.

33. See Baker, *Plain Ugly*, 71.

34. Francis Beaumont and John Fletcher, *The Captain*, ed. L. A. Beaurline, in Bowers, *Dramatic Works*, 1:541–670.

35. Whether or not the "swart complexion" that adds to this characterization is produced through theatrical prosthetics or only marked discursively, the lines partake of what Hall identifies (in a different context) as the "color complex, which is undergirded by a fundamental urge for whiteness." Hall, *Things of Darkness*, 69. On the practice of using cloth to signify skin color, see Smith, "Textile Black Body." On the changing technologies of paint used for blackface in early modern performance, see Stevens, *Inventions of the Skin*, chap. 2. On velvet patches and syphilis, see Margaret Healy, *Fictions*

of *Disease in Early Modern England: Bodies, Plagues, and Politics* (New York: Palgrave Macmillan, 2001), esp. chaps. 4 and 5.

36. I owe this formulation to Musa Gurnis.

37. Bruce Boehrer, "Alsemero's Closet: Privacy and Interiority in *The Changeling*," *Journal of English and Germanic Philology* 96, no. 3 (July 1997): 349; Kim Solga, *Violence against Women in Early Modern Performance: Invisible Acts* (Basingstoke, UK: Palgrave Macmillan, 2014), 143.

38. Gordon McMullan, "*The Changeling* and the Dynamics of Ugliness," in *The Cambridge Companion to English Renaissance Tragedy*, ed. Emma Smith and Garrett A. Sullivan Jr. (Cambridge: Cambridge University Press, 2010), 231, 222. Quoting Mark Cousins's assertion that ugliness "deforms a totality," McMullan observes that the excess of ugliness resists wholeness; "it is the thing that is over and above the whole" (224). See also Michael Neill's assertion that De Flores is the "agent of a reductive transformation" so that "unforming form (beauty) itself, De Flores is the true plague of *The Changeling*, its active principle of indistinction." Neill, *Issues of Death: Mortality and Identity in English Renaissance Tragedy* (Oxford: Clarendon Press, 1997), 174. On the double plot, see David Nicol, *Middleton and Rowley: Forms of Collaboration in the Jacobean Playhouse* (Toronto: University of Toronto Press, 2012).

39. On antipathy as an occult cause in *The Changeling*, see Mary Floyd-Wilson, *Occult Knowledge, Science, and Gender on the Shakespearean Stage* (Cambridge: Cambridge University Press, 2013), esp. chap. 4.

40. In Christopher Ricks's classic argument, the play engages in double entendre—repeating keywords such as "service" and "honour"—with a sexual meaning that Beatrice is unable to comprehend. Christopher Ricks, "The Moral and Poetic Structure of *The Changeling*," *Essays in Criticism* 10, no. 3 (1960): 293. Adapting his insight that Beatrice's defining character trait is "a tragic failure to see puns" (294), I read Beatrice's refusal to reckon with the contingency of her judgment—"His face loathes one" rather than "I loathe his face"—as a failure to parse verbs.

41. I quote the passage in the text without the editorially marked asides of the Oxford edition.

42. See Jeremy Lopez's observation that asides "demarcate theatrical space, isolating but insisting on the simultaneity of several different and very specific interpretive possibilities for the on-stage action," making the aside both one of the "most pervasive" and "most potentially disruptive" early modern dramatic conventions. Lopez, *Theatrical Convention and Audience Response in Early Modern Drama* (Cambridge: Cambridge University Press, 2003), 56. On asides in *The Changeling*, see Nora Williams, "'Cannot I keep that secret?': Editing and Performing Asides in *The Changeling*," *Shakespeare Bulletin* 34, no. 1 (Spring 2016): 29–45.

43. Frank Whigham, "Reading Social Conflict in the Alimentary Tract: More on the Body in Renaissance Drama," *English Literary History* 55, no. 2 (Summer 1988): 341.

44. See also Jonathan Dollimore's claim that "an act of transgression and its consequences actually disclose 'blood' and 'birth' to be myths in the service of historical and social forms of power, divested of which Beatrice becomes no more than what 'the act' has made her." Dollimore, *Radical Tragedy: Religion, Ideology, and Power in the Drama of Shakespeare and His Contemporaries* (Chicago: University of Chicago Press, 1984), 178.

45. Cristina Malcolmson, "'As Tame as the Ladies': Politics and Gender in *The Changeling*," in *Revenge Tragedy*, ed. Stevie Simkins (New York: Palgrave Macmillan, 2001), 156. See also Mark Thornton Burnett's observation that "De Flores might be a subversive, but he is equally a force for the reassertion of order." Burnett, *Masters and Servants in English Renaissance Drama and Culture* (Basingstoke, UK: Macmillan, 1997), 109.

46. John Reynolds, *The Triumphs of God's Revenge* [sic], *Against the crying, and execrable Sinne of Murther* (London: Felix Kyngston for William Lee, 1621). Annabel Patterson notes that "Middleton added the entire episode of the tests and the bed-trick, thereby making virginity and its overvaluation a central theme of his tragedy." Patterson, introduction to *The Changeling*, in Gary Taylor et al., *Middleton: Collected Works*, 1633. Reynolds's text was extremely popular, published in 1621, reprinted each year for the next three years, and then reprinted thirteen more times before 1680.

47. To account for this gap, modern editors of the play often add an explanatory note with conjecture that the two men must have seen Beatrice-Joanna and De Flores at some point prior to the scene's opening, as if the play, a text with a relatively stable print history, is missing a scene.

48. On the "black mask" as a form of racial marking, see Hall, *Things of Darkness*, esp. 85–92. Lara Bovilsky connects the "black mask" to a racialized marking of De Flores's ugliness in *Barbarous Play: Race on the English Renaissance Stage* (Minneapolis: University of Minnesota Press, 2008), esp. 150–51.

49. Baker, *Plain Ugly*, 84.

50. McMullan observes that Beatrice-Joanna "insists on *indistinction* as the only way to clean the stain of ugliness." McMullan, "Dynamics of Ugliness," 231. Whigham calls this plea "self-debasing, self-expelling" ("Reading Social Conflict," 340); see also Gail Kern Paster's insightful reading of Beatrice-Joanna's figuration as "waste liquid" that reconstitutes her relation to the world. Paster, "The Ecology of the Passions in *A Chaste Maid in Cheapside* and *The Changeling*," in *The Oxford Handbook of Thomas Middleton*, ed. Gary Taylor and Trish Thomas Henley (Oxford: Oxford University Press, 2012), 162.

51. See, for example, Neill's argument that the play "has been only superficially concerned with 'change'; the shaping metaphor behind the whole action is not one of metamorphosis but of discovery—the penetration and display of morbid secrets." Neill, *Issues of Death*, 175.

52. Algernon Charles Swinburne, "Thomas Middleton," *The Nineteenth Century* 19 (1886): 138–53, collected in Sara Jayne Steen, ed., *Ambrosia in an Earthen Vessel: Three Centuries of Audience and Reader Response to the Works of Thomas Middleton* (New York: AMS, 1993), 176.

53. William Empson, *Some Versions of Pastoral* (New York: New Directions, 1950), 50.

54. A. L. Kistner and M. K. Kistner, "The Five Structures of *The Changeling*," *Modern Language Studies* 11, no. 2 (Spring 1981): 47. The sense of Beatrice-Joanna's "revulsion as caused by De Flores's face" is shared by Joost Daalder and Antony Telford Moore in "'There's scarce a thing but is both loved and loathed': *The Changeling* I.i.91–129," *English Studies* 80, no. 6 (December 1999): 500.

55. Carol Thomas Neely, "Distracted Measures: Madness and Theatricality in Middleton," in *Thomas Middleton in Context*, ed. Suzanne Gossett (Cambridge: Cambridge University Press, 2011), 306. On the performance of madness in early modern drama,

see Neely's germinal work, *Distracted Subjects: Madness and Gender in Shakespeare and Early Modern Culture* (Ithaca, NY: Cornell University Press, 2004).

56. Quoted in Roach, *Player's Passion*, 50.

57. Farah Karim-Cooper, *The Hand on the Shakespearean Stage: Gesture, Touch and the Spectacle of Dismemberment* (London: Bloomsbury Arden Shakespeare, 2016), 82. Karim-Cooper defines the "iconic gesture" as a "formal hand (or body) movement" both "highly recognizable to an early modern audience" and represented with "graphic correspondences in paintings and engravings" (82–83).

58. Roach, *Player's Passion*, 50, 49.

59. Mary Baine Campbell suggests that Bulwer's text "might serve as magnetic center of several analyses: not only the histories of fashion, the body, and anthropology, but those of wonderbooks, monstrosity, abjection, semiosis, plastic surgery, nationalism, commodity capitalism, and subjectivity meet here, as well as histories of the concepts, central to all of these topics, of 'nature' and 'culture.'" Campbell, *Wonder and Science: Imagining Worlds in Early Modern Europe* (Ithaca, NY: Cornell University Press, 1999), 235–36. Bearden offers a useful corrective to the critical tendency to extract *Anthropometamorphosis* from Bulwer's broader body of work and offers a groundbreaking reading of Bulwer's treatment of deafness and sign language; see Bearden, *Monstrous Kinds*, chap. 2. On the political significance of monsters, see William E. Burns, "The King's Two Monstrous Bodies: John Bulwer and the English Revolution," in *Wonders, Marvels, and Monsters in Early Modern Culture*, ed. Peter G. Platt (Newark: University of Delaware Press, 1999); on the thin distinction between human and nonhuman, see Susan Wiseman, "Monstrous Perfectibility: Ape-Human Transformations in Hobbes, Bulwer, Tyson," in *At the Borders of the Human: Beasts, Bodies and Natural Philosophy in the Early Modern Period*, ed. Erica Fudge, Ruth Gilbert, and Susan Wiseman (London: Palgrave Macmillan, 1999); on body modification as a kind of monstrosity, see Elizabeth Stephens, "Queer Monsters: Technologies of Self-Transformation in Bulwer's *Anthropometamorphosis* and Braidotti's *Metamorphoses*," in *Somatechnics: Queering the Technologisation of Bodies*, ed. Nikki Sullivan and Samantha Murray (New York: Ashgate, 2009).

60. Bulwer, *Anthropometamorphosis*, title page. Bulwer published an initial edition in 1650, followed by two more editions, expanded in 1653 to include the appendix on the "English Gallant" that I discuss below.

61. This English gallant resembles the figure Christopher Marsh discusses in "A Woodcut and Its Wanderings in Seventeenth-Century England," *Huntington Library Quarterly* 79, no. 2 (2016): 245–62.

62. Discussing a similar juxtaposition in Bulwer's appendix, Hall notes that while the engraving associates a black woman and a white woman in a gendered critique of cosmetic artifice, the black woman is positioned as "imitative": my sense here, by contrast, is that the male figures slot less neatly into the hierarchy of opposition because the imitation works the other way around. Hall, *Things of Darkness*, 89.

63. Gosson insists that "every play to the world's end, if it be presented up on the Stage, shall carry that brand on his back to make him known," and even "such playes as contain good matter . . . cannot be played, without manifest breach of God's commandment." Stephen Gosson, *Playes Confuted*, sig. E6r.

64. Edmund Gayton, *Pleasant Notes Upon Don Quixot* (London: William Hunt, 1654), sig. T3v. I thank Musa Gurnis for pointing me to this reference.

65. John Ford et al., *The Spanish Gypsy*, ed. Gary Taylor, in Taylor et al., *Thomas Middleton: Collected Works*. See also Douglas Bruster's discussion of the textual relationship between the two plays in "The Changeling," in *Thomas Middleton and Early Modern Textual Culture: A Companion to The Collected Works*, ed. Gary Taylor et al. (Oxford: Clarendon Press, 2007), 1094.

5. Playing Time, or Sick of Feigning

1. Philip Barrough, *The Methode of Phisicke* (London: Thomas Vautroullier, 1583), sigs. C1r, C1v, C4r, C4v.

2. William Salmon, *Synopsis Medicinae* (London: W. Godbid for Richard Jones, 1671), sig. 3N4r. Unless otherwise noted, quotes preserve emphasis in the original text.

3. Lazare Rivière, *The universal body of physick in five books; comprehending the several treatises of nature, of diseases and their causes, of symptoms, of the preservation of health, and of cures*, trans. William Carr (London: Printed for Philip Briggs, 1657), sig. S4v.

4. Foucault suggests that "up to the end of the eighteenth century medicine related much more to health than to normality," rather than, by the nineteenth century, operating along "the medical bipolarity of the normal and the pathological." Michel Foucault, *The Birth of the Clinic: An Archaeology of Medical Perception*, trans. A. M. Sheridan Smith (New York: Vintage, 1994), 35. For accounts of this medical development in relation to disability studies, see Lennard J. Davis, *Enforcing Normalcy: Disability, Deafness, and the Body* (New York: Verso, 1995), and Deutsch and Nussbaum, "Defects."

5. Henri-Jacques Stiker distinguishes the affective association of disease with mortal threat from disability's "need not to be exiled, misunderstood, strange and a stranger." Stiker, *History of Disability*, 8.

6. Kafer, *Feminist, Queer, Crip*, 27. On cure as a "vanishing point" of a medical gaze that can only imagine correcting a disabled body, see Johnson Cheu, "Performing Disability, Problematizing Cure," in Sandahl and Auslander, *Bodies in Commotion*, 136. Accounts of cure in disability theory target an ideology of cure, a critique of medical intervention that is structural rather than individual.

7. Kafer points out that disability "becomes the future of no future" because "this kind of cure-driven future positions people with disabilities in a temporality that cannot exist fully in the present, one where one's life is always on hold, in limbo, waiting for the cure to arrive." Kafer, *Feminist, Queer, Crip*, 33, 44.

8. Eli Clare, *Brilliant Imperfection: Grappling with Cure* (Durham, NC: Duke University Press, 2017), 15.

9. Kafer, *Feminist, Queer, Crip*, 26. Thus, as Kafer puts it, "crip time bends the clock to meet disabled bodies and minds" (27); as Ellen Samuels observes in a profound meditation on crip time, "we who occupy the bodies of crip time know that we are never linear." Samuels, "Six Ways of Looking at Crip Time," *Disability Studies Quarterly* 37, no. 3 (2017), https://dsq-sds.org/article/view/5824.

10. Much critical work has focused on the relationship between the theater and plague: the classic account is Leeds Barroll, *Politics, Plague, and Shakespeare's Theater: The Stuart Years* (Ithaca, NY: Cornell University Press, 1991); valuable book-length studies include Rebecca Totaro, *Suffering in Paradise: The Bubonic Plague in English Literature from More to Milton* (Pittsburgh: Duquesne University Press, 2005), and Ernest B. Gilman, *Plague Writing in Early Modern England* (Chicago: University of

Chicago Press, 2009). On disease metaphors, see Jonathan Gil Harris, *Sick Economies: Drama, Mercantilism, and Disease in Shakespeare's England* (Philadelphia: University of Pennsylvania Press, 2004); on concepts of infection and the playhouse, see Carolyn Sale, "Eating Air, Feeling Smells: *Hamlet's* Theory of Performance," *Renaissance Drama* 35 (2006): 145–68, and Darryl Chalk and Mary Floyd-Wilson, eds., *Contagion and the Shakespearean Stage* (New York: Palgrave Macmillan, 2009).

11. MacKay, *Persecution, Plague, and Fire*, 121, 118.

12. Elam, *Semiotics of Theatre*, 7–8.

13. Sandahl, "Tyranny of Neutral," 255.

14. I discuss this critique in the introduction; see also Sandahl, "Tyranny of Neutral," and Kuppers, *Theatre and Disability*, esp. 11–32.

15. M. Remi Yergeau, *Authoring Autism: On Rhetoric and Neurological Queerness* (Durham, NC: Duke University Press, 2018), 10.

16. To take a modern example, we could think of Rita Marcalo's *Involuntary Dances* (2009), a durational performance in which the disabled artist attempted to induce an epileptic seizure before an audience. Most public responses to the piece critiqued the premise as inviting an "exploitative gaze," though other artists valorized the work's exploration of "visibility versus non-visibility, and control versus non-control" of disabled bodies. Bree Hadley, *Disability, Public Space Performance and Spectatorship: Unconscious Performers* (London: Palgrave Macmillan, 2014), 117, 120; see esp. 114–21. What this piece suggests, in my reading, is the relation between acting and constraint: Marcalo vividly poses the question of how involuntary bodily responses might be aestheticized.

17. Gosson, *Playes Confuted*, sig. E5r. I discuss this passage in the introduction.

18. Poole, *The English Parnassus, or, A Helpe to English Poesie* (London: Printed for Tho. Johnson, 1657), sig. L3v.

19. For a generative reading of the "discursive messiness" that brings disability theory to bear on the intersection of early medical discourse of epilepsy and Shakespeare's *Julius Caesar*, see Allison P. Hobgood, "'Caesar Hath the Falling Sickness.'"

20. Hippocrates of Cos, *The Sacred Disease*, vol. 21, trans. W. H. S. Jones (Cambridge, MA: Harvard University Press, 1923), 183. See also Galen, *On the Causes of Symptoms II*, trans. Ian Johnston (Cambridge: Cambridge University Press, 2006), which treats "abnormal movements" that run the gamut from convulsions and tremors to shivering and hiccups, to sneezing and yawning, distinguishing between movements that "are natural, but brought on by disease, and those that are not natural" (236). Galen's work was translated by Thomas Linacre and published in London by R. Pynson in the 1520s: see Richard J. Durling, "A Chronological Census of Renaissance Editions and Translations of Galen," *Journal of the Warburg and Courtauld Institutes* 24, nos. 3–4 (July–December 1961): 230–305.

21. Thomas Cogan, *The Haven of Health* (1584; repr., London: Printed by Anne Griffin for Roger Ball, 1636), sig. B1r.

22. John Trapp, "Brief commentary or exposition upon the Gospel according to St John," in *A commentary or exposition upon the four Evangelists, and the Acts of the Apostle* (London: A. M. for John Bellamie, 1647), sigs. X1v–X2r. Doctrinal disputes draw on the metaphor; for example, the sermon given by Nathanael Homes organizes its major points as the "Five Symptomes" of "the Falling-sicknesse of Apostacie from Religion, like to fall away from our Profession." Homes, *A sermon preached afore*

Thomas Andrews Lord Maior and the aldermen, sheriffs &c. of the honorable corporation of the citie of London in which discourse is held forth (London: Printed by T. R. and J. C., 1650), sig. D4v.

23. John Webster, *The Displaying of Supposed Witchcraft* (London: J. M., 1677), sig. 2T2r.

24. Lucinda McCray Beier discusses medical casebooks that identify epilepsy as a treatable disease in *Sufferers and Healers: The Experience of Illness in Seventeenth-Century England* (London: Routledge, 1987). Elsewhere I have discussed the wonky temporality of magical cure; see Katherine Schaap Williams, "'Strange Virtue': Staging Acts of Cure," in Iyengar, *Disability, Health, and Happiness*, 93–108.

25. I focus here on Scot's work in relation to a brief discussion of epilepsy, but the scholarship on witchcraft, gender, and medical history, as well as work on Harsnett's text as a Shakespearean source, is extensive. For a broad overview of witchcraft in the period, see James Sharpe, *Witchcraft in Early Modern England* (London: Routledge, 2001); on "jugglers" and illusion in medieval performance, see Philip Butterworth, *Magic on the Early English Stage* (Cambridge: Cambridge University Press, 2005); on witchcraft and Shakespeare's plays, see Deborah Willis, *Malevolent Nature: Witch-Hunting and Maternal Power in Early Modern England* (Ithaca, NY: Cornell University Press, 1995); on witchcraft and drama, see Marcus Harmes and Victoria Bladen, eds., *Supernatural and Secular Power in Early Modern England* (London: Routledge, 2015).

26. Reginald Scot, *The Discoverie of Witchcraft . . . verie necessarie to be knowne* (London: [Henry Denham] for William Brome, 1584), sig. C4r. See also Butterworth's discussion of Scot's effort to demonstrate that "jugglers created these effects by conscious, deliberate and purposeful skill." Butterworth, *Magic on the Early English Stage*, 151.

27. Shakespeare, *Second Part of King Henry the Fourth*.

28. Francis Beaumont and John Fletcher, *The Woman Hater*, ed. George Walton Williams, in Bowers, *Dramatic Works*, 1:145–260.

29. Thomas Tomkis, *Albumazar* (London: Nicholas Okes for Walter Burre, 1615), sig. B2v.

30. William Shakespeare, *The Second Part of Henry the Sixth*, ed. William Montgomery, in Orgel and Braunmuller, *Complete Pelican Shakespeare*, 1080–122.

31. For a generative reading of Simpcox's feigning, see Lindsey Row-Heyveld, "'The lying'st knave in Christendom': The Development of Disability in the False Miracle of St. Alban's," *Disability Studies Quarterly* 29, no. 4 (Fall 2009), https://dsq-sds.org/article/view/994/1178.

32. Gary Taylor, "History, Plays, Genre, Games," in Taylor and Henley, *Oxford Handbook of Thomas Middleton*, 47.

33. Thomas Middleton, *Hengist, King of Kent; or, The Mayor of Queenborough*, ed. Grace Ioppolo, in Taylor et al., *Thomas Middleton: Collected Works*, 1448–87.

34. William Shakespeare, *The Tragedy of Othello the Moor of Venice*, ed. Russ McDonald, in Orgel and Braunmuller, *Complete Pelican Shakespeare*, 1392–444.

35. Like the reported fit in *Julius Caesar*, Othello's fit is characterized as having "served admirably to increase the pathos of the impending, and, by now, inevitable tragedies." R. R. Simpson, *Shakespeare and Medicine* (New York: E. & S. Livingstone, 1959), 160. F. David Hoeniger, though he suggests Iago's report of Othello's prior fit is a lie, observes that "Othello's fit is merely a short-lived trance caused by his over-

wrought emotional state, though the fact that he falls on the ground symbolizes how successfully Iago has undermined his integrity." Hoeniger, *Medicine and Shakespeare in the English Renaissance* (Newark: University of Delaware Press, 1992), 204. For a foundational reading of disability in the play in relation to humoral variability, see David Houston Wood, "'Fluster'd with Flowing Cups': Alcoholism, Humoralism, and the Prosthetic Narrative in *Othello*," *Disability Studies Quarterly* 29, no. 4 (2009), https://dsq-sds.org/article/view/998/1182.

36. Frank Whigham, *Seizures of the Will in Early Modern English Drama* (Cambridge: Cambridge University Press, 1996), 1, 5.

37. Justin Shaw, "'Rub Him About the Temples': *Othello*, Disability, and the Failures of Care," *Early Theatre* 22, no. 2 (2019): 177. Though I concentrate on Iago here, Shaw's reading illuminates the failure of Cassio, as the other brief spectator in the scene, to care for Othello.

38. Peter Womack, *Ben Jonson* (Oxford: Basil Blackwell, 1986), 143, 143, 144.

39. Womack, *Ben Jonson*, 142, 143.

40. Womack, *Ben Jonson*, 143.

41. Montaigne, *Essayes*, sig. 2L6v.

42. Jonson, *Timber*, 537.

43. We could frame this insight in terms of theater phenomenology; if, as Bert O. States observes, "theater ingests the world of objects and signs only to bring images to life," in this case the object of the actor's body and the scripted signs may not be digested into the image. States, *Great Reckonings in Little Rooms: On the Phenomenology of Theater* (Berkeley: University of California Press, 1985), 37. Critics have also, of course, noted that such moments of perceiving through the spectacle seem to be part of the early modern theater's pleasure: see Lin's argument, for example, that *King Lear*, in "drawing attention to stage technologies . . . reminds spectators that what they see is *not* a blinding but a simulation of one." Lin, *Materiality of Performance*, 5.

44. Ben Jonson, *Volpone, or The Fox*, ed. Richard Dutton, in Bevington et al., *Works of Ben Jonson*, 3:1–192, 42. Dutton's edition is based on the 1606 quarto.

45. See, for example, Harriet Hawkins, "Folly, Incurable Disease, and *Volpone*," *Studies in English Literature, 1500–1900* 8, no. 2 (Spring 1968): 335–48; Anne Barton observes that "the sentences themselves, in which the punishments exquisitely fit the crimes, are unashamedly those of the dramatist." Barton, *Ben Jonson, Dramatist* (Cambridge: Cambridge University Press, 1984), 117.

46. As Barish observes, while "these countermines of theatricality seem sometimes to threaten to blow all antitheatrical doctrine sky high," nonetheless, "on the official level antitheatrical doctrine holds sway, as the ending of *Volpone* clearly shows." Barish, *Antitheatrical Prejudice*, 146.

47. See, for example, John Creaser's argument that a key "reason why our delight in Volpone is not neutralised by moral condemnation lies in his outstanding theatrical presence" and the actor's "unique rapport with the audience," produced by "the joy he takes in his roguery." Creaser, "*Volpone*: The Mortifying of The Fox," *Essays in Criticism* 25, no. 3 (1975): 344–45.

48. Lauren Coker, "'There is no suff'ring due': Metatheatricality and Disability Drag in *Volpone*," in Hobgood and Wood, *Recovering Disability*, 123. I discuss the charge of "disability drag" in the introduction; see also Siebers, *Disability Theory*, 114–16.

49. Maggie Vinter, *Last Acts: The Art of Dying on the Early Modern Stage* (New York: Fordham University Press, 2019), 134, 135. Thus, Vinter observes, Volpone's performance is "a sort of zero-degree acting" that "explores the limits of how far a performance can efface itself while still functioning as a performance" (134).

50. Frances Teague, "Ben Jonson and London Courtrooms," in *Solon and Thespis: Law and Theater in the English Renaissance*, ed. Dennis Kezar (Notre Dame, IN: University of Notre Dame Press, 2007), 35.

51. Lorna Hutson, *The Invention of Suspicion: Law and Mimesis in Shakespeare and Renaissance Drama* (Oxford: Oxford University Press, 2007), 317.

52. Katharine Eisaman Maus, *Inwardness and Theater in the English Renaissance* (Chicago: University of Chicago Press, 1995), 168.

53. See Ben Jonson, *Volpone*, in *The Workes of Benjamin Jonson* (London: William Stansby, 1616), sigs. 2T6v–2Ur. The speech below concludes with a question mark after "dissemble" (instead of the 1607 quarto's period); I follow the punctuation of the 1616 *Workes*, which emphasizes the formal continuity of the questions that structure Voltore's speech.

54. Ian Donaldson suggests that *Volpone*'s ending is among the best of Jonson's conclusions that "serve as metaphors and models of the mental, psychological, and moral state of the characters who inhabit them." Donaldson, *Jonson's Magic Houses: Essays in Interpretation* (Oxford: Clarendon Press, 1997), 110.

55. Jonson, *Volpone*, 37–38. Dutton's editorial note observes that the capital letters in the poem "leave it ambiguous as to whether it is the play, character or even possibly the author who is addressed" (37).

56. See James P. Bednarz, "Jonson's Literary Theatre: *Volpone* in Performance and Print (1606–1607)," in *Volpone: A Critical Guide*, ed. Matthew Steggle (London: Continuum, 2011) 83–104, which challenges critical assumptions about Jonson's scorn for the theater in relation to the 1607 quarto. On the importance of the commendatory poems to the quarto, see Dutton's fascinating argument in *Volpone and the Gunpowder Plot* (Cambridge: Cambridge University Press, 2008), 37–54.

57. Coker, "'There is no suff'ring due,'" 132.

58. John Dryden, *Of Dramatic Poesy and Other Critical Essays*, ed. George Watson (London: J. M. Dent & Sons, 1962), 1:61.

59. Barton, *Ben Jonson, Dramatist*, 107–8.

60. Stephen Greenblatt, "The False Ending in *Volpone*," *Journal of English and Germanic Philology* 75, nos. 1–2 (January–April 1976): 95. For Greenblatt, Jonson "offers the audience a resolution precisely the reverse of the one he will finally provide" so that they must contemplate a world in which Volpone evades justice (92).

61. John Dennis, "From *Letters on Several Occasions*, 1696," collected in *Volpone: A Casebook*, ed. Jonas A. Barish (London: Macmillan, 1972), 30.

62. Dennis, "From *Letters on Several Occasions*," 29.

63. Dennis, "From *Letters on Several Occasions*," 29.

64. Sidney, *Defence of Poetry*, 44.

65. Sidney, *Defence of Poetry*, 68.

66. In this sense, the play relies on what Tobin Siebers calls the "prejudicial reduction of a body to its disability." Siebers, *Disability Theory*, 81.

67. For a perceptive reading of these characters as a demonstration that "the tenuous superiority of the human disavows the inextricable mingling and fundamen-

tal kinship among beings," see Elizabeth D. Harvey, "Beastly Physic," *Shakespeare Studies* 41 (2013): 123.

68. William Congreve, "From *Letter to Dennis on Humour in Comedy, 1695*," in Barish, *Volpone: A Casebook*, 31.

69. Jonas A. Barish, introduction to *Volpone: A Casebook*, 12.

70. Dennis, "From *Letters on Several Occasions*," 29.

71. Yergeau, *Authoring Autism*, 4.

6. Making the Monster

1. Shakespeare, *The Tempest*, ed. Peter Holland, in Orgel and Braunmuller, *Complete Pelican Shakespeare*, act 2, scene 2, lines 29, 64, 88–89, 141–42, 142, 143, 144, 147–48, 151–52, 152, 155, 155–56, 162, 176, 176, 185.

2. I discuss Jonson's account of poetic form and Diamond's formulation of performance as both "doing" and "thing done" in the introduction.

3. See Laura Lunger Knoppers and Joan B. Landes, introduction to *Monstrous Bodies/Political Monstrosities in Early Modern Europe*, ed. Laura Lunger Knoppers and Joan B. Landes (Ithaca, NY: Cornell University Press, 2004); Surekha Davies, "The Unlucky, the Bad, and the Ugly: Categories of Monstrosity from the Renaissance to the Enlightenment," in *The Ashgate Research Companion to Monsters and the Monstrous*, ed. Asa Simon Mittman and Peter J. Dendle (Burlington, VT: Ashgate, 2013), 49–75; and Bearden, *Monstrous Kinds*, 1–32.

4. See Kathryn M. Brammall, "Monstrous Metamorphosis: Nature, Morality, and the Rhetoric of Monstrosity in Tudor England," *Sixteenth Century Journal* 27, no. 1 (Spring 1996): 6.

5. Bearden, *Monstrous Kinds*, 13. See Kathleen Long's discussion of how Aristotelian and Augustinian views "complement rather than contradict each other." Long, "'Nature Abhors Normality': Theories of the Monstrous from Aristotle to *The X-Files* (1993–2002)," in *Speaking of Monsters: A Teratological Anthology*, ed. Caroline Joan S. Picart and John Edgar Browning (New York: Palgrave Macmillan, 2012), 195–208, 195.

6. Julie Crawford, *Marvelous Protestantism: Monstrous Births in Post-Reformation England* (Baltimore: Johns Hopkins University Press, 2005), 11; Turner, "Introduction: Approaching Anomalous Bodies," 4; Stagg, "Representing Physical Difference," 24. As Stagg observes, "Although there is no simple correspondence between the overlapping discourses of disability and monstrosity, physical difference lies at their core" (21); the monstrous body appears a "passive spectacle of difference" (35).

7. Lennard J. Davis highlights the "inordinate amount of attention" directed at examples of "anomalous, strange births" that "were distinguished from disabilities that were acquired, particularly through disease." Davis, *Bending Over Backwards*, 53.

8. Rosemarie Garland-Thomson, "Introduction: From Wonder to Error—A Genealogy of Freak Discourse in Modernity," in *Freakery: Cultural Spectacles of the Extraordinary Body*, ed. Rosemarie Garland-Thomson (New York: New York University Press, 1996), 3.

9. See Michael Hagner, "Enlightened Monsters," in *The Sciences in Enlightened Europe*, ed. William Clark, Jan Golinski, and Simon Schaffer (Chicago: University of Chicago Press, 1999), which traces the eighteenth-century relocation of monsters from the wonder cabinet to the human sciences (179).

10. Pender, "In the Bodyshop," 99; Paul Semonin, "Monsters in the Marketplace: The Exhibition of Human Oddities in Early Modern England," in Garland-Thomson, *Freakery*, 77. Bearden's important account "uncover[s] a shared identity, specifically a disability identity, for these so-called monsters." *Monstrous Kinds*, 181.

11. Robert Bogdan, *Freak Show: Presenting Human Oddities for Amusement and Profit* (Chicago: University of Chicago Press, 1988), 3; Rachel Adams, *Sideshow U.S.A.: Freaks and the American Cultural Imagination* (Chicago: University of Chicago Press, 2001), 6. Thus, as Adams notes, "freakishness is a historically variable quality, derived less from particular physical attributes than the spectacle of the extraordinary body swathed in theatrical props, promoted by advertising and performative fanfare" (5).

12. Katharine Park and Lorraine Daston, *Wonders and the Order of Nature 1150–1750* (New York: Zone Books, 1998), 209. See esp. chap. 5.

13. Foucault, *Abnormal*, 65, 50.

14. Pender, "No Monsters," 156; Bearden, *Monstrous Kinds*, 6.

15. Wes Williams argues that the monster's "flight into metaphor, story, and rumour" is coterminous with the category's conceptual centrality: "Monsters find themselves characterized as in a strict sense unrepresentable, banished offstage, somehow obscene." Williams, *Monsters and Their Meanings in Early Modern Culture: Mighty Magic* (Oxford: Oxford University Press, 2011), 2.

16. I draw here on Jeffrey Jerome Cohen's observation that the monster is "pure culture" and "threatens to reveal that difference originates in process, rather than in fact." Cohen, "Monster Culture (Seven Theses)," in Cohen, *Monster Theory*, 4, 14–15. Likewise, Susan Stewart observes, "Often referred to as a 'freak of nature,' the freak, it must be emphasized, is a freak of culture." Stewart, *On Longing: Narratives of the Miniature, the Gigantic, the Souvenir, the Collection* (Durham, NC: Duke University Press, 1993), 109.

17. On monstrosity as artifice, see Marie-Hélène Huet, *Monstrous Imagination* (Cambridge, MA: Harvard University Press, 1993), esp. chap. 2, "The Renaissance Monster."

18. Bearden, *Monstrous Kinds*, 181–82.

19. Paré, *Workes*, sig. 4N3r.

20. Johnson's translation, Pallister has pointed out, is based an "extremely faulty Latin translation" of the *Oeuvres*. Pallister, introduction to Paré, *Monsters and Marvels*, xxviii. In Paré's original version, the two figures appear on different pages and with slightly different engravings.

21. *A Wonder Woorth the Reading* (London: William Jones, 1617), sig. A1r.

22. Crawford's *Marvelous Protestantism* offers a germinal account of the emblematic disorderings of monstrous births; on this pamphlet, see 98–100. On monstrous images, see Johns, "Grievous Burthen," esp. 50–56. On the cultural interpretation of monsters as transgression, see David Cressy, *Travesties and Transgressions in Tudor and Stuart England: Tales of Discord and Dissension* (Oxford: Oxford University Press, 2000), esp. 29–50.

23. The phrase is common: see, for example, the title page of *Strange Newes of a Prodigious Monster . . . of Aprill last, 1613* (London: J. P. for S. M., 1613).

24. See Cressy's observation that "here, locked in conflict, were the culture of Godly reformation and the culture of vulgar tradition." Cressy, *Travesties and Transgressions*, 46.

25. William Rankins, *A Mirrour of Monsters ... with the description of the subtile slights of Satan, making them his instruments* (London: J. C. for T. H., 1587), sig. B2r–v.

26. Burnett, *Constructing "Monsters,"* 10.

27. Burton, *Anatomy of Melancholy*, "Democritus to the Reader," 65.

28. Burnett, *Constructing "Monsters,"* 3.

29. Jasper Mayne, *The Citye Match* (Oxford: Leonard Lichfield, 1639), sig. G1v. N. W. Bawcutt notes that *The Citye Match* was written for the king's visit to Oxford in 1636 but was not performed; the edition includes separate prologues, one addressed to the king and queen and one for performance at Blackfriars. Bawcutt, "Puritanism and the Closing of the Theatres in 1642," *Medieval and Renaissance Drama in England* 22 (2009): 182.

30. Stewart, *On Longing*, 109. Compare Elizabeth Grosz's notion of "intolerable ambiguity," foregrounding "the inputs and effects of the subject's corporeality on its identity" by making the impairment signify as wondrous beyond bodily difference. Grosz, "Intolerable Ambiguity: Freaks as/at the Limit," in Garland-Thomson, *Freakery*, 55.

31. To follow Rosemarie Garland-Thomson's distinction between the normate stare and the staree, we could note that the monstrous staree cannot look back, and cannot speak back; see Garland-Thomson, *Staring*, esp. chap. 7.

32. Stewart, *On Longing*, 109.

33. Wrongly (if enthusiastically) attributed to Rowley and Shakespeare, the play's early criticism focused on authorship. N. W. Bawcutt demonstrates that licensing from the Master of the Revels confirms the performance date of 1622; see N. W. Bawcutt, ed., *The Control and Censorship of Caroline Drama: The Records of Sir Henry Herbert, Master of the Revels, 1623–73* (Oxford: Clarendon Press, 1996), 136. See also Joanna Udall's introduction to *A Critical, Old-Spelling Edition of* The Birth of Merlin *(Q 1662)*, ed. Joanna Udall (London: Modern Humanities Research Association, 1991).

34. For an overview of representations of Merlin, see Stephen Knight, *Merlin: Knowledge and Power Through the Ages* (Ithaca, NY: Cornell University Press, 2009). On early modern invocations of Merlin's political prophecies, see Howard Dobin, *Merlin's Disciples: Prophecy, Poetry, and Power in Renaissance England* (Palo Alto, CA: Stanford University Press, 1990).

35. Udall notes that the title page "links two playwrights ... whose literary reputations differ so radically as to make their complicity suspect to later readers." Udall, "Introduction," 23. On Shakespearean apocrypha, see Peter Kirwan, *Shakespeare and the Idea of Apocrypha: Negotiating the Boundaries of the Dramatic Canon* (Cambridge: Cambridge University Press, 2015).

36. Critical history remarks on jarring language difference between plots; A. F. Hopkinson suggests that "the play has probably descended to us in a mutilated condition, for many of the prose speeches read like blank-verse corrupted." Hopkinson, "Introduction to *The Birth of Merlin*," in *Shakespeare's Doubtful Plays*, ed. A. F. Hopkinson (London: M. E. Sims, 1892), 2.

37. William Rowley, *A Critical, Old-Spelling Edition of* The Birth of Merlin *(Q 1662)*, ed. Joanna Udall (London: Modern Humanities Research Association, 1991).

38. On the relation between demonic conception and Merlin's appearance, see Anita Obermeier, "Merlin's Conception by the Devil in William Rowley's Play *The Birth of Merlin*," *Arthuriana* 24, no. 4 (2014): 48–79.

39. Thomas Heywood, *The Life of Merlin: Sirnamed Ambrosius* (London: J. Okes for Jasper Emery, 1641). Geoffrey of Monmouth's *Vita Merlini* is a key source for Merlin's historiography: see Obermeier, "Merlin's Conception," and Neil Thomas's account of Merlin as a "problematic figure" in chronicle accounts. Thomas, "The Celtic Wild Man Tradition and Geoffrey of Monmouth's *Vita Merlini*: Madness or *Contemptus Mundi?*," *Arthuriana* 10, no. 1 (Spring 2000): 27.

40. These lines recall monster pamphlets that blame a woman for coupling with a devil, and critics interpret them to link Merlin and Caliban: Mark Dominik notes that Merlin's "identity as 'monster' links him to that other late-Shakespearean monster, Caliban, another half-human, half-devil prodigy." Dominik, *William Shakespeare and The Birth of Merlin* (Beaverton, OR: Alioth Press, 1985), 152. Alison Findlay notes that "the moon-calf's appearance is a visual sign of the demonic sexual liaison from which it was conceived," citing both Merlin and Caliban as "moon-calves with satanic parentage." Findlay, *Illegitimate Power: Bastards in Renaissance Drama* (Manchester: Manchester University Press, 1994), 49.

41. On the play's attitude toward Joan in relation to the other female characters, see Monika Karpinska, "Bawdily Manipulations: Spheres of Female Power in *The Birth of Merlin*," *Early Theatre* 9, no. 1 (June 2006): 123–29.

42. Ambroise Paré defines marvels as things that are "against nature'"; see Bearden's trenchant discussion in *Monstrous Kinds*, 15–16.

43. Udall, *Birth of Merlin*, 11.

44. The Clown's misguided apprehension of Merlin is perhaps balanced by his critique of the court; David Nicol notes that "in his self-written roles, Rowley himself encourages the audience to agree with some of the ideas put forward by the clown." Nicol, *Middleton and Rowley*, 72.

45. Howard Dobin observes that the play "is at once a parodic comedy and a serious political drama; it thus reproduces, in a radical and ultimately self-canceling way, the contradictions inhering in Britain's national prophet and the prophetic tradition." Dobin, *Merlin's Disciples*, 194.

46. Megan Lynn Isaac, "Legitimizing Magic in *The Birth of Merlin*," *Early Theatre* 9, no. 1 (June 2006): 117.

47. Both Royalists and Parliamentarians mobilized Merlin's figure in the political tussle over the future of the nation; on polemics of the 1640s, see Dobin, *Merlin's Disciples*, 207–9. Julia Briggs reads Merlin's preposterous appearance against John Foxe's discussion of Merlin's prophecies in "Middleton's Forgotten Tragedy *Hengist, King of Kent*," *Review of English Studies* 41, no. 164 (November 1990): 488.

48. On anachronism in the play as an "aesthetic irritant," see Lucy Munro, "'Nemp your sexes!' Anachronistic Aesthetics in *Hengist, King of Kent* and the Jacobean 'Anglo-Saxon' Play," *Modern Philology* 111, no. 4 (2014): 738.

49. Michael Baird Saenger, "The Costumes of Caliban and Ariel qua Sea-Nymph," *Notes and Queries* (1995): 334–36.

50. Saenger, "Costumes of Caliban," 336.

51. Anthony Munday et al., *Londons Love, to the Royal Prince Henrie, Meeting Him on the River of Thames, at his returne from Richmonde, With a Worthy Fleete of Her Cittizens, on Thursday the last of May, 1610* (London: Edw. Allde for Nathaniell Fosbrooke, 1610), sig. B4r.

52. Foundational work in critical race studies by Hall and Akhimie is cited below. A wealth of post-colonial criticism elucidated Caliban in relation to Prospero's exercise of colonial power; for overviews, see Peter Hulme and William H. Sherman, eds., *The Tempest and Its Travels* (Philadelphia: University of Pennsylvania Press, 2000); and Ania Loomba, *Shakespeare, Race, and Colonialism* (Oxford: Oxford University Press, 2002), esp. chap. 1. On Caliban's performance history, see Alden T. Vaughan and Virginia Mason Vaughan, *Shakespeare's Caliban: A Cultural History* (Cambridge: Cambridge University Press, 1991); on a post-colonial Caliban in performance, which perhaps "registers the bodily elements of Shakespeare's play as a corrective to the authority of the spoken text," see Susan Bennett, *Performing Nostalgia: Shifting Shakespeare and the Contemporary Past* (London: Routledge, 1996), 150; on racializing signifiers, see Margo Hendricks, "Visions of Color: Spectacle, Spectators, and the Performance of Race," in *A Companion to Shakespeare and Performance*, ed. Barbara Hodgdon and W. B. Worthen (Oxford: Blackwell, 2005), 511–26. Lauren Eriks Cline's generative reading of Caliban tracks performance "without fixing his shiftiness": see Cline, "Becoming Caliban: Monster Methods and Performance Theories," in Traub, *Shakespeare and Embodiment*, 710. On Caliban's enactment of the play's interest in "speculative *poesis*," see Debapriya Sarkar, "*The Tempest*'s Other Plots," *Shakespeare Studies* 45 (2017): 203–30.

53. Julia Reinhard Lupton, "Creature Caliban," *Shakespeare Quarterly* 51, no. 1 (Spring 2000): 3–4, 21. Lupton departs from critical accounts of Caliban that have "tend[ed] to naturalize his strangeness either within the macrocosmic synthesis of a general humanity (as either its exemplum or its exception) or—following the strain of much recent criticism—within the smaller worlds defined by race, nation, or culture" (3). See also Katherine Eggert's reading of Caliban as the character who "lays bare the flaws both of the seamless social body Prospero imagines and of the intellectual corpus underlying Prospero's magic." Katherine Eggert, *Disknowledge: Literature, Alchemy, and the End of Humanism in Renaissance England* (Philadelphia: University of Pennsylvania Press, 2015), 153.

54. Lupton's assertion that "Caliban's physical deformity mirrors his moral limitations" ("Creature Caliban," 18) is productively contradicted, I think, by her insight that from Caliban "another universalism might accrue, one that would acknowledge the creature's difference without resolving that difference into an identity" (20).

55. See esp. Lennard J. Davis, "The End of Normal" and "Dismodernism Reconsidered," in *The End of Normal: Identity in a Biocultural Era* (Ann Arbor: University of Michigan Press, 2013).

56. Akhimie, *Cultivation of Difference*, 152, 153.

57. On Caliban's service, see Urvashi Chakravarty, *Fictions of Consent: Slavery, Servitude and Free Service in Early Modern England* (Philadelphia: University of Pennsylvania Press, forthcoming), chap. 5.

58. On the repeated cues that build tension for Caliban's delayed entrance, see Simon Palfrey and Tiffany Stern, "The Cue-Space in *The Tempest*," in Palfrey and Stern, *Shakespeare in Parts*, 275–307.

59. Tsar Peter I, for example, was known for his avid interest in conscripting people deemed monstrous to display in his famous collection in St. Petersburg. See Hagner, "Enlightened Monsters," 180–86. For Burnett, this moment in *The Tempest*

"localizes" representations of monstrosity with a "peculiarly English purchase." Burnett, *Constructing "Monsters,"* 126; see also 125–53.

60. Burnett, *Constructing "Monsters,"* 135.

61. Hall, *Things of Darkness,* 148.

62. Suparna Roychoudhury, *Phantasmatic Shakespeare: Imagination in the Age of Early Modern Science* (Ithaca, NY: Cornell University Press, 2018), 181. My reading concurs with Roychoudhury's insightful claim that "what has been set on stage for us to see is not a monster, but rather the activity of looking at monsters" (181).

63. I am grateful to Ellen MacKay and Musa Gurnis for helping me think through this point.

64. William Davenent and John Dryden, *The Tempest, or, The Enchanted Island a comedy, as it is now acted at His Highness the Duke of York's Theatre* (London: J. M. for Henry Herringman, 1670), sig. A4v.

65. Hall, *Things of Darkness,* 152.

66. Hazlitt, *Characters,* 118.

67. Hazlitt, *Characters,* 118.

68. Thomas Betterton, *The Prophetess: Or, the History of Dioclesian* (London: Jacob Tonson, 1690), sig. A4v. I am grateful to John Kuhn for alerting me to this example.

69. Francis Beaumont and John Fletcher, *The Prophetess,* ed. George Walton Williams, in Bowers, *Dramatic Works,* 9:221–322.

Coda

1. Collier, *Short View,* sig. P6r.

2. Mac Wellman, "Speculations," in *The Difficulty of Crossing a Field: Nine New Plays* (Minneapolis: University of Minnesota Press, 2008), 328. In the quoted material here and in the epigraph, I have reproduced Wellman's double negative exactly as written, a negative concord embedded in the symmetry of the phrase.

3. Harley Granville-Barker, *On Dramatic Method* (London: Sidgwick & Jackson, 1931), 29.

4. Royal Society, "Of the Posture-Master," *Philosophical Transactions of the Royal Society of London (1683–1775),* 20, no. 242 (January 1698): 262.

5. Sander L. Gilman, *Stand Up Straight! A History of Posture* (London: Reaktion Books, 2018), 157. See also Tonya Howe's "'All deformed Shapes': Figuring the Posture-Master as Popular Performer in Early Eighteenth-Century England," *Journal of Early Modern Cultural Studies* 12, no. 4 (2012): 26–47.

6. See Steven Shapin and Simon Schaffer's classic account of the Royal Society's "literary technology," a narrative style that "make[s] virtual witnessing a practical option for the validation of experimental performances." Shapin and Schaffer, *Leviathan and the Air-Pump: Hobbes, Boyle, and the Experimental Life* (Princeton, NJ: Princeton University Press, 1985), 69.

7. Peggy Phelan's insight that performance disappears is generative here, although this account aims at surveillance, in contrast to Phelan's formulation of live performance as "representation without reproduction." Phelan, *Unmarked: The Politics of Performance* (London: Routledge, 1993), 3.

8. Madhavi Menon, *Indifference to Difference: On Queer Universalism* (Minneapolis: University of Minnesota Press, 2015), 1.

9. Menon, *Indifference to Difference*, 116.

10. José Esteban Muñoz, *Cruising Utopia: The Then and There of Queer Futurity* (New York: New York University Press, 2009), 1. Muñoz's argument develops Ernst Bloch's distinction between abstract utopias, those that "are untethered from any historical consciousness" and concrete utopias, which are defined by "educated hope" (Muñoz, 3), a hope in a methodology that "dwells in the region of the not-yet" and is "marked by an enduring indeterminacy." Bloch, *Literary Essays*, trans. Andrew Joron et al. (Palo Alto, CA: Stanford University Press, 1998), 341. See also Jill Dolan's discussion of utopian performativity as "never finished gestures toward a potentially better future." Dolan, *Utopia in Performance: Finding Hope at the Theater* (Ann Arbor: University of Michigan Press, 2005), 8.

11. As Carrie Sandahl puts it, "Whatever the acting style, the notion that actors' bodies should first be stripped of individuality and idiosyncrasy as a prerequisite to creating a role undergirds them all. . . . Implicit in the various manifestations of the neutral metaphor is the assumption that a character cannot be built from a position of physical difference." Sandahl, "Tyranny of Neutral," 262. Musa Gurnis insightfully complicates Sandahl's account of acting technique, showing how "neutral" is defined in classical acting practice as (in the Alexander Technique, for example) "any body free of habitual tension in an internal state of relaxed awareness"—which offers, at least theoretically, scope for the idiosyncrasy of individual bodies and their morphologies and contests the "false conflation of the neutral with the able." Gurnis, "Neutral Not Able: Disability in Classical Actor Training" (paper presented at the annual meeting of the Shakespeare Association of America, Washington, DC, April 2019), 5.

12. Davis, *End of Normal*, 37.

13. Davis, *End of Normal*, 37.

14. Paul Menzer, "Character Acting," in *Shakespeare's Theatres and the Effects of Performance*, ed. Farah Karim-Cooper and Tiffany Stern (London: Bloomsbury Arden Shakespeare, 2013), 143. On the practice of writing for particular actors, see Bart Van Es, *Shakespeare in Company* (Oxford: Oxford University Press, 2013).

15. Menzer, "Character Acting," 163.

16. States, *Great Reckonings*, 40.

17. Bérubé, *Secret Life*, 49.

Bibliography

Primary Texts

Armin, Robert. *The History of the Two Maids of More-clacke*. Edited by Richard Preiss. In *The Routledge Anthology of Early Modern Drama*, edited by Jeremy Lopez, 743–815. London: Routledge, 2020.

Bacon, Francis. *The Major Works*. Edited by Brian Vickers. Oxford: Oxford University Press, 1996.

Barrough, Philip. *The Methode of Phisicke*. London: Thomas Vautroullier, 1583. ESTC S112722.

Beaumont, Francis, and John Fletcher. *Beggars' Bush*. Edited by Fredson Bowers. In vol. 3 of *The Dramatic Works in the Beaumont and Fletcher Canon*, edited by Fredson Bowers, 225–362. Cambridge: Cambridge University Press, 1976.

———. *The Captain*. Edited by L. A. Beaurline. In vol. 1 of *The Dramatic Works in the Beaumont and Fletcher Canon*, edited by Fredson Bowers, 541–670. Cambridge: Cambridge University Press, 1966.

———. *Love's Pilgrimage*. Edited by L. A. Beaurline. In vol. 2 of *The Dramatic Works in the Beaumont and Fletcher Canon*, edited by Fredson Bowers, 567–691. Cambridge: Cambridge University Press, 1970.

———. *The Prophetess*. Edited by George Walton Williams. In vol. 9 of *The Dramatic Works in the Beaumont and Fletcher Canon*, edited by Fredson Bowers, 221–322. Cambridge: Cambridge University Press, 1994.

———. *The Woman Hater*. Edited by George Walton Williams. In vol. 1 of *The Dramatic Works in the Beaumont and Fletcher Canon*, edited by Fredson Bowers, 145–260. Cambridge: Cambridge University Press, 1966.

Bedford, Thomas. *A True and Certaine Relation of a Strange-birth*. London: Anne Griffin for William Russell, 1635. ESTC S12122.

Bellany, Alastair, and Andrew McRae, eds. Early Stuart Libels: An Edition of Poetry from Manuscript Sources. Early Modern Literary Studies Texts Series 1 (2005). Accessed September 20, 2020. http://purl.oclc.org/emls/texts/libels/.

Betterton, Thomas. *The Prophetess: Or, the History of Dioclesian*. London: Jacob Tonson, 1690. ESTC R2373.

Bodenham, John. *Bel-vedére, or, The Garden of the Muses*. London: F. K. for Hugh Astley, 1600. ESTC S102718.

Brome, Richard. *A Jovial Crew, or, The Merry Beggars*. London: J. Y. for E. D. and N. E., 1652. ESTC R6854.

Bulwer, John. *Anthropometamorphosis: man transform'd: or, the artificial changling*. London: William Hunt, 1653. ESTC R202040.

———. *Philocophus: or, The Deafe and Dumbe Mans Friend*. London: Printed for Humphrey Moseley, 1648. ESTC R3977.

Burton, Robert. *The Anatomy of Melancholy*. Edited by Holbrook Jackson. New York: Vintage Books, 1977.

Butler, Samuel. *Characters and Passages from Note-Books*. Edited by A. R. Waller. Cambridge: University of Cambridge Press, 1908.

Castiglione, Baldesar. *The Book of the Courtier*. Translated and edited by George Bull. London: Penguin, 1967.

Cavendish, Margaret. *The Worlds Olio*. London: Printed for J. Martin and J. Allestrye, 1655. ESTC R469142.

A certaine relation of the hog-faced gentlewoman called Mistris Tannakin Skinker. London: J[ohn] O[kes] for F. Grove, 1640. ESTC S117439.

Chamberlain, John. *The Letters of John Chamberlain*. Edited by N. E. McClure. Vol. 1. Philadelphia: American Philosophical Society, 1939.

Chapman, George. *The Blinde Begger of Alexandria most pleasantly discoursing his variable humours in disguised shapes full of conceite and pleasure*. London: Printed for William Jones, 1598. ESTC S104930.

Cibber, Colley. *An Apology for the Life of Colley Cibber*. Edited by B. R. S. Fone. Ann Arbor: University of Michigan Press, 1968.

———. *The Tragical History of King Richard III*. London: Printed for B. Lintott and A. Bettesworth, 1700. ESTC R14068.

Cogan, Thomas. *The Haven of Health*. 1584. Reprint, London: Printed by Anne Griffin for Roger Ball, 1636. ESTC S108449.

Collier, Jeremy. *A Short View of the Immorality, and Profaneness of the English Stage, Together With the Sense of Antiquity upon this Argument*. London: S. Keble, R. Sare, and H. Hindmarsh, 1698. ESTC R224353.

Congreve, William. "From *Letter to Dennis on Humour in Comedy, 1695*." In *Volpone: A Casebook*, edited by Jonas A. Barish, 30–31. London: Macmillan, 1972.

Copley, Anthony. *Wits fittes and fancies*. London: Richard [Jones], 1595. ESTC S111171.

Davenant, William, and John Dryden. *The Tempest, or, The Enchanted Island a comedy, as it is now acted at His Highness the Duke of York's Theatre*. London: J. M. for Henry Herringman, 1670. ESTC R17310.

Day, John. *The Ile of Guls*. London: Printed for John Trundle, 1606. ESTC S124593.

Day, John [and Henry Chettle]. *The Blind Begger of Bednal-green With the merry humor of Tom Strowd the Norfolk Yeoman*. London: Printed for R. Pollard and Tho. Dring, 1659. ESTC R6497.

Dekker, Thomas. *The Shoemaker's Holiday*. Edited by Jonathan Gil Harris. London: Methuen Drama, 2008.

———. *The Wonder of a Kingdom*. London: Robert Waworth for Nicholas Vavasour, 1636. ESTC S109551.

Deloney, Thomas. *The Gentle Craft*. Edited by Simon Barker. Aldershot, UK: Ashgate, 2007.

Dennis, John. "From *Letters on Several Occasions, 1696*." In *Volpone: A Casebook*, edited by Jonas A. Barish, 29–30. London: Macmillan, 1972.

Dryden, John. *Of Dramatic Poesy and Other Critical Essays*. Edited by George Watson. Vol 1. London: J. M. Dent & Sons, 1962.

The Fair Maid of the Exchange. Edited by Genevieve Love. In *The Routledge Anthology of Early Modern Drama*, edited by Jeremy Lopez, 816–81. London: Routledge, 2020.

The Famous Victories of Henry V. Edited by Brian Walsh. In *The Routledge Anthology of Early Modern Drama*, edited by Jeremy Lopez, 350–81. London: Routledge, 2020.

The Fayre Mayde of the Exchange: With The pleasuant Humours of the Cripple of Fanchurch. London: Henry Rockit, 1607. ESTC S106110.

Fletcher, John, and Philip Massinger. *The Little French Lawyer*. Edited by Robert Kean Turner. In vol. 9 of *The Dramatic Works in the Beaumont and Fletcher Canon*, edited by Fredson Bowers, 323–460. Cambridge: Cambridge University Press, 1994.

Ford, John, Thomas Dekker, Thomas Middleton, and William Rowley. *The Spanish Gypsy*. Edited by Gary Taylor. In *Thomas Middleton: The Collected Works*, edited by Gary Taylor and John Lavagnino, and Macdonald P. Jackson, John Jowett, Valerie Wayne, and Adrian Weiss, 1723–65. Oxford: Clarendon Press, 2007.

Galen. *On the Causes of Symptoms II*. Translated by Ian Johnston. Cambridge: Cambridge University Press, 2006.

Gayton, Edmund. *Pleasant Notes Upon Don Quixot*. London: William Hunt, 1654. ESTC R7599.

Gosson, Stephen. *Playes Confuted in Five Actions*. London: Thomas Gosson, 1582. ESTC S105757.

Hay, William. *Deformity: An Essay*. 2nd ed. London: Printed for R. and J. Dodsley, 1754. ESTC T111104.

Henslowe, Philip. *Henslowe's Diary*. Edited by R. A. Foakes. 2nd ed. Cambridge: Cambridge University Press, 2002. First published 1961 by Cambridge University Press (Cambridge).

Heywood, Thomas. *An Apology for Actors*. London: Nicholas Okes, 1612. ESTC S106113.

———. *The Life of Merlin: Sirnamed Ambrosius*. London: J. Okes for Jasper Emery, 1641. ESTC R10961.

Hic Mulier. In *Half Humankind: Contexts and Texts of the Controversy about Women in England, 1540–1640*, edited by Katherine Usher Henderson and Barbara F. McManus, 264–76. Chicago: University of Illinois Press, 1985.

Hill, Thomas. *The Contemplation of Mankinde*. London: Henry Denham for William Seres, 1571. ESTC 104092.

Hippocrates of Cos. *The Sacred Disease*. Translated by W. H. S. Jones. Vol. 21. Cambridge, MA: Harvard University Press, 1923.

The Historie of the Tryall of Chevalry, With the life and death of Cavaliero Dicke Bowyer. London: Simon Stafford for Nathaniel Butter, 1605. ESTC S111569.

Homes, Nathanael. *A sermon preached afore Thomas Andrews Lord Maior and the aldermen, sheriffs &c. of the honorable corporation of the citie of London in which discourse is held forth*. London: Printed by T. R. and J. C., 1650. ESTC R29231.

Huloet, Richard. *Huloets Dictionarie newelye corrected, amended, set in order and enlarged*. Translated by John Higgins. London: in aedibus Thoma[s] Marshij, 1572. ESTC S119246.

Jones, Richard. "To the Gentlemen Readers and others that take pleasure in reading Histories." In *Tamburlaine the Great*, by Christopher Marlowe. London: Richard Jones, 1590. ESTC 122101.

Jonson, Ben. *The Alchemist*. Edited by Peter Holland and William Sherman. In vol. 3 of *The Cambridge Edition of the Works of Ben Jonson*, edited by David Bevington, Martin Butler, and Ian Donaldson, 541–710. Cambridge: Cambridge University Press, 2012.

———. *Timber: or, Discoveries*. Edited by Lorna Hutson. In vol. 7 of *The Cambridge Edition of the Works of Ben Jonson*, edited by David Bevington, Martin Butler, and Ian Donaldson, 481–596. Cambridge: Cambridge University Press, 2012.

———. *Volpone, or The Fox*. Edited by Richard Dutton. In vol. 3 of *The Cambridge Edition of the Works of Ben Jonson*, edited by David Bevington, Martin Butler, and Ian Donaldson, 1–192. Cambridge: Cambridge University Press, 2012.

———. *The Workes of Benjamin Jonson*. London: William Stansby, 1616. ESTC S1256501.

Kendall, Timothy. *Flowers of Epigrammes*. London: John Sheppard, 1577. ESTC S107994.

[Kirkman, Francis?]. *The Wits, or, Sport upon sport*. London: Printed for Henry Marsh, 1662. ESTC R38726.

A Larum for London, or The Siedge of Antwerpe. London: Edward Allde for William Ferbrand, 1602. ESTC S122090.

Look About You. Edited by Paul Menzer. In *The Routledge Anthology of Early Modern Drama*, edited by Jeremy Lopez, 267–349. London: Routledge, 2020.

Manningham, John. *The Diary of John Manningham of the Middle Temple, 1602–3*. Edited by Robert Parker Sorlien. Hanover, NH: Published for the University of Rhode Island by the University Press of New England, 1976.

Marston, John. *The History of Antonio and Mellida*. London: Printed for Mathewe Lownes and Thomas Fisher, 1602. ESTC S109896.

Mayne, Jasper. *The Amorous Warre*. Oxford: Printed by Henry Hall for Ric. Davis, 1659. ESTC R31204.

———. *The Citye Match*. Oxford: Leonard Lichfield, 1639. ESTC S114462.

Middleton, Thomas. *Hengist, King of Kent; or, The Mayor of Quinborough*. Edited by Grace Ioppolo. In *Thomas Middleton: The Collected Works*, edited by Gary Taylor and John Lavagnino, and Macdonald P. Jackson, John Jowett, Valerie Wayne, and Adrian Weiss, 1448–87. Oxford: Clarendon Press, 2007.

Middleton, Thomas, and William Rowley. *The Changeling*. Edited by Douglas Bruster. In *Thomas Middleton: The Collected Works*, edited by Gary Taylor and John Lavagnino, and Macdonald P. Jackson, John Jowett, Valerie Wayne, and Adrian Weiss, 1632–78. Oxford: Clarendon Press, 2007.

Montaigne, Michel de. *The Essayes, or Morall, Politike, and Military Discourses*. Translated by John Florio. London: Val. Sims for Edward Blount, 1603. ESTC S111839.

More, Thomas. *The History of King Richard the Third: A Reading Edition*. Edited by George M. Logan. Bloomington: Indiana University Press, 2005.

Munday, Anthony, Michael Drayton, Robert Wilson, and Richard Hathway. *The first part of the true and honorable historie, of the life of Sir John Old-castle, the good Lord Cobham*. London: V. S. for Thomas Pavier, 1600. ESTC S106323.

———. *Londons Love, to the Royal Prince Henrie, Meeting Him on the River of Thames, at his returne from Richmonde, With a Worthy Fleete of Her Cittizens, on Thursday the last of May, 1610.* London: Edw. Allde for Nathaniell Fosbrooke, 1610. ESTC S103981.

Overbury, Thomas. *New and Choice Characters.* London: Thomas Creede for Laurence Lisle, 1615. ESTC S1323.

Paré, Ambroise. *On Monsters and Marvels.* Translated by Janis L. Pallister. Chicago: University of Chicago Press, 1982.

———. *The Workes of that famous Chirurgion Ambrose Parey.* Translated by Thomas Johnson. London: Th. Cotes and R. Young, 1634. ESTC S115392.

Perkins, William. *The Whole Treatise of the Cases of Conscience.* Cambridge: John Legat, 1608. ESTC S114500.

Phillips, Edward. *New World of English Words.* London: E. Tyler for Nath. Brooke, 1658. ESTC R14781.

Poole, Joshua. *The English Parnassus, or, A Helpe to English Poesie.* London: Printed for Tho. Johnson, 1657. ESTC R468961.

Prynne, William. *Histrio-Mastix: The players scourge, or, actors tragedie.* London: E[dward] A[llde, Augustine Mathewes, Thomas Cotes] and W[illiam] J[ones] for Michael Sparke, 1633. ESTC S115324.

Puttenham, George. *The Arte of English Poesy.* Edited by Frank Whigham and Wayne A. Rebhorn. Ithaca, NY: Cornell University Press, 2007.

Rainolds, John. *Th'overthrow of Stage Playes.* Middelburg, NL: Printed by Richard Schilders, 1599. ESTC S115568.

Rankins, William. *A Mirrour of Monsters . . . with the description of the subtile slights of Satan, making them his instruments.* London: J. C. for T. H., 1587. ESTC S115638.

Read, Alexander. *The Chirurgicall Lectures of Tumors and Ulcers.* London: I. H. for Francis Constable and E. B., 1635. ESTC S115690.

The Returne from Pernassus, Or the Scourge of Simony. London: G. Eld for John Wright, 1606. ESTC S114071.

Reynolds, John. *The Triumphs of God's Revenge* [sic], *Against the crying, and execrable Sinne of Murther.* London: Felix Kyngston for William Lee, 1621. ESTC 115836.

Rivière, Lazare. *The universal body of physick in five books; comprehending the several treatises of nature, of diseases and their causes, of symptomes, of the preservation of health, and of cures.* Translated by William Carr. London: Printed for Philip Briggs, 1657. ESTC R230160.

Rogers, Thomas. *A Paterne of a Passionate Mind.* London: Thomas East, 1580. ESTC S2952.

Rowley, William. *A Critical, Old-Spelling Edition of* The Birth of Merlin *(Q 1662).* Edited by Joanna Udall. London: Modern Humanities Research Association, 1991.

Royal Society. "Of the Posture-Master." *Philosophical Transactions of the Royal Society of London (1683–1775)* 20, no. 242 (January 1698): 262.

Salmon, William. *Synopsis Medicinae.* London: W. Godbid for Richard Jones, 1671. ESTC R4806.

Scot, Reginald. *The Discoverie of Witchcraft . . . verie necessarie to be knowne.* London: [Henry Denham] for William Brome, 1584. ESTC S116888.

Shakespeare, William. *The Second Part of Henry the Sixth*. Edited by William Montgomery. In *The Complete Pelican Shakespeare*, edited by Stephen Orgel and A. R. Braunmuller, 809–57. London: Penguin Books, 2002.

———. *The Second Part of King Henry the Fourth*. Edited by Claire McEachern. In *The Complete Pelican Shakespeare*, edited by Stephen Orgel and A. R. Braunmuller, 1080–122. London: Penguin Books, 2002.

———. *The Tempest*. Edited by Peter Holland. In *The Complete Pelican Shakespeare*, edited by Stephen Orgel and A. R. Braunmuller, 730–63. London: Penguin Books, 2002.

———. *The Third Part of Henry the Sixth*. Edited by William Montgomery. In *The Complete Pelican Shakespeare*, edited by Stephen Orgel and A. R. Braunmuller, 858–903. London: Penguin Books, 2002.

———. *The Tragedy of Julius Caesar*. Edited by William Montgomery. In *The Complete Pelican Shakespeare*, edited by Stephen Orgel and A. R. Braunmuller, 1295–336. London: Penguin Books, 2002.

———. *The Tragedy of King Richard the Third*. Edited by Peter Holland. In *The Complete Pelican Shakespeare*, edited by Stephen Orgel and A. R. Braunmuller, 904–57. London: Penguin Books, 2002.

———. *The Tragedy of Othello the Moor of Venice*. Edited by Russ McDonald. In *The Complete Pelican Shakespeare*, edited by Stephen Orgel and A. R. Braunmuller, 1392–444. London: Penguin Books, 2002.

Shakespeare, William, and George Wilkins. *Pericles Prince of Tyre*. Edited by Stephen Orgel. In *The Complete Pelican Shakespeare*, edited by Stephen Orgel and A. R. Braunmuller, 604–40. London: Penguin Books, 2002.

Sidney, Philip. *A Defence of Poetry*. Edited by J. A. Van Dorsten. Oxford: Oxford University Press, 1966.

Statutes of the Realm. Vol. 4, pt. 1, 2. London: Dawsons of Pall Mall, 1963. Originally printed in 1819.

Stellato, Marcello Palingenio. *The Zodiake of Life*. Translated by Barnabe Googe. London: Henry Denham for Rafe Newberye, 1565. ESTC S113950.

Strange Newes of a Prodigious Monster . . . of Aprill last, 1613. London: J. P. for S. M., 1613. ESTC S107360.

Tomkis, Thomas. *Albumazar*. London: Nicholas Okes for Walter Burre, 1615. ESTC S118449.

Trapp, John. *A commentary or exposition upon the four Evangelists, and the Acts of the Apostle*. London: A. M. for John Bellamie, 1647. ESTC R201354.

The True Tragedie of Richard the Third. London: Thomas Creede, 1594. ESTC S111104.

Tuke, Thomas. *A Discourse Against Painting and Tincturing of Women*. London: Printed for Edward Marchant, 1616. ESTC S118556.

Valerius, Cornelius. *The Casket of Jewels*. Translated by John Charlton. London: William How for Richard Johnes, 1571. ESTC S119018.

Webster, John. *The Displaying of Supposed Witchcraft*. London: J. M., 1677. ESTC R186333.

A Wonder Woorth the Reading. London: William Jones, 1617. ESTC S106531.

Woodall, John. *The Surgeons Mate, with A Treatise of Gangrena, and Sphacelos*. London: Rob. Young for Nicholas Bourne, 1639. ESTC S95910.

Secondary Texts

Adams, Rachel. *Sideshow U.S.A.: Freaks and the American Cultural Imagination.* Chicago: University of Chicago Press, 2001.
Agnew, Jean-Christophe. *Worlds Apart: The Market and the Theater in Anglo-American Thought, 1550–1750.* Cambridge: Cambridge University Press, 1986.
Ahmed, Sara. *Willful Subjects.* Durham, NC: Duke University Press, 2014.
Akhimie, Patricia. *Shakespeare and the Cultivation of Difference: Race and Conduct in the Early Modern World.* London: Routledge, 2018.
Anderson, Susan L. "Introduction: Disability in the Early Modern Theatre." *Early Theatre* 22, no. 2 (2019): 143–56.
———. "Limping and Lameness on the Early Modern Stage." In *Performing Disability in Early Modern English Drama*, edited by Leslie Dunn. New York: Palgrave Macmillan, forthcoming.
Appleby, Joyce Oldham. *Economic Thought and Ideology in Seventeenth-Century England.* Princeton, NJ: Princeton University Press, 1978.
Arab, Ronda. *Manly Mechanicals on the Early Modern English Stage.* Selinsgrove, PA: Susquehanna University Press, 2011.
Archer, Ian W. "Material Londoners?" In *Material London, ca. 1600*, edited by Lena Cowen Orlin, 174–92. Philadelphia: University of Pennsylvania Press, 2000.
Archer, John. "Citizens and Aliens as Working Subjects in Dekker's *The Shoemaker's Holiday*." In *Working Subjects in Early Modern English Drama*, edited by Michelle M. Dowd and Natasha Korda, 37–52. New York: Ashgate, 2011.
———. *Citizen Shakespeare: Freemen and Aliens in the Language of the Plays.* New York: Palgrave Macmillan, 2005.
Astington, John. *Actors and Acting in Shakespeare's Time: The Art of Stage Playing.* Cambridge: Cambridge University Press, 2010.
Aune, M. G. "The Uses of *Richard III*: From Robert Cecil to Richard Nixon." *Shakespeare Bulletin* 24, no. 3 (2006): 23–47.
Baker, Naomi. "'Happy and without a name': Prosthetic Identities on the Early Modern Stage." *Textual Practice* 30, no. 7 (2016): 1309–26.
———. *Plain Ugly: The Unattractive Body in Early Modern Culture.* Manchester: Manchester University Press, 2010.
Barish, Jonas. *The Antitheatrical Prejudice.* Berkeley: University of California Press, 1981.
———. Introduction to *Volpone: A Casebook*, edited by Jonas A. Barish, 11–23. London: Macmillan, 1972.
Barker, Roberta, and David Nicol. "Does Beatrice Joanna Have a Subtext? *The Changeling* on the London Stage." *Early Modern Literary Studies* 10, no. 1 (May 2004): 3.1–43.
Barroll, Leeds. *Politics, Plague, and Shakespeare's Theater: The Stuart Years.* Ithaca, NY: Cornell University Press, 1991.
Bartolovich, Crystal. "Mythos of Labor: *The Shoemaker's Holiday* and the Origin of Citizen History." In *Working Subjects in Early Modern English Drama*, edited by Michelle M. Dowd and Natasha Korda, 17–36. New York: Ashgate, 2011.
Barton, Anne. *Ben Jonson, Dramatist.* Cambridge: Cambridge University Press, 1984.

Bauman, H-Dirksen L., and Joseph J. Murray, eds. *Deaf Gain: Raising the Stakes for Human Diversity*. Minneapolis: University of Minnesota Press, 2014.

Bawcutt, N. W., ed. *The Control and Censorship of Caroline Drama: The Records of Sir Henry Herbert, Master of the Revels, 1623–73*. Oxford: Clarendon, 1996.

———. "Puritanism and the Closing of the Theatres in 1642." *Medieval and Renaissance Drama in England* 22 (2009): 179–200.

Bearden, Elizabeth B. *Monstrous Kinds: Body, Space, and Narrative in Renaissance Representations of Disability*. Ann Arbor: University of Michigan Press, 2019.

Bednarz, James. "Jonson's Literary Theatre: *Volpone* in Performance and Print (1606–1607)." In *Volpone: A Critical Guide*, edited by Matthew Steggle, 83–104. London: Continuum, 2011.

Beier, A. L. *Masterless Men: The Vagrancy Problem in England, 1560–1640*. London: Methuen, 1985.

Beier, Lucinda McCray. *Sufferers and Healers: The Experience of Illness in Seventeenth-Century England*. London: Routledge, 1987.

Bellany, Alastair. *The Politics of Court Scandal in Early Modern England: News Culture and the Overbury Affair, 1603–1660*. Oxford: Oxford University Press, 2007.

———. "Railing Rhymes Revisited: Libels, Scandals, and Early Stuart Politics." *History Compass* 5, no. 4 (June 2007): 1136–79.

Bennett, Susan. *Performing Nostalgia: Shifting Shakespeare and the Contemporary Past*. London: Routledge, 1996.

Bérubé, Michael. *The Secret Life of Stories: From Don Quixote to Harry Potter, How Understanding Intellectual Disability Transforms the Way We Read*. New York: New York University Press, 2016.

Besnault, Marie-Hélène, and Michel Bitot. "Historical Legacy and Fiction: The Poetical Reinvention of King Richard III." In *The Cambridge Companion to Shakespeare's History Plays*, edited by Michael Hattaway, 106–25. Cambridge: Cambridge University Press, 2002.

Bevington, David. "The Major Comedies." In *The Cambridge Companion to Ben Jonson*, edited by Richard Harp and Stanley Stewart, 72–89. Cambridge: Cambridge University Press, 2000.

———. "Theatre as Holiday." In *The Theatrical City: Culture, Theatre and Politics in London, 1576–1649*, edited by David L. Smith, Richard Strier, and David Bevington, 101–16. Cambridge: Cambridge University Press, 1995.

Bhabha, Homi K. *The Location of Culture*. 2nd ed. New York: Routledge, 2004.

Blau, Herbert. *Take Up the Bodies: Theater at the Vanishing Point*. Urbana: University of Illinois Press, 1982.

Bloch, Ernst. *Literary Essays*. Translated by Andrew Joron et al. Palo Alto, CA: Stanford University Press, 1998.

Boehrer, Bruce. "Alsemero's Closet: Privacy and Interiority in *The Changeling*." *Journal of English and Germanic Philology* 96, no. 3 (July 1997): 349–68.

Bogdan, Robert. *Freak Show: Presenting Human Oddities for Amusement and Profit*. Chicago: University of Chicago Press, 1988.

Booth, Stephen. "Doubling in Shakespeare's Plays." In *Shakespeare: The Theatrical Dimension*, edited by Philip C. McGuire and David A. Samuelson, 103–27. New York: AMS Press, 1979.

Boswell, James. *The Life of Samuel Johnson*. Vol. 2. London, 1791.

Bovilsky, Lara. *Barbarous Play: Race on the English Renaissance Stage*. Minneapolis: University of Minnesota Press, 2008.

Box, Ian. "Bacon's Moral Philosophy." In *The Cambridge Companion to Bacon*, edited by Markku Peltonen, 260–82. Cambridge: Cambridge University Press, 1996.

Bradbury, Jill Marie, John Lee Clark, Rachel Grossman, Jason Herbers, Victoria Magliocchino, Jasper Norman, Yashaira Romilus, Robert T. Sirvage, and Lisa van der Mark. "ProTactile Shakespeare: Inclusive Theater by/for the Deaf-Blind." *Shakespeare Studies* 47 (2019): 81–99.

Brammall, Kathryn M. "Monstrous Metamorphosis: Nature, Morality, and the Rhetoric of Monstrosity in Tudor England." *Sixteenth Century Journal* 27, no. 1 (Spring 1996): 3–21.

Breight, Curtis C. *Surveillance, Militarism, and Drama in the Elizabethan Era*. New York: St. Martin's Press, 1996.

Briggs, Julia. "Middleton's Forgotten Tragedy *Hengist, King of Kent*." *Review of English Studies* 41, no. 164 (November 1990): 479–95.

Bruster, Douglas. "*The Changeling*." In *Thomas Middleton and Early Modern Textual Culture: A Companion to The Collected Works*, edited by Gary Taylor and John Lavagnino, and Macdonald P. Jackson, John Jowett, Valerie Wayne, and Adrian Weiss, 1094–104. Oxford: Clarendon Press, 2007.

———. *Drama and the Market in the Age of Shakespeare*. Cambridge: Cambridge University Press, 1992. Reprint, 2005.

Bullough, Geoffrey, ed. *Narrative and Dramatic Sources of Shakespeare*. Vol. 5. London: Routledge and Kegan Paul, 1964.

Burnett, Mark Thornton. *Constructing "Monsters" in Shakespearean Drama and Early Modern Culture*. Basingstoke, UK: Palgrave Macmillan, 2002.

———. *Masters and Servants in English Renaissance Drama and Culture*. Basingstoke, UK: Macmillan, 1997.

Burns, William E. "The King's Two Monstrous Bodies: John Bulwer and the English Revolution." In *Wonders, Marvels, and Monsters in Early Modern Culture*, edited by Peter G. Platt, 187–204. Newark: University of Delaware Press, 1999.

Butterworth, Philip. *Magic on the Early English Stage*. Cambridge: Cambridge University Press, 2005.

Cahill, Patricia A. *Unto the Breach: Martial Formations, Historical Trauma, and the Early Modern Stage*. Oxford: Oxford University Press, 2008.

Campbell, Lily B. *Shakespeare's "Histories": Mirrors of Elizabethan Policy*. San Marino, CA: Huntington Library Press, 1947.

Campbell, Mary Baine. *Wonder and Science: Imagining Worlds in Early Modern Europe*. Ithaca, NY: Cornell University Press, 1999.

Carlson, Marvin. *Theories of the Theatre*. Ithaca, NY: Cornell University Press, 1993.

Carroll, William. *Fat King, Lean Beggar: Representations of Poverty in the Age of Shakespeare*. Ithaca, NY: Cornell University Press, 1996.

Casey, Jim. "'Richards Himself Again': The Body of Richard III on Stage and Screen." In *Shakespeare and the Middle Ages: Essays on the Performance and Adaptation of the Plays with Medieval Sources or Settings*, edited by Martha W. Driver and Sid Ray, 27–48. Jefferson, NC: McFarland, 2009.

Cecil, Algernon. *A Life of Robert Cecil, First Earl of Salisbury*. London: John Murray, 1915.

Chakravarty, Urvashi. *Fictions of Consent: Slavery, Servitude and Free Service in Early Modern England*. Philadelphia: University of Pennsylvania Press, forthcoming.

———. "'Live, and beget a happy race of kings': *Richard III*, Race and Homonationalism." In *Shakespeare / Sex: Contemporary Readings in Gender and Sexuality*, edited by Jennifer Drouin, 147–67. London: Bloomsbury Arden Shakespeare, 2020.

Chalk, Darryl, and Mary Floyd-Wilson, eds. *Contagion and the Shakespearean Stage*. New York: Palgrave Macmillan, 2009.

Charnes, Linda. *Notorious Identity: Materializing the Subject in Shakespeare*. Cambridge, MA: Harvard University Press, 1993.

Chen, Mel Y. *Animacies: Biopolitics, Racial Mattering, and Queer Affect*. Durham, NC: Duke University Press, 2012.

Chess, Simone. "Performing Blindness: Representing Disability in Early Modern Popular Performance and Print." In *Recovering Disability in Early Modern England*, edited by Allison P. Hobgood and David Houston Wood, 105–22. Columbus: Ohio State University Press, 2013.

Cheu, Johnson. "Performing Disability, Problematizing Cure." In *Bodies in Commotion: Disability and Performance*, edited by Carrie Sandahl and Philip Auslander, 135–46. Ann Arbor: University of Michigan Press, 2005.

Clare, Eli. *Brilliant Imperfection: Grappling with Cure*. Durham, NC: Duke University Press, 2017.

Clark, Arthur Melville. *Thomas Heywood: Playwright and Miscellanist*. New York: Russell & Russell, 1967. First published 1931 by Basil Blackwell (Oxford).

Cline, Lauren Eriks. "Becoming Caliban: Monster Methods and Performance Theories." In *The Oxford Handbook of Shakespeare and Embodiment*, edited by Valerie Traub, 709–23. Oxford: Oxford University Press, 2016.

Clode, Charles Mathew. *The Military Forces of the Crown: Their Administration and Government*. Vol. 1. London: John Murray, 1869.

Cohen, Jeffrey Jerome. "Monster Culture (Seven Theses)." In *Monster Theory: Reading Culture*, edited by Jeffrey Jerome Cohen, 3–25. Minneapolis: University of Minnesota Press, 1996.

Coker, Lauren. "'There is no suff'ring due': Metatheatricality and Disability Drag in *Volpone*." In *Recovering Disability in Early Modern England*, edited by Allison P. Hobgood and David Houston Wood, 123–35. Columbus: Ohio State University Press, 2013.

Coleman, Terry. *Olivier: The Authorised Biography*. New York: Bloomsbury, 2005.

Colley, John Scott. *Richard's Himself Again: A Stage History of Richard III*. New York: Greenwood Press, 1992.

Comber, Abigail Elizabeth. "'A Medieval King 'Disabled' by an Early Modern Construct: A Contextual Examination of *Richard III*." In *Disability in the Middle Ages: Reconsiderations and Reverberations*, edited by Joshua R. Eyler, 183–96. Burlington, VT: Ashgate, 2010.

Cook, Amy. *Building Character: The Art and Science of Casting*. Ann Arbor: University of Michigan Press, 2018.

Craik, Katharine A., and Tanya Pollard, eds. *Shakespearean Sensations: Experiencing Literature in Early Modern England*. Cambridge: Cambridge University Press, 2013.

Crane, Mary Thomas. "What Was Performance?" *Criticism* 43, no. 2 (2001): 169–87.

Crawford, Julie. *Marvelous Protestantism: Monstrous Births in Post-Reformation England*. Baltimore: Johns Hopkins University Press, 2005.

Creaser, John. "*Volpone*: The Mortifying of The Fox." *Essays in Criticism* 25, no. 3 (1975): 329–56.

Cressy, David. *Travesties and Transgressions in Tudor and Stuart England: Tales of Discord and Dissension*. Oxford: Oxford University Press, 2000.

Croft, Pauline. "The Reputation of Robert Cecil: Libels, Political Opinion, and Popular Awareness in the Early Seventeenth Century." *Transactions of the Royal Historical Society*, 6th ser., 1 (1991): 43–69.

Cruickshank, Charles Greig. *Elizabeth's Army*. Oxford: Oxford University Press, 1946.

Daalder, Joost, and Antony Telford Moore. "'There's scarce a thing but is both loved and loathed': *The Changeling* I.i.91–129." *English Studies* 80, no. 6 (December 1999): 499–508.

Davidson, Michael. *Concerto for the Left Hand: Disability and the Defamiliar Body*. Ann Arbor: University of Michigan Press, 2008.

Davies, Surekha. "The Unlucky, the Bad, and the Ugly: Categories of Monstrosity from the Renaissance to the Enlightenment." In *The Ashgate Research Companion to Monsters and the Monstrous*, edited by Asa Simon Mittman and Peter J. Dendle, 49–75. Burlington, VT: Ashgate, 2013.

Davis, Lennard J. *Bending Over Backwards: Disability, Dismodernism, and Other Difficult Positions*. New York: New York University Press, 2002.

———. *The End of Normal: Identity in a Biocultural Era*. Ann Arbor: University of Michigan Press, 2013.

———. *Enforcing Normalcy: Disability, Deafness, and the Body*. New York: Verso, 1995.

Davis, Natalie Zemon. *The Return of Martin Guerre*. Cambridge, MA: Harvard University Press, 1984.

Davison, Peter H. Introduction to *The Fair Maid of the Exchange*, edited by Peter H. Davison and Arthur Brown, i–xv. Oxford: Malone Society Reprints, 1963.

Day, Gillian M. "Determination and Proof: Colley Cibber and the Materialization of Shakespeare's *Richard III* in the Twentieth Century." In *Shakespeare Matters: History, Teaching, Performance*, edited by Lloyd Davis, 266–76. Newark: University of Delaware Press, 2003.

Desmet, Christy. *Reading Shakespeare's Characters*. Amherst: University of Massachusetts Press, 1992.

Dessen, Alan C. *Recovering Shakespeare's Theatrical Vocabulary*. Cambridge: Cambridge University Press, 1995.

Dessen, Alan C., and Leslie Thomson. *A Dictionary of Stage Directions in English Drama, 1580–1642*. Cambridge: Cambridge University Press, 1999.

Deutsch, Helen. "The Body's Moments: Visible Disability, the Essay, and the Limits of Sympathy." In *Disability and/in Prose*, edited by Brenda Brueggemann and Marian E. Lupo, 1–14. London: Routledge, 2008.

Deutsch, Helen, and Felicity Nussbaum, eds. *"Defects": Engendering the Modern Body.* Ann Arbor: University of Michigan Press, 2000.

Diamond, Elin. Introduction to *Performance and Cultural Politics*, edited by Elin Diamond, 1–12. London: Routledge, 1996.

Dickie, Simon. *Cruelty and Laughter: Forgotten Comic Literature and the Unsentimental Eighteenth Century.* Chicago: University of Chicago Press, 2011.

DiGangi, Mario. *Sexual Types: Embodiment, Agency, and Dramatic Character from Shakespeare to Shirley.* Philadelphia: University of Pennsylvania Press, 2011.

Dillon, Janette. *Theatre, Court, and City, 1595–1610: Drama and Social Space in London.* Cambridge: Cambridge University Press, 2000.

Dionne, Craig, and Steve Mentz. Introduction to *Rogues and Early Modern English Culture,* edited by Craig Dionne and Steve Mentz, 1–32. Ann Arbor: University of Michigan Press, 2004.

Dobin, Howard. *Merlin's Disciples: Prophecy, Poetry, and Power in Renaissance England.* Palo Alto, CA: Stanford University Press, 1990.

Dolan, Frances E. "Taking the Pencil Out of God's Hand: Art, Nature, and the Face-Painting Debate in Early Modern England." *PMLA* 108, no. 2 (March 1993): 224–39.

Dolan, Jill. *Utopia in Performance: Finding Hope at the Theater.* Ann Arbor: University of Michigan Press, 2005.

Dollimore, Jonathan. *Radical Tragedy: Religion, Ideology, and Power in the Drama of Shakespeare and His Contemporaries.* Chicago: University of Chicago Press, 1984.

Dominik, Mark. *William Shakespeare and The Birth of Merlin.* Beaverton, OR: Alioth Press, 1985.

Donaldson, Ian. *Jonson's Magic Houses: Essays in Interpretation.* Oxford: Clarendon Press, 1997.

———. "Note on *Richard Crookback*, Lost Play (1602)." In vol. 2 of *The Cambridge Edition of the Works of Ben Jonson*, edited by David Bevington, Martin Butler, and Ian Donaldson, 183–84. Cambridge: Cambridge University Press, 2012.

Durling, Richard J. "A Chronological Census of Renaissance Editions and Translations of Galen." *Journal of the Warburg and Courtauld Institutes* 24, nos. 3–4 (July–December 1961): 230–305.

Dutton, Richard. *Volpone and the Gunpowder Plot.* Cambridge: Cambridge University Press, 2008.

Eggert, Katherine. *Disknowledge: Literature, Alchemy, and the End of Humanism in Renaissance England.* Philadelphia: University of Pennsylvania Press, 2015.

Elam, Keir. *The Semiotics of Theatre and Drama.* 2nd ed. New York: Routledge, 2002. First published 1980 by Methuen (London).

Empson, William. *Some Versions of Pastoral.* New York: New Directions, 1950.

Enders, Jody. *Death by Drama and Other Medieval Urban Legends.* Chicago: University of Chicago Press, 2002.

Fawcett, Julia H. *Spectacular Disappearances: Celebrity and Privacy, 1696–1801.* Ann Arbor: University of Michigan Press, 2016.

Festa, Lynn. *Fiction Without Humanity: Person, Animal, Thing in Early Enlightenment Literature and Culture.* Philadelphia: University of Pennsylvania Press, 2019.

Fideler, Paul A. *Social Welfare in Pre-industrial England: The Old Poor Law Tradition.* New York: Palgrave Macmillan, 2006.
Field, Barron. Introduction to *The Fair Maid of the Exchange: A Comedy,* edited by Barron Field, v–ix. London: Printed for the Shakespeare Society, 1846.
Findlay, Alison. *Illegitimate Power: Bastards in Renaissance Drama.* Manchester: Manchester University Press, 1994.
Fischer-Lichte, Erika. *The Show and the Gaze of Theatre: A European Perspective.* Iowa City: University of Iowa Press, 1997.
Fisher, Will. *Materializing Gender in Early Modern English Literature and Culture.* Cambridge: Cambridge University Press, 2006.
Fissell, Mark Charles. *English Warfare, 1511–1642.* London: Routledge, 2001.
Floyd-Wilson, Mary. *Occult Knowledge, Science, and Gender on the Shakespearean Stage.* Cambridge: Cambridge University Press, 2013.
Foucault, Michel. *Abnormal: Lectures at the Collège de France, 1974–1975 (Volume 4).* Translated by Graham Burchell. Edited by Valerio Marchetti and Antonella Salomoni. New York: Picador, 2003.
——. *The Birth of the Clinic: An Archaeology of Medical Perception.* Translated by A. M. Sheridan Smith. New York: Vintage, 1994.
——. *Society Must Be Defended: Lectures at the Collège de France, 1975–1976 (Volume 5).* Translated by David Macey. Edited by Mauro Bertani and Alessandro Fontana. New York: Picador, 2003.
Freeburg, Victor O. *Disguise Plots in Elizabethan Drama: A Study in Stage Tradition.* New York: Columbia University Press, 1915.
Freeman, Lisa A. *Antitheatricality and the Body Public.* Philadelphia: University of Pennsylvania Press, 2017.
Fumerton, Patricia. "Making Vagrancy (In)visible: The Economics of Disguise in Early Modern Rogue Pamphlets." In *Rogues and Early Modern English Culture,* edited by Craig Dionne and Steve Mentz, 193–210. Ann Arbor: University of Michigan Press, 2004.
——. *Unsettled: The Culture of Mobility and the Working Poor in Early Modern England.* Chicago: University of Chicago Press, 2006.
Garber, Marjorie. *Shakespeare's Ghost Writers: Literature as Uncanny Causality.* New York: Methuen, 1987.
Garland-Thomson, Rosemarie. "The Case for Conserving Disability." *Journal of Bioethical Inquiry* 9, no. 3 (2012): 339–55.
——. "Dares to Stares: Disabled Women Performance Artists and the Dynamics of Staring." In *Bodies in Commotion: Disability and Performance,* edited by Carrie Sandahl and Philip Auslander, 30–41. Ann Arbor: University of Michigan Press, 2005.
——. *Extraordinary Bodies: Figuring Physical Disability in American Culture and Literature.* New York: Columbia University Press, 1997.
——. "Introduction: From Wonder to Error—A Genealogy of Freak Discourse in Modernity." In *Freakery: Cultural Spectacles of the Extraordinary Body,* edited by Rosemarie Garland-Thomson, 1–22. New York: New York University Press, 1996.
——. *Staring: How We Look.* Oxford: Oxford University Press, 2009.

Gibbons, Brian. *Jacobean City Comedy*. Cambridge, MA: Harvard University Press, 1968.

———. *Shakespeare and Multiplicity*. Cambridge: Cambridge University Press, 1993.

Gilman, Ernest B. *Plague Writing in Early Modern England*. Chicago: University of Chicago Press, 2009.

Gilman, Sander. *Stand Up Straight! A History of Posture*. London: Reaktion Books, 2018.

Gosse, Edmund. *The Jacobean Poets*. London: John Murray, 1894.

Granville-Barker, Harley. *On Dramatic Method*. London: Sidgwick & Jackson, 1931.

Green, Juana. "The Sempster's Wares: Merchandising and Marrying in *The Fair Maid of the Exchange* (1607)." *Renaissance Quarterly* 53, no. 4 (Winter 2000): 1084–118.

Green, London. "Edmund Kean's Richard III." *Theatre Journal* 36 (1984): 505–24.

Greenblatt, Stephen. "The False Ending in *Volpone*." *Journal of English and Germanic Philology* 75, nos. 1–2 (January–April 1976): 90–104.

———. *Renaissance Self-Fashioning: From More to Shakespeare*. Chicago: University of Chicago Press, 1980.

———. *Shakespeare's Freedom*. Chicago: University of Chicago Press, 2010.

Griswold, Wendy. *Renaissance Revivals: City Comedy and Revenge Tragedy in the London Theatre, 1576–1980*. Chicago: University of Chicago Press, 1986.

Grosz, Elizabeth. "Intolerable Ambiguity: Freaks as/at the Limit." In *Freakery: Cultural Spectacles of the Extraordinary Body*, edited by Rosemarie Garland-Thomson, 55–66. New York: New York University Press, 1996.

Gurnis, Musa. "Neutral Not Able: Disability in Classical Actor Training." Paper presented at the annual meeting of the Shakespeare Association of America, Washington, DC, April 2019.

Gurr, Andrew. *Shakespeare's Opposites: The Admiral's Company, 1594–1625*. Cambridge: Cambridge University Press, 2009.

Haber, Judith. *Desire and Dramatic Form in Early Modern England*. Cambridge: Cambridge University Press, 2009.

Hadley, Bree. *Disability, Public Space Performance and Spectatorship: Unconscious Performers*. London: Palgrave Macmillan, 2014.

Hagner, Michael. "Enlightened Monsters." In *The Sciences in Enlightened Europe*, edited by William Clark, Jan Golinski, and Simon Schaffer, 175–217. Chicago: University of Chicago Press, 1999.

Hall, Kim F. *Things of Darkness: Economies of Race and Gender in Early Modern England*. Ithaca, NY: Cornell University Press, 1995.

Hammer, Paul E. J. *Elizabeth's Wars: War, Government and Society in Tudor England, 1544–1604*. London: Palgrave Macmillan, 2003.

Handover, P. M. *The Second Cecil: The Rise to Power, 1563–1604, of Sir Robert Cecil, late first Earl of Salisbury*. London: Eyre & Spottiswoode, 1959.

Harbage, Alfred. *Annals of English Drama, 975–1700*, revised by S. Schoenbaum and Sylvia Stoler Wagonheim. London: Routledge, 1989. First published 1940 by University of Pennsylvania Press (Philadelphia).

Harmes, Marcus, and Victoria Bladen, eds. *Supernatural and Secular Power in Early Modern England*. London: Routledge, 2015.

Harris, Jonathan Gil. *Sick Economies: Drama, Mercantilism, and Disease in Shakespeare's England*. Philadelphia: University of Pennsylvania Press, 2004.
Harris, Jonathan Gil, and Natasha Korda. "Introduction: Towards a Materialist Account of Stage Properties." In *Staged Properties in Early Modern English Drama*, edited by Jonathan Gil Harris and Natasha Korda, 1–32. Cambridge: Cambridge University Press, 2002.
Hartley, Andrew James. "Character, Agency and the Familiar Actor." In *Shakespeare and Character: Theatre, History, Performance, and Theatrical Persons*, edited by Paul Yachnin and Jessica Slights, 158–76. New York: Palgrave Macmillan, 2009.
Harvey, Elizabeth D. "Beastly Physic." *Shakespeare Studies* 41 (2013): 114–24.
Hawkins, Frederick William. *The Life of Edmund Kean*. Vol. 1. London: Tinsley Brothers, 1869.
Hawkins, Harriet. "Folly, Incurable Disease, and *Volpone*." *Studies in English Literature, 1500–1900* 8, no. 2 (Spring 1968): 335–48.
Hazlitt, William. *Characters of Shakespear's Plays*. London: Printed by C. H. Reynell, for R. Hunter and C. and J. Ollier, 1817.
———. *Hazlitt on Theatre*. Edited by William Archer and Robert William Lowe. New York: Hyperion Press, 1980.
Healy, Margaret. *Fictions of Disease in Early Modern England: Bodies, Plagues, and Politics*. New York: Palgrave Macmillan, 2001.
Hendren, Sara. *What Can a Body Do? How We Meet the Built World*. New York: Riverhead Books, 2020.
Hendricks, Margo. "Visions of Color: Spectacle, Spectators, and the Performance of Race." In *A Companion to Shakespeare and Performance*, edited by Barbara Hodgdon and W. B. Worthen, 511–26. Oxford: Blackwell, 2005.
Henke, Robert. *Poverty and Charity in Early Modern Theater and Performance*. Iowa City: University of Iowa Press, 2015.
Hibbard, Laura A. "The Authorship and Date of the *Fayre Maide of the Exchange*." *Modern Philology* 7, no. 3 (January 1910): 383–94.
Hillman, David, and Carla Mazzio. "Introduction: Individual Parts." In *The Body in Parts: Fantasies of Corporeality in Early Modern Europe*, edited by David Hillman and Carla Mazzio, xi–xxix. London: Routledge, 1997.
Hindle, Steve. "Civility, Honesty and the Identification of the Deserving Poor in Seventeenth-Century England." In *Identity and Agency in England 1500–1800*, edited by Henry French and Jonathan Barry, 38–59. New York: Palgrave Macmillan, 2004.
Hirschmann, Nancy. "Disability as a New Frontier for Feminist Intersectionality Research." *Politics and Gender* 8, no. 3 (2012): 396–405.
Hobgood, Allison P. "Caesar Hath the Falling Sickness: The Legibility of Early Modern Disability in Shakespearean Drama." *Disability Studies Quarterly* 29, no. 4 (2009). https://dsq-sds.org/article/view/993/1184Caesar.
———. "'Teeth before Eyes: Impairment and Invisibility in Shakespeare's *Richard III*." In *Disability, Health and Happiness in the Shakespearean Body*, edited by Sujata Iyengar, 23–40. New York: Routledge, 2015.
Hobgood, Allison P., and David Houston Wood. "Disabled Shakespeares." *Disability Studies Quarterly* 29, no. 4 (2009). https://dsq-sds.org/article/view/991/1183.

———. "Early Modern Literature and Disability Studies." In *The Cambridge Companion to Literature and Disability*, edited by Clare Barker and Stuart Murray, 32–46. Cambridge: Cambridge University Press, 2018.

———. "Introduction: Ethical Staring: Disabling the English Renaissance." In *Recovering Disability in Early Modern England*, edited by Allison P. Hobgood and David Houston Wood, 1–22. Columbus: Ohio State University Press, 2013.

Hodgdon, Barbara. "Replicating Richard: Body Doubles, Body Politics." *Theatre Journal* 50, no. 2 (1998): 207–25.

Hoeniger, F. David. *Medicine and Shakespeare in the English Renaissance*. Newark: University of Delaware Press, 1992.

Hopkinson, A. F. Introduction to *The Birth of Merlin*. In vol. 2 of *Shakespeare's Doubtful Plays*, edited by A. F. Hopkinson, i–xiv. London: M. E. Sims, 1892.

Hotine, Margaret. "*Richard III* and *Macbeth*—Studies in Tudor Tyranny?" *Notes and Queries* 38, no. 4 (December 1991): 480–86.

Howard, Jean E. "Stage Masculinities, National History, and the Making of London Theatrical Culture." In *Center or Margin: Revisions of the English Renaissance in Honor of Leeds Barroll*, edited by Lena Cowen Orlin, 199–214. Selinsgrove, PA: Susquehanna University Press, 2006.

———. *Theater of a City: The Places of London Comedy, 1598–1642*. Philadelphia: University of Pennsylvania Press, 2007.

Howard, Jean E., and Phyllis Rackin. *Engendering a Nation: A Feminist Account of Shakespeare's English Histories*. New York: Routledge, 1997.

Howe, Tonya. "'All deformed Shapes': Figuring the Posture-Master as Popular Performer in Early Eighteenth-Century England." *Journal of Early Modern Cultural Studies* 12, no. 4 (2012): 26–47.

Huet, Marie-Hélène. *Monstrous Imagination*. Cambridge, MA: Harvard University Press, 1993.

Hulme, Peter, and William H. Sherman, eds. *The Tempest and Its Travels*. Philadelphia: University of Pennsylvania Press, 2000.

Hutchings, Mark. "*Richard III* and *The Changeling*." *Notes and Queries* 52, no. 2 (2005): 229–30.

Hsy, Jonathan. "Disability." In *The Cambridge Companion to the Body in Literature*, edited by David Hillman and Ulrika Maude, 22–40. Cambridge: Cambridge University Press, 2015.

Hutson, Lorna. *Circumstantial Shakespeare*. Oxford: Oxford University Press, 2015.

———. *The Invention of Suspicion: Law and Mimesis in Shakespeare and Renaissance Drama*. Oxford: Oxford University Press, 2007.

Hyland, Peter. *Disguise on the Early Modern English Stage*. Burlington, VT: Ashgate, 2011.

Isaac, Megan Lynn. "Legitimizing Magic in *The Birth of Merlin*." *Early Theatre* 9, no. 1 (June 2006): 109–21.

Iyengar, Sujata. "Introduction: Shakespeare's Discourse of Disability." In *Disability, Health, and Happiness in the Shakespearean Body*, edited by Sujata Iyengar, 1–19. New York: Routledge, 2015.

Jain, Lochlann S. "The Prosthetic Imagination: Enabling and Disabling the Prosthesis Trope." *Science, Technology, and Human Values* 24, no. 1 (1999): 31–54.

Jardine, Lisa, and Alan Stewart. *Hostage to Fortune: The Troubled Life of Francis Bacon*. New York: Hill & Wang, 1999.

Jeffrey, Cole. "'Here's Beauty Changed to Ugly Whoredom': Calvinist Theology and Neoplatonic Aesthetics in *The Changeling*." *Renaissance Drama* 47, no. 1 (Spring 2019): 21–39.

Johns, Geoffrey A. "A 'Grievous Burthen': *Richard III* and the Legacy of Monstrous Birth." In *Disability, Health, and Happiness in the Shakespearean Body*, edited by Sujata Iyengar, 41–57. New York: Routledge, 2015.

Johnston, Kirsty. *Disability Theatre and Modern Drama: Recasting Modernism*. London: Bloomsbury Methuen Drama, 2016.

Jones, Ann Rosalind, and Peter Stallybrass. *Renaissance Clothing and the Materials of Memory*. Cambridge: Cambridge University Press, 2000.

Jorgensen, Paul. *Shakespeare's Military World*. Berkeley: University of California Press, 1956.

Juárez-Almendros, Encarnación. *Disabled Bodies in Early Modern Spanish Literature: Prostitutes, Aging Women and Saints*. Liverpool: Liverpool University Press, 2017.

Kafer, Alison. *Feminist, Queer, Crip*. Bloomington: Indiana University Press, 2013.

Karim-Cooper, Farah. *Cosmetics in Shakespearean and Renaissance Drama*. Edinburgh: Edinburgh University Press, 2006.

———. *The Hand on the Shakespearean Stage: Gesture, Touch and the Spectacle of Dismemberment*. London: Bloomsbury Arden Shakespeare, 2016.

Karpinska, Monika. "Bawdily Manipulations: Spheres of Female Power in *The Birth of Merlin*." *Early Theatre* 9, no. 1 (June 2006): 123–29.

Kastan, David Scott. "Workshop and/as Playhouse: Comedy and Commerce in *The Shoemaker's Holiday*." *Studies in Philology* 84, no. 3 (1987): 324–37.

Kemble, John Philip. *Macbeth and King Richard the Third*. London: John Murray, 1817.

Kerwin, William. *Beyond the Body: The Boundaries of Medicine and English Renaissance Drama*. Amherst: University of Massachusetts Press, 2005.

Kinney, Arthur F. *Rogues, Vagabonds, and Sturdy Beggars: A New Gallery of Tudor and Early Stuart Rogue Literature*. Amherst: University of Massachusetts Press, 1973. Reprint, 1990.

Kirwan, Peter. *Shakespeare and the Idea of Apocrypha: Negotiating the Boundaries of the Dramatic Canon*. Cambridge: Cambridge University Press, 2015.

Kistner, A. L., and M. K. Kistner. "The Five Structures of *The Changeling*." *Modern Language Studies* 11, no. 2 (Spring 1981): 40–53.

Knight, Stephen. *Merlin: Knowledge and Power Through the Ages*. Ithaca, NY: Cornell University Press, 2009.

Knoppers, Laura Lunger, and Joan B. Landes, eds. *Monstrous Bodies/Political Monstrosities in Early Modern Europe*. Ithaca, NY: Cornell University Press, 2004.

Knowles, Ric. "Encoding/Decoding Shakespeare: *Richard III* at the 2002 Stratford Festival." In *A Companion to Shakespeare and Performance*, edited by Barbara Hodgdon and W. B. Worthen, 297–318. New York: Wiley Blackwell, 2005.

Knutson, Roslyn L. "Filling Fare: The Appetite for Current Issues and Traditional Forms in the Repertory of the Chamberlain's Men." *Medieval and Renaissance Drama in England* 15 (2003): 57–76.

Kostihová, Marcela. "Richard Recast: Renaissance Disability in a Postmodern Culture." In *Recovering Disability in Early Modern England*, edited by Allison P. Hobgood and David Houston Wood, 136–49. Columbus: Ohio State University Press, 2013.

Kreider, Paul V. *Elizabethan Comic Character Conventions: As Revealed in the Comedies of George Chapman*. Ann Arbor: University of Michigan Press, 1935.

Kunin, Aaron. *Character as Form*. London: Bloomsbury Arden Shakespeare, 2019.

Kuppers, Petra. "Deconstructing Images: Performing Disability." *Contemporary Theatre Review* 11, nos. 3–4 (2001): 25–40.

———. *Theatre and Disability*. London: Palgrave Macmillan, 2017.

Lake, Peter. *How Shakespeare Put Politics on the Stage: Power and Succession in the History Plays*. New Haven, CT: Yale University Press, 2016.

Lamb, Charles. *Specimens of English Dramatic Poets Who Lived about the Time of Shakespeare*. New York: Wiley & Putnam, 1845.

Lash, Alexander Paulsson. "'A delightful Proteus': Humors, Disguise, and the Actor's Skill in *The Blind Beggar of Alexandria* and *1 Henry IV*." *Shakespeare Studies* 47 (2019): 205–32.

Lawrence, William J. "Lengths." *The Stage*. February 11, 1932.

———. *Pre-Restoration Stage Studies*. Cambridge, MA: Harvard University Press, 1927.

Leggatt, Alexander. *Citizen Comedy in the Age of Shakespeare*. Toronto: University of Toronto Press, 1973.

Leinwand, Theodore B. *The City Staged: Jacobean Comedy, 1603–13*. Madison: University of Wisconsin Press, 1986.

———. *Theatre, Finance, and Society in Early Modern England*. Cambridge: Cambridge University Press, 1999.

Lew, Mike. *Teenage Dick*. London: Nick Hern Books, 2019.

Lewis, Victoria Ann. "Crip." In *Keywords for Disability Studies*, edited by Rachel Adams, Benjamin Reiss, and David Serlin, 46–48. New York: New York University Press, 2015.

Lin, Erika T. *Shakespeare and the Materiality of Performance*. New York: Palgrave Macmillan, 2012.

Long, Kathleen. "'Nature Abhors Normality': Theories of the Monstrous from Aristotle to *The X-Files* (1993–2002)." In *Speaking of Monsters: A Teratological Anthology*, edited by Caroline Joan S. Picart and John Edgar Browning, 195–208. New York: Palgrave Macmillan, 2012.

Loomba, Ania. *Shakespeare, Race, and Colonialism*. Oxford: Oxford University Press, 2002.

Lopez, Jeremy. "Imagining the Actor's Body on the Early Modern Stage." *Medieval and Renaissance Drama in England* 20 (2007): 187–203.

———. "Postmodern Gosson, or 1599 Is a Four-Letter Word." In *Thunder at a Playhouse: Essaying Shakespeare and the Early Modern Stage*, edited by Peter Kanelos and Matt Kozusko, 131–42. Selinsgrove, PA: Susquehanna University Press, 2010.

———. *Theatrical Convention and Audience Response in Early Modern Drama*. Cambridge: Cambridge University Press, 2003.

Love, Genevieve. *Early Modern Theatre and the Figure of Disability*. London: Arden Shakespeare, 2019.

Lupton, Julia. *Citizen-Saints: Shakespeare and Political Theology*. Chicago: University of Chicago Press, 2005.

———. "Creature Caliban." *Shakespeare Quarterly* 51, no. 1 (Spring 2000): 1–23.

MacKay, Ellen. *Persecution, Plague, and Fire: Fugitive Histories of the Stage in Early Modern England*. Chicago: University of Chicago Press, 2011.

———. "Indecorum." In *Early Modern Theatricality*, edited by Henry S. Turner, 306–26. Oxford: Oxford University Press, 2013.

Macleod, Randall / Random Cloud. "'The very names of the persons': Editing and the Invention of Dramatick Character." In *Staging the Renaissance: Reinterpretations of Elizabethan and Jacobean Drama*, edited by David Scott Kastan and Peter Stallybrass, 88–96. London: Routledge, 1991.

Mairs, Nancy. *Plaintext*. Tucson: University of Arizona Press, 1986.

Malcolmson, Cristina. "'As Tame as the Ladies': Politics and Gender in *The Changeling*." In *Revenge Tragedy*, edited by Stevie Simkins, 142–62. New York: Palgrave Macmillan, 2001.

Mann, David. *The Elizabethan Player: Contemporary Stage Representation*. London: Routledge, 1991.

Mann, Jenny C., and Debapriya Sarkar. "Introduction: Capturing Proteus." *Philological Quarterly* 98, nos. 1–2 (2019): 1–22.

Marsh, Christopher. "A Woodcut and Its Wanderings in Seventeenth-Century England." *Huntington Library Quarterly* 79, no. 2 (2016): 245–62.

Maus, Katharine Eisaman. *Inwardness and Theater in the English Renaissance*. Chicago: Chicago University Press, 1995.

Mazzio, Carla. *The Inarticulate Renaissance: Language Trouble in an Age of Eloquence*. Philadelphia: University of Pennsylvania Press, 2009.

McKeown, Adam N. *English Mercuries: Soldier Poets in the Age of Shakespeare*. Nashville, TN: Vanderbilt University Press, 2009.

McMullan, Gordon. "*The Changeling* and the Dynamics of Ugliness." In *The Cambridge Companion to English Renaissance Tragedy*, edited by Emma Smith and Garrett A. Sullivan Jr., 222–35. Cambridge: Cambridge University Press, 2010.

McRae, Andrew. *Literature, Satire and the Early Stuart State*. Cambridge: Cambridge University Press, 2004.

McRuer, Robert. *Crip Theory: Cultural Signs of Queerness and Disability*. New York: New York University Press, 2006.

———. *Crip Times*. New York: New York University Press, 2018.

———. "Fuck the Disabled: The Prequel." In *Shakesqueer: A Queer Companion to the Complete Works of Shakespeare*, edited by Madhavi Menon, 294–301. Durham, NC: Duke University Press, 2011.

Mehl, Dieter, Angela Stock, and Anne-Julia Zwierlein, eds. *Plotting Early Modern London: New Essays on Jacobean City Comedy*. Burlington, VT: Ashgate, 2004.

Menon, Madhavi. *Indifference to Difference: On Queer Universalism*. Minneapolis: University of Minnesota Press, 2015.

Menzer, Paul. *Anecdotal Shakespeare: A New Performance History*. London: Arden Shakespeare, 2015.

———. "Character Acting." In *Shakespeare's Theatres and the Effects of Performance*, edited by Farah Karim-Cooper and Tiffany Stern, 141–67. London: Bloomsbury Arden Shakespeare, 2013.

Metzler, Irina. *Disability in Medieval Europe: Thinking about Physical Impairment during the Middle Ages, c. 1100–1400*. London: Routledge, 2006.

Mitchell, David T., and Sharon L. Snyder. *Cultural Locations of Disability*. Chicago: University of Chicago Press, 2006.

———. *Narrative Prosthesis: Disability and the Dependencies of Discourse.* Ann Arbor: University of Michigan Press, 2000.

Moulton, Ian Frederick. "'A monster great deformed': The Unruly Masculinity of *Richard III.*" *Shakespeare Quarterly* 47, no. 3 (1996): 251–68.

Muldrew, Craig. *The Economy of Obligation: The Culture of Credit and Social Relations in Early Modern England.* Basingstoke, UK: Macmillan, 1998.

Muñoz, José Esteban. *Cruising Utopia: The Then and There of Queer Futurity.* New York: New York University Press, 2009.

Munro, Lucy. "'Nemp your sexes!' Anachronistic Aesthetics in *Hengist, King of Kent* and the Jacobean 'Anglo-Saxon' Play." *Modern Philology* 111, no. 4 (2014): 734–61.

Nardizzi, Vin. "Disability Figures in Shakespeare." In *The Oxford Handbook of Shakespeare and Embodiment,* edited by Valerie Traub, 455–67. Oxford: Oxford University Press, 2016.

———. "The Wooden Matter of Human Bodies: Prosthesis and Stump in *A Larum for London.*" In *The Indistinct Human in Renaissance Literature,* edited by Jean E. Feerick and Vin Nardizzi, 119–36. New York: Palgrave Macmillan, 2012.

Neely, Carol Thomas. "Distracted Measures: Madness and Theatricality in Middleton." In *Thomas Middleton in Context,* edited by Suzanne Gossett, 306–16. Cambridge: Cambridge University Press, 2011.

———. *Distracted Subjects: Madness and Gender in Shakespeare and Early Modern Culture.* Ithaca, NY: Cornell University Press, 2004.

Neill, Michael. *Issues of Death: Mortality and Identity in English Renaissance Tragedy.* Oxford: Clarendon Press, 1997.

Ngai, Sianne. *Ugly Feelings.* Cambridge, MA: Harvard University Press, 2005.

Nicol, David. *Middleton and Rowley: Forms of Collaboration in the Jacobean Playhouse.* Toronto: University of Toronto Press, 2012.

Nussbaum, Felicity A. *The Limits of the Human: Fictions of Anomaly, Race, and Gender in the Long Eighteenth Century.* Cambridge: Cambridge University Press, 2003.

Obermeier, Anita. "Merlin's Conception by the Devil in William Rowley's Play *The Birth of Merlin.*" *Arthuriana* 24, no. 4 (2014): 48–79.

Orlemanski, Julie. *Symptomatic Subjects.* Philadelphia: University of Pennsylvania Press, 2019.

Palfrey, Simon, and Tiffany Stern. *Shakespeare in Parts.* Oxford: Oxford University Press, 2007.

Pallister, Janis L. Introduction to *On Monsters and Marvels* by Ambroise Paré, translated and edited by Janis L. Pallister, xv–xxxii. Chicago: University of Chicago Press, 1982.

Park, Katharine, and Lorraine Daston. *Wonders and the Order of Nature, 1150–1750.* New York: Zone Books, 1998.

Paster, Gail Kern. *The Body Embarrassed: Drama and the Disciplines of Shame in Early Modern England.* Ithaca, NY: Cornell University Press, 1993.

———. "The Ecology of the Passions in *A Chaste Maid in Cheapside* and *The Changeling.*" In *The Oxford Handbook of Thomas Middleton,* edited by Gary Taylor and Trish Thomas Henley, 148–63. Oxford: Oxford University Press, 2012.

———. *Humouring the Body: Emotions and the Shakespearean Stage*. Chicago: University of Chicago Press, 2004.

Paster, Gail Kern, Katherine Rowe, and Mary Floyd-Wilson, eds. *Reading the Early Modern Passions*. Philadelphia: University of Pennsylvania Press, 2004.

Patterson, Annabel. Introduction to *The Changeling*. In *Thomas Middleton: The Collected Works*, edited by Gary Taylor and John Lavagnino, and Macdonald P. Jackson, John Jowett, Valerie Wayne, and Adrian Weiss, 1632–36. Oxford: Clarendon Press, 2007.

Pelling, Margaret. "Appearance and Reality: Barber-Surgeons, the Body, and Disease." In *London 1500–1700: The Making of the Metropolis*, edited by A. L. Beier and Roger Finlay, 82–105. New York: Longman, 1986.

Peltonen, Markku. "Rhetoric and Citizenship in the Monarchical Republic of Queen Elizabeth I." In *The Monarchical Republic of Early Modern England: Essays in Response to Patrick Collinson*, edited by John F. McDiarmid, 109–27. New York: Ashgate, 2007.

Pender, Stephen. "'No Monsters at the Resurrection': Inside Some Conjoined Twins." In *Monster Theory: Reading Culture*, edited by Jeffrey Jerome Cohen, 143–67. Minneapolis: University of Minnesota Press, 1996.

——— "In the Bodyshop: Human Exhibition in Early Modern England." In *Defects: Engendering the Modern Body*, edited by Helen Deutsch and Felicity Nussbaum, 95–126. Ann Arbor: University of Michigan Press, 2000.

Phelan, Peggy. *Unmarked: The Politics of Performance*. London: Routledge, 1993.

Pollard, Tanya. *Drugs and Theater in Early Modern England*. Oxford: Oxford University Press, 2005.

Porter, Martin. *Windows of the Soul: Physiognomy in European Culture, 1470–1780*. Oxford: Clarendon Press, 2005.

Preiss, Richard. *Clowning and Authorship in Early Modern Theatre*. Cambridge: Cambridge University Press, 2014.

Puar, Jasbir K. *The Right to Maim: Debility, Capacity, Disability*. Durham, NC: Duke University Press, 2017.

Pugliatti, Paola. *Beggary and Theatre in Early Modern England*. Aldershot, UK: Ashgate, 2003.

Quayson, Ato. *Aesthetic Nervousness: Disability and the Crisis of Representation*. New York: Columbia University Press, 2007.

Ricks, Christopher. "The Moral and Poetic Structure of *The Changeling*." *Essays in Criticism* 10, no. 3 (1960): 290–306.

Rivlin, Elizabeth. *The Aesthetics of Service in Early Modern England*. Evanston, IL: Northwestern University Press, 2012.

Roach, Joseph R. *The Player's Passion: Studies in the Science of Acting*. Newark: University of Delaware Press, 1985.

Rosenfeld, Colleen Ruth. *Indecorous Thinking: Figures of Speech in Early Modern Poetics*. New York: Fordham University Press, 2018.

Rossiter, A. P. "Angel with Horns: The Unity of *Richard III*." In *Angel with Horns: 15 Lectures on Shakespeare*, edited by Graham Storey, 3–23. New York: Longman, 1989.

Row-Heyveld, Lindsey. *Dissembling Disability in Early Modern English Drama*. Cham, Switzerland: Palgrave Macmillan / Springer Nature, 2018.

——. "'The lying'st knave in Christendom': The Development of Disability in the False Miracle of St. Alban's." *Disability Studies Quarterly* 29, no. 4 (Fall 2009). https://dsq-sds.org/article/view/994/1178.

Roychoudhury, Suparna. *Phantasmatic Shakespeare: Imagination in the Age of Early Modern Science*. Ithaca, NY: Cornell University Press, 2018.

Saenger, Michael Baird. "The Costumes of Caliban and Ariel qua Sea-Nymph." *Notes and Queries* (1995): 334–36.

Saintsbury, George. *A History of Elizabethan Literature*. New York: Macmillan, 1891.

Salamon, Linda Bradley. "Vagabond Veterans: The Roguish Company of Martin Guerre and *Henry V*." In *Rogues and Early Modern English Culture*, edited by Craig Dionne and Steve Mentz, 261–93. Ann Arbor: University of Michigan Press, 2004.

Sale, Carolyn. "Eating Air, Feeling Smells: *Hamlet*'s Theory of Performance." *Renaissance Drama* 35 (2006): 145–68.

Samuels, Ellen. *Fantasies of Identification: Disability, Gender, Race*. New York: New York University Press, 2014.

——. "Six Ways of Looking at Crip Time." *Disability Studies Quarterly* 37, no. 3 (2017). https://dsq-sds.org/article/view/5824.

Sandahl, Carrie. "Queering the Crip or Cripping the Queer? Intersections of Queer and Crip Identities in Solo Autobiographical Performance." *Gay and Lesbian Quarterly* 9, nos. 1–2 (2003): 25–56.

——. "The Tyranny of Neutral: Disability and Actor Training." In *Bodies in Commotion: Disability and Performance*, edited by Carrie Sandahl and Philip Auslander, 255–67. Ann Arbor: University of Michigan Press, 2005.

Sandhal, Carrie, and Philip Auslander. Introduction to *Bodies in Commotion: Disability and Performance*, edited by Carrie Sandahl and Philip Auslander, 1–12. Ann Arbor: University of Michigan Press, 2005.

Sarkar, Debapriya. "*The Tempest*'s Other Plots." *Shakespeare Studies* 45 (2017): 203–30.

Saunders, Ann, ed. *The Royal Exchange*. London: London Topographical Society, 1997.

Sawday, Jonathan. *The Body Emblazoned: Dissection and the Human Body in Renaissance Culture*. London: Routledge, 1995.

Schelling, Felix E. *Elizabethan Drama, 1558–1642*. Vol. 1. Boston: Houghton Mifflin, 1908.

Schoenfeldt, Michael C. *Bodies and Selves in Early Modern England: Physiology and Inwardness in Spenser, Shakespeare, Herbert, and Milton*. Cambridge: Cambridge University Press, 1999.

Schweik, Susan M. *The Ugly Laws: Disability in Public*. New York: New York University Press, 2009.

Schwyzer, Philip. *Shakespeare and the Remains of Richard III*. Oxford: Oxford University Press, 2013.

Seaver, Paul S. "The Artisanal World." In *The Theatrical City: Culture, Theatre and Politics in London, 1576–1649*, edited by David L. Smith, Richard Strier, and David Bevington, 87–100. Cambridge: Cambridge University Press, 1995.

Semonin, Paul. "Monsters in the Marketplace: The Exhibition of Human Oddities in Early Modern England." In *Freakery: Cultural Spectacles of the Extraordinary Body*, edited by Rosemarie Garland-Thomson, 69–81. New York: New York University Press, 1996.

Shapin, Steven, and Simon Schaffer. *Leviathan and the Air-Pump: Hobbes, Boyle, and the Experimental Life*. Princeton, NJ: Princeton University Press, 1985.

Sharpe, James. *Witchcraft in Early Modern England*. London: Routledge, 2001.

Shaw, Justin. "'Rub Him About the Temples': *Othello*, Disability, and the Failures of Care." *Early Theatre* 22, no. 2 (2019): 171–83.

Sheerin, Brian. *Desires of Credit in Early Modern Theory and Drama: Commerce, Poesy, and the Profitable Imagination*. London: Routledge, 2016.

Sher, Antony. *Year of the King: An Actor's Diary and Sketchbook*. London: Chatto & Windus / Hogarth Press, 1985.

Siebers, Tobin. *Disability Aesthetics*. Ann Arbor: University of Michigan Press, 2010.

———. *Disability Theory*. Ann Arbor: University of Michigan Press, 2008.

———. "Shakespeare Differently Disabled." In *The Oxford Handbook of Shakespeare and Embodiment*, edited by Valerie Traub, 435–54. Oxford: Oxford University Press, 2016.

Siemon, James R. Introduction to *King Richard III*, by William Shakespeare, 1–123. Edited by James R. Siemon. Arden Shakespeare 3rd ser. London: Bloomsbury Arden Shakespeare, 2009.

Silvers, Anita. "An Essay on Modeling: The Social Model of Disability." In *Philosophical Reflections on Disability*, edited by D. Christopher Ralston and Justin Ho, 19–36. Dordrecht: Springer, 2010.

Simpson, R. R. *Shakespeare and Medicine*. New York: E. & S. Livingstone, 1959.

Singer, Julie. Introduction to "Disability and the Social Body." *postmedieval: a journal of medieval cultural studies* 3, no. 2 (2012): 135–41.

Skuse, Alanna. "Missing Parts in *The Shoemaker's Holiday*." *Renaissance Drama* 45, no. 2 (2017): 161–79.

Slack, Paul. *The English Poor Law, 1531–1782*. Cambridge: Cambridge University Press, 1990.

———. *Poverty and Policy in Tudor and Stuart England*. London: Longman, 1988.

Slater, Michael. "'Shameless Collaboration': Mixture and the Double Plot of *The Changeling*." *Renaissance Drama* 47, no. 1 (2019): 41–71.

Slotkin, Joel Elliot. *Sinister Aesthetics: The Appeal of Evil in Early Modern English Literature*. Cham, Switzerland: Palgrave Macmillan / Springer Nature, 2017.

Smallwood, Robert L. Introduction to *The Shoemaker's Holiday*, by Thomas Dekker, edited by R. L. Smallwood and Stanley Wells, 1–70. Manchester: Manchester University Press, 1979.

Smith, Ian. "The Textile Black Body: Race and 'Shadowed Livery' in *The Merchant of Venice*." In *The Oxford Handbook of Shakespeare and Embodiment*, edited by Valerie Traub, 170–85. Oxford: Oxford University Press, 2016.

Snyder, Karl E. Introduction to *A Critical Edition of* The Faire Maide of the Exchange *by Thomas Heywood*, edited by Karl E. Snyder, 1–61. New York: Garland, 1980.

Sofer, Andrew. "Properties." In *The Oxford Handbook of Early Modern Theatre*, edited by Richard Dutton, 560–74. Oxford: Oxford University Press, 2009.

———. *The Stage Life of Props*. Ann Arbor: University of Michigan Press, 2003.

Solga, Kim. *Violence against Women in Early Modern Performance: Invisible Acts*. Basingstoke, UK: Palgrave Macmillan, 2014.

Somogyi, Nicholas de. *Shakespeare's Theatre of War*. Aldershot, UK: Ashgate, 1998.
Stagg, Kevin. "Representing Physical Difference: The Materiality of the Monstrous." In *Social Histories of Disability and Deformity*, edited by David M. Turner and Kevin Stagg, 19–38. London: Routledge, 2006.
States, Bert O. *Great Reckonings in Little Rooms: On the Phenomenology of Theater*. Berkeley: University of California Press, 1985.
———. *The Pleasure of the Play*. Ithaca, NY: Cornell University Press, 1994.
Steen, Sara Jayne, ed. *Ambrosia in an Earthen Vessel: Three Centuries of Audience and Reader Response to the Works of Thomas Middleton*. New York: AMS Press, 1993.
Stephens, Elizabeth. "Queer Monsters: Technologies of Self-Transformation in Bulwer's *Anthropometamorphosis* and Braidotti's *Metamorphoses*." In *Somatechnics: Queering the Technologisation of Bodies*, edited by Nikki Sullivan and Samantha Murray, 171–86. New York: Ashgate, 2009.
Stern, Tiffany. *Making Shakespeare: From Stage to Page*. London: Routledge, 2004.
Stevens, Andrea Ria. *Inventions of the Skin: The Painted Body in Early English Drama, 1400–1642*. Edinburgh: Edinburgh University Press, 2013.
Stewart, Susan. *On Longing: Narratives of the Miniature, the Gigantic, the Souvenir, the Collection*. Durham, NC: Duke University Press, 1993.
Stiker, Henri-Jacques. *A History of Disability*. Translated by William Sayers. Ann Arbor: University of Michigan Press, 1999.
Stone, Deborah A. *The Disabled State*. Philadelphia: Temple University Press, 1984.
Straznicky, Marta. "The End(s) of Discord in *The Shoemaker's Holiday*." *Studies in English Literature, 1500–1900* 36, no. 2 (Spring 1996): 357–72.
Swinburne, Algernon Charles. "Thomas Middleton." *The Nineteenth Century* 19 (1886): 138–53.
Targoff, Ramie. "'Dirty' Amens: Devotion, Applause, and Consent in *Richard III*." *Renaissance Drama* 31 (2002): 61–84.
Taylor, Gary. "History, Plays, Genre, Games." In *The Oxford Handbook of Thomas Middleton*, edited by Gary Taylor and Trish Thomas Henley, 47–63. Oxford: Oxford University Press, 2012.
Teague, Frances. "Ben Jonson and London Courtrooms." In *Solon and Thespis: Law and Theater in the English Renaissance*, edited by Dennis Kezar, 64–79. Notre Dame, IN: University of Notre Dame Press, 2007.
———. *Shakespeare's Speaking Properties*. Lewisburg, PA: Bucknell University Press, 1991.
Thirsk, Joan. *Economic Policy and Projects: The Development of a Consumer Society in Early Modern England*. Oxford: Clarendon Press, 1978.
Thomas, Neil. "The Celtic Wild Man Tradition and Geoffrey of Monmouth's *Vita Merlini*: Madness or *Contemptus Mundi*?" *Arthuriana* 10, no. 1 (Spring 2000): 27–42.
Torrey, Michael. "'The plain devil and dissembling looks': Ambivalent Physiognomy and Shakespeare's *Richard III*." *English Literary Renaissance* 30, no. 2 (Spring 2000): 123–53.
Totaro, Rebecca. *Suffering in Paradise: The Bubonic Plague in English Literature from More to Milton*. Pittsburgh: Duquesne University Press, 2005.
Totaro, Rebecca, and Ernest B. Gilman, eds. *Representing the Plague in Early Modern England*. London: Routledge, 2010.

Traub, Valerie. "Introduction: Feminist Shakespeare Studies." In *The Oxford Handbook of Shakespeare and Embodiment*, edited by Valerie Traub, 1–36. Oxford: Oxford University Press, 2016.

———. "The Nature of Norms in Early Modern England: Anatomy, Cartography, *King Lear*." *South Central Review* 26, nos. 1–2 (2009): 42–81.

Tribble, Evelyn. *Early Modern Actors and Shakespeare's Theatre: Thinking with the Body*. London: Bloomsbury Arden Shakespeare, 2017.

Turner, David M. "Disability Humor and the Meanings of Impairment in Early Modern England." In *Recovering Disability in Early Modern England*, edited by Allison P. Hobgood and David Houston Wood, 57–72. Columbus: Ohio State University Press, 2013.

———. "Introduction: Approaching Anomalous Bodies." In *Social Histories of Disability and Deformity*, edited by David M. Turner and Kevin Stagg, 1–16. London: Routledge, 2006.

Turner, David M., and Kevin Stagg, eds. *Social Histories of Disability and Deformity*. London: Routledge, 2006.

Turner, Henry S. *The Corporate Commonwealth: Pluralism and Political Fictions in England, 1516–1651*. Chicago: University of Chicago Press, 2016.

———. "Generalization." In *Early Modern Theatricality*, edited by Henry S. Turner, 1–23. Oxford: Oxford University Press, 2013.

———. "Lessons from Literature for the Historian of Science (and Vice Versa): Reflections on 'Form.'" *ISIS* 101 (2010): 578–89.

Udall, Joanna. Introduction to *A Critical, Old-Spelling Edition of The Birth of Merlin (Q 1662)*, edited by Joanna Udall, 1–116. London: Modern Humanities Research Association, 1991.

Van Es, Bart. *Shakespeare in Company*. Oxford: Oxford University Press, 2013.

Vaughan, Alden T., and Virginia Mason Vaughan. *Shakespeare's Caliban: A Cultural History*. Cambridge: Cambridge University Press, 1991.

Verity, A. Wilson. Introduction to *The Best Plays of the Old Dramatists: Thomas Heywood*, edited by A. Wilson Verity, vii–xxxii. London: Vizetelly, 1888.

Vinter, Maggie. *Last Acts: The Art of Dying on the Early Modern Stage*. New York: Fordham University Press, 2019.

Walsh, Brian. "Performing Historicity in Dekker's *The Shoemaker's Holiday*." *Studies in English Literature* 46, no. 2 (Spring 2006): 323–48.

———. *Shakespeare, the Queen's Men, and the Elizabethan Performance of History*. Cambridge: Cambridge University Press, 2009.

Waswo, Richard. "Crises of Credit: Monetary and Erotic Economies in the Jacobean Theatre." In *Plotting Early Modern London: New Essays on Jacobean City Comedy*, edited by Dieter Mehl, Angela Stock, and Anne-Julia Zwierlein, 55–74. Burlington, VT: Ashgate, 2004.

Weimann, Robert. *Author's Pen and Actor's Voice: Playing and Writing in Shakespeare's Theatre*. Edited by Helen Higbee and William West. Cambridge: Cambridge University Press, 2000.

———. *Shakespeare and the Popular Tradition in the Theater: Studies in the Social Dimension of Dramatic Form and Function*. Edited by Robert Schwartz. Baltimore: Johns Hopkins University Press, 1978.

Wellman, Mac. *The Difficulty of Crossing a Field: Nine New Plays*. Minneapolis: University of Minnesota Press, 2008.
Wells, Susan. "Jacobean City Comedy and the Ideology of the City." *English Literary History* 48, no. 1 (Spring 1981): 37–60.
West, William N. "Intertheatricality." In *Early Modern Theatricality*, edited by Henry S. Turner, 151–72. Oxford: Oxford University Press, 2013.
———. "What's the Matter with Shakespeare? Physics, Identity, Playing." *South Central Review* 26, nos. 1–2 (Spring–Summer 2009): 103–26.
Wheeler, Richard P. "History, Character, and Conscience in *Richard III*." *Comparative Drama* 5 (1971–1972): 301–21.
Whigham, Frank. "Reading Social Conflict in the Alimentary Tract: More on the Body in Renaissance Drama." *English Literary History* 55, no. 2 (Summer 1988): 333–50.
———. *Seizures of the Will in Early Modern English Drama*. Cambridge: Cambridge University Press, 1996.
Wiggins, Martin. *Shakespeare and the Drama of His Time*. Oxford: Oxford University Press, 2000.
Wiggins, Martin, in association with Catherine Richardson. *British Drama, 1533–1642: A Catalogue*. Vols. 1–8. Oxford: Oxford University Press, 2015.
Wilks, John S. *The Idea of Conscience in Renaissance Tragedy*. London: Routledge, 1990.
Williams, Katherine Schaap. "Demonstrating Disability." *Early Theatre* 22, no. 2 (2019): 185–97.
———. "Enabling Richard: The Rhetoric of Disability in *Richard III*." *Disability Studies Quarterly* 29, no. 4 (2009). http://dsq-sds.org/article/view/997/1181.
———. "'More legs than nature gave thee': Performing the Cripple in *The Fair Maid of the Exchange*." *English Literary History* 82, no. 2 (Summer 2015): 491–519.
———. "Performing Disability and Theorizing Deformity." *English Studies* 94, no. 7 (Fall 2013): 757–72. Reprinted in *Shakespeare and the Future of Theory*, edited by François-Xavier Gleyzon and Johann Gregory. London: Routledge, 2016.
———. "'Strange Virtue': Staging Acts of Cure." In *Disability, Health, and Happiness in the Shakespearean Body*, edited by Sujata Iyengar, 93–108. New York: Routledge, 2015.
Williams, Nora. "'Cannot I keep that secret?': Editing and Performing Asides in *The Changeling*." *Shakespeare Bulletin* 34, no. 1 (Spring 2016): 29–45.
Williams, Wes. *Monsters and Their Meanings in Early Modern Culture: Mighty Magic*. Oxford: Oxford University Press, 2011.
Willis, Deborah. *Malevolent Nature: Witch-Hunting and Maternal Power in Early Modern England*. Ithaca, NY: Cornell University Press, 1995.
Wills, David. *Prosthesis*. Stanford, CA: Stanford University Press, 1995.
Wilson, Jeffrey. "The Trouble with Disability in Shakespeare Studies." *Disability Studies Quarterly* 37, no. 2 (2017). https://dsq-sds.org/article/view/5430/4644.
Wilson, Luke. "Monetary Compensation for Injuries to the Body, A.D. 602–169." In *Money and the Age of Shakespeare*, edited by Linda Woodbridge, 19–37. New York: Palgrave Macmillan, 2003.

Wiseman, Susan. "Monstrous Perfectability: Ape-Human Transformations in Hobbes, Bulwer, Tyson." In *At the Borders of the Human: Beasts, Bodies, and Natural Philosophy in the Early Modern Period*, edited by Erica Fudge, Ruth Gilbert, and Susan Wiseman, 215–38. London: Palgrave Macmillan, 1999.

Withington, Phil. *The Politics of Commonwealth: Citizens and Freemen in Early Modern England*. Cambridge: Cambridge University Press, 2005.

Witmore, Michael. *Culture of Accidents: Unexpected Knowledges in Early Modern England*. Stanford, CA: Stanford University Press, 2001.

Womack, Peter. *Ben Jonson*. Oxford: Basil Blackwell, 1986.

Wood, Alice Ida Perry. *The Stage History of Shakespeare's King Richard the Third*. New York: Columbia University Press, 1909.

Wood, David Houston. "'Fluster'd with Flowing Cups': Alcoholism, Humoralism, and the Prosthetic Narrative in *Othello*." *Disability Studies Quarterly* 29, no. 4 (2009). https://dsq-sds.org/article/view/998/1182.

Woodbridge, Linda. *Vagrancy, Homelessness, and English Renaissance Literature*. Urbana: University of Illinois Press, 2001.

Worthen, W. B. *Shakespeare Performance Studies*. Cambridge: Cambridge University Press, 2014.

Wrightson, Keith. *Earthly Necessities: Economic Lives in Early Modern Britain*. New Haven, CT: Yale University Press, 2000.

Yachnin, Paul, and Jessica Slights. Introduction to *Shakespeare and Character: Theatre, History, Performance and Theatrical Persons*, edited by Paul Yachnin and Jessica Slights, 1–18. New York: Palgrave Macmillan, 2009.

Yergeau, M. Remi. *Authoring Autism: On Rhetoric and Neurological Queerness*. Durham, NC: Duke University Press, 2018.

Index

Adams, Rachel, 188, 268n11
aesthetic: as judgment, 27, 121–25, 141–42, 144, 235n56; as theatrical, 3, 6, 24, 44, 119, 223, 228, 231n12; as value, 9, 22, 75, 77–79, 123, 151, 189, 231n11, 256–7n10. *See also* disability
Agnew, Jean-Christophe, 104
Ahmed, Sara, 247n32
Akhimie, Patricia, 12, 212, 258n31
Anderson, Susan L., 230n9, 246n19
antitheatricality, 8, 16, 23, 43, 118, 174, 150, 170, 180, 191, 197–98, 202, 222, 265n46
Archer, John, 67, 248n36
Armin, Robert, 8
Astington, John, 235n57, 253n33
Aune, M.G., 243n74
Awdeley, John, 91

Bacon, Francis, "Of Deformity" by, 21, 27, 47, 50–53, 244n85
Baker, Naomi, 62, 116, 128, 140
Barish, Jonas, 172, 182, 240n30, 265n46
Barker, Roberta, 257n18
Barrough, Philip, *The Method of Physic* by, 23, 154–55, 159–60
Bartolovich, Crystal, 247n35, 248n40, 249n57
Barton, Anne, 179, 265n45
Bawcutt, N.W., 269n29, 269n33
Bearden, Elizabeth B., 6, 12, 188–89, 191, 234n46, 235n52, 241n40, 261n36, 267n3, 268n10, 270n42
Beaumont, Francis, works of: *The Captain*, 23, 129–31; *The Little French Lawyer*, 84–85; *Love's Pilgrimage*, 84; *The Prophetess*, 216–17; *The Woman Hater*, 165
Bedford, Thomas, 11
Bednarz, James, 178, 266n56
Beier, A.L., 58–59
Bellany, Alastair, 48, 50, 244n84
Bennett, Susan, 271n52

Bérubé, Michael, 20, 227, 235n56, 238n91
Besnault, Marie-Hélène, 26
Betterton, Thomas, *The Prophetess: Or, the History of Dioclesian* by, 216–17
Bhabha, Homi K., 251n10
biopower, 26
Bitot, Michael, 26
Blau, Herbert, 6, 232n18
Bodenham, John, 55
body: of actor, 3–4, 6–7, 9, 14, 16–17, 19–24, 45–47, 54, 57–58, 81, 84, 92, 106, 153, 157–58, 162, 169–72, 174, 180–81, 187, 190, 198, 202, 215–16, 265n43, 273n11; crippled, 3, 6–7, 21–22, 26, 56, 85–119, 187, 251n9; deformed, 3–4, 6, 8, 11–12, 16, 20–21, 25–54, 88–89, 102, 104, 106–07, 110–111, 114–116, 120–23, 127, 140, 144, 152, 182, 187, 190, 210, 212, 230n7, 241n41, 244n86; as embodiment, 7, 20, 22, 27, 32, 42, 44, 50, 85–86, 101, 150, 175, 189, 202, 215, 221, 229n4, 231n16, 234n44; lame, 3–4, 6, 10, 20–22, 30–33, 54–85, 88, 91, 95, 100–01, 106, 127, 171, 177, 187, 193, 212–13, 227, 247n31; monstrous, 2–3, 19, 21, 23–24, 36–38, 45, 48, 99, 137, 146, 148, 186–218, 221–22, 269n31, 271n59; sick, 3–4, 23, 91, 123, 153–185, 187; ugly, 3, 11–13, 21, 22, 23, 29, 119–153, 186–87. *See also* disability
Boehrer, Bruce, 131
Bogdan, Robert, 188
Booth, Stephen, 256n84
Brome, Richard, *A Jovial Crew* by, 97–98
Bruster, Douglas, 104, 255n61, 262n65
Bulwer, John, 12–13, 23, 125, 143–45, 147–52, 191, 193, 235n52; *Anthropometamorphosis* by, 23, 125, 144–51, 191
Burnett, Mark Thornton, 37, 197, 214, 260n45, 272n59
Burton, Robert, *The Anatomy of Melancholy* by, 11–13, 127–28, 136, 198

303

INDEX

Butler, Samuel, 118
Butterworth, Philip, 264n25–26

Cahill, Patricia A., 59, 61, 76, 245–46n10, 247n31
Campbell, Mary Baine, 261n59
Carlson, Marvin, 236n62
Carroll, William C., 91, 252n20
Castiglione, Baldassare, 12
Cavendish, Margaret, 121
Cecil, Robert, 21, 27, 29, 46–51, 53, 243n74, 244n76, 244n83
Chakravarty, Urvashi, 242n48, 271n57
Chapman, George, *The Blind Beggar of Alexandria* by, 22, 92–93
Charnes, Linda, 26, 39
Chen, Mel Y., 230n5
Chess, Simone, 253n37
Chettle, Henry, *The Blind Beggar of Bethnal Green* by, 93
Cheu, Johnson, 262n6
Cibber, Colley, 40, 42, 44–46, 53, 243n62
citizenship, 3, 22, 56, 58, 66–67, 85, 248n38
Clare, Eli, 156
Cline, Lauren Eriks, 271n52
Cohen, Jeffrey Jerome, 268n16
Coker, Lauren, 172, 179
Colley, John Scott, 46–47
Collier, Jeremy, 1, 24, 222, 25
Comber, Abigail Elizabeth, 27
comedy, 15, 66, 71, 82, 86, 92, 99–101, 104, 114–118, 131, 135, 181–81, 199, 219, 251n8, 255n73, 256n84, 270n45
Cook, Amy, 238n90
Copley, Anthony, 55, 86–87, 109, 117
Crane, Mary Thomas, 235n57
Crawford, Julie, 188, 268n22
Creaser, John, 265n47
Cressy, David, 268n22, 268n24
crip theory. *See* disability
cripping up, 7–9, 84–85, 157–58, 172–73, 232–33n28, 240n24, 251n7. *See also* disability
Croft, Pauline, 47–48, 244n83
cure, 5–6, 20, 73, 155–56, 159–62, 168, 176–77, 179, 224; ideology of, 155–56, 262n6; temporality of, 156, 262n7–9, 264n24

Daston, Lorraine, 189
Davenant, William, 215–16
Davidson, Michael, 220, 231n11
Davies, Surekha, 267n3

Davis, Lennard. J., 10, 50, 56, 226, 230n6, 231n14, 233n35, 239n3, 244n86, 267n7
Day, John, works of: *The Blind Beggar of Bethnal Green*, 93; *The Isle of Gulls*, 48
deafness, 11, 13, 174, 181–83, 238n83, 261n59
debility, 57
deformation, 22, 28, 31–32, 45, 53, 79, 144–46, 152–53, 170, 224, 228. *See also* performance
deformity, 10–18, 27–29, 31–40, 43–54, 56–58, 76–77, 101–03, 111, 114–18, 121–28, 134, 140–42, 147–48, 151–53, 171, 188–89, 212, 216, 231n14, 233n34, 239n1–2, 240n17, 257n19, 271n54. *See also* disability
Dekker, Thomas, works of: *The Shoemaker's Holiday*, 20, 22, 56, 66–74, 81–83, 247n35, 248n40; *The Wonder of a Kingdom*, 83
Deloney, Thomas, 68–69, 248n46–47
Dennis, John, 179–83
Dessen, Alan C., 238n83, 240n21
Deutsch, Helen, 244n85
Diamond, Elin, 18, 267n2
DiGangi, Mario, 20
disability: and acting, 2–3, 5–9, 14–15, 17–21, 26–28, 33, 37–38, 42–46, 49–50, 57–58, 80–81, 84–85, 91–92, 99, 105, 118–19, 143, 146–47, 151–53, 157–58, 165–70, 231n17, 263n16, 273n11; and bodily difference/impairment, 2–6, 10–13, 19, 22, 35, 53, 56–57, 83–85, 92–93, 98, 103, 117, 122–24, 128, 170, 181–83, 193, 215, 218, 233n36, 237n81, 269n30; and compulsory able-bodiedness, 124–25; and crip theory, 9, 124–25, 151, 221, 232–33n9, 240n24; and cripping up, 7–9, 44, 84–85, 157–58, 172–73, 231n16, 232–33n28, 240n24, 251n7; as cultural model, 3, 5, 6–7, 187–89, 221, 229n4; and dramatic character, 2–4, 6–8, 18–21, 22–24, 26–28, 38–46, 52–54, 60–62, 81–85, 87–89, 92–95, 97–102, 105–06, 114–19, 125, 128–31, 141–43, 150–53, 157–58, 164–72, 179–84, 187–90, 197–99, 203–04, 214–16, 218, 221–22, 226–27, 232n19, 238n89–91, 273n11; and environment, 3, 6, 26, 101, 229n3; and feigning, 2, 4, 8, 16–18, 22–23, 71–73, 83–85, 89–91, 94–7, 107–10, 124, 131, 151–53, 164, 170–72, 179–81, 198, 222, 224; as formal aesthetic, 3, 6, 9–10, 15, 24, 44, 118–19, 123, 131, 150–51, 223, 227–28, 231n11–12, 235n56, 256–7n10; as

medical model, 6–7, 27, 76–79, 155–56, 161–62; as moral interpretation, 5–6, 25–27, 122–24, 126–28, 133; as organizing logic, 4–5, 23, 115, 123, 133, 156, 181, 221; as overplus, 87, 89, 107, 114, 116–19; as site of singularity, 14–15, 57, 62–3, 88–89, 105, 112, 114, 131, 190, 223, 263n16; as site of theatrical iterability, 14–15, 17–19, 42, 53–54, 88–89, 152–53, 158, 164–70, 191; as stage semiotic, 4, 18, 20–21, 143, 157, 181, 184, 221; as social model, 3, 8–9, 26, 61, 76–79, 88, 221, 229n3. *See also* deformity

disease, 1, 23, 67, 75, 89, 124, 154–61, 164, 166, 169, 171, 173, 175, 177, 180, 184, 224, 262n5, 263n10, 267n7. *See also* illness

Dobin, Howard, 270n45, 270n47
Dolan, Jill, 273n10
Dollimore, Jonathan, 259n44
Donaldson, Ian, 243n73, 266n54
Drayton, Michael, 83
Dryden, John, 179, 215–16
Dutton, Richard, 178, 266n55

Eggert, Katherine, 271n53
Elam, Keir, 112, 157, 236n76
Empson, William, 142
epilepsy, 2, 20, 23, 154, 156, 158–61, 166–68, 184, 229, 263n19, 264n24–25

Fair Maid of the Exchange, The, 21–22, 87–89, 92, 96, 98–118, 182, 254n51, 256n84
Famous Victories of Henry V, The, 56, 69–70
Fawcett, Julia, 45, 243n62
Festa, Lynn, 105
Findlay, Alison, 270n40
Fischer-Lichte, Erika, 236–37n77
Fisher, Will, 105, 237n82
Fletcher, John, works of: *Beggars' Bush*, 22, 85, 94–97; *The Captain*, 23, 120–31; *The Little French Lawyer*, 84–85; *Love's Pilgrimage*, 84; *The Prophetess*, 216–17; *The Woman Hater*, 165
Foucault, Michel, 5, 155, 189, 230n6, 262n4
Freeburg, Victor O., 93
Fumerton, Patricia, 91, 252n23, 252n25

Garber, Marjorie, 28, 239n4
Garland-Thomson, Rosemarie, 35, 56, 103, 124, 188, 231n11, 232n20, 235n55, 249n56, 257n10, 269n31
Garrick, David, 19, 42, 46, 242n51
Gayton, Edmund, 120, 151–52

gesture, 5, 13–14, 16–17, 19, 22, 32, 40, 42, 52, 54, 64, 82–83, 100, 102, 120, 129, 143, 155, 157, 161, 168, 173, 184, 188, 209, 211, 213, 216, 218–220, 261n57
Gibbons, Brian, 26, 251n8
Gilman, Sander L., 224
Gosse, Edmund, 99
Gosson, Stephen, 16, 43, 150, 158, 181, 236n62, 261n63
Granville-Barker, Harley, 223
Green, Juana, 99, 103
Greenblatt, Stephen, 128, 179, 258n30, 266n60
Greene, Robert, 91
Grosz, Elizabeth, 269n30
Gurnis, Musa, 259n36, 273n11

Hadley, Bree, 263n16
Hall, Edward, 29
Hall, Kim F., 214–215, 242n48, 258n22, 260n48, 261n62
Hammer, Paul E. J., 246n11
Harman, Thomas, 91
Harsnett, Samuel, 161
Harvey, Elizabeth D., 266–67n67
Hathway, Richard, 83
Haughton, William, 93
Hazlitt, William, 216, 242n51
Hendren, Sara, 229n3
Henke, Robert, 91–92, 252–53n27
Heywood, Thomas, 120, 204, 250n5
Hill, Thomas, 36
Hillman, David, 75
Hindle, Steve, 233n31
Hirschmann, Nancy J., 229n3
Hobgood, Allison P., 5, 13, 27, 229n2, 231n12, 241n35, 263n19
Hodgdon, Barbara, 245n91
Hoeniger, F. David, 264–65n35
Holinshed, Raphael, 29
Howard, Jean E., 52, 99, 103, 214n34, 254n54
Hutchings, Mark, 230n7
Hutson, Lorna, 175, 238n89
Hyland, Peter, 107, 253n33, 255n71

illness, 56, 89–90, 143, 154, 156, 161, 164, 172–75, 181, 241n41. *See also* disease
imitation, 2, 13, 15–17, 22, 31, 35, 38, 88, 100–01, 105, 110–14, 118–19, 148–50, 157–58, 165, 169–71, 180–83, 224. *See also* mimesis
impersonation, 7, 52, 88–89, 98, 104–06, 108, 110–111, 113–19, 181. *See also* disability

involuntarity, 158, 183–84
Iyengar, Sujata, 5, 10

Johns, Geoffrey A., 27, 33
Johnson, Samuel, 19, 49, 74, 191
Johnston, Kirsty, 231n16, 232n22, 238n90
Jones, Ann Rosalind, 107
Jones, Richard, 16
Jonson, Ben, works of: *The Alchemist*, 92; *Richard Crookback*, 243n73; *Timber*, 17–18, 171; *Volpone*, 21, 23, 157, 169, 171–83, 266n54
Jorden, Edward, 161

Kafer, Alison, 156, 160, 233n28, 262n7, 262n9
Karim-Cooper, Farah, 143, 258n22, 261n57
Kerwin, William, 249n59
Kistner, A. L., 142
Kistner, M. K., 142
Knutson, Roslyn L., 59, 246n17
Kostihová, Marcela, 33
Kuppers, Petra, 7, 229n3, 231n16, 232n22, 238n9, 263n14
Kyd, Thomas, 41

labor, 9, 16, 22, 26, 28, 56–59, 61–72, 74, 80–85, 89–91, 98–100, 102–105, 110, 114, 123, 125, 150, 169, 197, 212, 226, 247n32, 252n23; artisanal, 22, 56, 65, 72. 82; martial, 22, 56–57, 62–63, 65–66, 68–69, 74, 80, 85
Lake, Peter, 243n74, 244n75
Lamb, Charles, 99
Larum for London, A, 21–22, 56, 58, 61, 63, 66, 85, 246n17
Lash, Alexander Paulsson, 92–93
Leinwand, Theodore B., 104
Lin, Erika T., 15, 109, 237n78, 265n43
Long, Kathleen, 267n5
Lopez, Jeremy, 82, 238n89, 253n32, 259n42
Love, Genevieve, 6, 8, 18, 20, 27, 59, 61–62, 88, 113, 115–16, 237n79, 238n85, 241n35, 247n28, 251n13, 255n68
Lupton, Julia, 67, 211, 248n38, 271n53–54

MacKay, Ellen, 123, 156, 232n24
Malcolmson, Cristina, 137
Mann, David, 237n78
Mann, Jenny C., 236n71
Marlowe, Christopher, 16
marriage plot, 99, 103, 116, 125, 129
Marston, John, *Antonio and Mellida* by, 15–16

Massinger, Philip, works of: *Beggars' Bush*, 22, 94–97; *The Little French Lawyer*, 84–85
materiality, 18, 31, 58, 156, 171–72, 203, 218
Maus, Katharine Eisaman, 175
Mayne, Jasper, works of: *The Amorous Warre*, 84; *The Citye Match*, 188, 199–203, 214, 269n29
Mazzio, Carla, 75, 235n51
McMullan, Gordon, 131, 259n38, 260n50
McRae, Andrew, 48, 243n74
McRuer, Robert, 9, 57, 124, 232–33n28, 240n24
Menon, Madhavi, 225
Menzer, Paul, 42, 53, 113, 226, 242n51, 251n14
Metzler, Irina, 233n36, 245n3
Middleton, Thomas, works of: *The Changeling*, 21, 23, 125, 131–32, 136–39, 141–44, 150–53; *Hengist, King of Kent*, 23, 156, 166–67; *The Spanish Gypsy*, 152
mimesis, 4, 9, 28, 40, 190, 225. See also imitation
Mitchell, David T., 6, 20, 25, 97, 106, 229n4, 241n34, 244n85, 251n9, 258n25. See also prosthesis
monstrosity, 6, 10, 23–24, 36–37, 46, 187–91, 197–199, 202, 205, 207–09, 211–12, 214–18, 222, 233n34, 239n3, 241n40, 249n58, 261n59, 268n17, 272n59
de Montaigne, Michel, 126–27, 134, 136, 170–71, 183, 258n25
More, Thomas, *The History of King Richard the Third* by, 29, 45
Moulton, Ian Frederick, 37, 241n40
Munday, Anthony, works of: *The Life of Sir John Oldcastle*, 83; *Londons Love*, 209–10
Muñoz, José Esteban, 225, 273n10
Munro, Lucy, 270n48

Nardizzi, Vin, 10, 27, 62, 74, 76, 80, 238n86, 243n59, 249n58
Neely, Carol Thomas, 143, 260–61n55
Neill, Michael, 259n38, 260n51
Ngai, Sianne, 257n14
Nicol, David, 257n18, 259n38, 270n44

Obermeier, Anita, 270n38–39
Overbury, Thomas, 19, 244n84
overplus, 87, 89, 107, 114, 116–19

Palfrey, Simon, 26, 43, 241n44, 271n58
palsy, 20, 23, 154–60, 164–66, 173–74, 177, 179–81, 183–84, 220, 223

INDEX 307

Paré, Ambroise, 5, 22, 37, 74–80, 90, 94, 129, 191–92, 200, 241n41, 268n20, 270n42
Park, Katharine, 189
Paster, Gail Kern, 234n44, 253n30, 260n50
Patterson, Annabel, 260n46
Pender, Stephen, 50, 189, 231n14, 241n41
performance: and actor's body, 3–5, 7–9, 15–18, 23–24, 27–28, 31–32, 53–54, 80–81, 83–85, 91–92, 106, 114–15, 151–53, 156–58, 164, 169–72, 177–78, 185, 187–90, 202, 217–18, 220–25, 231n11, 231n17, 235n56–58, 236n77, 252–3n27, 273n11; of feigned disability, 2, 22–23, 57, 73–74, 89–91, 94–97, 100, 107–10, 114–18, 157–58, 166–68, 172–81, 231n16, 252n23; and print, 16–17, 38, 41–42, 80–81, 95–98, 101–02, 111–12, 142–44, 147, 150–51, 169, 172, 189–90, 193, 196–97, 212, 225; and theater history, 8, 14–15, 40–44, 52–53, 83–85, 91–92, 105, 151–52, 157, 170, 207, 201–11, 215–16, 226–28, 242n51, 263n16, 242n51; theory, 3, 16–18, 30, 187, 237n78, 237n81; as transformation, 16, 38, 43–44, 54, 95–96, 85, 88, 90, 92–93, 108–10, 118–19, 150–53, 170–72, 179–81, 197–99, 203, 224–25, 253n32. *See also* deformation; theater
Perkins, William, 16
Phelan, Peggy, 272n7
Phillips, Edward, 121
Philosophical Transactions of the Royal Society, 223
physiognomy, 11, 13, 36, 50, 92, 125–129, 131–33, 147, 157, 258n23
pleasure, 4, 23, 51, 66, 92–94, 103, 108, 131, 133, 136, 164, 172, 216, 253n32, 265n43
Poole, Joshua, 154, 158
Porter, Martin, 11, 36, 258n23
Preiss, Richard, 28, 242n50
prosthesis: as bodily prosthesis, 3, 27, 74–80, 85, 90, 105–108, 113–15, 129, 191–93, 237n79, 243n59, 249n58, 258n35; as narrative prosthesis, 6, 20–21, 97, 106; as textual prosthesis, 95–97, 105–07, 110–12, 238n85–86, 255n64; as theatrical prosthetic, 3–4, 14–15, 18–20, 22, 27, 37–38, 45, 47, 57, 61–62, 80, 83–85, 88, 94–96, 105–08, 110–17, 128–9, 158, 189–90, 199–203, 227, 237n82, 247n28, 258n35. *See also* stage property
Prynne, William, 16, 181
Puar, Jasbir K., 57
Puggliati, Paola, 90
Puttenham, George, 10, 14–15, 28

Quayson, Ato, 25, 235n56, 257n16

Rainolds, John, 16
Rankins, William, 197–98
Read, Alexander, 123, 125
representation, 2–9, 16, 18, 22, 27–30, 39, 46–47, 50, 58, 91–92, 99, 103, 108, 118, 131, 143, 153, 157, 164, 169, 174, 177, 180, 187, 189, 190, 200, 210, 211, 222, 225–26, 228, 231n14, 235n56, 236n62, 237n78, 242n45, 245n10, 253n37, 257n16, 269n34, 272n59
Returne from Parnassus, The Second Part of the, 41, 154
Reynolds, John, 137, 260n46
Ricks, Christopher, 259n40
Rivière, Lazare, 155
Rivlin, Elizabeth, 81, 248n46–47
Roach, Joseph R., 8, 16, 143, 253n30
Rogers, Thomas, 123
Rosenfeld, Colleen R., 17, 256n4
Row-Heyveld, Lindsey, 8, 27, 88, 91, 110, 116, 238n83, 241n34, 251n13, 252n21, 264n31
Rowley, William, works of: *The Birth of Merlin*, 24, 188, 198, 203–09, 269n33, 270n39–47; *The Changeling*, 21, 23, 125, 131–32, 136–39, 141–44, 150–53
Roychoudhury, Suparna, 214, 272n62

Saenger, Michael Baird, 209–10
Salamon, Linda Bradley, 70, 245n9, 249n55
Salmon, William, 154–55
Samuels, Ellen, 91, 234n48, 262n9
Sandahl, Carrie, 7, 157, 231n17, 232n19, 233n28, 263n14, 273n11
Sarkar, Debapriya, 236n71, 271n52
Schaffer, Simon, 272n6
Schelling, Felix, 99
Schweik, Susan M., 124, 256–57n10
Schwyzer, Philip, 243n73
Scot, Reginald, *The Discoverie of Witchcraft by*, 23, 161–64
Semonin, Paul, 188
Shakespeare, William, works of: *Julius Caesar*, 1–2, 4, 157, 263n19; *King Henry IV, part 2*, 67–68, 164; *King Henry VI, part 2*, 165–66; *King Henry VI, part 3*, 23, 30, 45; *King Lear*, 24, 91, 222, 265n43; *King Richard III*, 5, 13, 19, 21–22, 25–54, 151, 187, 215, 220–21, 240n17, 241n35, 242n45, 242n48, 242n51, 242n54, 243n62, 243n73–74, 244n76; *Othello*, 23, 156, 168–69, 264n35; *Pericles*, 84; *The Tempest*, 21, 24, 186–87, 189, 209–16, 270n41, 271n52

308 INDEX

Shapin, Steven, 272n6
Shaw, Justin, 169, 256n37
Sher, Antony, 42–44, 242n52, 243n59
sickness, 1, 24, 92, 94, 128, 154–56, 159–61, 164, 166–72, 176–79, 181, 263n19
Sidney, Philip, *A Defence of Poetry* by, 21, 28, 182
Siebers, Tobin, 5, 9, 25, 27, 39, 172, 229n4, 231n16, 232n28, 240n17, 241n34, 257n10, 265n48, 266n66
Silvers, Anita, 56
similitude: in acting, 8, 109–10, 118, 150, 180–81, 214, 223; and antisimilitude, 148, 224; as simile, 72–73, 129, 160, 195–96, 201, 212–13
Simpson, R. R., 264n35
Skuse, Alanna, 80, 250n71
Slotkin, Joel Elliott, 230n7, 257n19
Smallwood, Robert, 66, 68, 82 248n49
Smith, Ian, 238n82, 258n35
Snyder, Sharon L., 6, 20, 25, 97, 106, 229n4, 241n34, 244n85, 251n9, 258n25. *See also* prosthesis
Solga, Kim, 131
Somogyi, Nicholas de, 59, 246n17, 247n30
spectacle, 4, 21, 211, 222, 227, 265n43, 268n10; of actor's body in performance, 18, 157–58, 162–64, 167–68, 209–11, 216–17; of deformity, 37–38, 53, 83, 112, 117, 130; of monstrosity, 188–91, 195–97, 199–203, 207–08, 213–14, 267n6; of sick body, 1–2, 157, 167–68, 175–77; of wounded soldier, 65–66, 73–74
spectatorship, 2, 4, 7, 14–16, 18, 23–24, 34–35, 37–38, 52–53, 56–57, 86–87, 108–10, 121–23, 146–47, 152–53, 161–64, 167–68, 171, 179, 183–85, 188–90, 195–96, 201–03, 224–25, 232n18, 237n78, 263n16
stage property, 3–4, 19–20, 22, 27, 37–38, 45, 47, 57, 61–62, 83–85, 88, 94–96, 105–08, 113–17, 128–29, 158, 189–90, 199–203, 227, 247n28, 258n35. *See also* prosthesis
Stagg, Kevin, 188, 252n19, 267n6
Stallybrass, Peter, 107
States, Bert O., 88, 227, 265n43
Stern, Tiffany, 26, 43, 237n82, 241n44, 271n58
Stevens, Andrea Ria, 237n82, 258n35
Stewart, Susan, 203, 268n16
Stiker, Henry-Jacques, 239n2, 262n5
Stone, Deborah, 90–91
surface reading, 23, 35, 119, 141–42, 153
Swinburne, Algernon Charles, 142
symptom, 1, 23, 153–61, 164–67, 169, 173–74

Taylor, Gary, 166
Teague, Frances, 175, 237n82
theater: early modern, 3–5, 9, 18–21, 24, 46–47, 52–53, 59, 62, 83–85, 91, 95, 98, 104–05, 156, 164, 182–85, 197–99, 215–17, 225–28, 234n44, 235n57–58, 237n78–79; and theatrical form, 6–9, 14–18, 22–23, 27–28, 50, 56–57, 82, 88–89, 125, 152–53, 157–58, 169–72, 179, 187–90, 220–23, 232n18, 236n71, 273n10; as theatrical medium, 1, 3, 6–7, 9, 15, 88, 118, 128–29, 141–42, 193, 203, 209–11, 217, 223, 235n56, 238n85, 265n43; and theatricality, 3, 15, 24, 39, 53, 91, 113, 125, 131, 147, 150–51, 170, 190, 198, 235n58; 237n81, 252n27, 265n46. *See also* performance
Tomkis, Thomas, *Albumazar* by, 165
Torrey, Michael, 36
tragedy, 29, 41, 100–01, 125, 131, 141, 219
transformation, 54, 85, 88, 90, 93, 109, 118, 123, 140, 144, 146–48, 150, 152–53, 170, 172, 181, 190, 197–98, 203, 210, 225, 254n55, 259n38, 241n59
Trapp, John, 160, 263n22
Traub, Valerie, 234n46, 235n51
Trial of Chivalry, The, 22, 56, 58–61, 66
Tribble, Evelyn, 237n78, 253n41
True Tragedie of Richard III, The, 21, 29, 240n27
Tuke, Thomas, 258n22
Turner, David M., 86, 188, 233n34
Turner, Henry S., 68, 83, 235n58, 236n71
type: as allegorical type, 210–11; as bodily variance, 13, 258n25; as dramatic character, 4, 20, 22, 54, 88–89, 101–02, 116–19, 143, 221; as print, 49; as stereotype, 6–8, 14, 22, 26–27, 49, 53, 69, 72, 91, 96–98, 109–10, 143, 161, 215, 224–25, 251n9; as typecast actor, 7–8, 84–85, 226–27, 231n16–17, 238n90. *See also* performance

Udall, Joanna, 207, 269n33
ugliness, 23–24, 120–135, 137, 140–44, 147, 150–51, 153, 259n38, 260n48, 260n50; logics of, 132, 135

Valerius, Cornelius, 66
Vinter, Maggie, 174, 266n49
visibility, 20, 38–39, 57–58, 73, 156, 175, 232n18, 256n10, 263n16
vulnerability, 1, 9, 12, 23, 43, 60, 109, 158, 169, 177, 183, 185, 212, 246n11

Walsh, Brian, 30, 240n27, 249n50
Waswo, Richard, 99, 116, 255n60
Weber, Max, 68
Webster, John, 160–61
Weimann, Robert, 28, 237n78, 241n33, 242n45
Wellman, Mac, 223, 272n2
Wells, Susan, 88
West, William N., 17, 28, 38, 237n81
Wheeler, Richard P., 39
Whigham, Frank, 136, 260n50, 265n36
Wiggins, Martin, 29, 85, 253n37, 253n40
Wilks, John S., 26
Williams, Nora, 259n42
Williams, Wes, 189, 268n15

Wills, David, 77, 105, 249n58, 255n64
Wilson, Robert, 83
witchcraft, 23, 37, 156, 161, 163, 264n25
Withington, Phil, 248n36, 248n39
Wits, The, 95–97
Womack, Peter, 169–70
Wonder Worth the Reading, A, 193–94
Wood, David Houston, 5, 13, 231n12, 265n35
Woodall, John, 22, 74–75, 79–80
Woodbridge, Linda, 90, 246n13
Worthen, W. B., 17, 237n78
wounded soldier, 22, 65, 72, 74, 80, 85
Wrightson, Keith, 254n55

Yergeau, M. Remi, 158, 184

www.ingramcontent.com/pod-product-compliance
Lightning Source LLC
Chambersburg PA
CBHW030116240426
43673CB00041B/1303